FIGHTING FASCIST SPAIN

FIGHTING FASCIST SPAIN

WORKER PROTEST from the PRINTING PRESS

MONTSE FEU

UNIVERSITY OF ILLINOIS PRESS
Urbana, Chicago, and Springfield

© 2020 by the Board of Trustees
of the University of Illinois
All rights reserved
1 2 3 4 5 C P 5 4 3 2 1
♾ This book is printed on acid-free paper.

Library of Congress Control Number: 2020936559

To Aaron K. Gillette, my beloved husband

Contents

List of Organizations ix

Spanish Terms xi

Principal Authors and Activists, *España Libre* xiii

Acknowledgments xvii

Introduction: The SHC's Opposition to Spanish Fascism 1

Part One. Print Culture, Activism, and Solidarity

1 Transnational Networks of Support 25
2 *España Libre*, the Antifascist Periodical 36
3 *España Libre* and Its Editors 53
4 The Struggle against Deportations 79
5 Solidarity for Political Prisoners 96

Part Two. Literary Representations and Aesthetics

6 We, the Antifascist People 113
7 Theater—*Género Chico* and Antifascism 133

8 Aurelio Pego, Antifascist Satirical Chronicler   145
9 Damned Cartoons! Workers' Identity and Resistance   159
   Conclusion: The SHC's Antifascist Legacy   171

Appendixes

A SHC-Affiliated Associations   183
B Supporting Networks and Individuals   189
C Sporadic Contributors, Writers, and Reprinted Authors   191
D Aided Refugees and Political Prisoners   195
E Popular Plays and Zarzuelas Produced by the SHC, 1939–1977   199
F Original Antifascist and Exile Plays, 1937–1950   203
G Regular Speakers and Performers, 1937–1977, and Their Roles   215

Notes   219
Bibliography   257
Index   269

Organizations

ACLU	American Civil Liberties Union
AFL	American Federation of Labor
AMA	Agrupación de Mujeres Antifascistas (Antifascist Women's Organization)
ANFD	Alianza Nacional de Fuerzas Democráticas (National Alliance of Democratic Forces)
ASE	Alianza Sindical Española (Spanish Union Alliance)
ASO	Alianza Sindical Obrera (Labor Union Alliance)
CIO	Congress of Industrial Organizations
CNT	Confederación Nacional del Trabajo (National Confederation of Labor)
ICFTU	International Confederation of Free Trade Unions
ILGWU	International Ladies' Garment Workers Union
POUM	Partit Obrer d'Unificació Marxista (Workers' Party of Marxist Unification)
SHC	Sociedades Hispanas Confederadas (Confederation of Hispanic Societies)
SIA	Solidaridad Internacional Antifascista (Antifascist International Solidarity)
SRA	Spanish Refugee Aid
UGT	Unión General de Trabajadores (General Union of Workers)

Spanish Terms

apropósito	topical one-act play
astracán	absurdist comedy
Caudillo	military dictator (Francisco Franco)
cenetista	member of the CNT
crónica	chronicle
cuadro	skit/vignette
género chico	popular, farcical genre
esperpento	grotesque
juguete cómico	farce or comic play
lector	reader (at a factory)
patria chica	national or regional identity
revista	musical comedy
sainete	one-act play
zarzuela	operetta

Principal Authors and Activists, *España Libre*

Carmen Aldecoa (Turón de Mieles, Asturias, date unknown–Madrid, 1988). Teacher for the Confederación Nacional del Trabajo during the Spanish Civil War. Arrived in New York in 1941 after short stays in France and Cuba. Executive member of the SHC and occasional lecturer. Staff writer and contributor for *España Libre*. Author of *Del sentir y pensar* (Mexico, 1957). Adjunct professor of Spanish at New York University. Left the United States in the 1980s and settled in Madrid.

Sergio Aragonés (Castellón, Spain, 1937–). His family arrived in Mexico in 1944 escaping the Spanish Civil War and the Nazi occupation of France. Served as editorial cartoonist for *España Libre* from 1962 to 1965. Participated in several fundraising events as spokesman until 1965. Cartoonist for *Mad* magazine.

Josep Bartolí Guiu (Barcelona, 1939–New York, 1995). Political cartoonist, founder of the professional cartoonists' syndicate. Fought as a militiaman in the Spanish Civil War (1936–1939), escaped French internment camps and the Gestapo. Lived in Mexico and became friends with Frida Kahlo. In the 1940s, started to draw for *Holiday* magazine and was part of the 10th Street group, along with Willem de Kooning, Franz Kline, Jackson Pollock, and Mark Rothko. Cartoonist for *España Libre* in the 1950s and 1960s.

Principal Authors and Activists

Alfonso Camín (La Peñuca, Spain, 1890–Porceyo, Spain, 1982). Migrated to Cuba in 1905 and worked for the periodicals *La Noche, Apolo,* and *Diario de la Marina.* In 1914 returned to Spain to cover the First World War. Founded the magazine *Norte* in 1929. Regular contributor for *Gráfico* (New York), *El Cronista del Valle* (Brownsville, Texas), *Evolución* (Laredo, Texas), *Las Novedades* (New York), *La Prensa* (San Antonio), *Via Libre* (New York), *La Voz* (New York), and *Cultura Proletaria* (New York). Submitted poetry to *España Libre* from Mexico.

José Castilla Morales (Huelva, Spain, 1893–New York, 1961) Migrated to Cienfuegos, Cuba, in 1909. Staff writer for *El Sembrador, El Progreso,* and *Tierra.* Fled the Gerardo Machado administration's political repression and arrived in New York with anarchists Avelino Iglesias and Paulino Díez. Staff writer for the anarchist newspaper *Solidaridad Obrera* (Mexico, 1918–1930) and assistant director of *La Voz* (New York, 1939). SHC founder, leader, and playwright; editor and satirist for *España Libre*. Worked as a Spanish advertising manager for a chemical laboratory in New York.

Carmen Cordellat (Cuba, unknown–New York, unknown) Piano teacher and performer at the SHC's fundraisers. Served as the SHC's secretary in the 1940s and the 1950s. Worked closely with pro bono lawyers and the Second Spanish Republic government-in-exile to prevent deportations and relocate refugees.

Miguel Giménez Igualada (Iniesta, Spain, 1888–Mexico, 1973). Settled in Mexico after surviving the internment camps of France. Author of several books on anarchism and contributor to several Spanish periodicals in the Americas. Essayist for *España Libre*. He often wrote under the pen names Miguel Ramos Giménez and Juan de Iniesta. Pursued many means of earning a living from street vendor to teacher.

Jesús González Malo (Santander, Spain, 1903–New York, 1965). President of the Santander Dock Workers Union and editor of the leftist newspaper *La Región* in Santander, Spain, before the Spanish Civil War. Militiaman during the Spanish Civil War. Arrived in New York in 1940 after short stays in France and Cuba. SHC leader and *España Libre* staff writer and editor. In New York, he worked as a welder.

Adolfo Jiménez Colón (Jumilla, Spain, 1884–place unknown, 1995). Arrived in New York in 1918. Founding member of the SHC and composer of many of the zarzuelas performed at fundraisers. *España Libre* published his satiric poetic attacks on the Franco regime and fascism until 1952. Author of *Bombas de mano* (1938). Profession unknown, he possibly taught music.

Félix Martí Ibáñez (Cartagena, 1911–New York, 1972). Contributor for the Spanish anarchist press and general director of Public Health and Social Services in Catalonia during the Spanish Civil War. Arrived in New York in 1939. *España Libre* essayist and short story writer. Professor of medical humanities at New York University.

Aurelio Pego (Valladolid, 1899–La Coruña, 1973). Arrived in New York in 1919. Contributor for several Spanish-language periodicals in the Americas. Joined *España Libre* in 1940 as a staff writer. His satirical columns ran until the paper closed its doors in 1977. In the United States corresponded for several Hispanic newspapers and worked as a clerk in several businesses.

Mary Reid (Marita Reijal) (Place unknown, 1895–Gibraltar, Spain, date unknown). Arrived in New York in 1921 with La Compañía de Teatro Español. Formed her own company, Compañía Marita Reid, and played the circuit of mutual aid societies. Founding member of the Centro Andaluz in 1929. Served regularly as stage star, director, and playwright in workers' associations in the 1930s. An SHC founding member. Acted, directed plays, and was the master of ceremonies in hundreds of antifascist fundraisers.

Ramón J. Sender (Huesca, 1901–San Diego, 1982). Spanish novelist, essayist, and journalist. Essayist for *España Libre*. Taught Spanish at several universities, including the University of New Mexico.

Acknowledgments

Writing this book has been a precious experience for me. I felt uneasy when I could not devote time to the Sociedades Hispanas Confederadas and its periodical, *España Libre*. I hope that my research provides new insights on the fight of common people against fascism and this recovered story soothes those who still today suffer the effects of their tragic and broken family histories. I wish that no one else ever suffers war and fascism.

Fighting Fascist Spain originated at the Recovering the United States Hispanic Literary Heritage Project in 2007. I thank the directors, Nicolás Kanellos and Carolina Villarroel, for their support. Professors involved in my initial research, Gabriela Baeza Ventura, Maria Elena Solino, and Victor Fuentes, further encouraged my work, which has continued to evolve into databases, articles, and monographs. Geoff Eley's seminar "Fascism, Modernity, Politics, Aesthetics" in the School of Criticism and Theory at Cornell University in 2009 critically developed my research project.

I thank the Department of World Languages and Cultures and the College of Humanities and Social Sciences at Sam Houston State University, and in particular Debra Andrist, Leif French, and Dean Abbey Zink, for their support in funding my travel to conferences and archives. I also thank SHSU Office of Research and Sponsored Programs for faculty research enhancement grants, which allowed me to travel to archives and advance this work.

Although my research first focused on exile and antifascism, the anarchist ideology and practice of *España Libre* and the SHC became more distinct the more I read the periodical and other archival materials. While attending conferences and visiting archives, I was fortunate to learn from the research networks Grupo de Estudios de Exilio Literario, the North American Anarchist Studies Network, and the Research Society for American Periodicals. I have now befriended people whom I admire, among them Jon Bekken, Christopher Castañeda, Jesse Cohn, Peter Cole, Andy Cornell, Jorge De Hoyos Puente, Carmen de la Guardia, Chris Ealham, Donna R. Gabaccia, Amanda Gailey, Jennifer Guglielmo, Olga Glondys, Tom Goyens, Andrew Hoyt, Jean Lee Cole, Jorell Melendez-Badillo, Kirk Shaffer, Dave Struthers, Susana Sueiro Seoane, Mar Trallero, and Kenyon Zimmer, among others. My academic networks continue to grow, and I am grateful for researchers who inspire me every day. Their knowledge and friendship have improved this book and my life in multiple ways. I am especially indebted to Chris Castañeda, always available and knowledgeable.

I would like to acknowledge José Nieto Ruiz, *España Libre* staff writer and SHC member. I was extremely lucky to meet him, and this book is enriched by his testimony. His enthusiastic assessment of my work in our first telephone call—"It was exactly like that, Montse!"—will always be in my heart. I am glad my research and publications have inspired those who disseminate antifascist history in social and mass media.

I thank also librarians, archivists, and editors. SHSU librarians Sarah Greenmyer, Michael Hanson, Erin Owens, and Sammie Phelps have always been there with a solution. Likewise, I am thankful to James Engelhardt, University of Illinois Press editor, for his reading and assistance throughout the process of bring this book to publication. I am grateful to Christopher Lura and Marilyn Campbell for their thoughtful editing.

All translations of quotes are mine.

FIGHTING FASCIST SPAIN

Introduction

The SHC's Opposition to Spanish Fascism

Agapito, the Spanish migrant protagonist of Prudencio de Pereda's novel *Windmills in Brooklyn* (1960), dreams of retiring in Galicia, Spain. Agapito first moves to New York from Spain in the 1890s in search of better-paying work, hoping to save enough money to return home with a nest egg. However, his dream is shattered by the Spanish Civil War and by the rise to power of Franco's regime. In *Windmills in Brooklyn*, de Pereda novelizes what the ascendance of Francisco Franco regime meant for Spanish workers in the United States: those opposed became exiles who could not return to their home country.

At the turn of the twentieth century, Spaniards were working across the United States—from the far western agricultural fields of Hawaii and California, to the prairies of Idaho and Nevada, and to the West Virginia mines and the Vermont quarries. They congregated in the industrial centers of Chicago, Detroit, and New York City, and ranged as far south as the cigar factories in Florida in Key West and Tampa, as well as in the Panama Canal construction zone.[1] Many Spanish workers arrived in the United States already imbued with radical traditions rooted in the socialism or anarchism of their homeland, and they went on to found cultural and mutual aid societies in large urban cities and in smaller rural and mining areas. Radicals had fled persecution in Spain during the Primo de Rivera dictatorship (1923–1930), something that further radicalized the Spanish diaspora. Often, they formed politically radical enclaves, such as in Paterson, New Jersey, or Brooklyn, New York. These radicals would play a critical role in the broader antifascist political efforts in the years during the Spanish Civil War (1936–1939) and the Francisco Franco dictatorship (1939–1975). In the United States, they created their own alternative press and participated in vigorous transnational, radical countercultures. These international collaborations became a powerful element in their antifascist fight during the Spanish Civil War and Franco's dictatorship.

At the outbreak of the Spanish Civil War, most Spanish workers in the United States supported the Government of the Second Spanish Republic, which had been democratically elected in 1931. When war broke out and Franco came to power, the Spaniards and radicals living in the United States and elsewhere began to organize against the new regime. About two hundred U.S. Spanish cultural and mutual aid societies came together in what became known as the Sociedades Hispanas Confederadas (SHC, Confederation of Hispanic Societies).[2] The SHC was devoted to its antifascist cause, particularly through its activism and print culture. For nearly forty years, from 1939 until 1977—when Spain held the first democratic elections after Franco—the SHC published the bilingual periodical *España Libre* (Free Spain) in Brooklyn. The periodical denounced the Franco regime; raised funds to help refugees, political prisoners, and the underground resistance in fascist Spain (both financially and legally); helped workers feel part of a broader community; and energized their culture and politics. Although membership in the SHC was open to anyone advocating freedom for Spain, *España Libre* followed the principles of two specific unions: the Spanish anarchist union—Confederación Nacional del Trabajo (CNT)—and the Spanish socialist union—Unión General de Trabajadores (UGT). These principles were expressed through journalism, political essays, literature, and theater. Following the radical legacy of Spanish immigrant communities that settled earlier in U.S. industrial and rural centers, the SHC heavily focused on the development of its community and political network. An active print culture helped the confederation to expand its membership and reach broader reading audiences—two critical objectives for the maintenance of such a large grassroots organization over the course of several decades.

This book is an effort to recover for contemporary scholars and readers this major collective grassroots political project, one that has never been fully recognized. *España Libre* continued an antifascist, progressive, and radical legacy in the United States while Franco intended to destroy progressive and radical expressions in Spain. It also constituted an alternative progressive path to modernity, albeit an exiled one, and one that has been largely lost until now.

Fighting Fascist Spain pieces together the story of modern Spanish immigrants to the United States in their fight against fascism through the narrative arc of the periodical *España Libre* and the grassroots activism of the organization that sustained that periodical, the Sociedades Hispanas Confederadas, or the SHC. Although *Espana Libre* was run by Spanish immigrants and exiles in the United States, during its antifascist exile, the confederation had a clear transnational consciousness: old migrants and new exiles coalesced in overlapping communities that were linked to similar antifascist networks in other countries. These transnational communities were brought together by the publishing networks of *Espana Libre*. By studying this publication and its networks, it is possible to bring to light crucial narratives that have remained hidden in the past.

The Foundation of the Sociedades Hispanas Confederadas

On July 18, 1936, the same day that the Spanish military attempted to seize control of the country's major cities with the help of European fascist forces, Jesús Arenas, a Galician immigrant who would become one of the SHC's founding members, stepped off the steamship *Oriente* and onto the docks of New York. Arenas was already active in anarchist politics in Spain and he was traveling to the United States to escape the increasingly dangerous political climate for radicals there. When he arrived in New York that day in July, the anarchist sojourner found the political atmosphere tense among the Spanish workers' organizations in New York as a result of the news about a military coup in Spain. Soon after arriving, Arenas attended an antifascist meeting in Union Square where anarchist José Patín and communist Daniel Alonso—two active members of radical communities in New York—addressed dozens of Spanish workers and argued for the importance of fighting against fascism in Spain and across the European continent. During the rally, Arenas joined Patín and Alonso to create a new organization—Comité Antifascista Español (Spanish Antifascist Committee, CAE)—and the members of the Ateneo Hispano, a migrant labor activist organization, offered its headquarters in New York City as a base. Founded by Arenas, Patín, and Alonso, along with several other active members in the Ateneo at that time, the CAE was the predecessor of the Sociedades Hispanas Confederadas.[3] A series of meetings with other proletarian associations soon followed. By July 25, only a week after the uprising, the Ateneo had become the Spanish workers' center of antifascist operations and held its first fundraising event: an inspirational speech by Luis Zugadi Garmendia, a Basque anarchist who would also become one of the SHC's founders. That same month, the CAE began publishing *Frente Popular* (Popular Front, 1936–1939). This publication was the precursor to *España Libre* (Free Spain, 1939–1977), which the

SHC would begin publishing three years later. Both periodicals articulated the confederation's political stance by publishing antifascist protest.

The Ateneo Hispano was an offshoot of a previous social center—the Centro Instructivo y Recreativo (Instructional and Recreational Center)—which served as a meeting place for Spanish, Italian, and Anglo-American anarchists and labor activists in New York. Many of the Ateneo Hispano's members would join the antifascist CAE. The members and sympathizers of the Ateneo Hispano already had an established record of organizing grassroots political activism, and they brought their experience to their work with the CAE. Run by workers, Ateneo Hispano breathed labor militancy. Its labor and political activism included projects in education, print culture, and theater and collaborations with American and international unions. The organization had long maintained a focus on education and the tradition of performing radical and popular theater. In 1934, one of the first events sponsored by the Ateneo Hispano was a conference featuring Columbia University Spanish professors Federico de Onís and Ángel del Río speaking on Spanish culture, an event for which the painter Juan Eugenio Domingo Mingorance (1906–1979) decorated the stage. Later, when the organization sought to raise money to move to new premises at 59 Henry Street, Brooklyn—which would have its own theater—the members held performances every Saturday, including a drama, a comedy, and a zarzuela.[4] The SHC's inclusive artistic, educational, and intellectual practices first developed in these earlier workers' associations would be maintained by the organization throughout its existence.

As a labor and cultural organization for migrant workers, the Ateneo Hispano paid close attention to Spanish news that arrived via newspapers brought by sailors, or from the sailors' firsthand accounts of the situation in Spain. After learning about the Second Republic's repression of the miners' strikes in Asturias, Spain, in October of 1934—one of the most important confrontations between workers and the Republic—the Ateneo Hispano organized a series of events to protest.[5] Anarchist and socialist workers in Spain and in the United States questioned the repressive policies of the Republic. In addition to sparking unrest among the workers, the Republican government in Spain also roused the Spanish right-wing and traditionalist groups to opposition. However, the right wing's concerns were less about repressive labor policies and were instead focused on the far-reaching educational, social, and institutional reforms that the Republic sought to impose, including institutional secularization and new agrarian laws that threatened the traditional oligarchy. Also, the Republic's attempts at national federalization aroused hostility from proponents of the centralization of political and economic power. Other workers' organizations in the United States besides the Ateneo Hispano in New York followed this broader political situation in Spain and sought to influence events in Spain as much as they could.

The tension between vanguard progressive movements and Spain's reactionary factions only partially explains the Spanish Civil War. When looking at the European continent more generally, it's clear that the rising fascist movements in Europe had a central role in the Spanish Civil War and the resulting Franco regime.[6] According to Ferran Gallego and Francisco Morente, "The fascistization of the Spanish right visibly began in 1933–34, with the creation of the Falange Española (Spanish Falange) in October 1933 and its fusion with the JONS to create FE-JONS (Falange Española–Juntas de Ofensiva Nacional-Sindicalista, Councils of the National-Syndicalist Offensive) in early 1934."[7] Spanish fascists and extreme-right groups shared a set of principles that was to be achieved through a totalitarian state, vertical syndicalism, vehement imperial rhetoric, National Catholicism, cultish dedication to a single leader and to the absolute dominance of a ruling minority, political indoctrination of the youth through educational policies, and a "deep purging of society through unbridled violence."[8] The example in Italy at this time was an important one. As Matteo Albanese and Pablo del Hierro have stated: "Many authoritarian and conservative politicians, frustrated by political turmoil and social unrest in the Republic, found a solution in the Italian model precisely because it appeared to ensure political stability and prosperity."[9] Eager to encourage the reforms in Spain similar to those passed in Italy, Benito Mussolini and his military and diplomatic agents engaged in fascist cultural penetration and propagandist pressure in the Spanish media, as well as in Spain's business and educational sectors.[10] Over time, features already promoted by the Spanish right—such as social corporatism, Catholicism, and traditional nationalism—combined into "a sort of Hispanized fascism" with the prominent leadership of the military and the Church.[11] Reactionary and fascist forces coalesced in these objectives, and their opposition to the democratic republic climaxed with a military coup on July 18, 1936, organized by leading military generals—most notably General Francisco Franco.

The Migrant Communities and Their Manifold Support for the SHC's Antifascism

During the Spanish Civil War and Franco's dictatorship, the SHC fought fascism in a variety of ways. As a port city, New York gave working-class residents "an unusual worldliness . . . sailors returned from sea with firsthand accounts of the rise and fall of fascism."[12] In particular, Hispanic sailors attended SHC fundraisers and rallies when in port in New York and collected funds on their ships. Several articles in *España Libre* list the names of contributing steamships and the amount of their regular collections. From their migrant enclaves, members came together and extended the scope of *España Libre* by participating in the associated organizations' fundraisers and submitting articles, subscriptions, and donations to the periodical. Their biographies, as published in the periodical, testify to their radical and antifascist migrant experiences.

However, workers' solidarity went beyond print protest and fundraising. Some traveled to Spain and were killed in battle. In his memoirs, Bernardo Vega recalls the fervent antifascist sentiment during the war from people living in the United States: "The democratic people of the United States stood alongside the Spanish people as they rose up in arms. Hundreds of young men of all nationalities wanted nothing more than to join the popular forces and did so."[13] Pablo de la Torriente Brau, the Puerto Rican–Cuban author and member of the Cuban Club Martí in Manhattan, left New York on August 28, 1936, carrying press credentials for the *New Masses, El Machete* (Mexico), and *Frente Popular* (which changed its name to *España Libre* in November 1939). Six months later, the SHC delegate was killed in Spain.[14]

SHC members also traveled to Spain. Already devoted anarchists, Basque brothers Luis and Ignacio Zugadi Garmendia immigrated to Cuba as young boys in 1917. From Cuba, they moved to New York where they joined Cultura Obrera, an anarchist organization, and worked with Pedro Esteve in writing for the association's periodical. When news of the Spanish Civil War arrived in New York, they joined with Arenas, Alonso, Patin, and several other founding members of the CAE. Luis Zugadi Garmendia, who also wrote for the New York anarchist periodicals *Aurora* and *Cultura Proletaria*, traveled to Spain to fight against fascism in 1937 and was killed in action in March 1938. In keeping with the ideals of solidarity among workers that were representative of the anarchist and socialist goals of the publication, the notice of his death, published in *Frente Popular*, asserted that not much was known about the life of this antifascist, because "workers have no history."[15] However, the obituary mentioned that like many other workers, he had migrated from the mines of Vizcaya to Cuba, and arrived in New York wandering the world with no other riches than his hopes and dreams.[16]

The SHC often shared membership with other unions, and migrants active in those other unions often supported the antifascist fight. For example, Cándido Villa, who worked as a coal miner in Virginia, came to the United States in 1905 from Pontevedra, Spain. He became an active affiliate of the Industrial Workers of the World (IWW). His obituary in *España Libre* noted that he had always supported the SHC's fundraising efforts. Similarly, Canary Islander Matías de la Rosa immigrated first to Cuba and then to New York, where he worked in the tobacco industry in the early 1890s. In the 1940s, he was president of La Fraternidad, an affiliated Masonic organization, and also served as the SHC's treasurer.[17]

Members of the SHC did not all live in major urban centers; many lived throughout the United States and its territories. But this did not diminish their opportunities for engagement in the organization's work. For example, one of the SHC's founding members, anarchist Rogelio Fernández, escaped the draft for the Spanish Second Melillan Campaign in Morocco and worked on crews constructing the Panama Canal.[18] When the Spanish Civil War broke out, he joined the Panamanian affiliate association Amigos de Sociedades Hispanas Confederadas. Fernández was able to connect to the work of the broader SHC through that organization's long-term sponsorship of *España Libre*, something it maintained until its last issue in 1977.[19] Andalusian labor leader Félix Lunar arrived in the United States in 1920; he first worked in the West Virginia coal mines. In 1924, he moved to work in the agricultural fields of California. Committed to fight fascism, Lunar was one of the most loyal article contributors to *España Libre*. From another important migrant enclave, Tampa, Florida, José Martínez Gil, cigar roller and then *lector* (factory reader), regularly contributed to *España Libre* with writing and funds. In Tampa, he also directed the periodical *El Internacional*, a publication of the AFL Journeymen Cigar Makers International Union. Martínez Gil later moved to New York and wrote antifascist plays for antifascist fundraisers. In New York, he also edited *Hércules*, the magazine of the Sociedad Gallega (Galician Society).[20]

Through shops, restaurants, boarding houses, and vacation villas, people engaged in cultural, commercial, and political communities financially sponsored the SHC by fundraising and advertising in *España Libre*. The stories of family businesses run by Domingo González, Manuel Montero López, Antonio Sánchez, and Esteban Roig are representative of some of the ways migrants from all walks of life sustained the SHC. Galician Spaniard Domingo González landed in New York as a stowaway in 1923 and worked as a kitchen helper until he could open his own business, Ebro Restaurant, located at 151 8th Street. After years of working on merchant ships, Manuel Montero López opened another popular meeting place, the United Café, on 11th Street in 1928.[21] One of the SHC's founders, Antonio Sánchez, was another well-known small business owner in the community that also advertised in *España Libre*. From 1919 to 1926, Sánchez had worked on merchant ships and on the Manhattan docks off-loading oil. He opened a small bar and four years later partnered with F. Calza and bought the Restaurante Castilla at 35 Madison

Street.²² These restaurants, like many others owned by migrants, ran advertisements for many years in *España Libre* and donated to fundraisers. Esteban Roig, a bookstore owner, ran an advertisement in the periodical announcing that Spanish music as well as anarchist and socialist books could be found in his bookstore at 576 Sixth Avenue. His band, the Happy Boys, enlivened many fundraisers and social events.²³

Equally important, the establishments mentioned above, among others, served as gathering places for the development of migrant networks. In this respect, boarding houses are depicted as social pillars of the migrant community in Prudencio de Pereda's *Windmills in Brooklyn*. De Pereda remembers Spaniards visiting the boarding houses that had originally welcomed them upon their arrival to the United States, where they would play cards and eat paella with other Spanish migrants.²⁴ In *Memoirs of Bernardo Vega*, the author likewise recalls the exquisite cuisine in the boarding house of Puerto Rican anarcho-feminist Luisa Capetillo.²⁵ Despite these rosy portrayals, living accommodations in boarding houses during the first decades of the century were often inhumane for poor newcomers to New York. According to Puerto Rican Joaquín Colón, dangerous gas lamps illuminated cold, rented rooms already filled with "territorial" rats and insects.²⁶ Nevertheless, the boarding houses—among other types of establishments—remained a critical site of contact for migrants.

Other types of lodgings also offered important points of contact for the Spanish migrants. Several SHC members ran vacation villas that offered affordable living arrangements for arriving Spaniards and provided inexpensive vacation spots for workers. El Cortijo, a vacation home in Fostertown, Wallkill, New York, was a very successful forty-five-room villa. To reach potential clients and support the work of the SHC, El Cortijo regularly purchased advertisements in *España Libre*. Like El Cortijo, Aldea Borines was another popular vacation house advertised in *España Libre*.²⁷ These villas were informal meeting places that helped workers cross regional, linguistic, ethnic, religious, racial, and gender lines, fostering a cosmopolitan culture based on multiethnic unions and mutual aid societies. Their support to the SHC and *España Libre* was long-lasting.

Spanish migrants working in numerous other industries also supported the work of the SHC across the United States. Many Spanish migrants worked for construction companies, sugar refineries, and cigar manufacturers owned by their compatriots, some of which were well established by the 1930s.²⁸ Valencian Vicente Martínez Ybor and Ignacio Haya, the most prominent manufacturers of Havana cigars in the nineteenth century, are a well-known example. They had been established in Florida since the nineteenth century, having purchased land in Tampa in 1885.[29] In Florida, as elsewhere in the country, publications helped form networks through which migrants in these areas and industries could both support antifascist work and fellow Spanish migrants. Spanish mutual aid societies and unions in Ybor City and neighboring Tampa alleviated the emotional hardships of living in a foreign country through subscriptions to their migrant periodicals and other forms of aid. *La Gaceta* (Tampa), a local Spanish-language periodical, was among the first publications to denounce the "fascist aggression towards the Spanish Republic [in the United States]," according to its director, Victoriano Manteiga.[30] Moreover, many Ybor City residents subscribed to *España Libre* until its last issue in 1977. Businesses in Florida also took out advertisements. For example, the tobacco manufacturer Miguel Alonso's advertisement read: "Miguel Alonso. Tobacco plant storehouse. Manufacturers of the famous Madrigal cigar."[31] Through subscriptions and advertisements, they were able to sponsor the publication and its cause.

From the first accounts of fascism brought by sailors, to fervent antifascists who traveled to fight in Spanish soil, to workers and activists fundraising and protesting in the United States, and to the publishers of *España Libre*, the antifascist fight of SHC members only ended with the first democratic elections after the Franco regime in Spain in 1977.

Solidarity and Protest against Spanish Fascism after the Spanish Civil War

Dictator Francisco Franco had a clear strategy inspired by his Italian military advisers. In February 1937, he told Colonel Emilio Faldella: "In a civil war, a systematic occupation of territory accompanied by the necessary cleansing is preferable to a rapid rout of the enemy armies which leaves the country still infested with enemies."[32] Franco's postwar repression continued this approach, beginning with the Law of Political Responsibilities (February 9, 1939) designed to economically punish dissenters, while also extracting resources for the victors.[33] Defining factors of this process were the role of National Catholicism, the cult of violence, and the militarization of the state. Spanish fascism "encompassed symbolic and doctrinal aspects, social control, mass organization and mobilization, the construction of the educational system, youth organizations, representations channels, the union apparatus, the articulation of local powers, and the establishment of clientelistic patterns at all levels of a modern power system."[34]

After the defeat of the Axis powers in World War II, Franco embraced a Christian and anticommunist agenda and sought to suppress the memory of his alliances with Adolf Hitler and Benito Mussolini. The defeat of Hitler and Mussolini accelerated Franco's desire to present his fascist government in different ways, and he did so through the transformation of the national-syndicalist state into a Catholic state, "dressing it in an 'organic democracy' capable of integrating itself into the new European order."[35] Traditional scholarly approaches divide fascism in Franco's Spain into two periods: a clear fascist period until 1941, and a less obvious fascist period after 1945.[36] For Stanley G. Payne, "Franco's political style, though always retaining fundamental principles of authoritarianism, nationalism, traditionalism, and Catholicism, was always eclectic."[37] Paul Preston titled his 2008 book *El gran manipulador* (The great manipulator), to reflect the chameleonlike capacity of the Caudillo. The dictatorship in Spain became a lesser evil for the United States and its European allies who were at the time fighting international communism. To define these adaptive characteristics of the Franco dictatorship, the regime has been characterized as "para-proto-pseudo-fascism" or "fascist-ized."[38]

From 1975 to 1977, the transition to democracy in Spain was guided by "the Francoist political elite and rigidly supervised by the pro-Franco army, backed by civilian Falangists, thousands of whom still had the right under Spanish law to carry arms. The price demanded by this powerful coalition for its support of institutional change was an amnesty for itself, and public silence over the past."[39] Whereas there is general acceptance that the Third Reich was responsible for mass murder, there has been no public condemnation of the Franco regime's fascist terror nor of the hideaway given to fascists and Nazis in Francoist Spain.[40] The cult of deadly fascist power in Spain, as far as it has not yet been tried, judged, and condemned, has continued to diminish Spanish democracy.

During the tumultuous decades spanning the Franco dictatorship, the SHC in the United States protested against Spanish fascism in the streets and on the pages of its bilingual periodical *España Libre*. The confederation grew to 65,000 members at its height.[41] Approximately two hundred affiliated grassroots associations organized fundraisers to support Spaniards under fascism and expressed their protest against the regime on the page and in the streets. From their migrant enclaves, the affiliated societies, clubs, centers, and athenaeums facilitated the safe arrival of Spanish Civil War exiles to the Americas. Earlier migrants and Spanish Civil War exiles subscribed to *España Libre*, submitted contributions, and advertised their family businesses in the periodical.

A close examination of *España Libre* reveals that workers early on understood Spanish fascism as a complex and adapting interlocking of fascist, extreme-right, and capitalist values. In 1940, one announcement about fascism in the April 12 *España Libre* issue claimed that fascism was a "political system based on the annihilation of liberty, maintained with the most barbaric repression. The arts, science, and peace disturb Nazism. For this reason, it hates books. German people live this way. Spanish people live this way."[42] In an essay published in *España Libre* two decades later, anarchist Manuel Villar Mingo, in exile in Buenos Aires, expressed the despair felt by Spaniards over the seeming permanence of Spanish fascism: "Democratic, popular, and progressive Spain was, once again, disappointed. For the Spaniards, the long night that began in April 1939 remained impenetrable in its darkness. It seems that we belong to another world, inhabitants of another planet, that our destiny counts little. For the Spaniards, Hitler won the war. This is the absurd and tragic result." Sharing a perception held by other exiles and readers of *España Libre*, Villar Mingo questioned the American notion that the Allied powers of the Second World War stopped fascism. Instead, he accurately claimed fascism continued in Spain.[43] Like other writers for *España Libre*, Jesús González Malo elaborated on the several reasons for claiming that fascism was continuing, not only in Spain but in the world. González Malo, an anarcho-syndicalist, argued that the anarchists and socialists failed to unite, communists and Russia served as justification for a fascist Spain, and the liberal democracies allowed it to happen. In doing so, González Malo claimed that world democracies "se han fascistizado" (fascistized themselves).[44]

The common usage of the term "fascistization" in *España Libre* referred to the complex ideological overlap of values between traditionalists and fascists in Franco's Spain.[45] *España Libre* claimed that Franco's Spain underwent an ongoing and adaptive fascistization process in which the political culture of fascism played a fundamental role in maintaining a system of domination over Spaniards. Franco embraced the regeneration of the nation, conceived of as a biological and historical community of like-minded individuals threatened by foreign elements. In this mindset, destruction was a precondition for reconstruction. Fascism initially responded to the "dangerous" progressive possibilities of the Second Republic, voted into office in April 14, 1931. *España Libre*'s contributors denounced not only the fascist violence and militarization that kept Franco in power but also how the regime kept Spain in complete backwardness: the limited development of a representative parliamentary state, the archaic rural economy, and the powerful, Christian, and conservative oligarchy.

España Libre helped create an antifascist, progressive, and radical legacy in the United States, one that represented an alternative, progressive path to modernity. Sophia A. McClennen criticizes some postmodern interpretations of an exilic mind as a metaphor for being "free of the repressive state of national identity."[46] Celebrating the condition of exile as an emancipator to transcend time and space disregards the fact that a displaced author must contend with questions of language, publication, and audience.[47] McClennen advocates for a greater attention to the émigré's historical context because to dehistoricize an experience outside the homeland is to glorify it and to strip it of its tragic meaning.[48] Following McClennen, I acknowledge the pain of members, staff, and contributors to avoid ignoring their historical marginalization. As McClennen stated: "Simply put, the condition of exile is directly a result of the social and political climate occupied by the author, making ahistorical exile literature a contradiction in terms."[49] Spanish Civil War exile scholarship has been particularly oblivious of Spanish workers exiled in the United States, whose struggle, and whose political and cultural legacy, has not been examined or anthologized, erasing them again from history.

In the United States, the SHC never ceased to organize various forms of condemnation of Spanish fascism despite being monitored by the Spanish Consulate in New York and its activities reported to the FBI. The SHC provided solidarity for the victims of fascism: migrants subscribed to *España Libre*, submitted written pieces to the periodical, organized fundraisers, and protested in the streets. For members, exile meant participatory antifascism but also the endurance of tragic circumstances, such as poverty, undocumented refugee status, and the haunting memory of relatives and friends killed in the Spanish Civil War or tortured in Franco's prisons. The same Law of Political Responsibilities that outlawed dissenters and confiscated their possessions was also applied to those who participated in pro-Republic efforts abroad, and the Spanish state sought to outlaw and dispossess them in the same way.[50] As a result, radical workers were never able to return to see their homes, their relatives, or friends in Spain while the dictator was alive.

Over the years, *España Libre* and the SHC's activism grew increasingly arduous, particularly during the Cold War. The United States had a non-interventionist policy toward Franco's Spain. At that time, U.S. opposition to communism coincided with General Franco's anticommunist doctrine, helping shield the Caudillo's fascist practices from international condemnation. Meanwhile, Franco fascistized Spain with a culture of National Catholicism and cult of military power that enforced social cleansing of dissenters and terrorized the population. However difficult, workers continued to play a key role in the transnational circulation of antifascist ideas. Jesús González Malo, anarcho-syndicalist exile and leader of the SHC, was determined to denounce Spanish fascism in *España Libre*, and to circulate antifascist literature to Spain.

Introduction

To avoid the Spanish regime's censorship, González Malo established a communication mechanism, contacting sailors in merchant ships arriving in New York, Boston, and Baltimore,[51] and he found sailors and maritime workers willing to smuggle reports on civil rights infringements out of Spain, or, on the other hand, to smuggle copies of *España Libre* into the country. Traveling Spaniards also volunteered to act as messengers and overcame Franco's surveillance network by camouflaging stacks of *España Libre*, antifascist documents, or correspondence with clandestine dissidents in Spain under their clothes.

González Malo's previous experience as president of the Union of Dock Workers in Santander, Spain, provided him with contacts who smuggled information to and from the underground opposition. This "under the radar" system also permitted the circulation of anarchist and exile periodicals in New York. However, on November 7, 1942, J. Edgar Hoover ordered FBI special agents in Baltimore to monitor González Malo and apprehend him if he was seen giving letters, documents, or parcels to any Spanish sailors at the docks.[52] The FBI interrogated González Malo several times in his home. Nonetheless, González Malo continued sending and receiving these periodicals and smuggling letters. By publishing censored information, González Malo's undercover communications played a key role in *España Libre*'s ability to document the fascist terror in Spain.

By resurrecting the antifascist activism and culture of *España Libre*, this book joins the work of other scholars in exploring the interaction of culture and radical ideologies.[53] In *Italian Immigrant Radical Culture*, Marcella Bencivenni highlights the role of culture in the subversive's radical world. Likewise, in *Underground Passages: Anarchist Resistance Culture, 1848–2011*, Jesse Cohn explains how anarchists have disseminated their ideology by creating attractive countercultural spaces with borrowings from artistic movements and subcultures.[54] Following Bencivenni and Cohn, *Fighting Fascist Spain* shows how a print culture that emphasized humor and documentary evidence encouraged both solidarity and the resistance to Franco. Spaniards' experiences in the United States, as progressive and radical migrants, show how common strategies of cultural production helped ethnic migrant communities to play a role in constructing antifascist America. Intimately linked to the history of European radical migrations to the United States, *Fighting Fascist Spain* contributes to the broader fields of American and Hispanic cultural studies. By looking at the role that literature, theater, and cartoons played in the antifascist fight of the SHC, a distinctive antifascist identity comes into view.[55]

The story of the SHC also foregrounds strategies of cultural production that demonstrate how migrant women navigated structures of power in ways that resonate with recent scholarship on immigrant radical women.[56] It is a distinctive characteristic of the SHC's cultural production that women did not often write or sign their work for *España Libre*, although they participated alongside men in political meetings and lectures and played a central role as organizers and performers in fundraisers.

Research on the modern migrant world of Spaniards in the United States has grown since the publication of Gary R. Mormino and George E. Pozzetta's seminal work, *The Immigrant World of Ybor City* (1987).[57] Though crucial to any study of Spaniards in the United States, recent publications focus on the decades prior to the Spanish Civil War, rather than providing an in-depth examination of the antifascist activists and their cultural production during the Franco era. Similarly, none of the research on the American organizations that aided Republican Spain, like the Abraham Lincoln Brigade and others, have examined the SHC's contributions to ethnic, labor, and literary history.[58] *Fighting Fascist Spain* applies an interdisciplinary approach that builds on scholarship about Spanish Civil War exiles, anarchist culture, and antifascist humor, as well as ethnicity, migration, and radical politics. With a transnational methodology, this book explores the web of interactions among migrants and exiles, cultural and political encounters, and literary and artistic exchanges that flourished in the confederation and the periodical. It describes the networks that Spanish exiles established within their home country, in the United States, and across the globe—networks that were crucial in the broader fight against fascism. It describes, for example, how the anarchist Hispanic milieu brought together labor leader and playwright José Castilla Morales, actress and director Mary Reid, and musician and satirist Adolfo Jiménez Colón (Lirón)—all of whom met in the workers' association Ateneo Hispano. The Spanish Civil War exile network was instrumental in assisting *España Libre* editor Jesús González Malo, contributor Carmen Aldecoa, and cartoonist Sergio Aragonés in immigrating to New York City. Similarly, the networks enabled by the U.S. Spanish-language periodicals provided satirist Aurelio Pego and poet Alfonso Camín with the professional and social connections required to sustain their zealous anti-Francoism. The personal and professional relations established through these radical and migrant networks coalesced in the SHC and extended the fight against fascism.

Fighting Fascist Spain also identifies the web of anarchist, anarcho-syndicalist, and socialist connections that facilitated the political engagement of local activists and organizations to enlarge the global reach of the organization. After the execution of Francesc Ferrer i Guàrdia in Barcelona in 1909, more than twenty Modern Schools were set up in New York and continued the influential educator's pedagogy. Several friends of the Modern Schools became influential patrons of the SHC. Of German origin, anarchist intellectual Rudolf Rocker arrived in the United States in 1933. Soon after, Rocker became one of the leading intellectual forces behind the Modern School at the Mohegan community in Crompond, New York, a role that he maintained until his death in 1958.[59] Over the years, a close friendship and collaboration developed between Rocker and *España Libre* editor González Malo. Rocker's friends Roger Nash Baldwin and Norman Thomas also helped the SHC by focusing international attention on the incarcerations and executions of resistance leaders in Spain. The connections extended to Victor Reuther (United Automobile Workers of America) and Nancy Macdonald (Spanish Refugee Aid), who financially and politically assisted the SHC. In turn, Baldwin, Macdonald, Reuther, Rocker, and Thomas opened access to labor and progressive American networks of activism and solidarity that aided refugees as well as the underground resistance during the Franco regime.

In re-creating their cultural world, *Fighting Fascist Spain* recovers talented working-class authors and artists who were no longer invested in imminent revolutions but instead adapted to the demands of exile and the Cold War. Although Castilla Morales, Lirón, Pego, and Reid are almost completely erased from history by Americanization and Francoism, they influenced migrants in ways similar to earlier anarchist activists Luisa Capetillo, Pedro Esteve, the Flores Magón brothers, and Lucy G. Parsons, among others. Also, these recovered authors form part of a broader antifascist movement in exile, which in Chris Vials's words: "helped to create the Adornos, Marcuses, and Gramscis."[60] The SHC empowered members to resist fascism and redefine their political and cultural values. Aware that Francoist repression was undermining people's voices, Aldecoa, Miguel Giménez Igualada, González Malo, and Ramón J. Sender documented or fictionalized Spanish anarcho-syndicalist history and validated diversity and interdependence as tools of everyday resistance in exile. Likewise, Félix Martí Ibáñez's fiction, Aragonés's and Josep Bartolí Guiu's cartoons, Castilla Morales's comedies, and Pego's satirical chronicles aesthetically re-created this resistance. In the United States, these authors were successful in refuting fascist myths and in revitalizing people's history and culture. Spanish migrants brought with them progressive, popular, and humorous traditions that helped shape their response to fascism. However, authors also adapted those ideas in their American exile. Although veiled, Martí Ibáñez's anarchist values continued to be the root of the alternative strands of representation in some of his short stories published in the highly regarded medical magazines *MD*, which featured pieces on medicine, culture, and literature.[61] Also, Aragonés's editorial experience in *España Libre* transferred to his playful artistic sensibility, which continued to be nurtured in *Mad* magazine. By examining such adaptations, *Fighting Fascist Spain* reveals the varied and flexible practices of anarchists and antifascists in exile and their influence in American culture. Notably, a rich migrant culture was at the heart of these authors' antifascist sentiment.

The Interlocked Nature of Antifascist Activism and Culture

The rich artistic production found in exile periodicals is a powerful demonstration of the way humans cannot be forcibly detached of their culture.[62] *España Libre*, as a site of culture, kept close to the activists' hearts their radical and progressive working-class identity. Indeed, political resistance also meant the cultural continuity of radical Spain in exile. Far from assimilating into the dominant Spanish Republican exile and U.S. cultures, *España Libre* re-created an independent, working-class, caring antifascist culture. The intellectual, political, and cultural engagement that was offered through literature, theater, and cartoons by the SHC protected members from the steady trauma of exile and prevented them from being paralyzed or worn down. Instead, satire and sarcasm empowered them, and humor maintained their capacity to laugh in distress. As a result, this witty, engaged, and caring culture that fostered solidarity was a forceful blow against fascist power. As Audre Lorde has stated, caring culture was not an indulgence in the antifascist fight, it was "an act of political warfare."[63] For the SHC to remain strong in its efforts to fight antifascism and not to yield to fascist repression required the conviction that working-class identity, history, and culture mattered, and that it was worth documenting and re-creating in exile. *España Libre*, as a site of cultural production, fought this "good fight." For the antifascist workers, *España Libre* became their voice in exile all the way from the late 1930s until the 1970s.

The antifascist and anarchist ideas that the SHC expressed in the pages of *España Libre* were presented in an array of journalistic, literary, and visual forms. These ideas and genres developed over the course of several decades within specific historical, political, and cultural contexts. In order to clarify the intellectual and literary development—and the broader contexts that fostered that development—*Fighting Fascist Spain* is organized thematically and is broken out into two parts. The first part (chapters 1–5) describes the organizational development of the SHC and *España Libre* as well as the solidarity exemplified by them. The second part (chapters 6–10) focuses on the cultural production that sustained the antifascist exile more generally, such as the literary genres that were published in the periodical, many of which were intrinsic to anarchist thought and culture.

Looking at the SHC and its work through these historical and literary lenses brings into view the robust cultural world that was the strength of the SHC's antifascist solidarity. Both during the Spanish Civil War and the decades of Franco dictatorship, Spanish progressives of all social classes went into exile. Although the SHC's predominant focus was its opposition to fascism, and the organization would remain the most important point of contact for antifascist Spaniards in the United States, the SHC was also supported and influenced by a broader confluence of networks of anarchists, antifascists, Hispanics, Spanish Civil War exiles, and labor radicals. These ethnic and radical networks strengthened the SHC's commitment to generating its own non-institutionalized modes of organization in its fight against fascism.

España Libre: The Voice of Antifascist Workers

Although there were other antifascist and pro-Republic periodicals published in New York City, none were published by and for a community of workers for the entire period of Franco's rule until the dictator died and elections were celebrated again in Spain in 1977. Affiliation to *España Libre* was instrumental in disseminating workers' ideology and culture. On average, 4,000 weekly copies circulated in the United States and worldwide, and about 500 copies were smuggled into Spain. Tellingly, *España Libre* never abandoned its anarchist and antifascist militancy, and it continued rallying, fundraising, and protesting on the page and on the stage during the McCarthy era. One of the important sections of the periodical was the book service that organized the distribution of books and magazines to members and readers. By looking at the circulation patterns of these books and the periodical, it's possible to trace the ways radical political ideas were disseminated beyond the borders of postwar Europe and in Cold War America. Throughout the many changing historical contexts during its existence, *España Libre* employed a vast range of strategies on the page to fight fascism from the United States. This book reveals how these strategies changed over time, even though their longer-term goal of ending fascism remained constant.

Helped by numerous staff writers, the editors and main contributors to *España Libre* were political leaders who thrived on debate and activism but who were also sophisticated chroniclers of Spanish politics and culture. In their commitment to denouncing Franco's Spain and cultivating radical thought, the periodical's editors ensured the continuation of *España Libre* for thirty-eight years by volunteering, fundraising, and soliciting contributors. In particular, the story of González Malo exemplifies how labor leaders gained access to a public sphere through their work as editors of *España Libre*, which allowed them to converse with prominent thinkers in the United States, and with clandestine dissidents in Spain. The extremely active editors and contributors conducted the periodical's editorial work through a bottom-up approach that helped in the formation of an antifascist transnational print network connecting the United States, Latin America, and Europe.

España Libre had an unprecedented catalytic role in fostering solidarity for victims of Spanish fascism. Some members had fought in the civil war and lost their homeland. Most had family members and friends who had been executed, imprisoned, or were living under fascist rule. Their own migrant status in the United States was uncertain because they were never granted refugee status, and both the FBI and Spanish consular officials were surveilling them for their socialist and anarchist affiliations. Pro-Republic Spaniards in the United States became people "without a country" with no right to U.S. citizenship and unable to seek the services of Spanish embassies and consulates in the United States. Despite this precarious situation, the SHC sent funds, goods, and ambulances to Republican fronts during the Spanish Civil War. After the war, the confederation helped relocate fellow refugees to visa-granting countries, and sent aid to the underground resistance in Spain. The history and literature of the exiled working class in the United States during the war has been disregarded on the assumption that workers were not politically organized and their cultural production was not diverse or innovative. However, the texts published in *España Libre* prove that this preconceived notion is not accurate.

When Franco came to power, those who supported the Second Republic were incarcerated or executed. In order to protest this imprisonment or execution of political prisoners in Spain, the SHC demonstrated, boycotted, and fundraised in the streets of cities across the United States. While the international press overlooked the execution of dissenters in Spain, *España Libre* disseminated information about the ongoing political killings to the world and clandestinely in Spain. In order to accomplish this critical resistance effort, which was central to the work of the SHC, the organization undertook numerous fundraising campaigns over the years. Women members in the SHC led the street protests and fundraisers for political dissenters and prisoners in Spain. These events—which had been organized by the SHC and publicized in *España Libre*—are documented in archival photography. The last *España Libre* issue, published in 1977, announced that the SHC had raised a total of two million dollars since the beginning of the publication in 1939.

España Libre's writers debated how best to approach and support the resistance efforts—from intellectual and aesthetic debates, to ones focused on action. I trace the adaptive nature of anarchist and antifascist culture published in *España Libre* by examining the transformation of the literary archetypes prevalent at the end of the conflict into exile literary representations. For example, Alfonso Camín, one of the writers in *España Libre*, encouraged a combative antifascism that would appeal to the Spanish symbol for freedom, Don Quixote, while anarchist Miguel Giménez Igualada promoted a maternalist approach, in which women took the role of caregivers of antifascist homes. *España Libre* also played a critical role in preserving and interpreting the memory of those fallen in the Spanish Civil War and those tortured or executed by Franco's regime. Although readers were exposed to warlike rhetoric and traditional perspectives on gender, *España Libre*'s literature also foreshadowed a more intersectional world. In particular, Martí Ibáñez's short stories had a significant role in the transformation of anarchist literature from the revolutionary Spanish context to the fight against fascism in exile. His narratives foregrounded affective engagement with others as means of a lifestyle of resistance. Similarly, migrant texts documented and poeticized *España Libre* readers' lives in the United States and provided them with a developing ethnic identity and history in the United States.

Several *España Libre* writers and editors reexamined anarchism in exile.[64] The adaptability of anarchism in its fight for its ideal of a free society was particularly evident in exile and these efforts were active until democracy was restored in Spain. Contributors documented Spanish labor print culture that was being systematically erased by the regime, contested stereotypes of anarchists, and viewed workers, migrants, and minorities as politically key actors against fascism. Spanish anarchism among exiles in the United States was not rigid or anchored in the past; rather, it underwent an ideological evolution that was tied to the authors' exile experience and marked by postwar antifascism. Anarchists no longer sought violent insurrection against the state but instead sought spontaneous prefiguration of a free society enacted by everyday acts of mass organizing, cooperation, and cultural transformation. Instead of eliminating the idea of revolution, exiles integrated their revolutionary principles into everyday life in the United States. Moving toward a postmodern approach, revolution was exercised by inclusion of subjectivities rather than through violent contest of political power. These anarchist developments constitute critical outcomes in the broader history discussed in *Fighting Fascist Spain*.

The comic and farcical theater of the SHC had a crucial significance in raising funds and creating working-class identity in exile. Although the original plays are now mostly lost, it is nevertheless possible to find information about them through the reviews published in *España Libre* of these vibrant anarchist and popular theatrical traditions. In an effort to encourage attendance and raise funds, the periodical published the plays' opening day, the names of the affiliations in charge, as well as the names of the amateur actors. Indeed, for the SHC, theater was a collective venture. José Castilla Morales, an active member, playwright, and writer for *España Libre*, and Mary Reid, an active actress and director, transformed their community's tragic exile into a meaningful struggle for ethnic and working-class solidarity through artistic works of parody and wit. Both original and popular plays were performances of género chico (popular, farcical genre), a popular Hispanic theatrical form, known for its sharp-witted action, skilled dialogues, farcical humor, and working-class protagonists. The performances exhibit a clear hybrid nature: the cross-cultural influences, the parody of canonical drama, the nostalgia of popular plays and dances, the blurred distinctions between popular and high cultures in operettas and zarzuelas, and the grotesque and satirical sketches about current political news. These theatrical works redefined possibilities of artistic vigor to awaken political consciousness in exile.

In addition to theater, essays and editorials by numerous writers helped develop community and solidarity and inspire activism among readers. One of the main writers for *España Libre*, Aurelio Pego, articulated in his works a sharp, humorous attack on fascism that also helped turn exile into a livable experience. Defeated exiles needed comic relief and community, and sarcasm provided both. His insightful humor greatly appealed to exiles and it cultivated their will to resist while proclaiming the urgency of change. Pego's wit was incisive in countering fascist myth-making with a satiric worldview that was grounded in an attack on the imperial representation of the Caudillo, National Catholicism, and fascist exercise of power and political repression. With spirited chronicles, Pego lampooned American and exiles for their inaction.

Varied visual strategies were put forth in the periodical. Some authors ridiculed fascists in gendered terms while others sought compassion for refugees. Comic art grew awareness of the threat of fascism and exposed the state of terror perpetrated by Hitler and Franco. When Aragonés translated the Spanish underground resistance reports into visual language on the front page of *España Libre*, he perceptively counteracted the regime's propaganda. Similarly, Bartolí Guiu's illustrations humanized political prisoners for readers. Compared with the flashy sarcasm with which Pego wrote his crónicas, caricaturists attacked fascism with polished and precise strokes. Cartoons delivered *España Libre*'s mission powerfully until the last issue of the periodical, even after many founders had passed away and fundraising had decreased.

In exile, the SHC was as organized and politically active against Franco as were their underground comrades in Spain. From the United States, associations fought against incarcerations and the extermination of dissenters in fascist Spain with activism, print protest, and solidarity. *España Libre* writers denounced fascism and transformed political discourse into participatory collective action by devoting their lives to antifascist activism and culture. The history of *España Libre* reveals an unknown dimension of political and cultural antifascism in the United States. While the mainstream press celebrated the defeat of fascism in Europe, *España Libre* published about the fascist regime that persisted in Spain until 1977: unified national movement, the role of the Falange, the fascist conception of Spanish economy, the systematic social cleansing, the cult of the heroes of Movimiento, and the normalization of violence and state of terror in Spain. For decades, the SHC did not stop its prolabor and antifascist militancy and continued its contacts with U.S. labor leaders, leading rallies and developing funding. Moreover, *España Libre* cultivated a rich set of literary and cognitive tools that interrogated how Spanish fascist power operated.

The broad objective of *Fighting Fascist Spain* is not merely to recover a neglected migrant activism and literature but to articulate how workers' culture and politics shaped their antifascism. Using extensive and previously ignored literary, visual, and archival sources, the book explores abounding anarchist literature and antifascist humor. *Fighting Fascist Spain* contends that workers' public protest was fashioned by traditions and institutions: grassroots associations, the alternative press, and the comic and farcical theater that provided opportunities for anarchist practice and humorous antifascism. Spanish and American twentieth-century political repression of anarchism has kept the movement marginal. The workers' legacies have been forgotten or misrepresented by fascist and Cold War discourses. Therefore, the story of the SHC is one of academic recovery.

The playwright and writer José Castilla Morales foresaw and denounced this historical erasure. In an article published in *España Libre*, Castilla Morales recalled a conversation about Julián Amo and Harmion Shelby's *La obra impresa de los intelectuales españoles en América 1936–1945* (The print works of Spanish intellectuals in America 1936–1945), published in 1950. Referring to the publication, Castilla Morales claimed: "I knew it all before it came out."[65] He agreed that the book, published by Stanford University Press, looked magnificent, but protested: "There are many known names that are missing, among them, mine."[66] The antifascist activists are also often missing in the remaining associations' websites or related social media. In particular, anarchists' stories have often been disregarded or even dehumanized for their radical perspectives on state power. However, their important antifascist interventions can be found in the same associations' minutes, periodicals, and other publications. Only by uncovering these untold narratives can we make sense of our present and rediscover the communities and practices that keep fighting for civil rights. *España Libre* was the means by which the SHC developed a public institution that could facilitate the work of this confederation of antifascist workers, and ultimately invite the solidarity from other organizations and individuals across the world.

Part One

Print Culture, Activism, and Solidarity

1

Transnational Networks of Support

The extraordinary story of SHC's antifascist activism comes alive on the pages of *España Libre*. United by a print culture of solidarity and political protest, various networks helped the working-class confederation. Active members from these networks met at fundraisers at athenaeums and workers' associations, creating a confluence of antifascist, Hispanic, and radical hubs of resistance whose members influenced and aided one another. The periodical also evidences the ways in which, by virtue of their elite positions, Spanish politicians, intellectuals, and professors assisted displaced exiles. *España Libre* reveals significant networking with labor leaders in the United States as well. By facilitating contacts with local unions, activists, and radical intellectuals, influential patrons of the SHC attracted international attention to the incarcerations and executions of resistance leaders in Spain.

By publishing reviews of antifascist fundraisers and developing its network of professional and social connections internationally, the SHC was able to use *España Libre* to extend the scope of its zealous antifascism among other ethnic radical and migrant print cultures in the United States and around the world. These included networks associated with the Second Spanish Republican government and politicians in exile; labor unions both within and outside the United States; educators including exiled Spanish academics and the Modern Schools; as well as Spanish-language and radical publishers operating in Europe and South America.

The Government of the Second Spanish Republican in Exile

The Government of the Second Spanish Republic continued to be active in exile after the victory of Francisco Franco's forces in the Spanish Civil War. Its officials resided in various countries until the restoration of democracy in Spain in 1977. Although the United States did not recognize it, the government had diplomatic relations with Mexico, Panama, Guatemala, Venezuela, Poland, Czechoslovakia, Hungary, Yugoslavia, Romania, and Albania. Communicating across national boundaries, the SHC worked with the exiled government in aiding refugees. Several politicians and members of the government contributed to *España Libre* from the countries where they were residing, and their speeches were reproduced in the periodical.

Despite working with the government-in-exile in important ways, because of the SHC's radical politics and its long-term commitment to anarchist and socialist ideas, the confederation was still active in promoting its core agenda. For example, although the SHC shared many goals with the government-in-exile, *España Libre* still published critiques of the government and accused it of applying ineffective strategies, some of which led to heated responses. Discussions arose during several attempts to institute a government-in-exile representative in the United States. On each of these occasions, the SHC reminded the government of the powerful position of the confederation, which was the result of its political diversity and its networking with numerous hubs of support with labor leaders and politicians in the United States. In 1961, for instance, when the then-minister of foreign affairs in exile, Fernando Valera Aparicio, visited an SHC assembly in its headquarters in New York, he accused affiliates of impeding the possibility of establishing a government-in-exile representative there. González Malo, then one of the executive members of the SHC, replied to Valera Aparicio by stating that the government-in-exile had to *earn* representation in New York instead of demanding it. Outraged, Valera reminded the audience that government-in-exile representatives were too busy escaping arrest and deportation to be seeking support from the SHC.[1] Consequently, *España Libre* published an article with the ironic title "Grata visita" (A Pleasant visit), informing its readers that the government-in-exile was to designate a representative in the United States in consultation with the various exile organizations settled in the United States.[2] Thus, the efforts of the government-in-exile to lead the exiles were in tension with the radical efforts of SHC members to organize the community from below. Although the SHC regularly worked with the government-in-exile and the broader Spanish Civil War exile network, it remained independent, and editorial decisions for *España Libre* were taken by members in regular assemblies.

Spanish Professors

At the turn of the twentieth century, the Junta para la Ampliación de Estudios del Ministerio de Instrucción Pública (Board for the Extension of Studies of the Ministry of Public Instruction, 1907–1939) granted study-abroad stays for Spanish professors and Spanish intellectuals.[3] Before the democratic government was overthrown in Spain in the 1930s, a number of Spanish academics had already settled in the United States. Many of these individuals would provide support and sponsorship for *España Libre*. Notably, Federico de Onís and Ángel del Río often worked with the organization. De Onís, from the University of Salamanca, arrived at Columbia University in 1916 to teach Spanish language and literature. He founded the Instituto de las Españas in New York in 1920. De Onís was awarded honorary membership in the SHC in 1954 for he often gave speeches at fundraisers. De Onís also became a member of the SHC International Advisory Committee in 1960, and he was appointed to help Spanish political prisoners. Del Río, who had arrived at Columbia University in 1929, also participated in numerous ways in the work of the periodical and the confederation. He penned several essays for *España Libre* and opened a round of conferences for members at the mutual aid society La Nacional.[4]

Other professors assisted several fleeing exiles in relocating to the United States and helped them into teaching posts. Américo Castro, who joined the faculty at Princeton University in 1940, helped José Rubia Barcia to receive a temporary contract with the university in 1943. In 1947, Rubia Barcia became a professor in the Department of Spanish and Portuguese at the University of California, Los Angeles. There, Rubia Barcia joined the affiliated association Leales Españoles de California (Loyalist Spaniards in California), and participated in fundraising activities for the SHC and *España Libre*. He also became a long-term contributor to *España Libre*, and he submitted opinion columns to the periodical from the 1940s until the last issue in 1977.

Even exiled professors and politicians, who lived penurious lives and were often marked by the psychological effects of exile, constituted a strong support network for *España Libre* and devoted their limited resources to fighting fascism and restoring democracy in Spain.[5] In 1939, Carmen Aldecoa and Jesús González Malo fled Spain to Cuba because Rubia Barcia invited Aldecoa to be part of the faculty of La Escuela Libre in Havana. Aldecoa then secured an adjunct position teaching Spanish in the Romance Languages Department at New York University. Her husband, González Malo, found work as a welder. He became affiliated with the United Auto Workers (UAW) District 65, the SHC, and then served as chief editor of *España Libre* from 1961 to 1965. In turn, Aldecoa and González Malo provided legal assistance to fleeing Spaniards for decades.

Through the years, González Malo continued to reach out to Spanish professors, politicians, and professionals in exile and to ask them to help the SHC. In one instance, he asked exiled journalist Víctor Alba for possible sponsors and contributors, who referred him to professors in the United States and abroad who could help.[6] González Malo also contacted Ramón J. Sender, exiled author and professor at the University of Albuquerque. Sender became a regular contributor to *España Libre* and through his eminence helped to support its distribution. From 1939 to 1977, several other professors in the United States and in other countries where exiles found refuge contributed to the periodical and attended fundraisers, including Francisco Ayala (Chicago, Princeton, Rutgers, New York University), Alonso Ayensa y Sánchez de León (Universidad Nacional Autónoma de México), Bernando Clariana (Middlebury College), and José Rubia Barcia (University of California, Los Angeles). With their written submissions, speeches, acts of solidarity, professional contacts, and donations, they supported *España Libre* and the SHC.

The Hispanic Press in the United States

The Hispanic press operating in the United States was another network of support for the SHC. As an ethnic community group, the SHC participated in the already well-established Hispanic networks within the country. Dating back to the early nineteenth century, Spanish-speaking and immigrant communities in the United States have published periodicals that have articulated radical, gender, class, political, and ethnic interests; protected and fostered the language, education, and culture of their ethnic minorities; and denounced totalitarian rule abroad.[7] The labor and ethnic periodicals connected to workers' associations educated their members in similar ways. Several Spanish-language newspapers praised *España Libre*'s antifascist journalism and reviewed their fundraisers. Among the publications that supported *España Libre*'s work were *La Prensa* (San Antonio), *Pueblos Hispanos* (New York), *Liberación* (New York), and *Ecos* (New York). Each of these publications would often review commemorations and fundraisers.[8] Anarchist Armando del Moral, a syndicated journalist for Spanish-language newspapers in the United States, lauded Hispanic comradeship during the commemoration of the Second Republic held by the affiliated association Los Leales in Los Angeles. Del Moral, a Spanish Civil War refugee himself, recalls how Spaniards cheered "Mexico" at the event, one of the few countries granting resident visas to fleeing Spaniards.[9] Antifascism united Hispanic communities in the United States.

These long-established newspapers offered jobs to Spanish migrants and exiles. Making use of this broader network among the Spanish-language press, Sergio Aragonés moved from Mexico to New York to further his career as a cartoonist in 1962. His uncle, Manuel Aragonés, who worked with González Malo to provide Mexican visas to refugees, asked him to help his nephew become established in New York. After his arrival, Aragonés's drawings illustrated signs at the regular demonstrations in front of the Spanish Consulate and the United Nations in New York. Aragonés also contributed to *España Libre* with his antifascist cartoons until 1965, the year of González Malo's death.[10] Helped by Cuban Antonio Prohibas, Aragonés secured a contract with *Mad* magazine and went on to become a renowned cartoonist.

Members also reinvented themselves in the United States as U.S.-based correspondents for Spanish-language periodicals outside the United States. This was the case for Aurelio Pego, who developed his career as a journalist, writing as an unpaid correspondent for Spanish and Latin American newspapers soon after his arrival in New York in 1919. By 1921, he was writing commissioned chronicles for several Spanish-language and labor journals and was copy-writing for advertising companies. Not only a prolific author but also a staunch anti-Francoist, Pego joined *España Libre* in 1940 as a staff writer. His satirical columns mocking fascists ran until the paper closed its doors. By joining the newspaper as staff members and contributors and otherwise reporting on news from Spain, these lesser-known journalists were able to serve as key vehicles for antifascist protest and solidarity organized from below.

The Anarchist Press

The SHC significantly participated in global communities fashioned by the anarchist press. Many of the connections to these global communities came through the anarchist print cultures already existing in the United States at this time. The U.S. Hispanic literature scholar Nicolás Kanellos distinguishes three major interconnected nodes of anarchist print cultures in the United States: New York, Ybor City in Florida, and the Southwest.[11] Anarchist periodicals, which often shared their membership, maintained close ties with their networks. During the Spanish Civil War and the Franco regime, these links were vital for the relocation of refugees. This was the case of José Nieto Ruiz, who escaped Spain after being subjected to torture for his syndicalist activities in 1960. Anarchists helped him flee Spain and eventually reach Canada. He was detained there at an immigration center. Canadian anarchists contacted comrades in Cuba, who arranged for a visa for him to travel to the island. From Cuba, he then went to Miami in 1962. There, Cuban anarchists in the city paid for him to join González Malo in New York. Nieto Ruiz became one of the staff writers of the periodical and González Malo's closest associate.[12]

Anarchist networks extended to all countries where Spaniards found refuge and served to connect antifascist writers and editors. The first interaction between journalist Zwy Aldouby and González Malo was through the Spanish anarchist exile community in Paris, France. In 1964, anarcho-syndicalist Juan Manuel Molina Mateo referred Aldouby to González Malo because the journalist was preparing a manuscript on the Spanish Civil War and inquired about *España Libre*.[13] After meeting González Malo, Aldouby volunteered to edit the English section of the exile periodical. Indeed, the Spanish-language anarchist press network was one of the most important pillars for the organic strength of the SHC.

This intricate involvement in the SHC also brought disputes. For example, the naming of communist Daniel Alonso as the first secretary of propaganda of the initial Comité Antifascista Español (CAE) was a contentious issue for the anti-Stalinist anarchist community. Anarchists were concerned about party-driven decisions by communists in the CAE.[14] Although CAE leaders vehemently rejected the accusations, the complaints prompted *España Libre* (and its precursor *Frente Popular*) to publish data on aid collected and sent to Spain.[15] Stalinist and anti-Stalinist perspectives continued to create tension within the organization. When Alonso stepped down in November 1939, the communists decided to leave with him, and the organization and the periodical adopted new names to reflect the changes. In November 1939, the CAE evolved to the Sociedades Hispanas Confederadas (SHC) and the periodical *Frente Popular* stopped publication and *España Libre* was launched. When Alonso died in 1962, anarchist Jesús Arenas Ruiz revealed the secret pact he had made with Alonso: they had signed an honor agreement by which they promised each other to put the CAE antifascist mission first before any ideological dogma or party lines.[16] However, distrust continued in the anarchist press where there was discontent about the SHC's cooperation with the non-anarchist left and the Government of the Second Spanish Republic in exile.[17]

Because of political disagreements, the anarchists often relied on personal relations for the survival of their networks. Catalan anarchist Pedro Esteve, who edited Spanish and Italian newspapers in Barcelona, Cuba, Tampa, New York, and Paterson, worked with anarchist Adrián del Valle, who also wrote for anarchist newspapers in Barcelona and Cuba and was in contact with the Italian anarchist print culture of New York. Del Valle was, in turn, a close friend of Asturian-born Alfonso Camín, who migrated to Cuba in 1905. Two decades later Camín became a prolific and popular contributor to the Hispanic and anarchist press in the Americas and became *España Libre*'s most appreciated poet. With his weekly submissions, Camín contributed to the periodical's antifascist mission through poetry, short stories, and essays.

These networks based on friendships lasted decades and extended to other radical ethnic print cultures. Only after a few days after Pedro Esteve's death in 1925, his friend Salvador Espí met Castilla Morales in the Círculo Instructivo y Recreativo on 23rd Street in New York. As an SHC delegate in Paterson during the Spanish Civil War, Espí and other members fundraised as much as they could to fight Spanish fascism. An interview published in *España Libre* after Espí's death in 1943 noted that numerous Italian Americans contributed to the funds raised by Espí for the periodical and the confederation.[18] In the end, the anarchist press and its writers weighted personal relations—and shared antifascist sentiment—more than distrust of coalitions in their political projects. The anarchist press participated in *España Libre*'s antifascist efforts, providing network support through their personal connections, and supporting the publication with announcements and reviews about fundraisers.[19]

Labor Unions in the United States and Canada

Relying upon the exchange of publications and interpersonal networks, Spanish migrants involved in the work of the SHC built a strong presence among labor unions in several industries in the opening decades of the twentieth century in the United States. In the maritime industry, for example, Hispanics played a major role in the Atlantic Coast maritime trade—primarily working as firemen (*fogoneros*) on ships sailing out of ports in the United States.[20] The anarchist periodical *Cultura Obrera* had a direct relationship with dock workers and seamen, and became an official publication of the Marine Firemen, Oilers, and Watertenders Union of the Atlantic and the Gulf, a union founded by Jaime Vidal, an anarchist journalist and activist colleague of Pedro Esteve, one of the other writers at *Cultura Obrera*.[21] These sailors helped distribute radical propaganda around the world. Also, many Spanish migrants who worked in the maritime industry and had become members of the Industrial Workers of the World (IWW) also joined the SHC when the Spanish Civil War broke out. This was the case of *España Libre* editor José Castilla Morales, who organized maritime workers in Cuba before migrating to New York where he edited the IWW's *Solidaridad* (1918–1930).[22]

SHC members and *España Libre*'s editors and writers also actively communicated with numerous other labor unions within the United States and internationally. For example, seeking printing funds as editor of *España Libre*, González Malo contacted the International Ladies' Garment Workers Union (ILGWU), IWW, the UAW and the American Federation of Labor and Congress of Industrial Organizations (AFL-CIO). As part of their support for their fellow workers under fascism in Spain, and in response to the constant requests from González Malo, American unions supported the antifascist publication with small donations. In turn, *España Libre* featured on its front pages the unions' resolutions against Franco's regime and their support to Spanish workers.[23] Throughout the years, conjoined demonstrations were also featured in the periodical, in particular those in front of the Spanish Consulate on Madison Avenue. Unions also lent their associations' spaces for fundraisers or meetings. For example, in 1960, the Liga Democrática Española, an affiliated association of the SHC, and the socialist federation Workmen's Circle Center in Montreal, Canada, worked together to commemorate April 14, the anniversary of the Second Republic, and fundraised with popular performances and plays.[24] On another occasion, Juan Bacofra, one of the *España Libre* contributors, gave a talk, "The Current Spanish Situation," at an event organized by the Socialist Party (SP) and the Democratic Socialist Federation (DSF) at the Workmen's Circle Center in New York in 1962.[25] Making sure that refugees and dissidents in Spain received as much help as possible, González Malo navigated American union rivalries and disputes in diplomatic ways. In a letter to Julián Gorkin in November 1962, González Malo alerts the editor of *Cuadernos del Congreso de la Libertad de la Cultura* (Paris) about the rivalry between Jay Lovestone (AFL) and Victor Reuther (CIO). Gorkin was seeking help from Lovestone for the underground resistance in Spain, and González Malo was afraid their conversations might affect Reuther's commitment to help the SHC.[26]

In their effort to assist the clandestine resistance in Spain, González Malo and Manuel Dorado, SHC general secretary, sent numerous letters to individuals, institutions, and unions around the world asking for donations for *España Libre*. They described the periodical as the organ of the SHC, a North American apolitical grassroots initiative fighting Spanish fascism. Thanks to their efforts, in August 1967, the UAW granted two thousand dollars to pay one of *España Libre*'s debts to a printer.[27] According to its correspondence, there were several UAW donations to the SHC from 1966 to 1976. In addition to the help with the debt for printing, donations totaling another three thousand dollars were documented in the donor pages in *España Libre*.[28] The ILGWU also supported *España Libre* with several five-hundred-dollar donations.[29] The periodical published notices of these and other American unions helping Spanish workers in Spain. As I discuss in more detail in later chapters, González Malo conducted a notable mailing campaign where he achieved several donations for Spanish unions in exile. This effort led to five hundred dollars being sent to the Socialist General Union of Workers (UGT) in Toulouse on November 30, 1951.[30] The historical and transnational connections between American unions and Spanish migrants within the United States and elsewhere played an important role in the support the SHC received.

The Modern School Network

Like the labor and anarchist press, radical associations supported the mission of the SHC. The Modern Schools, which were meeting grounds where anarchists interacted with progressive thinkers and artists, were part of the confluent circuits of kinship that aided the SHC. After the execution of Francesc Ferrer i Guàrdia in Barcelona in 1909, more than twenty Modern Schools were set up in New York that continued the influential educator's pedagogy.[31] Directed by workers, the Modern Schools provided instruction for their children and became focal points of cultural and political activity into the 1960s. The most celebrated intellectuals of the day, including Jack London, Upton Sinclair, Emma Goldman, and Charlotte Perkins Gilman, joined artists, political radicals, and feminists in giving lectures to progressive, and ethnically diverse, audiences.[32] On one occasion, Spanish anarchist Maximiliano Olay introduced Carlo Tresca to an audience of two hundred people at the Ferrer School located at the corner of 107th Street and Park Avenue in New York.[33] Anarchist intellectual Rudolf Rocker arrived in the United States in 1933 from Nazi Germany; soon after his arrival, Rocker became one of the leading intellectual forces behind the Modern School at the Mohegan Colony in Crompond, New York.[34] Rocker gave speeches in antifascist meetings sponsored by several organizations. In 1938, he joined Félix Martí Ibáñez in his pro-Republic tour of the United States during the Spanish Civil War.[35] In the 1940s, Rocker gave several antifascist speeches at events organized by the SHC in New York's Ateneo Hispano.[36] For his contributions to the SHC, Rocker gained honorary membership in 1954.[37]

Like Rocker, several friends of the Modern Schools became influential patrons of the SHC and *España Libre*. Roger Nash Baldwin, one of the founders of the American Civil Liberties Union (ACLU), was a lecturer at the Mohegan Colony in 1934. In June 1950, an advertisement announced an event at the Waldorf-Astoria Hotel in New York bestowing the One World Award to Roger Baldwin for his defense of human rights.[38] A friend of Rocker, Baldwin was invited to speak to an audience of three hundred antifascists at the Freedom House in New York on March 25, 1952. The meeting, organized by the SHC, denounced the execution of five syndicalist workers in Spain.[39] Baldwin's participation in similar events was regularly noted in the 1950s and 1960s, and his monetary donations were listed, along with others, as was customary, in *España Libre*. The newspaper also published Baldwin's letters of protest to General Franco, to the Spanish ambassador in Washington, and to the United Nations.[40] A sponsor of *España Libre*, Baldwin went on to serve as an advisory member of the SHC.[41] In 1954, for his continuous support, Baldwin was awarded an honorary membership.

In 1956, Baldwin wrote to the *New York Post* demanding coverage of the disappearance of Jesús de Galíndez, a member of the SHC.[42] His help was never forgotten. On March 20, 1970, the SHC sent a telegram to Harry Rappaport, chair of the League for Mutual Aid, to join its homage to Roger Baldwin. The SHC thanked Baldwin "for the thoughtful and aggressive part he has played in our movement . . . we laud him for bringing your estimable League into being. And we voice unending gratitude for his help to countless Spanish exiles through so many years."[43]

Norman Thomas, a leading socialist and founder and executive director of the ACLU, was another vital patron of the Modern Schools. He gave lectures along with Rocker and Baldwin at the Summer Institute on Social, Economic, and Political Problems at the Mohegan Colony in 1934. Thomas also served on the board of Manumit, an experimental school for workers' children in Pawling, New York.[44] In 1943, a story about the funeral of Carlo Tresca published in *España Libre* mentioned Thomas's eulogy at the Manhattan Center in front of a multitude of six thousand attendees.[45] Like Rocker and Baldwin, Thomas often spoke at fundraisers for *España Libre* and at SHC's meetings. Most importantly, Thomas contributed to the SHC by focusing international attention on the execution of dissenters in Spain. Thomas's letters addressed to Francisco Franco formally protesting these executions were reprinted and praised in *España Libre*. In May of 1947, Thomas wrote to the Department of State and requested an investigation into the sudden disappearance of anarchist Progreso Alfarache, ex-director of Solidaridad Obrera (Mexico) while in Spain. The notice, published on the front page of *España Libre*, alerted readers to the possibility that Alfarache could have been victim of "Falangist ferocity."[46] In 1953, Thomas wrote González Malo to inform him that he had contacted George Delaney, Jay Lovestone, and Victor Reuther about the situation of political prisoners in Spain and had discussed how the CIO and the AFL could help them.[47] In 1962, González Malo continued to inform the AFL-CIO about civil rights infringements in Spain to encourage its continued assistance.

In September 1952, the SHC invited Ferrer i Guàrdia's daughter, Sol Ferrer Sanmartí, to lecture to the mutual aid society La Nacional, New York, which often offered its headquarters to the SHC. A graduate of the Sorbonne, Ferrer Sanmartí was at the University at Buffalo, New York, writing her dissertation on her father's work when she visited the headquarters. In her speech, she noted that the antifascist work of the SHC and *España Libre* were well known, and that she was grateful for their regular remembrance of her father's work in the periodical.[48]

The Modern Schools' web of connections facilitated the political engagement of local activists and organizations that enlarged the global reach of the SHC. Without the connections that extended from the Modern Schools, the SHC would not have been able to aid political prisoners and refugees with long-lasting efficiency and in coordination with other organizations and unions in the United States and abroad.

The SHC was the most important point of contact for antifascist Spaniards arriving in the United States, who collaborated with U.S. unions and workers' associations, according to *España Libre*. Despite the ideological differences, as well as the doctrinal confrontations among leaders and theorists, antifascist sentiment encouraged the confluence of socialist, republican, and anarchist militants. The personal and professional relations established through several networks were indeed instrumental for the global reach of *España Libre*. The anarchist and Hispanic cultures brought together migrants and exiles who became leaders in fundraising for the victims of fascism and in aiding refugees in transit. The Modern Schools were emblematic of the transnational and intersecting clusters of mutual aid and global antifascism. Through the alternative press and the fundraisers, exiles met like-minded individuals in migrant, ethnic, and radical organizations and maintained a sense of trust and community so necessary to avoid the isolation of exile. On the contrary, despite fascism and the Red Scare, ethnic and radical networks strengthened the SHC in its commitment to generating its own non-institutionalized modes of collective organization. Its tireless solidarity and unprecedented antifascist culture, which will be discussed in the following chapters, grew from the cultural and political richness of the transnational migrant, anarchist, and ethnic hubs discussed in this chapter.

2

España Libre, the Antifascist Periodical

"We offer our files and our house to you to help the Spanish people. The interest of whom, like ours, is to preserve the freedom of the world and the peace of all peoples."[1] With these words, from a 1952 article, *España Libre* offered its archives to the U.S. ambassador to Spain, Lincoln MacVeagh. The print publications and archives of such periodicals as *España Libre* provided vast troves of information on the political repression in Spain and the political activities of resistance movements. With this gesture, *España Libre* underlined the importance of people's history. Franco's rule had a devastating effect on workers in Spain: not only were workers' unions suppressed and their leaders either shot or sent to prison or to exile, but their political activities and archives were censored and destroyed.[2] It is evident that *España Libre*'s editors saw their periodical as a repository of workers' thought in exile and were determined to publish their experiences through the Cold War years and beyond.

Exiles are generally assumed to be part of a social, intellectual, or political elite escaping political persecution, whereas immigrants are working class, motivated by economic need. However, in Francoist Spain, those driven into exile by the repressive regime included not only politicians or other elites, but dissenters and people of broad and diverse social status with politically progressive leanings. The Spanish Popular Front government during the Second Republic—which would continue as the Government of the Second Spanish Republic in exile after the civil war—besides traditional politicians and intellectuals, comprised large contingents of grassroots activists, workers, trade union groups, and other members of the laboring classes—a coalition that remains unique in the history of the Spanish government. From 1939 to 1977, the diversity of *España Libre*'s editors, staff writers, contributors, and subscribers is parallel to the social diversity of the diaspora. For this varied group of Spanish progressives, *España Libre,* headquartered in New York, was an antifascist, public, and popular forum.

Throughout its existence, *España Libre* was committed to a horizontal organizational structure. *España Libre's* editorial focus reflected the ideas of all the organization's members, as all members in the organization had executive powers and decisions were taken in regular open assemblies.[3] Following the proletarian culture of the constituent associations, the SHC wrote guidelines and celebrated regular assemblies and yearly national congresses.[4] With these initiatives, the SHC maintained a confederative structure, in which members and readers had their say in the writing and printing of *España Libre*. The many affiliated organizations of the SHC were hubs from which *España Libre* reached the networks that extended transnationally from the United States. Conferences, congresses, demonstrations, and rallies, as well as regular visits to the SHC of individuals from these exile and anarchist networks were advertised in the periodical, and readers were encouraged to attend. These ads and notices facilitated direct encounters among a diverse array of politicians, intellectuals, and workers.

Although editorials articulated the periodical's main antifascist goals, as it will be seen in the next chapter, regular sections informed and influenced readers on a range of subjects related to progressive causes. *España Libre*'s editors and contributors had a clear understanding of their role to preserve the diverse legacy of progressive and radical workers, something that was documented in each issue in the form of essays, reviews of books and fundraising events, historical writing, theater, fiction, and poetry.

España Libre's Main Characteristics

España Libre was published weekly from November 1939 to 1953; from 1954 and until it folded in June 1977, it was published less frequently. Its editions dropped from weekly to bimonthly in 1954, and then to monthly in 1963. From 1967 to 1977, the periodical was published every two months. It was distributed at newsstands, places of business, and by subscription. Circulation, subjected to available funds, was uneven. For each edition, a minimum of 1,500 and a maximum of 4,000 copies circulated in the United States and to exiles worldwide, of

Figure 1. *España Libre*'s front page, dated October 16, 1953. Fryer's cartoon, "Por bulerías," depicts Franco as a female flamenco dancer who is dancing to the tune played by Uncle Sam. Courtesy of Recovering the U.S. Hispanic Literary Heritage.

which 500 copies were smuggled into Spain.[5] Although modest in the numbers of copies in circulation, issues were often shared among readers in the United States, abroad, and clandestinely in Spain. The political objective was to reach as many people as possible. The SHC sent at no charge 30 percent of the periodical's circulation to refugees and exiles as a service. Although *España Libre* suffered from chronic financial shortfalls, the SHC maintained this dignified action throughout the course of its existence.

España Libre maintained an open submissions policy that mirrored the collective ethos of the SHC. Within the complexities of exile in the United States, the most notable quality of *España Libre* was its diversity of authorship: the periodical had regular and sporadic staff and contributors, some using pen names, others hiding under anonymity.[6] But where authors' names have been hidden, information on authorship can still be deduced from the minutes, personal letters, and obituaries. In general, beyond the magazine's staff, the authors included both prominent members from affiliate organizations in New York and around the country and the world, as well as regular members with no significant public reputation. The handful of members in charge of the newspaper were workers who would take on many responsibilities at once: editor, director, staff writer, treasurer, and so on. Neither the columnists nor the staff writers received any remuneration for their work; in fact, they often helped defray publishing costs.[7] Finally, *España Libre* was overwhelmingly written by men.

Community societies sponsored *España Libre* by purchasing advertising space in the newspaper, by lending space in their headquarters for fundraisers, and of course, by affiliating with the SHC. Mutual aid societies, often organized along regional lines from the "old country," welcomed arriving Spaniards. For a moderate fee, these societies—*sociedades de beneficencia* (charitable organizations), *sociedades de socorros mutuos* (mutual aid societies), and *sociedades de instrucción y recreo* (education and recreation societies)—promoted the general wellbeing of workers, and were the civic, recreational, and educational centers of the community. One of these societies, La Nacional, founded in Brooklyn in 1868, held many of the fundraisers at its headquarters free of charge. Although Spanish immigrants confronted draining and difficult working conditions, they ran small enterprises that constituted one of the most important financial pillars of the SHC. Family-run restaurants and shops distributed *España Libre* and collected donations.[8] This way funds were collected from regular subscribers and advertisers, as well as through donations collected by constituent organizations. Notices of these modest donations were published in the periodical to encourage further bequests. However, some members, who lived under invasive governmental watch, opted to keep their donations secret. This was the case of Rita Hayworth's uncle, Jaime Devesa, who asked Aurelio Pego to make sure their family's financial contribution was not published because they had relatives in Spain and they were afraid of retaliation.[9]

Beyond providing financial donations, sponsors gained international attention for the SHC and *España Libre*'s mission. In a letter to Mexican president Lázaro Cárdenas, editor Jesús González Malo revealed that printing the name of recognized sponsors in letterheads would protect the organization and its periodical from anticommunist persecution.[10] In a sarcastic statement, González Malo told the Mexican president that the SHC feared "anticommunist hysteria, which can mock us as subversives or attack against us if they think we lack powerful affections and contacts."[11] The list of sponsors was reproduced not only in letterheads but also in the periodical itself. In a letter thanking Albert Einstein for agreeing to be listed as a sponsor in *España Libre*, SHC executive members Manuel Dorado and González Malo assured him that "sponsorship of a person like yourself will help to bring the issue of Spanish democracy before the American people."[12] The list of sponsors or distinguished members changed year to year, although most maintained their support throughout the existence of the periodical.[13]

España Libre's Makeup

In general, in order to keep costs to a minimum, *España Libre* maintained a similar format throughout its publication history. Each edition was published in eight pages (occasionally, the periodical was published in twelve to twenty pages). Pages 1 to 3 would provide the latest Spanish news on economics, politics, and culture, as well as reports on civil rights infringements under the regime. News on the Government of the Second Spanish Republic in exile and the broader Spanish Civil War exile community were published in these first pages and in the editorial pages that followed. Page 4 was devoted to the editorial and opinion columns; editorials also appeared on page 2 or 5 in some issues. In the 1960s, *España Libre* published the writing of the Paris-based anarchist thinker and novelist Federica Montseny (1905–1994), who wrote essays on anarchist history and Spanish anarchism in exile in *España Libre*. Her essays also elaborated on Spanish and global issues from an anarchist perspective.

Pages 4 and 5 also reprinted articles from other Spanish Civil War exile publications. For example, in the 1940s, *España Libre* reprinted Adolfo García Fernández's essays that had appeared in *Facetas de actualidad*, the exile magazine he directed in Havana. In the 1950s, *España Libre* reprinted Gabriel Pradal's essays (published under the pen name Pericles Garcia) from the Toulouse publication *El Socialista*, which discussed economic matters and censorship of the press in Franco's Spain. In general, these reprinted articles were chosen because of their clear relevance to *España Libre*, and they spurred commentary and responses among readers.

Pages 6 and 7 of *España Libre* reviewed social and fundraising activities, and published information about the SHC's accounts (donations and expenses), which included a summary of the latest audit. On pages 6 to 8, some current issues of other Spanish Civil War exile magazines and U.S. Latino periodicals were summarized or reviewed. Publication of books on the Spanish Civil War were announced and reviewed on these final pages. The books that were reviewed in these pages promoted ideas on anarchism, labor movements, socialism, Spanish republicanism, Spanish-language literature, and denounced communism, Franco's political repression, National Catholicism, and the diplomatic relations of the United States with Spain.

The Bookstore Service

España Libre offered a bookstore service, which was a common practice in anarchist newspapers. Located at the periodical's headquarters, the service sold books, mostly written by Spanish Civil War exiles, worldwide. The books were about the Spanish Civil War, anarchism, socialism, communism, Spanish politics, Franco's infringements of civil rights in Spain, and fascism. The service also sold books on Spanish-language literature and American topics. Until 1942, the bookstore service was run by Manuel Castro.[14] On page 8 of *España Libre*, the bookstore advertised its services and reviewed books. The section was entitled "Librería del Ateneo Hispano" (Ateneo Hispano Bookstore) and listed about fifty titles in most issues. The exile network was the main source of the distribution of books for the SHC. Several small publishing houses, mainly in Mexico and Buenos Aires, sold their books on *España Libre*'s library service.[15]

In the 1950s and 1960s, Eduardo Vives, the son of a CNT member and militiaman in the Spanish Civil War, ran the section entitled "Servicio de Librería" (Bookstore service) and offered about thirty titles in most issues. Local bookstores, like the one run by SHC member Esteban Roig in New York, started to distribute books for the exile community. Books published by the CNT (Toulouse), Libro Mexicano (Mexico), and Ibérica Publishing Co. (New York) were the most popular. Books on the relations between the United States and Spain, the dictatorship, and the Spanish labor movement were the most read, although increasingly, books on other American topics from American publishers were announced.[16] In the 1960s and 1970s, José Nieto Ruiz, originally from Orihuela, Spain, and born in 1937, ran the library service. In these last decades, more books on fiction, economics, and science were distributed.[17] In these decades, books were acquired from several sources. Esteban Roig, originally from Alicante, Spain, made available his bookstore catalog, which was announced in *España Libre*. Roig's bookstore, located at 576 Sixth Avenue, also advertised in the periodical. Members were surely delighted to know that "Spanish music and books could be found" at the store.[18] Books were also distributed with the help of Ibérica Publishing Co., owned by Victoria Kent, a Spanish socialist politician exiled in New York. Epistolary relations with exile networks facilitated the distribution of books and some authors donated their books to assist with the fundraising efforts of *España Libre*.[19] Poet Alonso Camín was among those who donated his poetry books and copies of his magazine *Norte* (Madrid, Mexico, 1929–1977).[20] *España Libre* also distributed several anarchist and exile periodicals. It was customary among Spanish Civil War exiles to exchange periodical issues. These distribution systems assured that members had access to affordable books and at the same time raised funds for the SHC.

Reading was seen as an emancipatory practice in anarchist circles. In Benedict Anderson's terms, *España Libre* and its bookstore service displayed workers' "imagined community," which helped them to comprehend and interpret their historical context. Although as *España Libre*'s editor, González Malo spent endless hours editing the periodical, reading other periodicals and publications related to the Spanish Civil War, and attending to correspondence, the anarcho-syndicalist still expressed in a letter to Josep Peirats that he felt less worthy of expressing his opinion because he lacked the time he wished to devote to reading. González Malo admitted: "I'm absorbed in work and so much to do brutalizes me, I have not read a book at ease I do not know for how long."[21] González Malo's comment shows the shared belief in anarchist circles that reading was a fundamental to sustaining a free spirit. In exile, the SHC made sure books and periodicals were inexpensive and accessible to secure members' engagement with literary and political ideas as an everyday practice, which was central to the maintenance and development of the exile and radical networks.

Many members, who worked in mines, fields, factories, and restaurants, were not formally educated. However, *España Libre* and its bookstore service provided members with critical tools for self-education. Books distributed, cultural fundraisers, and subscriptions to exile and anarchist newspapers provided workers with a rich political and cultural knowledge. This informal educational system was central to the development of the critical skills necessary for political activism. Their education was pieced together through multifaceted networks of informal education that included exile and anarchist print networks, community organizing, and political affiliation. These networks embraced the practices of reading, public lectures, theater, and cultural performances.

Félix Lunar's autobiography exemplifies the SHC's approach to knowledge as provided in its book service. Lunar's *A cielo abierto* (Open-pit mining, 1953) was one of the books sold and distributed by the bookstore service. Lunar, son of "humble field workers," got his first pair of shoes on his eighth birthday. His father saw it as an investment because with new shoes Lunar could start working in the fields.[22] An agricultural worker and miner both in Spain and in the United States, Lunar claimed to have suffered "all the injustices that I could not escape. None I agreed to."[23] Despite his defenseless childhood, Lunar taught himself to read and organized two workers' societies that provided access to health care and education to its members in the Riotinto mines in Huelva, Spain.[24] While in Spain, he published two workers' newspapers, *La Frontera* (The border) and *Via Libre* (Free way), before fleeing to the United States to protect himself from prosecution for his labor leadership.[25] In the United States, Lunar worked in the California fields and contributed antifascist essays to *España Libre*.

English Pages, 1953–1977

In 1953, Spanish socialist Victoria Kent and her partner Louise Crane began publishing a high-quality, English-language, republican exile newspaper, *Ibérica* (1953–1974) in New York. In response, *España Libre* began to include English-language pages to remain competitive because of the concern that the launch of *Ibérica* would decrease *España Libre*'s subscriptions. The English-language pages summarized and translated each issue's editorial section, some of its news articles, and several opinion columns. They also reprinted articles or sometimes excerpts from labor newspapers, such as *Freedom*, *Saturday Review*, *The Nation*, *AFL-CIO Free Trade Union News*, *Free Labor World*, and *Midstream*, among others. These pages also covered news on rallies, strikes, and major decisions undertaken by American unions concerning Spanish fascism.

The English-language pages had some recurring contributors. This included Jim Peck, who was a radical pacifist with strong anarchist connections, author of *Freedom Ride* (1962), and a member of the War Resisters League with Dwight Macdonald.[26] He often denounced human rights violations in Franco's Spain in his English-language section in *España Libre*. Each April 14, Peck would accompany González Malo to the demonstrations in front of the Spanish Consulate in New York to commemorate the Second Republic.

The English pages also covered news about American supporters of the SHC. In 1969, *España Libre* covered Roger Nash Baldwin's Human Rights Award by the International League for Human Rights, in recognition for his lifetime human rights efforts.[27] Baldwin had founded the International League for Human Rights in 1942. He was also the founder of the American Civil Liberties Union and the editor of *Kropotkin's Revolutionary Pamphlets* (1927). In 1970, the English pages celebrated the fiftieth anniversary of the League for Mutual Aid and noted that Baldwin had "engineered its founding."[28]

John Nicholas Beffel, the newsman who covered the Sacco-Vanzetti trial in Dedham, Massachusetts, in 1921 for the *New York Daily Call* and *New York World*, became editor of the consolidated English pages in 1960. Beffel, who had also worked for the *Morning World* and *Herald Tribune*, among other papers, extended the periodical's network of contacts. To encourage submissions, he contacted authors to thank them for their publications on Spain and sent them information about *España Libre* in case they were interested in contributing.[29] Beffel asked Lawrence Fernsworth for reprints of his articles in *The Nation*, and Fernsworth's contributions were then reprinted in the English-language pages. Fernsworth covered the Spanish Civil War for the *London Times* and wrote special articles about the war for the *New York Times*.[30] As a friend of Nancy Macdonald, leader of Spanish Refugee Aid (SRA), Beffel often discussed with her the best way to cover the aid sent to refugees in France.[31] The first sentence of the obituary Beffel wrote of Rose Pesotta was emblematic of the way the SHC sought to celebrate its members and bring attention to their legacy: "Many Spanish-American and countless other workers were saddened by the recent death of Rose Pesotta, a sponsor of the Confederated Spanish Societies for 15 years and member of Spanish Refugee Aid's executive board ever since its formation in 1953."[32] On April 1, 1963, Beffel retired and Miguel P. Ortiz became editor of the English pages for the next several months.

In 1964, anarcho-syndicalist Juan Manuel Molina Mateo, in exile in France, referred Zwy Herbert Aldouby to González Malo because the Jewish journalist was preparing a manuscript on the Spanish Civil War and inquired about *España Libre*.[33] That same year, Aldouby started to edit the English pages. Aldouby, born Herbert Dubinsky, enhanced the periodical with his life experiences: from a graduate student of Columbia University School of Journalism to a Zionist avenger imprisoned in Spain. In the late 1940s, he worked for the Israeli Army intelligence. He joined the General Zionist party in 1952 and became the Foreign Desk editor of its newspaper, *HaBoker*. In 1961, he was arrested by Spanish authorities in company of Jacques Simon Feinsohn for trying to kidnap Leon Degrelle, a Belgian Nazi collaborator, in Spain. Aldouby was sentenced to nine years in prison.[34] Aldouby's Zionist sympathies, however, were never explicitly mentioned in *España Libre* or in SHC's documents.[35]

As the editor of the English language section, Aldouby ran articles about events in the United States where he himself was one of the main participants. In 1965, an article reviewing the commemoration of the Second Republic in the premises of La Nacional, Aldouby was praised as main speaker. The event was well attended. Some supporting individuals and organizations were Nancy MacDonald (Spanish Refugee Aid), Partido Socialista Americano, Ernest Fleishchman (SHC legal adviser), Georgina Pupo (Círculo de Escritores y Poetas Iberoamericanos), Alberto Uriarte (Centro Vasco-Americano), and Antonio Calvo (La Nacional). Aldouby addressed the audience by remembering how he had commemorated April 14, the Spanish Republic Day, the previous three years while incarcerated in Spain. He noted that right then political prisoners in jails and students in the streets were commemorating the Republic in unison with the exile community in the United States. Aldouby established links with the Jewish exile community when he declared that Spaniards always concluded events with the sentence: "Next year we will celebrate in Spain" while the Jewish community would also say: "Next year in Jerusalem." Aldouby claimed that instead of wishful thinking, there was the need for active coalitions with liberal forces against fascism and communism. His editorial focus in the sections he edited for *España Libre* was consistently reflective of his activist interests.

Regular Contributors: Progressive and Radical Writers

España Libre testifies to the bottom-up approach of the SHC. Editors were workers who sought contributions from workers as well as from established writers, intellectuals, and journalists. The diverse ideological leanings of contributors attest to the inclusive nature of *España Libre*. Its notable quality was this numerous and diverse authorship—at least in terms of walks of life; in terms of gender, however, this was not the case, since most authors were men. It had both regular and sporadic contributors, some using their real names, others using pen names or remaining anonymous.[36] Like the editors, contributors were unpaid, and often even gave small donations to sustain the periodical. The variety of regular and long-term contributors exemplified some of the main characteristics that marked the trajectory of *España Libre*, from its satirical workers' perspective to its stern antifascism. Two persistent characteristics of the contributors were their independence from the Spanish government-in-exile and the way they adapted to the needs of the periodical.

España Libre published numerous journalistic and literary genres: essays and satires, cartoons, book and cultural reviews, personal narratives, poetry, and short stories.[37] Reprints of announcements, essays, and manifestos from the Government of the Second Spanish Republic in exile and from Alianza Sindical Obrera (ASO) were also published. The predominant topics of discussion were the Spanish Civil War, the spread of fascism in the Americas, Franco's Spain, the hoped-for restoration of democracy in Spain, the legacy of anarchism and socialism, and antifascist activism.

Several contributors denounced fascist Spain. Musician Adolfo Jiménez Colón (1884–1955) wrote satirical antifascist poems in *España Libre* and composed the music for antifascist plays staged at fundraisers. Originally from Murcia, Spain, Jiménez Colón arrived in New York in 1918 and later became one of the SHC's founders. Under the pen name of Lirón, his poems sarcastically attacked National Catholicism in Franco's Spain and mocked the Spanish exiles for their inefficiency in fighting fascism.[38] In 1938, some of his poems published in the SHC's earlier periodical, *Frente Popular* (1936–1939), were compiled in *Bombas de mano* (Hand grenades). Lirón also used humor to denounce the United States' economic relations with Franco in the 1950s. Contributors also contested any sanctioning of Franco's government. In the 1930s, Asturian Luís Montés wrote for the New York *Cultura Proletaria* and in 1939 directed the Los Angeles periodical *Antifascista*. Montés was an active member of an affiliated organization, Leales Españoles, based in Los Angeles, and reported on its antifascist fundraisers. In the 1950s and 1960s, Montés wrote from Mexico City. He authored opinion columns denouncing the Franco regime and warned of the need to remember the antifascist legacy of the Spanish Civil War exiles. He published similar essays in the San Antonio periodical *La Prensa*. These contributors reminded readers that Franco's regime was illegitimate and the result of an antidemocratic revolt that succeeded thanks to the help of Fascist Italy and Nazi Germany.

Many contributors wrote from countries other than the United States and their works preserved the cultural history of progressive and radical Spain. From Cuba and México, Álvaro de Albornoz Limiana (1879–1954) became an important historical chronicler for *España Libre*. Albornoz Limiana was one of the founders of the Radical Socialist Party and the Second Republic. During the Republic, he served as minister of justice and minister of public works. With Jesús Vázquez Gayoso, the consul in Caracas, Venezuela, for the Government of the Second Spanish Republic in exile, Albornoz Limiana founded the magazine *Nuestra España* (Our Spain) in Cuba. From 1940 to 1945, he served as president of the Government of the Second Spanish Republic in exile. In the 1940s, Albornoz Limiana spoke at several SHC fundraisers with a most impressive command of the audience. An *España Libre* editorial of March 21, 1941, proudly announced that Albornoz Limiana submitted original articles to his ongoing column "España Adentro" (Inside Spain), an act that attested to his commitment to the periodical.[39] Albornoz Limiana wrote about radical historical figures such as French anarchist Pierre-Joseph Proudhon, Russian anarchist Mikhail Bakunin, and Catalan federalist Franscesc Pi i Margall. Even after his death in 1954, his columns continued to be reprinted in *España Libre* in the 1960s and 1970s. By publishing on radical history in *España Libre*, which was regularly smuggled into Spain, Albornoz Limiana strengthened the bond between members of a radical transnational community, whose history was forcefully banished by the Franco dictatorship.

From Grand Rapids, Michigan, exiled Galician author Jesús Prado Rodríguez (dates unknown) contributed original articles about Franco's Spain and exile in the United States. In "Confesiones de Juan Picador y Picadillo" (Confessions of Juan Picador y Picadillo), a regular column published in *España Libre* in 1940, the author denounced the difficult exile experience for most members: "Spanish migrants without formal education do not have the advantages of other migrants from northern Europe, and have to do the lowest of the jobs, but we get better jobs if fatigue does not break our back."[40] Under the pen names of Jesús Equis, Juan Picador, and Picadillo, Prado Rodríguez wrote two regular columns, "Remansos de paz" (Peace refuges) in 1940 and "El espejo de las horas" (The mirror of the hours) in 1940 and 1941. Some of his articles were compiled in *Gritos de carne* (Flesh screams, 1941). He was also the author of the poetry collection *Polvo y camino: Poemas en prosa y verso* (Dusty road: Poems in prose and in verse, 1968). Both books were illustrated by Juan Eugenio Domingo Mingorance.

In the 1950s and 1960s, Prado Rodríguez also published in *Solidaridad Obrera* (Paris) and *Espoir* (Toulouse). In his articles, he often showed the difficulties of adaptation to exile for workers and for writers. Aurelio Pego reviewed his work in 1970 and noted: "To be a writer in the United States is not easy. For American readers, you do not exist. For Hispanic readers you are far away or hidden."[41] Writers like Prado Rodríguez or Ángel Samblancat Salanova evidence the cross-border exchanges that promoted the transnational culture of *España Libre*, while still entangled in overreaching notions of state and nationality.

From the 1940s to 1963, Samblancat Salanova (1885–1963) wrote from Mexico. Before fleeing Spain, he was a regular in anarchist gatherings in Barcelona and wrote for one of the city's anarchist papers, *Solidaridad Obrera* or *Floreal*.[42] With a characteristically baroque style, he reviewed Spanish politics, world culture, and historical topics. Besides *España Libre*, he contributed to several anarchist periodicals, *Solidaridad Obrera* (Paris), *Solidaridad Obrera* (New York), and *Tierra y Libertad* (Mexico), and authored numerous fiction and nonfiction books.

José Rubia Barcia (1914–1997), a professor at the University of California, Los Angeles, published in *España Libre* against Franco's Spain. Some of these essays were later collected in *Prosas de razón y hiel* (Prose of reason and sorrow) (1976).[43] A student of the socialist professor Fernando de los Ríos at the University of Granada, Rubia Barcia went into exile in Cuba after his name appeared on a list of individuals to be executed by the Franco regime.[44] There, he founded the Escuela Libre de la Habana in 1940, which ran until 1943.[45] Cambridge researcher June Namias interviewed him in 1976 about his immigrant story in the United States. Rubia Barcia used the pseudonym Andrés Aragón for this occasion and told about his persecution by U.S. authorities for being mistaken for a communist.[46] Rubia Barcia also published in *España*

Libre articles about his academic work on authors in the United States such as Américo Castro or Eugenio F. Granell.

Alonso Ayensa y Sánchez de León escaped Spain in 1936; he first lived in Paris and later migrated to Mexico in 1952. There he worked as a librarian at the Universidad Nacional Autónoma de Mexico. From Mexico, he reviewed the works of exiled Spanish authors and intellectuals in *España Libre*. Ayensa y Sánchez de León denounced Franco's devious judicial system, published on the economy of Franco's Spain and the students' protests in Spain in the late 1950s. He opposed the monarchy after the demise of the Franco regime.

Francisco Ayala (1906–2009) was lecturing in Latin America when his father and brother were killed during the Spanish Civil War. He first taught at the University of Puerto Rico, and in the 1960s at Princeton University, Rutgers University, New York University, and the University of Chicago. In 1961, Ayala published a series of articles in *España Libre* about past and contemporary geopolitics under the titles "De la preocupación de España" (The concern of Spain) and "La defensa del occidente: America y Europa" (The defense of the West: America and Europe); these were later republished in his several collections of essays. Throughout the decades of publication, Albornoz Limiana, Prado Rodríguez, Samblancat Salanova, Rubia Barcia, Ayensa y Sánchez de León, and Ayala submitted regular contributions to *España Libre*, as well as to other anarchist periodicals, even when they knew they were watched by the FBI and their political involvement was sometimes frowned upon by their respective institutions.

Olga Glondys has underscored the relevance of personal contacts among anti-Stalinist exiles in their fight to democratize Spain in the 1950s and later decades. The main leaders of these efforts were in contact with the SHC, including Víctor Alba (Pere Pagès) and Julián Gorkin, who belonged to the quasi-Troskyite Partit Obrer d'Unificació Marxista (POUM, Worker's Party of Marxist Unification); socialist politician and journalist Luis Araquistáin; and liberal writer Salvador de Madariaga. Their articles were published in *España Libre*, along with the correspondence they exchanged with a transnational network of contacts that started in Mexico in the 1940s between post-Troskyite intellectuals and activists associated with the New York magazine *Partisan Review*.[47] The SHC played an important role in maintaining contacts with the CIO, led by Walter and Victor Reuther, along with the AFL of David Dubinsky and Jay Lovestone.[48]

Affiliated with the POUM, Catalan journalist Pere Pagès (1916–2003), who often wrote under the pen name of Víctor Alba, was director of *La Batalla* (The battle) during the Spanish Civil War. He escaped to France in 1945; his exile continued for some time in Mexico. In 1957, he moved to Washington, D.C., where he worked as a translator for the World Health Organization.[49] During this time, he reviewed books published by Spanish Civil War exiles and wrote pieces about the Spanish labor movement in *España Libre*. He also directed the Mexican magazine *Panoramas* (1963–1965). He himself was the author of numerous books about Spanish labor history. His involvement with the SHC went beyond his written submissions to its periodical. Alba became one of *España Libre*'s sponsors and advisors to the journal, and its delegate in Washington, D.C.[50] In this capacity and upon request, Alba advised González Malo in his contacts with labor unions in the United States and helped him in his efforts to get them to sponsor the clandestine resistance in Spain.

Beginning in the 1920s and until his death, Luis Araquistáin Quevedo (1886–1959), a Spanish socialist politician, journalist, and intellectual, published original pieces and reprints on Hispanic politics, culture, and sociology in *Las Novedades* (New York), *La Prensa* (San Antonio), and *El Heraldo* (Los Angeles), among others. As Spanish ambassador to the Weimar Republic, Araquistáin Quevedo lost faith in the power of parliamentary democracy to stop fascism. This experience influenced Araquistáin's socialist radicalization during the Second Republic.[51] Araquistáin also worked at a secret war propaganda bureau for the so-called Wellington House Committee in Britain.[52] Despite his earlier doubts, during his London exile Araquistáin regained his trust in liberal democracy. In the 1940s, Araquistáin published his regular *España Libre* column "London." *España Libre* noted his essays were originals, which spoke to his commitment to the mission of the SHC.[53] His essays were important enough to be reprinted in the 1950s. Araquistáin argued for the unity of pro-Republic factions as a way to defeat Franco and considered reinstallation of the monarchy as a possible political strategy for unification against Franco. He also published on the relations between Spain and England, England's role in the Second World War, international politics from a European perspective, and Spain under the Franco regime.

From Paris, Julián García Gómez (1901–1987) directed a Parisian magazine, *Cuadernos del Congreso de la Libertad de la Cultura* (Journal of the Congress for Cultural Freedom, 1953–1965). He sporadically wrote for *España Libre*.[54] Under the pen name of "Julián Gorkin," he elaborated on politics in the Hispanic world and the restoration of democracy in Spain. In one of his articles, Gorkin highlighted the fact that members were workers who had become journalists, activists, and intellectuals in their exile in the United States.[55] Gorkin spoke at several fundraisers in New York. He also worked with González Malo in seeking endorsements for ASO from American and international labor unions.

From the 1950s to the 1970s and from Oxford, England, Salvador de Madariaga (1866–1978), a Spanish intellectual and journalist of prestige, reprinted his antifascist and anticommunist articles in *España Libre*. Madariaga also published in several Spanish Civil War exile periodicals, such as the New York *Ibérica* and the Paris *Congreso por la Libertad de la Cultura*. Madariaga's famous 1959 BBC broadcasts against Franco were compiled in the volume *General márchese usted* (General leave now) and published by *Ibérica*'s publishing arm. Although Madariaga refrained from publishing his elitist views on democracy in *España Libre*, contributors would contest his privileged opinion even when published in other periodicals. In one occasion, González Malo published an open letter to Madariaga in *Comunidad Ibérica* (Mexico), in which he questioned Madariaga's orientalist characterization of Spaniards in *Anarchy and Hierarchy* (1937). For Madariaga, Spaniards were driven by passion rather than reason. González Malo wondered why the intellectual forgot to mention the anarchic idiosyncrasy of Spaniards.[56] Since the periodical encouraged all opinions, there were numerous responses addressed to Madariaga's monarchic sympathies. Despite his elitist conception of democracy, Madariaga was an asset for *España Libre*'s reach and distribution for his staunch antifascism and anticommunism.[57] His work in exile and mainstream publications was often reviewed in *España Libre*. The articles of Víctor Alba, Julián Gorkin, Luis Araquistáin, and Salvador de Madariaga renewed the fight for the unity against the Francoist regime by strengthening ties with Western political and cultural powers. Their correspondence with *España Libre* editors shows these intellectuals recognized the need to find common ground to make possible the restitution of democracy in Spain.

Regular and long-time contributors were convinced radicals who thrived on debate and political activism but were also sophisticated chroniclers of antifascist politics and culture and adapted to *España Libre*'s objectives. For example, Adolfo Jiménez Colón (Lirón) contributed to the satirical approach that Castilla Morales established in the first years of the publication and Luis Montés kept up his militant anti-Francoism until the day of his death. Other contributors kept alive progressive and radical histories and culture: Álvaro de Albornoz Limiana, Alonso Ayensa y Sánchez de León, and Francisco Ayala brought the Republican exile network to the pages of *España Libre* with their reviews of the political and cultural production of exiles. Similarly, José Rubia Barcia was the radical professor who contributed always to *España Libre* with his research in the United States. Samblancat Salanova and Jesús Prado Rodríguez provided with their baroque style models of prolific engagement with ideas in proletarian publications in exile.

These writers had lost a civil war and were exiled from their homeland, and most of their families and friends had been executed or imprisoned or were living under a repressive regime given to employing terror against its dissidents. Their own residency status as migrants in the United States was uncertain because they were never granted refugee status, and both the FBI and Spanish consulate officials were watching them for their radical leanings. Under the extremely difficult conditions of exile, their shared economic, legal, and emotional ties strengthened their devotion to the SHC and *España Libre*. They fought fascism and worked with the underground resistance in Spain.

In exile or underground in Spain, contributors kept their commitment to *España Libre*. Knowing their historical circumstances, one gains a deeper appreciation for their continuing fight for freedom and social justice and their adherence to participatory practice. Recovered biographies and publications reveal that most of them had much in common, despite their political diversity. Their biographies and obituaries show that they lived on next to nothing, ate little, had few articles of clothing, owned scanty furniture, and worked long hours but served with their work and contributed with funds they could barely scrape together for the dream of Spanish freedom. Their exile experiences were conscious and visionary.

Although political migrants might form new solidarities and develop new identities in the host country, an exile periodical such as *España Libre* concentrated on denouncing the home country's oppression. *España Libre* remained the primary communication system for progressive and radical Spanish workers in the United States, whose sense of self was conditional because their political legitimacy had been taken away from them. *España Libre*'s coverage proves the centrality of immigrant and exile periodicals, such as *España Libre*, in disseminating progressive and radical thought and literature beyond national borders. Staff and contributors, nongovernmental organizations, and the larger antifascist community published political protest in *España Libre*, which demonstrates the transnational reach and distribution of the periodical.

The lists of books and magazines sold through the periodical give evidence of the dissemination of radical political ideas beyond the borders of postwar Europe and within migrant networks. The bookstore, the periodical's English-language pages, reviews of cultural fundraisers, and the obituaries show the sheer number of common people who fought fascism daily in extraordinary ways. Beyond editorials and sections, the adherence of *España Libre* to anarchistic practices in its intellectual approach and publication practices is the most salient characteristic of the periodical. It points to the kind of society that the participants sought to achieve: one that maintained a committed critique of authoritarianism and a commitment to an ethical balance of ends and means. Once democracy was restored in Spain, in 1977, *España Libre*, the voice of popular antifascism, was discontinued. The last front page announced that "The fight for freedom returns to Spain."[58]

3

España Libre and Its Editors

Information about the editors of *España Libre* is, at best, partial because the periodical did not always publish personal information, or editors and staff writers published under a variety of pseudonyms, in order to protect members from the U.S. immigration authorities, who could detain them for their undocumented status in the United States or for their radical affiliations. As Aurelio Pego stated: "If we end up in prison we are of no use."[1] Also, this publishing tactic safeguarded underground correspondents in Spain from political persecution. Lastly, anonymity was common among anarchists, whose attitudes on authorship valued collective work. Nevertheless, there is enough information in personal papers and correspondence of those who worked at the publication, and those of other exile periodicals, to establish the years in which a given editor exerted the greatest influence and to demonstrate that staff and editors took on several responsibilities at once and served as needed.

España Libre's editors—who were progressive and radical writers whose antifascist publishing has largely remained unknown until now—not only adapted to changing historical circumstances in their exile in the United States but also invigorated the periodical's proletarian counterculture to fascism and elitism. Notably independent, José Castilla Morales, Aurelio Pego, and Jesús González Malo subversively shaped ideas, strategically influenced exile politics, and sustained ongoing resistance during times of harsh repression in Spain and Cold War political tensions in the United States. Marcos C. Mari and Alberto Uriarte, who served as editors in the 1960s and 1970s, sought to keep alive Spanish progressive culture in the last decades of the periodical with Joaquim Maurín Julià and Eugenio F. Granell.

The Editorial Evolution of *España Libre*

España Libre as the organ of the SHC was the only Spanish-language periodical published in the United States that specifically fought fascism throughout the years of the Franco dictatorship.[2] *España Libre* made the immediate needs of the victims of the Spanish Civil War, the Second World War, and Franco's Spain its focus even while its writers exchanged ideas for local and global responses to fascism. The publication's anarchist leaders encouraged strategic progressive coalitions and searched for political alternatives to Francoism.

In the years before *España Libre* was launched, the SHC struggled to find a common ground with other political groups during the Spanish Civil War and the Second World War. Communist members disapproved of antifascist coalitions, while anarchist members criticized the party-driven decisions by communists on distribution of funds and favoring propaganda over aid to comrades in Spain and in exile.[3] The conflict came to a head when the leader of the communists, Daniel Alonso, was expelled from the Spanish Communist Party because Galician anarcho-syndicalist Jesús Arenas Ruiz had replaced him as the secretary of propaganda. Alonso's act of sharing governance with an anarcho-syndicalist was perceived as disloyalty to the Communist Party.[4] After this upheaval, the SHC launched *España Libre* (1939–1977) to mark the organization's expulsion of communist leaders on November 3, 1939. This same day, the previous periodical, *Frente Popular* (1936–1939), was discontinued.[5] Editorials claimed that the working class was better served by socialists and republicans than by communists.

Without the communists, the antifascist confederation found common political ground among anarchist, socialist, and republican Spaniards. *España Libre* defined the SHC as a U.S. organization with no political agenda, which supported the Government of the Second Spanish Republic in exile. Nevertheless, the SHC's endorsement of ideological inclusion never lessened its advocacy of labor unionism. *España Libre* editorials reiterated its subscription to the principles dictated by the Spanish anarchist union (CNT) and the Spanish socialist union (UGT).[6] During the Spanish Civil War, writers would insist on the importance of the unions for the political and ethical education of the Spanish people,[7] and continued to contest propaganda against Spanish unions after the war. The editorial of February 12, 1943, stated that the SHC was a lawful organization with the objective of returning democracy to Spain: "We are convinced democrats and we will continue to fight for the freedom of subjugated peoples... and will protest against all the injustices perpetrated against the Spanish people... until we exhale our last breath of life."[8]

After the Spanish Civil War, many pages of the periodical were devoted to analyzing the conflict, and particularly the effect of fascist powers on the outcome.[9] Staff writers and essayists denounced the foreign intervention in the Spanish Civil War. Covering the bombing of Italy by the Allies in 1943, Félix Martí Ibáñez remembered the day he listened to Benito Mussolini on the radio broadcasting from la Piazza di Venezia and announcing the entrance of Italian forces into Barcelona. Martí Ibáñez only wished in his article that it was the Spaniards who had defeated Mussolini instead.[10]

Editorials in the 1940s discussed the fascistization of Spain. They denounced the consolidation of the Francoist regime and the influence of the Spanish fascist party, Falange, in Spanish domestic politics, in the economy, and in the construction of a new antiliberal state committed to eradicating the social and intellectual legacies of the Second Republic. *España Libre* was concerned about the promotion of the military virtues of sacrifice and violence against the dissenting Spanish population. In the 1940s, numerous articles denounced random assassinations of progressives and radicals, which were silenced by the Spanish mainstream press but communicated to *España Libre* by the clandestine resistance. When the Spanish Congress declared that Franco would be able to nominate his successor in 1947, *España Libre* announced that Spain now had an absolute leader with the protection of the Church.[11] *España Libre* regularly denounced the absolute power of a total leader, the mystical exaltation of violence and death, the institutional control of social life, and Catholic Nationalism, pillars of Spanish fascism.

The Falange leaders were portrayed as socially and politically powerful in Franco's Spain. In one of his satirical chronicles, editor and contributor Aurelio Pego attacked the Spanish journalist Eugenio Montes. The chronicle imagines Montes walking down one of the main streets of Madrid where "he leaves behind a whiff of incense, sulfur, press ink, and burial dust."[12] Pego's statement left little doubt about the fact that evil assassinations were being covered up by Falangist journalists. With contributors like Pego, *España Libre* condemned the Falange's infiltration of education and the media, and its role in the formation of new fascist Spain.

On May 1937, *España Libre*'s processor, *Frente Popular*, documented the foundation of the organization Casa de España by pro-Franco Marcelino García Rubiera and Manuel Díaz, both from the Spanish-American shipping industry, and regularly posted pictures of its members with the headliner "Fascists in New York." After the foundational meeting, members, among them Ramón Castroviejo, Juan Gallego, José María Torres Perona, and Francisco Larcegui, sent a telegram to Francisco Franco announcing the new organization and their unconditional service to Franco.[13] *Frente Popular* and *España Libre* covered news on the Falangists sent by General Wilhelm von Faupel to the United States: Miguel Echegaray, Juan Adriensens, Joaquin Sunyé, Francisco de Amat, José Martín, and the U.S. periodicals or publications they subsidized in the United States: *Spain, Cara al Sol, España Nueva*, and *Época*.

Likewise, contributors reproached Spanish professors for encouraging American students to enroll in study abroad courses in Spain. Published in June of 1948, one piece cautioned that the Falange was infiltrating American universities with tactics copied from the Nazis because American students were valuable assets for Francoist propaganda and the diffusion of fascism in the Americas.[14]

Several *España Libre* contributors and staff writers warned against the threat of the spread of fascism in the Americas through Franco's imperial concept of Hispanism, which proclaimed the universal task of assimilating the former colonies into the defense of Catholicism and the fascist Movimiento.[15] The Spanish fascist identity was, in this respect, inseparable from the imperial one. For instance, the periodical was concerned about the Consejo de la Hispanidad (Hispanic Council, 1941–1944), supposedly as a supranational diplomatic council dedicated to unifying Latin American cultures and economies. However, *España Libre* columnists denounced it as a covert Spanish fascist organization in Latin America.[16] Earlier, in 1940, an SHC ally and the former Spanish ambassador in the United States, Fernando de los Ríos, had published "Nazi Infiltration in Ibero-America" in *Social Research*, the academic journal published by the New School for Social Research.[17] Similarly, *España Libre*'s editorials published alerts on Nazi and Francoist agents in New York, who were forcing Spaniards to collaborate by threatening their families in Spain. Falangists, Nazis, and antifascists were warily watching each other in the United States. The editorial of January 12, 1940, dramatically imagined what pro-Franco and Falangists experienced in the street of New York: "So much fear, so much horror that they feel for the abuses committed, that from Franco to the youngest Falangist dandy, they see in every salute a password, in every look a reproach, in every word a threat, in every cry a vengeance, in every mourning the expiation of a crime."[18] In *Falange*, Allan Chase names the Spaniards in the United States who contributed to "one of the most effective of the Falange Exterior Fifth Columns in the world." In his book, Chase wrote, "When the history of the Second World War is written, the role the Falange Exterior played in the successful American campaign to prevent the lifting of the Arms Embargo on Loyalist Spain will fill some of the blackest pages in that tragic chronicle."[19]

España Libre also denounced Franco's warm diplomatic relations with the United States.[20] Franco's diplomats in the Unites States worked with domestic intelligence in attempting to force SHC members to spy on Spanish radicals in the United States. If they refused to do so, American agents threatened to denounce their potential informers to the Immigration Services due to their undocumented refugee status, or to inform the House Un-American Activities Committee (HUAC) about their socialist or anarchist sympathies.

When the Second World War broke out, it naturally came to occupy the pages of *España Libre*, not only for its political significance but because several members served in the war.[21] While the front page of January 1, 1943, listed the 160 SHC members "fighting on the trenches of democracy," in Europe, the Spanish assistance to Axis powers was often denounced in *España Libre*. For example, Thomas J. Hamilton's *Appeasement's Child* (1950), which denounced the fact that Nazi submarines operated from Spanish ports, was reviewed several times. This was also the case for Allan Chase, *Falange: The Axis Secret Army in the Americas* (1943), and the author was invited to participated in one of the SHC's fundraising rallies.[22] In *España Libre*'s pages, Chase chronicled the involvement of the Spanish fascist party, Falange, with German U-boats in the Atlantic, the pro-Nazi activities in the Americas, and the role of the Compañía Transatlántica Española in carrying supplies and spies for Germany and Spain. Another regular contributor, Álvaro de Albonoz Limiana, called for transnational coalitions of antifascist exiles from France, Italy, and Spain as a way to collaboratively resist the alliances that helped build fascist movements in Europe.[23] Essayists and staff members published articles on progressive and radical Spanish history to prove that there was another Spain than the traditional and Catholic one imposed by fascist forces. In January of 1943, the renewed alliance of CNT and UGT in Mexico was celebrated with articles in *España Libre*, assuring that the political and social reconstruction of Spain could only be done with the transformative societal role offered by free workers' unions.[24]

After the Second World War, editorials focused on support for refugees and the underground resistance. The periodical praised the U.S. aid given to European antifascist refugees, while simultaneously condemning the denial of refugee status to Spaniards arriving in the United States. Spanish Civil War exiles found themselves in limbo: they could not register at the Spanish Consulate in New York, nor could they easily obtain residency status in the United States.[25] *España Libre* emphasized the immediate needs of these Spanish exiles.

Its limited funds were devoted to aiding individuals rather than to antifascist propaganda. Not surprisingly, the announcements and reviews of cultural fundraisers for these causes were featured in the periodical's pages. Throughout the United States, the 200 affiliated associations held an average of thirty-nine fundraisers each year. These fundraisers encouraged donations by political speeches, lectures, theater performances, vaudeville shows, dinners, and dances. Generally, events were conducted at the social halls of the constituent organizations. When more space was needed, nearby theaters, such as the Palm Garden Theater or Webster Hall in New York, were rented. In addition, fundraising picnics and soccer games were organized in the summer. These events, beyond raising funds and fostering political commitment, also helped maintain anarchist values of horizontal power and reciprocity, of mutually beneficial relationships in the fight for social justice.

Although securing financial aid was the driving force of *España Libre* in the 1940s, the periodical kept progressive and anarchist thought alive in exile. When a periodical with similar political goals and with the same name, *España Libre*, started publishing in Paris in 1945, regular contributors to *España Libre* in New York both reprinted its articles and wrote original ones for the periodical in France. This helped increase circulation and interest in each publication while informing readers of a wider print culture network.[26] The *España Libre* in Paris was the publication of the CNT, the national anarchist exile organization in France, and it was directed by Félix Lorenzo Páramo. After its seventieth issue, it moved to Toulouse, directed there by several exiled anarchists, among them Mateo Santos and Emilio Vivas. Some texts from the New York *España Libre* were reprinted in the Toulouse *España Libre* as well.[27] The Toulouse *España Libre* issued its last edition on July 2, 1961.

While the New York *España Libre* continued to receive international aid in the 1950s, this support would decline in the following years as enthusiasm began to wane, a decline surely caused by the disheartening course of events that occurred at that time. While the close relationship with Fascist Italy and Nazi Germany forced the exclusion of Spain from the Marshall Plan—which helped Western Europe rebuild after the war—the Cold War soon made Francisco Franco a valuable ally in the fight against communism, and President Harry S. Truman restored diplomatic relations with Spain in 1951. Two years later, the Pact of Madrid offered economic and military aid to Spain in exchange for the establishment of U.S. military bases there. The Caudillo's successful transformation into an American ally led to Spain's incorporation into Western and world organizations. Spain's admission to the United Nations in 1955 marked a devastating turning point for the staff writers of *España Libre*. The country where the SHC had established its free press was now supporting the dictatorship. Dismayed by the increasing international recognition of Franco, *España Libre* intensified its dialogue with underground dissidents in Spain, as did most of the pro-Republic exile press. During Jesús González Malo's term as editor of the newspaper (1961–1965), the interaction with the clandestine resistance in Spain was prominent.[28]

In the 1960s, *España Libre*'s editorials contested the Francoist propaganda about the alleged years of domestic peace under Franco. Writers questioned Franco's rise to power and the way he sought to hold onto it, which was the result of a fratricidal war and years of revenge acts that ended in imprisonments and deaths.[29] One article powerfully dismantled Francoist propaganda, quoting a letter from a socialist in Spain: "I have had the disgrace of having my father executed in Jaen and my brother in Teruel. I and two other brothers were detained, tortured, and sentenced to prison several years. We have lost all of our possessions."[30] In the 1950s and 1960s, editorials continued to document Franco's criminal purge of dissenters.

In these last decades of *España Libre*, staff writers had to renew the antifascist fight. In conjunction with other international organisms, the periodical maintained its solidarity with the clandestine opposition movement in Spain. Editorials proposed a cohesive front against Franco by strengthening ties with other antifascist and anti-Franco international organizations, along with the main Western cultural powers. Toward this goal, *España Libre*'s editors exchanged correspondence and invited contributions from liberal and monarchic opponents to Franco. Juan García Duran, a Detroit member of the SHC, wrote an article in *España Libre* on August 5, 1960, urging for an anti-Francoist assembly to take place in London. García Duran called for Spanish unions, the government-in-exile, as well as intellectuals and politicians to be present at the anti-Francoist assembly. In addition, García Duran's article noted the anti-Francoist work of liberal and promonarchic forces, including Salvador de Madariaga, Pablo Casals, Indalecio Prieto, Americo Castro, Dionisio Ridruejo, Tierno Galván, Jiménez Fernández, and Sánchez Albornoz. González Malo also contacted a number of other liberal writers and politicians in Spain, including Raúl Morodo and Julián Gorkin, as support of this liberal coalition against Franco.[31]

During the 1960s, the SHC also had to devise new ideas and editorial approaches to reach readers. The language and discourse of the magazine—formed through its members, who had experienced wars and holocausts in Europe—was becoming less and less relevant for new generations of potential supporters. More than ever before, the publication needed a journalistic style that would hold together its readership. After González Malo's death (December 1965), the terms "people" and "masses" that had populated *España Libre* were increasingly replaced by "democracy" and "freedom" to effectively adapt to a Spanish American ethnic identity transformed by the civil rights movement in the United States. During its last years of publication, the periodical covered international and cultural news to attract the second generation of Spaniards in the United States.

However, the antifascist community was not forgotten. *España Libre* recognized members' contributions to anarchism and antifascism with heartfelt farewells to deceased members in editorials and eulogies. Death notices accompanied this public recognition and often requested donations to defray funeral costs and provided information on the place and time of the funerals and memorial events. Bereavement notices also illuminated the vast range of common people who fought fascism and who merited recognition. A short profile of deceased members and their involvement with the antifascist confederation and its periodical kept the legacy of departed members alive in the hearts and minds of readers. For example, satirist Aurelio Pego dedicated one of his columns to Pedro Díez, a member who worked for *España Libre* and who passed away in April 1954. Pego remembered Díez as a hardworking and discreet man who dealt with *España Libre*'s many logistic needs: its distribution, archive, correspondence, errands, visitors, or other tasks. Pego assured readers: "I will never forget him. But I do not think the Spanish Republic should forget him either for, within its modest sphere of action, he did so much for its cause, fought so hard, and suffered so much."[32] Similarly, José Castilla Morales wrote a eulogy for Antonio Martínez, a *lector* (reader) in a tobacco factory, who contributed to the antifascist theater by volunteering as prompter for many years.[33] As in the case of Díez or Martínez, other eulogies and obituaries were the first instances that an active member was safely mentioned in *España Libre*. Such recognition of their contributions was an homage to the fight of anonymous people against fascism, the "blood and bones" of the SHC.

José Castilla Morales: Editor, Playwright, and Satirical Chronicler

José Castilla Morales (Huelva, Spain, 1893–New York, 1961) is the editor who best represents the first decades of the newspaper. Originally from Huelva, Spain, young Castilla Morales migrated to Cienfuegos, Cuba, to avoid "serving the king" (possibly conscription for the Melilla War in 1909). In Cuba, he served as a labor leader in the Unión Marítima de Cuba (Cuban Maritime Union) along with anarchists Avelino Iglesias and Paulino Díez.[34] During the two decades he stayed in Cuba, he worked as staff writer for the anarchist newspapers *El Sembrador, El Progreso,* and *Tierra.* During this period, Castilla Morales married Teresa Puig, who later immigrated to the United States and organized the SHC's affiliated group Agrupación de Mujeres Antifascistas del Bronx (Association of Antifascist Women of the Bronx, AMA).[35] In Cuba, President Gerardo Machado unleashed a wave of political violence designed to establish a dictatorship over the country. Machado executed Castilla Morales's comrades Baldomero Dumenio and Alfredo López. Consequently, Castilla Morales, Iglesias, and Díez fled the island. Upon his arrival in New York in 1930, Castilla Morales edited the IWW's *Solidaridad* (1918–1930), served as assistant director of *La Voz* in 1939, and joined several workers' associations in the city.[36]

From 1939 to 1961, Castilla Morales took on many roles on the *España Libre* staff: editor, playwright, satirist, and writer. He was the main editor until 1951 but continued to be part of a team of editors after that year. Pedro Sellarés (editor) and Pedro Díez (managing editor) served in the 1940s. Exceptionally active in the SHC, Castilla Morales served several times as advertising secretary, assistant secretary, and secretary general. He also directed and hosted its daily radio program, called "La voz de Sociedades Hispanas Confederadas" (The voice of the Confederation of Hispanic Societies). Castilla Morales was one of the main writers of the periodical and he also wrote numerous antifascist plays that affiliated organizations performed at fundraisers. Under pen names, Castilla Morales also published chronicles that documented the everyday fighters of fascism.[37] With a light humorous tone, Castilla Morales described local meetings and fundraisers, as well as national congresses, and most importantly for readers, who attended them. Castilla Morales also published several interviews with the most active members of the antifascist exile community and was able to capture their personalities in just a few lines. In doing so, Castilla made these members real people for readers, recognized their commitment to freedom and justice, and hope to inspire others to emulate their good fight. A notice referring to his work for *España Libre* claims that his interviews maintain "the umbilical cord" that kept the community united.[38]

Throughout this time, Castilla Morales reported to *España Libre*'s headquarters after his paying work and pursued the multiple and pressing tasks at the periodical.[39] SHC founder Gregorio Garay, who first met José Castilla Morales in the IWW premises in front of the transatlantic company Compañia Transatlántica Española in Cuba, where they had both been labor organizers, admired him deeply. In his eulogy, Garay highlighted Castilla Morales's dedication to the antifascist periodical:

> I can see him in the SHC headquarters, at the Brooklyn Hispanic Athenaeum . . . ; I see him go down those stairs, weary, exhausted, to take a sip of coffee and return to his tasks. And I, who loved and admired him so much, I felt sorry for him, seeing him work without rest. . . . Ah, Castilla, Castilla! You were small, but you had a titanic spirit. I've known you for over thirty years, comrade Castilla; I first met you in the Local I.W.W., opposite the docks of the company Transatlántica Española. . . . I close my eyes and I see you and I hear you in the assemblies of SHC! "Take a moment . . . a moment, comrades" . . . always fair and thoughtful, conciliatory, how great and good you were, Castilla![40]

Garay finished his eulogy asking members to continue fighting for a Spain free from fascism in memory of the fallen comrades such as Castilla Morales.

During Castilla Morales's tenure as editor, several members undertook administrative and writing tasks on the periodical. They were politically committed migrants and exiles and greatly reinforced the antifascist and anarchist sentiment of *España Libre*. This was the case of Galician John Carnero, whose family arrived in New York in 1916, and who served as staff writer as well as secretary general, a position that Alberto Uriarte also filled when necessary. Carnero also became president of La Nacional, a mutual aid society for Spanish migrants that helped the SHC raise funds.[41] A regular *España Libre* administrator and staff writer, socialist José Castro Barral also worked with Castilla Morales. Castro Barral was a Galician émigré who worked in the 1940s and 1950s for the U.S. State Department's Voice of America radio service and served as a director of La Nacional as well. He wrote articles under the pen name "Xan D'Oleiros." Along with socialist Manolo Alonso, from Pontevedra, Spain, Castro Barral wrote most of the editorials in the 1940s (particularly in 1943).[42] Basque anarchist Hipólito Cristóbal, a printer and secretary of the Ateneo Hispano, served as treasurer during Castilla Morales's leadership. From Los Angeles, Julian Benedet served as secretary of Acción Demócrata de San Francisco (San Francisco Democratic Action), an SHC-affiliated association, and reported about antifascist actions in the West Coast. Benedet was an actor and an anarchist from Zaragoza, who also wrote regularly for the bi-weekly *Antifascista* in Los Angeles (1937–1939).

Sebastián Palmer Terrassa was another one of the staff writers working with Castilla Morales. Palmer was a Majorcan actor who arrived in New York in the 1920s and took part in the city theater company Compañía Lírica Española

Figure 2. Announcement for "Hora de Radio en Nueva York," a program of the Confederadas, in *España Libre*, April 5, 1940. Courtesy of Recovering the U.S. Hispanic Literary Heritage.

(Spanish Lyrical Company). He wrote on the Spanish Civil War and Franco's Spain. He also directed and edited *España Libre* in 1943 when Castilla took a break from this responsibility. Another staff writer working with Castilla Morales in the 1940s was Jacinto Toryho. Toryho wrote on anarchism and the Spanish Civil War. He had been a main leader of the Federación Anarquista Ibérica (National Anarchist Federation) and director of the anarchist paper *Solidaridad Obrera* (Barcelona) from 1936 to 1938. He renewed *Solidaridad Obrera* with a new editorial staff that included Federica Montseny and Diego Abad de Santillán.[43] Over the years, other members continued to lead the SHC and continued to contribute their writings to *España Libre*. This included Daniel Alonso, Manuel Alonso, Jesús Arenas, José Asensio Torrado, Avelino Iglesias, Peter G. Lanza, Manuel P. Martínez, José Patín, Emilio Rego, Andrés Rodríguez Barbeito, Antonio García Vallín, and Ignacio Zugadi Garmendia.

Aurelio Pego: Journalist and Staunch Antifascist

Soon after his arrival in New York in 1919, Aurelio Pego (Valladolid, Spain, 1899–La Coruña, Spain, 1973) began his journalistic career as a volunteer correspondent for Spanish and Latin American newspapers. By 1921, he was writing commissioned chronicles and copywriting for advertising companies.[44] Until the 1970s, Pego published essays on current affairs in numerous newspapers, magazines, and labor journals in the United States and the Hispanic world.[45] He was named president of the Asociación de Publicistas y Traductores Hispanoamericanos (Hispanic Publicists and Translators Association) in New York in the 1950s.[46] In an article published in *CNT* (Mexico), Pego admitted that he would have preferred to devote his writing career entirely to labor newspapers, but he had to make a living.[47]

A staunch antifascist, Pego joined *España Libre* as a staff writer in 1940 and helped José Castro edit *España Libre* from 1941 to 1943. His humorous chronicles and his sharp wit gave piercing coverage of European news during World War II. However, economic circumstances forced him to take employment as a regional manager of McCann-Erickson Corporation and, in 1952, he moved to Puerto Rico for his work. Around the time of his departure from New York, an *España Libre* article professed that Pego had been "the soul and support of *España Libre* and that he will continue to send his chronicles. He was in charge of *España Libre* in difficult times.... In 1936 Pego was already a renowned journalist and he put his talent to serve the freedom of the Spanish people."[48] The article also recalled Castilla Morales's praise of Pego's work and admitted that oftentimes they were the only two people editing the periodical. After his tenure as editor, Pego generously mentored other editors and his popular satirical chronicles ran until the paper closed its doors in 1977. In Puerto Rico, with Federico de Onís, Pego acted as executive member of Pro-Democracia Española (Pro-Spanish Democracy), an affiliated association, and reported on antifascist activism in Puerto Rico.

General José Asensio Torrado (1892–1961) succeeded Pego as editor.[49] In one of his chronicles, Pego lauded Asensio Torrado for his support of *España Libre*. Asensio Torrado was best known for his command during the Spanish Civil War and from his service as the Second Republic's sub-secretary to the minister of war. For these reasons, Asensio Torrado was one of the best-known Spaniards in the United States and the Americas, particularly in international political circles. He was also known in Washington, D.C., and in the United Nations, many of whose assemblies he attended as an observer, often with Pego. He was the cousin of playwright Adolfo Torrado, whose plays were staged in fundraisers. Despite his reputation, exile in the United States meant personal and economic hardship for the general. With a truncated military career, Asensio Torrado lived in poverty and earned a humble living with his translations. Nonetheless he dedicated many hours of work to *España Libre*, following in Pego's footsteps as an editor and continuing to build on the editorial work of Pego and the other editors before him.[50]

3. España Libre *and Its Editors*

Jesús González Malo: Supporter of the Resistance in Spain

Jesús González Malo (Santander, Spain, 1903–New York, 1965) served as a staff writer on *España Libre* from his arrival in New York in the early 1940s, and as editor of the periodical from 1961 to 1965. Before the Spanish Civil War, González Malo had been president of the Santander Dock Workers Union and editor of the leftist newspaper *La Región* in Santander, Spain.[51] During the conflict, González Malo fought in a mixed socialist and anarchist militia in Santander and Barcelona. Later, along with Carmen Aldecoa, whom I discuss more below, González Malo traveled to France and then to Cuba before moving to New York.[52]

González Malo's editorial strategy sought to make of *España Libre* a public forum open to readers to discuss social and political views, as well as to publish literature. González Malo perceived *España Libre* as a means of developing community among the members. At one point during his time as editor, some members complained about intellectuals and professors who used the periodical for self-promotion rather than dedicating themselves to the fight against fascism. In response to one such comment about the writings of Félix Martí Ibáñez, which occurred during an SHC assembly, González Malo defended Martí Ibáñez's essays and short stories from such accusation.[53] González Malo stressed that the priority of *España Libre* was to foster community rather than finding fault, and that each contribution was important for the periodical's mission. He personally contacted people from exile, labor, and North and South American networks and requested written submissions from them.[54] In his eulogy of González Malo, Joaquim Maurín Julià noted that, "Thanks to Malo, all the Spanish democrats, whether republicans, socialists, anarcho-syndicalists, Catholics or liberals, were included in SHC."[55] Other obituaries stressed his determined inclusiveness.

Several members of the SHC worked with González Malo on *España Libre*. In the 1950s and 1960s, Alberto Uriarte, who also served as general secretary and president of the Basque-American Center in New York, assisted González Malo in his job as managing editor of the periodical. Agustín Carcagente, who would also serve as vice president and president of the Fundraising Festivals Committee—and as the secretary general in the 1970s—was an administrator and staff writer with González Malo in the 1950s, and then an assistant manager in the 1960s. José Nieto Ruiz volunteered as a staff writer, helping with the correspondence and the bookstore.[56] At various times, Miguel R. Ortiz and Arturo Conde also served as vice secretaries, Carmen Conchado as administrator, and Josefina Gómez as treasurer.

With the help of sailor volunteers and correspondents in Spain, González Malo established an undercover correspondence system with the clandestine resistance in Spain. To protect his correspondents in Spain, González Malo used pseudonyms, coded language, and disguised handwriting in his correspondence. One of his pseudonyms, Martínez, was a tribute to a fellow militiaman, José María Martínez, who fell in combat in Sotiello, Asturias.[57] In his correspondence, González Malo asked contacts for "safe" addresses (individuals in Spain who volunteered to receive mail from the SHC). Once an address had become "wasted" (used a few times), it was replaced with a new one. The necessity to protect relatives and friends made personal information scarce. From Spain, his cousin "Julio" explained why: "Your good friends . . . do not think that they do not write to you because they have forgotten you. They do not write to you because they are afraid."[58] "Julio" reasoned that frightened collaborators would endanger the clandestine dissidents by mishandling codes, and asked González Malo to focus on the fight for freedom.

These strategies avoided Franco's censorship. The underground resistance's descriptions of fascist terror in Spain were increasingly highlighted during González Malo's tenure as editor of *España Libre*. González Malo knew that the periodical had the power to expose Franco's cruelty to the world.[59] However, under Franco's rule, the frequent raids on people's homes led to detention and incarceration of many members of the clandestine resistance. In 1947, several of these members collaborating with González Malo were imprisoned for organizing donations to support political prisoners' families. The Spanish military police, the Guardia Civil, found the lists of donations given to aid families of political prisoners in one its raids.[60]

FBI agents interrogated González Malo several times at his home. The first visit occurred on April 19, 1942, after the Office of Censorship intercepted his private correspondence. González Malo declared that he was not an anarchist, but a syndicalist. He told the agents he felt grateful to the United States for having given him refuge; however, he informed them that he did not plan to stop his relief aid to other Spanish refugees. On September 23, 1943, FBI agents ordered González Malo to register as a "Foreign Agent" because he was secretary of the sub-delegation of the Spanish anarchist union CNT in the United States and he was sending funds to France, Santo Domingo, Africa, and Cuba. Furthermore, González Malo had circulated the anarchist paper *Solidaridad Obrera* (Mexico) in the United States and written essays for *Solidaridad Obrera* and *España Libre*. Six days later, pro bono lawyer Jesse Rosenberg unregistered González Malo with a written declaration that his involvement with the CNT was limited to humanitarian relief for war refugees. Nonetheless, the

FBI interrogated González Malo again in 1944, 1964, and 1965. Each time he restated that his CNT membership was dedicated exclusively to relief aid for Spanish refugees.[61]

Despite the FBI surveillance, González Malo elaborated his postwar conception of anarcho-syndicalism not only in *España Libre* (New York) but also in *Comunidad Ibérica* (México), *CNT* (Toulouse), and *España Libre* (Toulouse). Additionally, González Malo wrote several books and pamphlets.[62] His articles prompted responses by other anarchists in these periodicals and his books were reviewed as well. The title of one of González Malo's books, *La incorporación de las masas* (The incorporation of the masses, 1952), referenced José Ortega y Gasset's *La rebelión de las masas* (*The Rebellion of the Masses*, 1932). In the context of prerevolutionary Spain, Ortega y Gasset warned against the pernicious effect of the people's revolutionary impulse. González Malo criticized Ortega y Gasset for such "elitist paternalism" which "grotesquely" reduced people to a violent, amorphous, unitary, and homogenous entity.[63] For González Malo, the elites, politicians, and union leaders too often assumed that workers needed tutelage, and portrayed them as disorganized, passive, and ingenuous, underestimating the common people's ability to organize independently and transform society.[64] Considering the people's historical role in bettering society, González Malo refuted the elite's dismissal of workers as inconsequential. Although common people might not have the opportunity to make the fateful decisions of political leaders, they were not simply victims of society; they were a force for progress.

González Malo's experience as leader of the Santander Dock Workers Union before his exile, and as a member of the District 65 Retail Wholesale and Department Store Union in New York, gave him insights into workers' successful self-organization. For González Malo, the Santander Dock Workers Union was a valuable example of how workers governed themselves because the 700-member union distributed responsibilities among 50 delegates. González Malo demanded that union leaders be elected regularly, and their pay limited, to prevent the abuse of power. Using members' dues, the Santander union offered unemployment, accident, and life insurance, as well as courses on accounting and English.[65] In 1957 and 1958, González Malo wrote about the achievements of District 65 in the periodical *CNT* (Mexico) and *España Libre* (Toulouse) to show similar goals achieved by the union. At the time, it functioned as a cooperative: members served as administrators, and decisions were made in open assemblies. The union provided insurance and cultural and educational activities to its members. Its Hispanic committee represented 2,000 members.[66] In his writings, González Malo provided examples of how workers had structured work, the economy, and the army during the Spanish Civil War, and had continued to build an antifascist resistance movement, like the clandestine ASO, during Franco's rule.[67] He published several articles in *España Libre* covering the same points.

In *La incorporación de las masas*, González Malo discussed the pre- and post–Civil War history of the Spanish workers' movement. Only after becoming conscious of their societal rights and responsibilities, González Malo felt, would people confront repressive power. Despite being self-taught, workers evolved from merely being represented in the body politic to becoming their own political actors. In exile, González Malo continued his fight to empower workers, and challenged exile coalitions to ensure workers would remain a political force in a free Spain.[68] González Malo also elaborated on the individual development of workers. In 1959, he published ten articles in *España Libre* that drew links between anarcho-syndicalism and Fernando de los Ríos's (1879–1949) humanist socialism based on the "ennoblement of individual responsibility."[69] De los Ríos was the Second Republic's ambassador to the United States and remained in the United States after the Spanish Civil War. In the 1940s, he gave sixteen speeches in fundraisers. De los Ríos's political thought was influenced by anarchism, Karl Krause's "harmonic rationalism," and Neo-Kantianism—a philosophical synthesis that characterized his most important work, *El sentido humanista del socialismo* (1926).[70] For de los Ríos, humanist socialism should inform every daily action, but would only be fully achieved when rationalism and idealism complemented each other, in what he called "realización armónica" (harmonious attainment).[71] De los Ríos's "realización armónica" shared with González Malo's "emancipación ética" (ethical emancipation) the aspiration for individual self-realization through an ethical and participatory life. González Malo believed that love of oneself was an essential ingredient of postwar anarchism; as he put it, "self-love is the source of all individuality. By learning to love oneself, one loves everything else. This fact is denied by many ideologies because they have the degrading purpose of mediatizing the natural feeling of self-esteem, educating man according to prescribed doctrine."[72] To González Malo, such self-love and participation in society led to the emancipation from tyranny. *España Libre* provided an important venue for González Malo's writings and the development of his political thought. In addition to his books and publications in other periodicals, his essays and correspondence while working for *España Libre* trace the arc of his broader intellectual commitments and development.

Not only de los Ríos but another SHC member, Dwight Macdonald (1906–1982), influenced González Malo in his conception of workers as political and ethical actors. Macdonald, who edited the periodical *Politics*, explored the legacy of humanism to find a new, radical means of achieving a more inclusive American society. Macdonald's "radical critical consciousness" formulated a humanist radicalism, whose purpose was to create a truly participatory democracy.[73] His notion of radical humanism contrasted with the use of humanism as the rhetorical rallying point in the common antifascist discourse during War World II in Europe and with humanism in the United States, which looked for ways to counterbalance the disruption of tradition by modernity and mass culture.[74] De los Ríos's "realización armónica" and González Malo's "emancipación ética" echoed Macdonald's central motif of a "radical critical consciousness," which looked for a more inclusive and ethical society that included the marginalized.

Rudolf Rocker (1873–1958) is another writer and thinker who greatly influenced González Malo as editor of *España Libre*.[75] Rocker had fled from Germany when Hitler came to power. He eventually settled in the United States, and formed part of the Modern School movement. He was fascinated by Spanish anarchism and in his writing, he often cited Spanish anarchists such as Tarrida del Mármol, Ricardo Mella, and Anselmo Lorenzo.[76] In turn, some of his works were translated into Spanish and reviewed in Spanish-language anarchist newspapers. *España Libre* regularly mentioned his work. In March 1956, *España Libre* partially reprinted Rocker's piece on the Spanish anarchist Fermín Salvochea.[77] In Salvochea's honor, Rocker had named his own son Fermín.[78] Additionally, Rocker's books were sold in *España Libre*'s bookstore service until the last day the periodical was published. González Malo and Rocker exchanged books about Spanish anarchism and González Malo translated Rocker's correspondence with Spanish anarchists.[79] In a letter that González Malo translated for him addressed to CNT Toulouse, Rocker proclaimed that since the end of the nineteenth century he admired the Spanish anarchist movement as much as Max Nettlau did.

Rocker's *Anarcho-syndicalism* (1938) was a decisive influence on González Malo's elaboration of anarcho-syndicalism in exile. González Malo attributed to Rocker the paternity of modern anarcho-syndicalism because Rocker had developed the theoretical description of what Spanish workers had put into practice before and during the Spanish Civil War. For González Malo, Rocker articulated anarcho-syndicalism as a series of practical objectives for the well-being of workers, such as the proposal of the syndicate as a unit of production, and the cooperative as a unit of distribution of goods. Repudiating both economic exploitation and political coercive institutions, González Malo believed that people should self-govern with these entities. Following Rocker,

La incorporación de las masas lays out a blueprint for an ideal, emancipated organic society based on local syndicates that become the fundamental social and economic organs in the form of cooperatives of production, unions, schools, and cultural organizations.[80] The anarcho-syndicalist blueprint included the federative model of Francesc Pi i Margall, a Catalan libertarian socialist and president of the First Spanish Republic, who dreamt of a federalist Spain in the nineteenth century. Influenced by Rocker's work, González Malo perceived syndicates as the vanguard of such a federalist and municipalist structure.[81]

The correspondence between González Malo and Rocker matured into a life-long friendship and their families became close.[82] Their letters often exchanged personal commiserations on the tragedy of exile. In 1946, Rocker told González Malo about his difficulties in obtaining a U.S. resident visa and the anguish he suffered over the possibility that he might be deported to Berlin: "under the horrible circumstances in Germany it would mean the same for me as to commit suicide."[83] Fortunately, Rocker obtained the visa. In 1956, a year after Milly Witkop(-Rocker)'s death, Aldecoa wrote an article commemorating her in *España Libre* (Paris) that Rocker appreciated and which helped his grieving.[84] After Rocker's death in 1958, González Malo noted in *España Libre* that some of Rocker's works remained to be translated into Spanish and encouraged readers to do so.[85] When González Malo died in 1965, Fermín Rocker, Rocker's artist son, published a eulogy with an original drawing in *España Libre* and portrayed him as "an idealist of the old school ... a man of strong convictions and loyalties, he was nevertheless too human to be a fanatic."[86]

González Malo defined himself as an anarcho-syndicalist or a libertarian, specifying that he believed in people and liberty above any ideology. To him, people, skeptical of their leaders, grew cognizant of their interdependency and created a fruitful "unity in independence."[87] By using this phrase, González Malo expressed the synthesis of individualism and solidarity ingrained in Spanish culture, which he saw exemplified in the most recognized Spanish literary pair: the symbiotic relationship of a laborer (Sancho Panza) and a knight (Don Quixote). He asked orthodox anarchists to free workers of constraining dogmas: "The popular movements must be liberated from all dogmatic subjugation. The philosophy of the masses is eclectic and instinctive."[88] González Malo mentioned Rocker as the thinker that understood such dialectics of the Spanish character.[89] Citing Ricardo Mella, González Malo called for fostering people's individualism in an intersectional society: "The man will be more man by his individuality and the human collectivity will have to be surpassed by true solidarity—two enormous forces that concur to the fullness of humanity. Separated, they will rise to barbarism: flocks of lambs and herd of wolves."[90] Similar to the philosophy expressed in Félix Martí Ibáñez's short stories, González Malo regarded anarchism in exile as a revolutionary intersection with others.

In his review of González Malo's *La incorporación de las masas* in *Solidaridad Obrera* (Paris), the anarchist Mariano Viñuales alerted his readers that González Malo's book would no doubt scandalize orthodox anarchist thinkers but claimed that González Malo's revisionist approach was well argued and necessary for the future of popular movements in Spain.[91] González Malo's exasperation grew in exile. In 1955, he wrote thirteen articles responding to Victor Sawdon Pritchett's *The Spanish Temper* (1954), in which he agreed to some extent with Pritchett's claim that Spaniards could be inflexible and violent.[92] In these articles, González Malo cited Miguel de Unamuno, Ricardo Mella, and Anselmo Lorenzo to encourage the Spanish people, for the sake of their own survival, to learn to be sympathetic to others.

Despite complaining about not having time to read because of his activism and work editing *España Libre*, González Malo nevertheless read extensively and incorporated the ideas of thinkers he was encountering in exile into his own writing. He was on a search for common ground from where anarchism intersected with the ideas of other progressive and radical thinkers. He named numerous influences in his writings. In his manuscripts, González Malo cited his contemporary and preceding anarchist and anarcho-syndicalist thinkers, mainly Diego Abad de Santillán, Mikhail Bakunin, Marin Civera, Joaquín Costa, J. García Pradas, M. González Prada, Peter Kropotkin, Anselmo Lorenzo, Ricardo Mella, Juan Peiro, Ángel Pestaña, Joseph Proudhon, Élisée Reclus, José Viadiu, and Manuel Villar. In his capacity as editor of *España Libre*, González Malo eagerly read Spanish exile and American progressive periodicals. In his articles, he mentions these periodicals as sources of documentation on the workers' role in a society free of fascism.

After the Henry George School of Social Science invited the SHC to attend a course on economics, González Malo published thirteen articles entitled "Por una economía libertaria" (For a libertarian economy) in *España Libre* (Toulouse) based on Henry George's *Progress and Poverty* (1879).[93] Upon reading the articles, Gaston Leval, a French anarcho-syndicalist, expressed his indignation at González Malo's approach to a libertarian economy and complained that, instead of writing about Henry George, John Stuart Mill, John Maynard Keynes, and Ortega y Gasset, González Malo should be writing about anarchist founders such as Pierre-Joseph Proudhon, Mikhail Bakunin, Peter Kropotkin, Ricardo Mella, and Errico Malatesta, among others. With a sarcastic: "Sin acrimonias: A Gaston Leval, erudito de la ortodoxia" (Without acrimony: For Gaston Leval, well-educated in orthodoxy), Malo responded that he was merely sharing what he had learned about other economic theorists in his course at the George School, and putting those ideas in conversation with anarchist thinkers.

In 1956, González Malo approved of the anarchist periodical *CNT* (Mexico) publishing an article by the liberal thinker Salvador de Madariaga, because González Malo believed that inclusionary efforts were important in the development of a more just society, "[just as] we celebrated the presence of our [anarchist] men in the athenaeum of Madrid and in the mainstream press. If we had done so more frequently, we would be singing a different tune now."[94] González Malo was often criticized for his reformist approach. In *CNT* (Mexico), he responded to both progressive and conservative critics: "We are revolutionaries precisely because we believe in the evolution of society."[95] He concluded in another article: "In this collectivist era, which revolves around the overwhelming advance of the applied sciences and technology for the material well-being, we need to strengthen both human bonds and theoretical nuances so that spiritual values do not perish. The time of orthodox ideological minorities and narrow nationalisms has ended. Avoiding being inclusive is to commit suicide."[96] In one of his last and most forceful articles, entitled "Con el mismo espíritu" (With the same spirit), the editor clarified *España Libre*'s reformist approach to anarchism after the Spanish Civil War. "We cannot affirm our libertarian spirit more clearly," he wrote. "We are staunch supporters of freedom, who fight tyranny in all its forms and manifestations, without hesitation or delay. Such expressions as 'just us' or 'all or nothing,' are long gone in our discourse because they deny the libertarian spirit, because they invoke the theory and practice of exclusionism."[97]

Editors in Later Decades (1960s and 1970s)

Carmen Aldecoa González (Turón de Mieles, Asturias, date unknown–Madrid, 1988) served as managing editor of *España Libre* after González Malo's death in 1965; however, she was only able to do so until March 1966 for health reasons.[98] Aldecoa had originally fled from Spain with González Malo to Bordeaux, France, in the 1930s. She had been living in Santander and working as a teacher at the time the Spanish Civil War broke out. The CNT asked her to teach the militia's children and she organized a school, the Casa Hijo del Miliciano (House of the Militia's Children). When the city of Santander fell to rebel forces in 1937, Aldecoa and González Malo fled to Bordeaux. In Lyon, Aldecoa started an orphanage named Iberia for refugee children.[99] Aldecoa and González Malo crossed again into Barcelona, still under pro-Republic forces. In the city, he worked at the port and she taught in two schools. In 1939, they crossed the border again but were imprisoned in an internment camp in France.[200] They received help from anarchists in Cuba and Aldecoa was invited by Spanish exile José Rubia Barcia to teach in La Escuela Libre in Havana. After living in Cuba, the couple moved to New York where Aldecoa secured an adjunct position teaching Spanish in the Romance Languages Department at New York University and later coordinated the Spanish teaching assistants of the department in the 1950s and 1960s.[101] After her arrival in New York in 1941, Aldecoa was involved with the SHC in several ways. She helped with the writing of the newspaper and gave several speeches in workers' associations, which discussed labor history and the cultural and political aspects of exile. She spoke on the role of women in the antifascist effort, remembering those who lost their lives in the fight for democracy in Spain and those who were still incarcerated in Franco's prisons. She implored women in the audience to continue the fight for justice in Spain.[102] She was also involved in several aid committees helping families in Spain. Possibly because of her adjunct position at New York University, Aldecoa kept a low profile within the SHC and *España Libre* but published in Mexico and France and was active in supporting political refugees.

Aldecoa's childhood among mining communities was an important influence in her life-long fight for social and political justice for the working class. She spent her childhood playing with miners' children because her father was an engineer in the Mieres, Asturian mines. In fact, a miner taught young Aldecoa how to read. Years later, in U.S. exile, she published *Del sentir y pensar: Libro primero*, in Mexico with the exile editor Bartomeu Costa Amic in 1957. The compilation included her articles in *El Diario Montañés* (Santander, 1936), *España Libre* (New York, 1940), *España Libre* (Toulouse 1941, 1955), and *La Prensa* (New York, 1951), as well as unpublished material.[103] Most importantly, *Del sentir y pensar* sought to preserve Spanish workers' history through an encyclopedic review of pre–Spanish Civil War labor periodicals. In her manuscript, Aldecoa noted that the workers' revolution started in Spain when anarchists and socialists discussed authors and thinkers such as Étienne Cabet, Pierre Joseph Proudhon, and Charles Fourier in workers' newspapers, associations, and schools. In this respect, Aldecoa cited Renée Lamberet's recognition of Spanish labor and print networks for their success before the First International of 1864.[104]

In *Del sentir y pensar*, Aldecoa criticizes elitist and colonialist perspectives that disregarded the historical contributions of common people in Spain and in the Americas.[105] To document proletarian print culture, Aldecoa makes sure to list the names of those involved in writing and editing periodicals. She includes labor leaders and journalists, as well as progressive thinkers and politicians. The author counts 582 newspapers from 1869 to 1936, and mentions among others *La Federación* (1869), *Solidaridad* (1870), *El Eco de la Clase Obrera* (1855) edited by Ramón Simó i Badía, *La Emancipación* (1872) edited by Pablo Iglesias and Anselmo Lorenzo, and the clandestine *La Fraternidad* (1947). She is troubled that such periodicals were not being preserved and thus the historical legacy of workers was being lost. Therefore, Aldecoa invites scholars to consult the archives of proletarian journals and examine workers' writing of the era, which she finds "full of confidence, and illuminated by poetic, utopian thought. Since then, [workers' journalism's] concern has been the discussion of doctrinal principles and solidarity. Its foundation is the critical-philosophical essay that urges readers to study and be informed."[106] Before Franco, proletarian journalism instructed workers. In exile, anarchist newspapers continued to promote "emancipatory ideas and human dignity."[107] Aldecoa mentions more than fifty periodicals written by exiles, among them *El Socialista, CNT, Adelante, La Batalla, Solidaridad Obrera, Ruta, Renovación, Cenit, Tierra y Libertad*, and *España Libre*.[108]

The goal of instructing workers also appears in her recovery of anarchist print culture. Aldecoa highlights the role of periodicals in publishing serialized and translated books, and in doing so, educating the people, "who deeply felt their illiteracy in their flesh and blood."[109] Two years later, González Malo would recall this goal and further provided the context of the pedagogical role of workers' periodicals in their associations. He refers to the many schools organized in workers' athenaeums in his article "Socialismo humanista IX" (Humanist socialism IX). These athenaeums offered books and periodicals to workers. González Malo notes that each union published its own newspaper when the popular sentiment was: "¡A la libertad por la cultura!" (To liberty through culture!). Workers read a lot "perhaps disorganized and hastily, but people read and studied with unequaled frenzy."[110]

In *Del sentir y pensar*, Aldecoa continues recovering authors published or translated in many proletarian periodicals.[111] She then reviews some of the authors popular among the proletariat: Ángel Gavinet, Clarín (Leopoldo García-Alas y Ureña), Vicente Blasco Ibáñez, Benito Pérez Galdós, Miguel de Unamuno, Ramiro de Maeztu, Azorín (José Martínez Ruiz), Pío Baroja, Ramón Pérez de Ayala, and José García Pradas. Also, she highlights newspapers devoting pages to literature and the arts, such as *Estudios* (1930), Marín Civera's *Cuadernos de Cultura* (1930), and *La Revista Blanca* (1899). She laments that such authors were not found in anthologies of Spanish literature when "with their thoughts and feelings [these authors] elevate the spirit and broaden the world's vision."[112] Finally, Aldecoa recognizes some commercial publishers that printed philosophy and literature at affordable prices for workers.[113]

In her book, Aldecoa praises the ways *España Libre* fought fascism; however, she also stressed the need to define exile beyond solely an antifascist identity: "We know that we are against this and that but not what we are.... Forgetting what we said we were yesterday, we are now preoccupied with insisting on what we are *not* today."[114] Aldecoa asks anarchists in exile to go beyond a simply reactive project against fascism, and to construct a new world. With this in mind, Aldecoa interviewed *España Libre* anarchist contributor Miguel Giménez Igualada about his experience in French internment camps. Giménez Igualada described how he survived by remembering his readings of Leo Tolstoy, Peter Kropotkin, Ernst Haekel, Jean-Marie Guyau, Charles Darwin, Romain Rolland, Mahatma Gandhi, José Enrique Rodó, Miguel de Cervantes, and Jiddu Krishnamurti. His book, *Más allá del dolor* (Beyond pain, 1946), urged readers to overcome the paralyzing power of pain through the prophetic power of literature. Aldecoa agreed with Giménez Igualada on the power of literature to deliver "a flowering virgin thought ... a new nuance of feeling, since humanity seems to have lost the ability to feel."[115] In this respect, Aldecoa aligned herself with *España Libre*'s inclusion of literature as a fundamental aspect of the anarchist and antifascist fight.

Miguel R. Ortiz (dates unknown) became managing editor after Aldecoa.[116] Ortiz, a Spanish university student who fled Franco's Spain in 1962, continued González Malo's legacy of opening the pages of *España Libre* to the underground resistance in Spain. However, he wanted to introduce changes to the publication. In January and February 1966, Ortiz changed the format of the periodical into a magazine with better-quality paper and more pages. But only a month later, in March, members voted to go back to the previous, more economical format to devote the maximum funds possible to aiding refugees and the underground opposition. This decision reinforced the members' desire to maintain "full support of the norms established by Jesús González Malo," which meant focusing on political commitment and assistance to refugees and the underground dissidents.[117] After Ortiz, Marcos C. Mari served as *España Libre*'s editor from November 1966 to 1972. Alberto Uriarte was the editor of the periodical from 1973 to 1977, and Agustín Carcagente managing editor. Endorsing the inclusiveness that had characterized González Malo's term, Mari sustained the clandestine distribution of *España Libre* in Spain. Staff writers Alberto Luis Ruiz, Alberto Lozano Barrios, and Zwy Aldouby (English-language pages) were particularly active during Mari's term.

During the last years of the periodical's existence, Joaquim Maurín Julià (Bonansa, Spain, 1896–New York, 1973) and Eugenio F. Granell (A Coruña,

Spain, 1912–A Coruña, Spain, 2001) became part of the editorial team. Both had been affiliated with POUM in the 1930s in Spain. Maurín Julià founded *La Batalla* (The battle) and Granell was a newspaperman for *Nueva Era* (New era), which were POUM periodicals. Granell also directed *Combatiente Rojo* (Red fighter) before going into exile. Maurín Julià escaped execution in Spain thanks to his wife's campaign from the United States and his brother-in-law's contacts with French president Léon Blum.[118] Once he was in the United States, Fernando de los Ríos, who began meeting with him at the Hispanic Society of America, wrote in support of his obtaining a visa. He described Maurín Julià as a man with a "highly individual attitude, completely separated from that of the communist minority . . . and who defended theses and policies absolutely divorced from those which communism propounds both nationally and internationally."[119] To make ends meet, Maurín Julià founded the American Literary Agency (ALA) in the 1940s, which placed journalistic essays in numerous newspapers in the Americas. The syndicating agency offered the services of Latino journalists to newspapers in the Americas with the promise of featuring U.S. news with a Hispanic perspective.[120] Maurín Julià published *Hacia la segunda revolución* (Toward the second revolution) in 1935 about the workers' revolutionary movement in Barcelona in 1934. It was reprinted in 1937 and 1966 with the title *Revolución y contrarrevolución* (Revolution and counterrevolution).[121]

While Maurín Julià paid attention to international and cultural news, the anarchist exile community was not forgotten in *España Libre*. Maurín Julià's regular *España Libre* column "Columna de honor" featured short biographies of members and the organization's sponsors. These essays documented the historical legacy of the Spanish Civil War exile community. In other columns, under the pen names A.B.C., John Anderson, Félix R. Anderson, W. K. Mayo (guacamayo), and Julio Antonio Roy, Maurín Julià elaborated on his political experience before and during the Civil War, discussed the legacy of the Second Republic, and denounced Franco's fascist Spain.[122]

Eugenio Fernández Granell became part of the editorial team of *España Libre* in the last years its life. Granell was a painter and writer and served as a militiaman during the Spanish Civil War. He went into exile in France, Guatemala, Puerto Rico, and the Dominican Republic before arriving in the United States. The SHC financially sponsored Granell (as well as other Spaniards) while he was in the Dominican Republic. In Puerto Rico, Granell was anonymously accused of being a dangerous communist. Throughout his exile, Granell corresponded with POUM comrades and published in several Spanish periodicals and journals.[123] The FBI, which had been watching Granell since 1951, interrogated the painter several times there.[124]

3. España Libre and Its Editors

Once in New York, Granell received assistance from various intellectual circles. André Bretón, who had met Granell in the Dominican Republic in the 1940s, introduced his friend to New York's intellectuals and artists, who included Mayer Shapiro, Jackson Pollock, and Robert Motherwell. In addition, Francisco García Lorca helped Granell obtain a summer teaching post at Middlebury College in 1947.[125] Later, Ángel del Río recommended him for an adjunct post at Brooklyn College, where he taught Spanish from 1957 to 1985.[126]

In 1947, Granell published his surrealist novel about the Spanish Civil War, *La novela del indio Tupinamba*, which of course was commented upon in *España Libre*, and soon after he was invited to contribute to the periodical and in the SHC. Granell's articles denounced Franco's Spain, and reviewed Spanish and exile literature (Azorín, Federico García Lorca, Antonio Machado, Unamuno).[127] With his cultural reviews, he brought to *España Libre* the artistic environment that welcomed him during his exile in the United States.

España Libre occupied an intersection of a multifaceted and participatory community composed of politically conscious workers and intellectuals. Helped by numerous staff writers and contributors, editors were natural leaders. In the 1940s editorials focused on alerting readers about the spread of fascism and fundraising for refugees. *España Libre* denounced the conditions in Spain where the population was dominated by the educational, social, and violent aspects of the Movimiento and National Catholicism. By the 1950s, the increasing international recognition of the Franco dictatorship disquieted members. The editorials published during that decade were heavily focused on denouncing that recognition. However, by the 1960s the periodical concentrated its efforts on supporting the weakened underground labor opposition in Spain and in coordinating efforts with other political forces. In the 1970s, *España Libre* published homages to exiles for the antifascist resistance they had lived. With more focus on culture and the migrant lives of members, the periodical also reveals that the second and third generations were progressively more preoccupied with issues of civil rights in U.S. society. Over decades of publication and with different strategies that adapted to changing times, *España Libre* kept up its fight from U.S. soil for a free Spain.

The harsh conditions of exile meant that the publication relied heavily on both sporadic and staff writers. However, the goals and personalities of a few of the editors notably marked the trajectory of *España Libre*. José Castilla Morales infused the periodical with humor and connections to anarchist and Hispanic associations in the United States. Aurelio Pego made a fierce antifascism the uniting goal for members. Jesús González Malo kept the paper independent from the Republican government-in-exile and focused instead on the needs of refugees and the clandestine resistance in Spain.

By connecting socialist and anarchist concepts, González Malo incorporated the people into a non-elitist version of humanism.[128] González Malo made workers central to a radical Spanish ethos and rejected elitist political strategies that he considered hierarchical at best, such as political democracy; or corrupted at worst, such as fascism.[129] He foregrounded the possibility of radical change with his vision of a non-elitist, inclusive, participatory, and self-managed postfascist society.

After the defeat of the Spanish Civil War, González Malo was concerned about the survival of anarcho-syndicalism and resolutely protected the sovereignty and legitimacy of workers. However, Rocker's *Nationalism and Culture* (1937) highly influenced González Malo in reconceptualizing the nation as reactionary in nature and bound to fascist tendencies. In exile, Rocker inspired González Malo to encourage people to engage in politics and strive for freedom, justice, and solidarity. *La incorporación de las masas* demanded a satisfactory integration of workers in society. González Malo's blueprint for an emancipated society predicted a slow, non-authoritarian, nonviolent evolution from oppression to self-incorporation into the body politic.

Carmen Aldecoa was the only woman who directed *España Libre*, but for a short time. Her experience testifies to the patriarchal culture of the periodical. Miguel R. Ortiz brought a new era of editors more attuned to the readers' needs in the 1960s and 1970s. Marcos C. Mari, Alberto Uriarte, Joaquim Maurín Julià and Eugenio F. Granell focused on cultural production with the support of many contributors. In this respect, *España Libre* played an important role in the democratization of Spain. Several of these late contributors, such as Madariaga or Araquistáin, facilitated dialogue within Spanish exile groups and fostered alliances with international organizations that offered, at the time, hope for a democratic Spain.

With *España Libre*, editors created an inclusive exile community that extended beyond the United States. Through the resilience and adaptation of its members in exile, the SHC and *España Libre* achieved some of the greatest political and cultural milestones of progressive and radical antifascism through the transformative role of solidarity and literature.

4

The Struggle against Deportations

España Libre's journalistic coverage of refugees fleeing Spain was a powerful tool to raise awareness for the antifascist cause. Moved by the stories of these refugees that regularly appeared in the periodical, members felt compelled to meet ships arriving from Europe at the Port of New York and trying to locate refugees in need. An anonymous short story published in *España Libre* on November 29, 1939, describes the apprehension refugees felt at their arrival and the comfort SHC members offered them: "The faces of the Spaniards look infinitely sad.... We know that no one is waiting for us.... Suddenly two strangers approach us, 'Are you refugees?' they ask. We nod. 'On behalf of the Sociedades Hispanas Confederadas, welcome to New York.' We did not answer. We were so moved."[1]

The SHC's solidarity with refugees, rather than being perceived as aid, was portrayed as an honor given to the first fighters of fascism. In a review published in *España Libre*, the Grupo Antifascista del Bronx (Bronx Antifascist Group) claimed: "We need to specially mention our help to the Spanish refugees, who were the first who faced Nazism," and encouraged other affiliated organizations to follow them.[2] Likewise, an editorial that appeared in *España Libre* mourned two tragic deaths of exiles in Mexico, that of playwright Antonio Fernández Escobés and journalist Fabián Vidal: "Many refugees who could not get back on their feet, and had not even the help of their countrymen.... Some of these unfortunate refugees have died of hunger, misery, anguish, and solitude. . . .

Figure 3. Members of the SHC at the Port of New York raising their antifascist fists. Courtesy of José Nieto Ruiz and Brandeis Special Collections.

We the early migrants, we have a clear conscience.... We do all we can."[3] The forceful editorial concluded that those who could help a countryman, and turn their back on him, and let him die "were accomplices of Franco."[4]

The stories of these kinds of tragic cases published in *España Libre* greatly disturbed readers. In June 1940, during the German occupation of France, the SHC invited socialist Francisco Largo Caballero, who had been the Spanish prime minister from 1936 to 1937, to participate in one of its fundraisers as a speaker, possibly a graceful attempt to help Largo Caballero escape occupied France. However, Largo Caballero declined the invitation, arguing that he was needed in Europe. Only shortly afterward he was arrested by the Gestapo.[5] In the face of his arrest, the SHC could only attempt to prevent Largo Caballero's imminent extradition to Spain, where he would surely have been executed. José Asensio Torrado, a general who fought under Largo Caballero's orders in Madrid during the Spanish Civil War, and Andrés Rodríguez Barbeito, an exiled journalist, were at the time executive members of the SHC. They enlisted Norman Thomas, a leading socialist, to help.[6] Thomas wrote to President Franklin Roosevelt about the case, and launched an international campaign that

4. The Struggle against Deportations

successfully led to the cancellation of Largo Caballero's extradition order.[7] Largo Caballero himself reasoned that international opinion might have deterred his extradition to Spain because Franco wanted to avoid further light shining on the inhumanities of his regime.[8] Nonetheless, Largo Caballero was interned at the Sachsenhausen concentration camp and died soon after his liberation at the end of the Second World War. In 1959, *España Libre* continued to remember his heroic act to remain in France, an example of "our Spanish dignity and hope for a free Spain."[9]

The suicide of twenty-eight-year-old Eusebio López Gallarta was another tragic case. Originally from Bilbao, Spain, the Spanish sailor arrived in New York in early autumn of 1949. Not having an entrance visa, he was detained by immigration officers upon his arrival at Ellis Island.[10] In the absence of a standing refugee policy to help people fleeing the repression of Franco's regime, López Gallarta was ordered to be deported. On October 8, 1949, López Gallarta committed suicide in his New York prison cell the day before deportation.[11] Another tragic case involved the disappearance of the SHC member Jesús de Galíndez in New York on March 12, 1956.[12] Galíndez, a Spanish exile who initially lived in the Dominican Republic before moving to the United States, wrote his doctoral dissertation at Columbia University on that Caribbean country's dictator, Rafael Leónidas Trujillo. One year after the completion of this study, Galíndez suddenly disappeared. Investigating Galíndez's disappearance, José Nieto Ruiz, a staff member at *España Libre*, along with Manuel de Dios Unanue, a journalist for the New York *La Prensa*, eventually concluded that Trujillo's men had killed Galíndez. They detailed their findings in *España Libre* in multiple articles in from 1956 to 1959. Their investigative journalism into Galíndez disappearance was the genesis of Spanish author Manuel Vázquez Montalbán's acclaimed novel *Galindez* (1990), which was inspired by Montalbán's interview with de Dios Unanue.[13]

Solidarity was needed during the Spanish Civil War but even more so during the decades following. After their victory, the Francoist forces began systematically rounding up those who had sided with the Second Republic. Although borders were sealed, Spaniards continued to clandestinely flee from the brutal political repression and execution sentences. However, they were not granted refugee status by North American law. In the United States, Spanish refugees fleeing Francoist Spain became people without a country with no right to U.S. citizenship and unable to seek the services of Spanish embassies or consulates in the United States. U.S. isolationist sentiment played against the SHC's goals: "Because of the pressure of isolationist public opinion . . . American quota regulations were not relaxed even after the defeat of France

Print Culture, Activism, and Solidarity

in June of 1940, when thousands of refugees in the United States appeared to be the only salvation from death."[14] Moreover, "given the passivity and indifference at the governmental level, refugee aid was left up to private organizations."[15] It was within the context of this dangerous absence of institutional aid that the SHC and *España Libre* operated. Because of the governmental indifference, refugees and SHC members were frequently forced to leave the United States and seek other host countries. For example, Jesús Arenas Ruiz, one of the SHC founders, could not resolve his immigration status with U.S. authorities and he was forced to move to Venezuela in 1940. In 1951, the SHC collaborated with the Government of the Second Republic in exile to influence the United Nations to redefine the concept of refugee so that it could also protect Spaniards.

España Libre's work expressing, fostering, and organizing solidarity for refugees catalyzed the community to be proactive. Money, medicines, and ambulances were sent to Republican fronts, numerous Spaniards who were held in internment camps were relocated, and refugees' passages to Latin American countries were paid with the SHC's funds.[16] The periodical was instrumental in seeking out and providing aid for arriving refugees and relocating them. The information in the SHC archive details the aid for refugees and tells a story of extraordinary grassroots solidarity fighting fascism against all odds. *España Libre* was the weekly advocate and reminder of this critical fight.

Advocating for Refugees Abroad

Among the crucial projects that *España Libre* undertook was its advocacy for refugees abroad. As a first step, *España Libre* informed its readers about the needs of refugees. It also published information about the related work by the SHC and its allies. *España Libre* published requests sent by the SHC to find out information about refuges in France, North Africa, the Dominican Republic, and any other country in which they were waiting for visas or help. For example, on June 25, 1943, *España Libre* published a letter from the Department of State sent to an executive member of the SHC, Sebastian Palmer, on its front page. Charles W. Yost, assistant chief of the Division of European Affairs, confirmed that the United States was unable to help the 2,000 Spanish refugees in North Africa until the Mexican government expressed its final concurrence to its arrangement for visas.[17] On July 2, 1943, a follow-up article was published on the front page: the American armed forces in the area were helping released refugees by offering them work while their Mexican visas were resolved.[18] On another occasion, *España Libre* published on the front page of its November

26, 1943, issue a letter addressed to executive member Maria Cordellat from Eldred D. Kuppinger, assistant chief of the Special Division in the Department of State. The letter explained how the SHC could send aid to the Dominican Republic via the War Relief Board.[19]

Throughout the decades, the periodical advocated for a wide array of refugee needs. In 1948, *España Libre* campaigned to free Spanish refugees from an internment camp in Karaganda in the Soviet Union. Members of the Francoist Division Azul, as well as other Spanish residents in the country, had been detained after the end of the Second World War. The periodical claimed that the residents' anticommunism and their desire to leave the USSR caused them to be apprehended. *España Libre* published about fifty names of Spanish antifascists detained in the camp.[20]

The periodical also helped in the resettlement of refugees. Upon arrival in their host countries, some refugees published notices in *España Libre* trying to find regional connections in the Americas. One such notice read: "The Spanish refugee, Demetrio Llorden, who comes from the concentration camps in África, and has just arrived in México, is interested in establishing contact with Onobre Benaño, and brothers Ardila, all from Nerva, Spain, and whom he thinks must reside in the United States."[21] Similarly, refugees in France and other locations also published notes in *España Libre* to locate family. For example, in June of 1947, Joaquin Gonzalez, who was in exile in France, published a note in *España Libre* in an effort to locate family in the United States: "Joaquin Gonzalez, Spanish refugee in France, wishes to contact his relative Serafin Gonzalez who lives in Brooklyn."[22] Publishing information about the transnational circumstances of refugees was a long-lasting service provided by the periodical.

Aid Sent to Spain, France, and the Dominican Republic

There are only a few surviving reports and balance sheets—mostly undated and incomplete—from the period during the Spanish Civil War. Nevertheless, the surviving records speak to the scope of material support the SHC provided to refugees and antifascist groups. At this time, *España Libre* had not yet been officially launched and the organization was still publishing its periodical under the title *Frente Popular*. For example, illustrated cards and stamps were sold to collect funds. For this goal, the SHC was in communication with the CNT group in Catalonia, Comité de Ayuda a Euzkadi y Norte (Aid Committee for Basque Country and the North) in 1937. 7,600 illustrated cards were sent to the SHC to be sold to members and readers.[23] According to one treasurer's report, from January 1936 to December 1939 the SHC sent a total of $445,184.77 in cash and goods to Spain, which included canned food, clothes, and medicines. Between 1937 and 1938, the SHC also sent eight ambulances.[24]

Partiality in the early records also hinders research: only men's names are noted; women are referenced as "wife of" or listed with their children as "family." A second undated balance sheet reports $89,047.48 spent in refugee aid, along with payments for fifty-seven fares to transport refugees to Latin America (at a cost of $6,814.13). A third undated report lists a total 150 refugees aided by the SHC.[25] Another handwritten report lists an additional 189 people evacuated on several ships. Some names and ships are annotated: 17 in the *Ipanema*, 15 in the *Borinquén* and *Coamo*, 15 in the *Winnipeg*, 14 in the *Santa Lucía*, 11 in the *Mexique*, 9 in the *Westernland*, 12 in the *Statendam*, and 9 in the *LaSalle de Burdeos*.[26] *Frente Popular* published information stating that during the war years the SHC paid the passages of 1,141 refugees who traveled from France to Mexico.[27]

At the end of the war, two executive members, José Castro and Marcos Mari, traveled to France, where most refugees were held in camps, with the mission of organizing evacuation of one thousand Spanish refugees and paying their passages to Mexico.[28] They sent to the SHC numerous lists of the names of Spaniards held in the camps, barracks, and shelters in Algeria (Ksar Boukhari), France (Adge Herault, Argeles sur Mer, Bergerac-Dordogne, Bram Aude, Camp du Larzac, Camp de la Saret per Grasse, Gurs, Le Barcarès, Ille-et-Vilaine, Patts de Mollo, Ponyatruc-Calongues, Saint Cyprien, Sandillon-Loiret, Tarn-et-Garonne, Vernet d'Ariege) and Tunisia (Mines du Meheri Zebbeus-Maknassy). These lists recommended inmates for sponsorship because of their antifascist commitment during the Spanish Civil War.[29] Castro and Mari paid numerous passages for refugees to travel to visa-granting countries in Latin America.[30]

Some of the data in the reports from this time can be verified with refugees' accounts of their experiences. Remarkably, Juan García Oliver, an anarchist leader and minister of justice (1936–1937), escaped occupied Paris and resided in Sweden until he obtained a visa to Mexico thanks to the SHC.[31] The confederation also helped anarchist Diego Abad de Santillán and a companion, and anarchist José Prego Vieiro, to escape France to Latin America.[32] Additionally, some data was published in *Frente Popular* and *España Libre* by constituent organizations. For example, Grupo Vasco published its refugee aid balances from July 1937 to December 1942. The Basque Group gave the SHC a total of $12,434.50 and directly spent $212.82 on refugee aid.[33] The periodical section "Cuentas claras" (Transparent accounting) shared with readers the costs involved in refugee aid efforts such as "Police permits, suit rental, telegram," which might have been derived from the organization of fundraisers or the legal representation of refugees.

4. The Struggle against Deportations

Also, individuals and affiliated and allied organizations published in *España Libre* their donations or funds raised to help refugees abroad. For example, in the 1940s, funds were sent to support refugees in the Dominican Republic, while in the 1950s, the SHC worked in close cooperation with the Spanish Refugee Aid (SRA): both organizations shared their membership lists, and the executive committee members attended the other organization's meetings. Nancy Macdonald, who was the leading figure of the SRA since its founding in 1953 until her retirement in 1983, raised over $5 million and aided 5,500 cases.[34]

On November 3, 1960, Macdonald wrote a letter of support and congratulations to the SHC "[for] keeping both native and Spanish-born Americans informed about what is happening from week to week in Spain under the Franco dictatorship, and for the vital necessity of restoring democracy in that unhappy country." She continued:

> Meanwhile Spanish Refugee Aid will continue, to the limits of its abilities and facilities, to help as many as possible of the 120,000 Spanish refugees now in Southern France. They lost their homes when Franco seized power ... but look hopefully toward the time when the Franco regime will fall, and the Spanish people can be free again. When that happy day comes, I am sure that large credit will be due to the Confederated Spanish Societies for all that they have done to make the long-time dream of a New Spain come true.[35]

There were numerous ways that the SRA and the SHC collaborated. For example, Macdonald had SRA lawyers, including Ernest Fleischman and several others, gather information for the SHC about the status of Spanish refugee deportation cases inside the United States; at the same time, the SHC offered its help to the SRA.[36] The SRA had established a system of "adoptions" by which a North American donor would send regular stipends to a refugee in France. Macdonald requested that the SHC verify the refugees' identities with the help of the exile community's contacts. *España Libre* endorsed SRA's petitions by asking the broader Spanish Civil War exile community about specific cases, in this way avoiding the risk that nonrefugees could abuse SRA's aid.[37] The SHC also raised funds for the SRA to send to Spanish refugees in France.[38] In 1961 the Women's Committee, formed for the purpose of raising funds for refugee children, sent $1,000 to the SRA.[39] *España Libre* invited readers to send monetary contributions as well.

The mutual support efforts between these two organizations is illustrated in the SRA's assistance to María Isabel Aldecoa, the cousin of SHC member and editor of *España Libre* Carmen Aldecoa. Franco's forces had executed Maria Isabel Aldecoa's father, Francisco Aldecoa González, and sentenced her sister to prison where she died. María Isabel was in exile in France and sponsorship for her was provided by a donor in Pennsylvania—a woman identified in the records only as Ms. Guerrero. In this relief effort, the SRA worked with another organization, Solidaridad Internacional Antifascista (SIA). Volunteers for the SIA, Margaret Hawkins and Suzanne Chatelet, visited María Isabel in France. Ms. Guerrero and SIA's support for Aldecoa included funds for living and medical expenses; this support would continue over the course of two decades until Aldecoa's death in 1985. SIA's reports describe the hard conditions of exile in France. In one occasion, the volunteer found Aldecoa's apartment's floor covered with newspapers, possibly to insulate against the cold. In another occasion, the volunteer realized María Isabel needed a nightshirt.[40] SIA's volunteers reported basic needs, often medicines, eyeglasses, and warm clothes. Their visits dignified the last years of refugees like M. I. Aldecoa. In 1985, the SIA wrote to Ms. Guerrero to inform her that M. I. Aldecoa had died and thanked her for twenty years of quarterly contributions of $150 that helped the Spanish refugee. In the same letter, SIA encouraged her to continue supporting Spanish refugees in France and mentioned a widower who needed help.[41] For the SRA aid given to refugees in France, Macdonald was appointed a distinguished member of the SHC in April 1954. In 1956, to honor Macdonald's work with the SRA and her support to refugees in France, she received the Medal of Dama de la Orden de la Liberación de España (Dame of the Liberation Order of Spain) conferred by Republican president-in-exile Diego Martínez Barrio. In 1982, King Juan Carlos I bestowed on Macdonald the honorific recognition of El Lazo de Isabel la Católica (Ribbon of Isabel the Catholic).[42] In 1987, Macdonald published her book *Homage to the Spanish Exiles: Voices from the Spanish Civil War* based on taped interviews and thus disseminating the voice of the victims of fascism.[43]

During these years, Carmen Aldecoa and Nancy Macdonald forged a lifelong friendship. To help Macdonald with her work in France, Aldecoa connected Macdonald and the SRA with the socialist union leader Pascual Tomás Taengua and the anarcho-syndicalist Roque Santamaría Cortiguera, both exiled in France. Before coming to the United States, Carmen Aldecoa had been the director of the Iberia orphanage in Lyon, France, for Spanish refugee children. Aldecoa published several articles in *España Libre* upon arriving in the United States to promote funding for these refugee children. At the fifth SHC National Congress, held in New York in 1941, Aldecoa demanded that money be spent on humanitarian causes, such as refugee children, rather than on political propaganda.[44] The SHC responded positively to her petition, and raised funds for refugee children in France.

4. The Struggle against Deportations

Avoiding Deportations from the United States: Relocations of Refugees

The SHC provided legal support to prevent deportations back to Spain, and they paid for passages for people to travel to visa-granting countries. Refugees often escaped Spain as stowaways in ships or enrolled as sailors and would desert on arrival in port. The SHC would then try to support these refugees. For example, in January 1964, González Malo wrote an internal report to other SHC members to support the legal case of Emilio Martínez Augusto, a sailor who deserted from a Spanish ship upon his arrival in New York.[45] In addition to these kinds of internal reports—which were commonly produced among the SHC—fundraising ads in *España Libre* also alerted the public about the needs of newly arrived Spaniards in the United States. In October 1943, Juan Reyes Ramos, a Spanish refugee, was detained on Ellis Island. González Malo contacted Reyes Ramos, and learned more about his case from a fundraiser for his benefit. Fundraisers for refugees such as Reyes Ramos were common among the exile communities and encouraged donations for refugees stuck in detention. *España Libre* published the SHC's estimates of legal defense and traveling costs of such Spanish refugees.[46]

España Libre prominently published information on the refugees relocated to Latin American countries. For example, in 1945, a front-page notice celebrated the relocation of refugees to Venezuela (José García Lariño and family, Carlos Carmelo Palacin Cruz and family, Emilio Saiz Abascal, Manuel Mendoza Requena, and Pedro Embid Herraiz), and Colombia (Pedro Durán Vernet).[47] The periodical published the costs related to relocation in the above-mentioned section "Cuentas claras." For instance, on January 31, 1947, refugees detained in Ellis Island were being relocated to Mexico and Venezuela, and *España Libre* published the costs for this relocation, which included clothes, food, and legal services, for a total of $758.24.[48] On March 28, 1947, *España Libre* continued reporting on these cases; this time the SHC spent $2,616.78 to pay passage for some refugees to Mexico and Venezuela, as well as clothes and food for refugees detained in the United States.[49] These regular notices were published in each issue of the periodical in the 1940s and 1950s.[50]

In general, the effort to prevent deportations was a collaboration that involved several organizations and institutions. In August 1947, there was a notice in *España Libre* of relocating Federico Fabas García, Ramón Díaz Pestaña, and José Asensi Selles, Spanish refugees who had been detained in Ellis Island. The International Rescue and Relief Committee (IRC), founded at the request of

Albert Einstein, paid for their passages to Latin American countries. On September 12, 1947, the published announcement in *España Libre* noted that the cost of the passages have been shared among the IRC, the affiliated organization Centre Català, and friends of the SHC.[51] Throughout the existence of *España Libre*, other announcements were published about collaborations with the IRC.[52] The Workers Defense League and the American Civil Liberties Union also assisted the SHC by providing legal services to refugees.

Lawyers worked against the clock because Spanish embassies and consulates in the United States aggressively sought information about these fleeing antifascist émigrés and reported them to immigration authorities for deportation. Franco's agents in the United States also notified immigration authorities about earlier migrants, who were at the time members of the SHC, for their radical political leanings or irregular visa statuses. In one of these notifications, the Spanish Consulate in New York reported Rafael Guerra Cuoto from La Coruña, Spain, to the Immigration Services after he was seen giving books and periodicals to sailors in New York to be clandestinely smuggled into Spain. Guerra Cuoto asked the SHC to help him obtain a Mexican visa to avoid deportation to Spain. The Masonic Lodge of New York, Logia Masónica, supported the veracity of Guerra Cuoto's account. A practice of double local and transnational checks ensured the validity of accounts for help addressed to the SHC. González Malo contacted Martínez Feduchy, the Second Republic consul in Mexico, for a visa for the Spaniard.[53] To avoid being apprehended by Immigration Services, some stowaways jumped into the ocean and swam to American shores. That was the case for José Bernardo Andreu, José Eduardo Fernando, and Félix Rincón Peñalba (who even had an artificial limb), who were apprehended nonetheless in the Delaware River.[54]

Although unsuccessful at causing antifascists to back down, Francoist coercive measures, which extended to reprisals against members' friends and relatives in Spain, were meant to deter *España Libre*'s solidarity and to scare the antifascists. Refugees were also aware of the Francoist representation of them as "dangerous radicals," something which, although it didn't frighten the antifascists, didn't necessarily help their cause in the United States at this time. Nonetheless, some deportation cases were widely covered in the periodical and crossed into other Spanish-language newspapers such as *La Prensa* (New York). In July 1951, *La Prensa* covered a story that *España Libre* had already published on the adventures of some Spaniards who had arrived in the United States as sailors, but who, after deserting their ships, were now en route to Mexico, a country that had granted visas to those deserting antifascist sailors. The photograph caption read: "Mexico Grants Asylum." In the photograph, taken in San Isidro, California, five deserters from the Spanish Navy are seen at the moment they crossed the border into Mexico, which has granted them political asylum: Manuel Fernández Rodríguez, Agustín Croza Cabrera, Ginés Jiménez Nortez, Enrique Medina Fernández, and Víctor Rodríguez.[55]

Ernest Fleischman and Legal Help for Refugees

Many lawyers played critical roles in the legal aid efforts for refugees, and *España Libre* often thanked these lawyers for their work in its pages. For example, upon the death of John González Moscoso, a lawyer who provided pro bono work in numerous cases involving the threatened deportation of antifascist Spaniards, *España Libre* published a heartfelt obituary where they praised him for his support of refugees.[56]

Ernest Fleischman also worked with the SHC for several decades to provide legal help for the antifascist cause. Fleischman was a partner in a large, progressive Park Avenue firm that allowed him to keep a personal portfolio of refugees, union organizers, civil rights activists, and other "little" clients who could not afford his defense.[57] *España Libre* staff member José Nieto Ruiz (1937–) was one such beneficiary. In 1959, Nieto Ruiz was detained and tortured in Barcelona for distributing CNT flyers. Anarchist networks helped him cross the Pyrenees. Spanish, Canadian, and Cuban anarchists facilitated his safe arrival in New York.[58] Once in the United States, however, he was ordered deported because he did not have a visa to be in the country. Thanks to *España Libre's* campaign, José Nieto Ruiz's trial and deportation case reached the mainstream press and brought attention to the humanitarian mission of the SHC.[59] *España Libre's* cartoonist Sergio Aragonés dedicated one of his editorial strips to highlighting the discrepancy in welcoming Cubans and not Spaniards to the United States—despite the fact that dissidents from both countries advocated for democracy. Several countries offered Nieto Ruiz political asylum, including Sweden, Denmark, Switzerland, Mexico, and France. Fleischman, who took up the case as he had taken so many others for the SHC, would ultimately succeed in obtaining a visa for Nieto Ruiz, even inviting Nieto Ruiz to live with him until his case was settled.[60] Nieto Ruiz was lucky—it was uncommon for the U.S. government to issue such visas. More often, Spanish refugees were forced to settle in whichever Latin American countries accepted them.

In a radio address published in *España Libre* on May 2, 1941, Jesse L. Rosenberg, one of the lawyers who voluntarily helped the SHC with deportation cases, congratulated the organization for "performing a unique and splendid task on behalf of the refugees" but asked fellow Americans to take responsibility in aiding Spaniards to escape fascist rule.[61] According to Rosenberg, the SHC saved countless lives by "transshipping refugees to friendly South American countries... with the understanding cooperation of our Department of Justice and formerly our Department of Labor."[62] Rosenberg continued: "It has been my greatest pride and satisfaction to be able to utilize my education, training and experience to alleviate the suffering of those whose lives and fortunes have been ruined.... I feel that we Americans must atone in some way for our failure to have performed our obvious duty."[63] Fleischman is one of the Americans who took up Rosenberg's call for this kind of justice work, and he spent decades fighting for the safety and rights of Spanish refugees in the United States.

When Fleischman's wife, Josephine Teresa Bridge Cowan Fleischman, passed away in 1968, Fleischman sent a thank-you card to *España Libre* for the numerous expressions of sympathy he had received and he expressed his own shared commitment to social justice. The card read: "My wife was in every sense a comrade, both in her public attitude and actions and with respect to our children, friends, and myself. I am enclosing a gift in her name.... With every wish for the success of the quest of the Spanish people for independence, socialism, and freedom."[64] For his contributions, the Government of the Second Spanish Republic in exile granted Fleischman the title of Caballero de la Orden de la Liberación de España (Knight of the Liberation Order of Spain) in November 1966.

Exceptional Activism of the SHC's Executive Members

The individuals who participated in the SHC's work and administration were dedicated individuals who left behind a record of heroic activism and support for refugees. This work included a commitment to obtaining visas to welcoming host countries for Spanish exiles, fundraising, promoting awareness of refugees, and otherwise supporting both psychologically and materially exiles who were at legal and physical risk.

Examples of this kind of dedicated and successful activism by members of the SHC abound. In 1950s, for example, Manuel Dorado, an executive member and the SHC's general secretary, played a critical role in helping refugees obtain visas to Mexico. Dorado often corresponded with Salvador Etcheverria and Antonio González Cárdenas at the Government of the Second Spanish Republic in exile consulate in Mexico to obtain visas for refugees. Among those for whom Dorado obtained a visa was the anarchist illustrator, painter, and cartoonist Shum (Alfons Vila i Franquesa). Shum had lived undocumented in the United States for many years and by 1952 was at risk of deportation.[65] With his friend and *España Libre*'s cartoonist Bartolí Guiu, Shum was part of the Grup del Sis (Group of the six), artists who funded the Sindicat pels Dibuixants Professionals (Union for Professional Cartoon Artists) in Barcelona. He published in both anarchist and mainstream newspapers.[66] In New York and later in Mexico, Shum worked as an illustrator and his exhibitions were reviewed in the *New York Times*. The work of Manuel Dorado in assisting Shum's transit to Mexico is exemplary of the broader activism undertaken by numerous SHC members.

Another individual who played a significant role in the SHC's work with refuges was Maria Cordellat, a Cuban who sympathized with the Second Republic, and who served as the SHC's secretary for several years. Cordellat was an active member: she played the piano in the fundraisers and antifascist plays. Her husband, the Valencian baritone Vicente Cordellat, also performed for fundraisers.[67] The Cordellats had been performing for variety shows since the 1920s in the United States. Because of her extraordinary work for the SHC, Aurelio Pego would once describe Cordellat as "the heroine of the organization." She aided refugees in several ways: informed lawyers and assisted with the paperwork, found ways for the ships' insurance to pay for the fares of the transship of arriving stowaways, sought funds with other organizations to aid refugees, corresponded with North American government officials, and visited detainees. Cordellat also provided much-needed answers to relatives seeking information about their family members. For example, Cordellat located Juan Múgica Arbelca after his family contacted the SHC in 1944. He was detained in the Ellis Island Immigrant Station after he had arrived in the SS *Queen Mary*. The SHC defrayed his food costs at Ellis Island.[68] Despite their limited means, members often helped with donations. In one instance, on February 1951, Deogracias Rojo, a cook, paid with his savings the $600 bond to release Manuel Giráldez, who was being detained at Ellis Island.[69]

Cordellat utilized her broader refugee support networks with other aid organizations, such as the International Relief and Rescue Committee (IRRC). In April 1948, she sought funds for the cases of Anastasio López Becerra and Ricardo G. Socas, two exiles who were being held in detention upon their arrival in the United States. Thanks to her efforts, the detained pair was permitted to transship and travel to Latin American countries instead of being deported to Spain, where they would have been sentenced or executed.[70] She contacted immigration detention centers and the Department of Justice to inquire about Spanish refugees. She informed American officials that the SHC would obtain Venezuelan and Mexican resident visas for refugees and that her organization would pay for the passages. To provide these refugees with visas, Cordellat worked with the Government of the Second Spanish Republic in exile consuls in Venezuela and Mexico.[71] The development of this broader network allowed her to be in a position to both hear about and help refugees. For example, in January 1948, she received notices about several stowaways being detained at different detention centers.[72] The next month, she was able to locate anarchist Juan López Moyano, who was being detained at Montgomery, Alabama. In March, she continued her efforts. Cordellat inquired about the legal status of Jesús Bartolomé Álamo, another detainee. Having been sentenced for four years in Spain for distributing left-wing republican flyers, Bartolomé Álamo had escaped to New York in a merchant ship but when told he was going to be detained at arrival he jumped into the Atlantic Ocean and swam to Staten Island.[73] Eventually Cordellat succeeded in getting him a Venezuelan visa and the SHC paid his fare.

Thanks to these types of regular interventions, Cordellat was contacted about other Spaniards in need. For instance, in March 1948, the Federal Correctional Institution in Danbury, Connecticut, wrote a letter to ask Cordellat to aid Mr. Máximo Echevarría Imaz "as well as two other individuals in similar circumstances who needed [your] assistance."[74] In another instance where refugees were being held in a similar facility, Cordellat processed reports about three stowaways, Miguel Martínez Mislata, José Luis Degoniz Valle, and Alfonso Sánchez Frade, who were being detained at the Federal Reformatory in Petersburg, Virginia, in August 1948. Evidence suggests that Cordellat's efforts in these kinds of cases were successful.[75] In February 1949, for example, after learning about the case of Josefa Tallón, a refugee being detained at Ellis Island, Cordellat was able to provide the necessary administrative support to obtain a visa for her to Venezuela.[76]

Cordellat was a perseverant woman committed to saving lives even when her personal safety was at risk. An exchange of letters with a man impersonating a Spanish refugee proved that she was not easily intimidated. She contacted Latin American consuls to make sure he did not get a visa using a fraudulent letter of recommendation from the SHC, and advised Immigration Services to deport him despite the menacing letter she received from the individual, who told her: "you treat me with little politeness.... At my release I will come immediately to New York as I have many matters to discuss with you."[77] Aurelio Pego's chronicle published in *España Libre* in November 1948 was dedicated to Cordellat and praised her extraordinary humanitarian work:

> Although the Spanish refugees in France figure that SHC works automatically, I am sorry to say that it is not true.... SHC is a poor organization—because all poor members are poor and, in the colony, there is a lot of miserable Spaniards

that do not contribute to its sustainability with even a penny.... The heroine of the organization, Maria Cordellat, carries, tirelessly, resigned, suffering, the bureaucratic weight of the organization.... She goes to Ellis Island, manages the cases... and gets [refugees] sent to a country of our America.... she brings them clothes and shoes and words that are worth more than all the money in the world.[78]

Various letters testify to the horrifying consequences of exile for some refugees. In January 1949, the Immigration and Naturalization Service of Portland, Oregon, contacted Cordellat because Antonio Alonso Falero had attempted to commit suicide. He was hospitalized and was to be deported back to Spain. The immigration officers even questioned his sanity. Cordellat explained to the official that Falero was known in the SHC because he used to receive his mail at its headquarters. He was illiterate, and members would read letters to him from his family. Cordellat believed he was anxious because of his exile and his family's poverty. She asked for an extended stay while she arranged a visa for him and assured the officer that she would request his former employer to send a written guarantee that Falero was an honest and hard-working man.[79]

Not surprisingly, González Malo worked with Cordellat and was one of the most active members in seeking support for Spanish Civil War exiles. González Malo's networking and correspondence was crucial in numerous cases throughout his tenure with the SHC. Already well known in the exile circles for his union and militia past, he would put this past to work in his efforts to help others. For example, González Malo wrote to Jesús Revaque Garea, director of Colegio de Madrid in México, asking for assistance in obtaining a visa for Cayetano Diego, who was being detained in California.[80] González Malo also solicited help from Vázquez Gayoso, the Government of the Second Spanish Republic in exile consul in Caracas, Venezuela. González Malo shared that Diego was a militia captain in Santander during the Spanish Civil War, and "thanks to his loyalty I can be here writing because he saved me from an attack that was being prepared against me; He does not remind me of this, but I will not forget it."[81] Carmen Aldecoa was in correspondence with Diego too, and she eventually was able to notify him that the lawyer Enrique R. Ramos had acquired a Venezuelan visa for him.

The SHC received numerous petitions for help from refugees because of the transnational reach of *España Libre* and its clandestine infiltration in Spain. In February 1961, González Malo asked for advice on some of these cases from politician Indalecio Prieto, a socialist exiled in México. Spanish civil servants who grew disillusioned with the regime had contacted the SHC for help to leave Spain, and González Malo wanted to know how to check the veracity of their accounts.⁸² Simultaneously, González Malo consulted Martínez Feduchy about a letter he received from Faustino Reija Vieto. In his letter, the ex-Falangist had presented himself as a dissident willing to desert the regime but in need of protection and a Mexican visa.⁸³ In response to many of these kinds of petitions, the SHC would diligently seek ways to help. But because of the risks of imposters or individuals seeking to take advantage of the SHC, it was also forced to be wary and verify the stories as much as possible.

One of González Malo's other key contributions to the organization's work was his commitment to keeping the SHC an independent organization. While the close collaboration between the SHC and the government-in-exile was very successful in helping refugees, the confederation was determined to maintain its own independence. González Malo was at the forefront of this effort. In a letter from November 28, 1969, to Martínez Feduchy, González Malo along with other members acerbically responded to the consul's insistence on dealing directly with Asensio Torrado, at the time the government-in-exile delegate in the United States. The letter reminded the consul that Asensio Torrado was not part of the executive committee and specified that the collaboration between the government and the SHC benefited both institutions, not just the SHC. The letter, signed by general secretary Alberto Uriarte, treasurer John Carnero, and vice-secretary J. González Malo, sarcastically ended with: "Grateful for your courteous condescendence, we send you our regards."⁸⁴

Nonetheless, when Asensio Torrado died, the SHC proposed Martínez Feduchy as the new North American representative for the government-in-exile.⁸⁵ Upon the naming of Martínez Feduchy as the Republican government's representative in the United States, *España Libre* congratulated him and his work for the government-in-exile. However, the published announcement also reminded readers of their primary mission: to resurrect the sovereignty of the Spanish people. As *España Libre*'s announcement put it,

> The Government of the Republic presided over by Claudio Sánchez Albornoz has appointed Martínez Feduchy as chief of the unofficial diplomatic mission to the United States.... The SHC wishes to state that ... to find a pacific solution to the Spanish problem, the restoration of the Republic is not necessary as a matter of principle; rather, the SHC looks forward to the day when the Spanish people can freely and democratically express their political will.⁸⁶

Besides his continuous collaboration with the government-in-exile, González Malo also contacted labor networks to coordinate efforts in the support of refugees.⁸⁷ Unions, labor newspapers, and institutions helped the SHC by sharing their membership rosters.⁸⁸ The ACLU, the American Socialist Party,

4. The Struggle against Deportations

and SRA provided a total of 10,000 new addresses. Also, Frances Grant shared 200 addresses of members of the International League for Human Rights.[89] The SHC launched several fundraising campaigns and reached all these potential contributors by mail. Anarcho-syndicalists abroad also aided with pro-refugee efforts. From Montreal, Canada, Francisco Rebordosa, a member of the SIA, worked with González Malo in preventing the deportation of anarchist Bernabé García Polanco in January 1964.[90] Anarchists in Cuba and Miami also helped staff writer Nieto Ruiz get to New York from Canada.

España Libre was an agent of change for refugee relief. Fundraisers, donations, aid sent abroad, evacuation of refugees in France, and deportation cases were covered in every single issue of the periodical. The networks of solidarity established by the SHC continued to aid Spanish refugees because of its grassroots, goal-based, inclusive activism, which achieved solidarity against fascism. As records show, numerous members and activists helped the SHC in its efforts on behalf of Spanish refugees. Aldecoa and Macdonald coordinated efforts and information to better serve exiles in France. Lawyers Ernest Fleischman, John Gonzalez Moscoso, Enrique R. Ramos, and Jesse L. Rosenberg, as well as Nancy Macdonald, working with Carmen Aldecoa, Maria Cordellat, and Jesús González Malo, efficiently led the SHC's efforts to help to refugees. Members went to the Port of New York to gather information on the needs of arriving refugees before they were detained by Immigration Services. Cordellat contacted immigration facilities and penitentiaries to find further details about detained Spaniards. González Malo wrote to allies in the labor and Spanish Civil War networks to solicit visas for Latin American countries. Beyond exercising solidarity, helping refugees was the prime antifascist activity, since it recognized a refugee's personal contestation of fascism.

Whereas Spanish anarchism is generally depicted as defeated after the Spanish Civil War, the SHC's story shows workers' strength, organization, and promise. *España Libre* informed and reminded its readers about refugees' needs so that members never ceased the help to antifascists. The last *España Libre* issue, published in 1977, announced that the SHC had raised a total of two million dollars over the years, which had sustained not only refugees but also political prisoners and underground resistance leaders.[91] Eventually, even the American government acknowledged the SHC's immigration activism on behalf of refugees. President Lyndon Johnson invited its leaders to the signing of the Immigration and Nationality Act of 1965.[92] The recovery of *España Libre*'s careful documentation of names and locations is relevant today because numerous Spaniards still cannot trace their family history. The following chapter, focused on street protest, will further explore efforts channeled to help the clandestine opposition in Spain.

5

Solidarity for Political Prisoners

España Libre extensively covered the SHC's demonstrations, rallies, and fundraisers that denounced political persecution perpetrated by Franco's regime. The periodical also published lists of political prisoners who were given life sentences or executed, followed by commentary. As late as 1974, *España Libre* still published news about political executions on its front page. That year, the journal exposed the brutal strangulation of Catalan anarchist Salvador Puig Antich with a torture device known as a "garrote vil."[1] As Janet Pérez describes, "Depending upon the circumstances (and especially whether they had friends or relatives on the winning side), such persons were either summarily executed or jailed as political prisoners. Some were tried and later executed, others sentenced to death but eventually pardoned, and others released after serving sentences of varying lengths."[2] One of the first laws promulgated under Franco, the February 9, 1939, "Ley de Responsabilidades Políticas" (Law of Political Responsibilities), dictated that political parties and cooperatives not sanctioned by the state were outlawed, and their members were to lose all their rights and possessions, which were taken by the state. Those who had helped pro-Republic efforts in Spain or abroad were similarly outlawed and dispossessed.[3] During the Franco years, *España Libre* published news about collaborations with the undercover resistance members, being careful to shield identities, and donations for prisoners, which were mainly channeled to their dispossessed families.

Over the course of its history, the SHC and its supporters held hundreds of rallies, pickets, and demonstrations across the United States and cultural fundraisers to aid Spanish victims of fascism.[4] Antifascist plays were performed alongside many other artistic and cultural performances; artists danced and sang, speeches were delivered, dinners were served, dance orchestras played, lotteries were held, and funds subsequently collected. Not only amateurs but some professional actors performed in these theatrical endeavors. *España Libre* covered the extraordinary activism for political prisoners in each of its issues. Protest was extended to other media too. Members published letters of protest in American mainstream papers and rented time on several radio stations. The SHC's numerous forms of protest in public spaces garnered international attention to the incarcerations and executions of dissenters in Spain.

Protest in the Street

In one of its first protest actions, the SHC took to U.S. streets with demonstrations to raise awareness of civil rights infringements in Franco's Spain.[5] During the Spanish Civil War, the SHC demonstrated in front of the British Consulate in New York for months demanding that the British help loyalist Spain. Demonstrations did not diminish after the war during Franco's rule. The SHC regularly picketed in front of the Spanish Consulate and the Spanish tourism office in New York.[6] Members of the SIA and the American Socialist Party often joined these demonstrations. Among the numerous protests, one that stands out is the demonstration against the announced visit of Franco's minister of information and tourism, Manuel Fraga Iribarne, to New York in 1964. Fraga was attending several events in Washington, D.C., and New York to commemorate October 12, el Día de la Raza. Members of the Socialist Party, Social Democrat Federation, Catholic Workers, Libertarian League, Iglesia Evangélica Española, and Sociedades Hispanas Confederadas protested in front of the New York Hilton Hotel. Leaflets, claiming that Fraga Iribarne was the Spanish Joseph Goebbels, were distributed. Another significant rally occurred in 1976 when King Juan Carlos I visited the United States after Franco died. The SHC protested in front of the Waldorf while a reception for the king was held inside. The congregated shouted: "Amnistía-Libertad" (Amnesty-Freedom).[7]

As part of these demonstrations, members undertook a boycott of consumer goods from Franco's Spain—like the Jewish American boycott of German products in the early 1930s. In 1937, each issue of the *Frente Popular* had big printed banners that proclaimed: "Boycott to fascist products!"[8] These demonstrations and boycotts continued throughout the late 1930s and into the 1940s. In December 1939, an article signed by the Agrupación de Mujeres Antifascistas (Antifascist Women's Association, AMA), and published in *España Libre*, asked readers to boycott Spanish commercial products sold in the

United States.[9] Similarly, Florida-born Violeta Miqueli González, who also performed as an amateur actress for the fundraisers at this time, published an article on March 15, 1940, that addressed "Spanish, Czechoslovakian, Polish, and Finnish mothers, all mothers who have suffered the horror of seeing their children torn apart by the bullets of Hitler, Mussolini, Franco and Stalin."[10] She asked women to inform shopkeepers about the need to boycott products from Franco's Spain. Miqueli González's emotional call for action also addressed the SHC's goal of involving workers in the antifascist fight: "Women can do a lot of good when we ignore the conventions of bourgeois society and accept the responsibility of our destiny as the vanguard of the people."[11] Because of her advocacy, *España Libre* published several notices encouraging the boycott of any product from Spain in the 1940s.[12]

Consequently, the SHC demonstrated in front of shops that sold products from fascist Spain. Shops that sold fascist products (Spanish, Italian, German, Japanese, or Portuguese) were often picketed during the Spanish Civil War, among them Casa Moneo and Casa Victori in New York. To show that members

Figure 4. Demonstrations in front of the Spanish Consulate on Madison Avenue, New York, date unknown. Members of the SHC, the American Socialist Party, and the Evangelical Church protested against the forthcoming visit of President Dwight D. Eisenhower to Generalissimo Francisco Franco. González Malo's sign reads, "España Sí; Franco No." Another demonstrator holds a sign that reads "No synagogue can bear any sign in Spain." Courtesy of José Nieto Ruiz and Brandeis Special Collections.

5. Solidarity for Political Prisoners

Figure 5. In the photo, González Malo holds a sign reading "We are against dictatorships anywhere." Next to González Malo, Dorothy Day holds a sign that says, "The Catholic Worker supports this picketing." Behind González Malo, Nieto Ruiz holds the sign "Franco—No, Khrushchev—No, Liberty—Yes." Alberto Uriarte stands behind Dorothy Day. Courtesy of José Nieto Ruiz and Brandeis Special Collections.

were not afraid of intimidation, *Frente Popular* printed the names of about 150 picketers. Nonetheless, the Judge Philip McCook prohibited the continuous demonstrations in front of the shops.[13] Theaters who supported Francoist artists were affected by the picketers as well. More than three thousand banners were made to demonstrate in front of the Fleisher Auditorium in Philadelphia and the Lewisohn Stadium in New York on the occasion of concerts of composer and pianist José Iturbi.

Fundraisers

Soon after its foundation, the SHC held cultural fundraisers on the streets as well. Funds were raised by and from workers. For this reason, fundraisers were held outside of working hours, after 8 p.m. on Saturdays. As one of *España Libre*'s reviews reminded readers, most attendees worked on Saturday mornings.[14] In other words, the show times, the themes, the venues—kept both accessible and affordable—were all decided while considering the needs and interests of

Figure 6. In the demonstrations on Madison Avenue, González Malo is holding the sign, "Lea *España Libre*" (Read *España Libre*). Pacifist and freedom rider James Peck, in front of him, holds a sign that says, "Give Spanish Sailors Perez & Prieto Political Asylum." A woman in the line behind González Malo holds a sign that says, "10 anti-Franco women have served 160 years in prison." Courtesy of José Nieto Ruiz and Brandeis Special Collections.

the working-class audience. Similarly, the formal characteristics of the plays that were performed at the events, with few actors and few scenes, were adapted to the limited and contingent resources of the SHC (including rehearsal time)—something that showcased the creativity of its members. Although organized by and addressed to workers, these events were inclusive and were open to anyone interested in antifascist themes. The creative process belonged to the people who organized the conferences, lectures, political rallies, demonstrations, and pickets, along with the more festive events, and large numbers of members and artists participated: Juan Eugenio Domingo Mingorance painted sets, Adolfo Jiménez Colón composed music, Maria Cordellat played the piano, and Esteban Roig's band the Happy Boys played music.[15] In one dramatic instance, in March 1940, a Mingorance mural, entitled *Éxodo*, was raffled off at Ateneo Hispano.[16]

Women were active in all fundraising efforts. To control costs, they cooked meals, sold tickets, prepared decorations, sewed costumes, and helped in the overall organization of the fundraisers. Yuyita Concheiro danced Spanish

5. Solidarity for Political Prisoners

Figure 7. SHC demonstrating in front of the Spanish Consulate on Madison Avenue. A member holds a sign with Sergio Aragonés drawing titled "July 18, 1939," that depicts a rebel bayoneting the Second Spanish Republic, depicted as a common man wearing a liberty cap. Courtesy of José Nieto Ruiz and Brandeis Special Collections.

regional dances as did Carmen López, who also sang. Elena and María Trujillo, both natives from Malaga, Spain (and possibly sisters), danced flamenco and performed as amateur actresses in many plays. Fay Torrens and Dorita Montero danced Spanish regional dances and acted in theatrical performances. These names represent only a few of the many volunteers who danced, sang, and acted in numerous cultural events to raise funds. Some people's assiduous work remained anonymous. Only a few names are revealed in the pages of *España Libre*, such as the October 21, 1953, obituary for Dolores Bouveta, which noted that: "she did not miss any of the events and cooperated daily in all the festivals organized by the affiliated Galicia Committee and by the Confederadas at large."[17] An anonymous article on August 28, 1942, praised "women, [who] spent interminable hours voluntarily cooking for [fundraisers] ... having done their duty—which was their only satisfaction."[18]

These activities were extremely successful, attracting thousands of participants and raising thousands of dollars for refugees and political prisoners.

España Libre's coverage of these benefits was enthusiastic. Although there were events celebrated in all affiliated associations scattered around the country, fundraising in New York, Pennsylvania, and Virginia were particularly successful. In the decade of the 1940s, the SHC held an average of thirty fundraisers per year; at its height, in 1940 and 1941, there were eighty-four and eighty-two events respectively.[19] Most of these fundraisers, which included theater performances, vaudeville shows, dinners, and dances, were conducted at the social halls of constituent organizations. These events often attracted several hundred people and collected, on average, less than a thousand dollars per event. However, April 14, the anniversary of the Second Republic, and July 19, the date that commemorated the people's defense of the Republic from the military revolt, were solemn dates and the largest theaters and halls were rented, such as Madison Square Garden or Manhattan Hall in New York.[20] On some of these occasions, as many as six thousand people attended, and up to twenty thousand dollars was collected.[21] Theatrical shows were accompanied by political and cultural speeches and other fundraising activities. Prominent Spanish politicians and intellectuals were invited to take part in these events and supported them with speeches and performances.[22]

The already mentioned AMA, founded in October 1939 in the Bronx, is an example of a women-led affiliated organization.[23] The AMA was active from 1939 to 1944.[24] Its first antifascist action was to collect food and toiletries for Spanish refugees held on Ellis Island while en route to Mexico.[25] In the next five years, AMA organized eleven fundraisers, two theatrical performances, two popular dances, and twelve fundraising dinners. In March 1940, AMA sent 11,500 French francs to disabled Spaniards exiled in Caussade, France.[26] The obituary of Flora Restoy, an AMA leader, claimed that the distinction that Restoy deserved should be extended to "other exemplary women, whose actions constitute one of the worthiest chapters of our honorable organic trajectory. The memory of one evokes that of all; our gratitude and esteem are unlimited. Distinguished compañeras: know that the memory of Flora increases our affection for all of you."[27] Other women's associations throughout the United States were also active, such as the Spanish American Women's Club of Niagara Falls; the Club Femenino of Massillon, Ohio; the Damas Auxiliares of the Spanish-American Citizen's Club, of Bayonne, New Jersey; and the Comité Femenino de Ayuda al Pueblo Español, of East St. Louis, Illinois. They organized on average about three major fundraisers per year in the 1940s.

Picnics and soccer games were also popular ways of fundraising. The Comité Español de Staten Island, for example, organized an annual picnic on Grant City Park in Grant City, on Staten Island. There were regional dance contests (including Spanish jota, Galician muñeira, and Catalan and Cuban rumba), games (such as running with a spoon holding a potato), and performances of bands and bagpipers (Esteban Roig Orquesta or the Gaiteros de Cherry Street Terra a Nosa).[28] In other places in the United States soccer games and other activities kept raising funds, and the organization Leales Españoles in Los Angeles organized a picnic in Verdugo Woodlands Park on August 22, 1943. The announcement in *España Libre* hoped for a day of fundraising, fraternal comradeship, and protest.[29]

From the 1950s to the 1970s the fundraising events progressively diminished in number and in the amount of money collected. On average, the SHC organized between ten and twenty events per year during this time, and its meetings were transformed more into social and cultural occasions rather than fundraisers.[30] *España Libre* proposed psychological and economic reasons for this growing "apathy" and "pessimism."[31] After a decade of almost weekly political speeches and antifascist-themed fundraisers, the exiled community, mainly the second generation, had lost interest in denouncing Franco's fascist Spain. Most importantly, members were exhausted and disheartened after Franco's Spain joined the United Nations in 1955.[32] The remaining committed members continued humanitarian and political efforts, such as supporting the undercover resistance in Spain, publishing *España Libre*, and condemning Spanish fascism until democracy was restored to Spain in 1977.

Protest on Air: "La Voz de Sociedades Hispanas Confederadas"

Radio programming, as a protest action, started with the precursor of *España Libre, Frente Popular*. As with any other project of the SHC, it was a success because of the collective force of the confederation. From March 1938 to 1943, the SHC broadcast thirty minutes of radio programming every day.[33] José Castilla Morales was director and presenter of the daily radio program, called "La voz de Sociedades Hispanas Confederadas." It was broadcast over several radio stations: WBBC (Brooklyn Broadcasting Corporation), WARD, WEVD (New York, NY, Debs Memorial Radio Fund), WLTH, and WVFV. In his book *Pioneros puertorriqueños en Nueva York 1917–1947* (2003), Joaquín Colón, a Puerto Rican activist and writer, mentions that Boricua Santiago Greví presented "La voz de Sociedades Hispanas Confederadas" in 1938 and 1939.[34] In the 1940s, Ignacio Zugadi Garmendia, Sebastián Palmer Terrassa, Carmen Novo, and Andrés Rodríguez Barbeito were popular presenters on the program.[35] Palmer Terrassa hosted the radio program for several years, acted in fundraising plays, and served as secretary of the affiliated association Grupo Salmerón. In a eulogy to his grandmother published in *España Libre* and most surely broadcast, Palmer Terrassa shared his family trauma, knowing that such longing for distant loved ones was common among exiles. His grandmother, who died in Spain, would tell neighbors that she was able to listen to her grandson's radio program in New York from the local Civil Guard headquarters. In reality, his grandmother, who suffered dementia in her last years, listened to a radio tuned to a local station in the Civil Guard headquarters, but the longing for her grandson made her believe she could distinguish his voice broadcasting from New York.[36]

Like Palmer Terrassa, Galician Andrés Rodríguez Barbeito, a journalist and diplomat connected to the socialist UGT, participated in fundraisers and radio programs. Before his arrival to New York, Rodríguez Barbeito had been the Second Republic's consul to Santos, Brazil, during the Spanish Civil War. There, Rodríguez Barbeito had organized the support for the Second Republic through the publication of the newspaper *Gaceta Hispana* and the radio program "Hora Hispana Brasileira de España Republicana," as well as the organization of fundraisers.[37] In New York, under the pen name Amadios, he condemned pro-Franco propaganda and criticized the silence of influential Spaniards in the United States.[38] Only a few radio scripts have survived, mostly from the Second World War era. At that time, Rodríguez Barbeito broadcast several programs about the war. On May 30, 1942, the program "La voz de las Sociedades Confederadas" announced the creation of a Hispanic committee presided over by businessman Valentín Aguirre that would sell war stamps and bonds to help defeat fascism in Europe.[39] During those years, José Argibay, under the pen name of Cascabeles, read witty letters on air for the delight of the listeners.[40] Throughout the decades, the SHC's radio broadcasts, public protests, and extensive fundraising events and rallies demonstrated not only a long and extraordinary commitment to its cause but also a powerful organizational ability to engage the public through these kinds of outreach activities.

Occupying the Mainstream Press

Addressing letters to the American mainstream media was a way in which members continuously occupied the public sphere in the United States. Several contributors regularly wrote letters contesting supportive views on Franco's Spain. Most notable among these was José María Martínez Novella—a naturopathic doctor who regularly published in anarchist periodicals *El Sembrador de Igualada* and *Estudios* before the Spanish Civil War in Spain, and *El Ateneo* (1938) and *Frente Popular* (1936–1939) in New York—who wrote such letters

5. Solidarity for Political Prisoners

Figure 8. Sociedades Hispanas Confederadas' stamps, sold to members as a fundraising strategy. Courtesy of José Nieto Ruiz.

for at least a couple of decades. One of the SHC's founders, Martínez Novella, also published a regular column in *España Libre* about fascism and medicine. He wrote from Tampa and from Miami, where he practiced nudism and veganism.[41] He was the author of several books on naturalism and syndicalism.[42] *España Libre* would regularly mention or republish Martínez Novella's letters to the American and global press where he countered claims favoring Franco and representations of Spanish loyalists as "dangerous radicals." He usually wrote to the *Havana Post*, the *Miami Herald*, the *Miami Daily News*, the *New York Times*, *Thought* (Fordham University), the *Wall Street Journal*, and *Catholic World*, as well as to the Columbia Broadcasting System, New York, WCBS-TV. Martínez Novella also sent his letters to politicians and public personalities with the same goal of contesting their public defense of Franco.[43] He rebutted publications by people in the clergy and higher education such as the Rev. Joseph F. Code or Professor Lawrence H. Kibbe from Le Moyne College, Syracuse, for example. For his continuing antifascist work, he received a medal from the Second Spanish Republic Government in exile.

Protest on the Page

Just as the SHC was unrelenting in its campaigns in support of refugees, *España Libre*'s coverage of the political persecutions under Franco's rule was equally implacable and fueled the public denunciations of the SHC. The underground anarchist national confederation, CNT, lost many of its most militant members through brutal repression, incarceration, and executions in Franco's Spain. Between 1945 and 1960, the CNT lost 80 percent of its members.[44] Exile culture in France, Mexico, and the United States emphasized solidarity for comrades in Spain. Lists of sentenced and executed dissenters of all political leanings and extensive coverage of specific cases were published, literature and cartoons were dedicated to the victims, and the underground dissidents' reports on civil rights infringements in Franco's Spain were prominently featured in *España Libre*.

España Libre published censored news on civil rights infringements thanks to the work of the undercover resistance in Spain and the periodical staff's collaborative and incisive journalism. This was particularly true in lesser-known cases of torture or execution. For example, in October 1940, a number of editorials denounced the political executions taking place in Spain, such as that of Catalonian president Lluís Companys. The issue's editorial, entitled "Double Monstrosity," shamed "distinguished" Spaniards in the United States for their compromised silence.[45] By pointing fingers at the exile community, *España Libre* equated the murder of the Catalan president with the lack of outraged protest in the public sphere in North America.

The terror against common people was also documented in the periodical. In September 1961, the SHC sent to its print, labor, and exile contacts (as well as the UN and President John F. Kennedy) a release for publication about the torture of eighty Basque citizens in Spain. The confederation also organized a demonstration in front of the Spanish Consulate in New York to that effect. The Workers Defense League, the Young People's Socialist League, the Catholic Worker's staff, and the Libertarian League joined the demonstration.[46] Staff writer Nieto Ruiz investigated and published several articles about the execution of Manuel Moreno Barranco in Spain. Barranco traveled to France in 1963 to present a reading of his poetry. On his return, he was tortured and killed by Franco's agents, who mistakenly thought he was working with the resistance in exile. The SHC sent smuggled photos of Moreno Barranco's corpse to Senator Jacob K. Javits of New York; however, upon being confronted, Spanish diplomats claimed that Moreno Barranco committed suicide in prison.[47] The publication of the Spanish regime's terror contested the indifference of the American mainstream media to victims of fascism in Spain. Ultimately, the SHC's claims were able to reach American politicians.

España Libre dedicated several of its front pages to denouncing Franco's state terror and praising the works of American antifascists. In early March 1952, *España Libre* published the text of a telegram that socialist Norman Thomas sent Francisco Franco asking him to halt the execution of five underground anarcho-syndicalist leaders.[48] Next to it, an editorial from *The Nation* about the execution was partially reprinted. The Workers Defense League demonstrated in front of the Spanish Consulate each week during March 1952, and *España Libre* published the dates and times of the demonstrations, encouraging readers to attend.[49] As part of these efforts, Thomas, who was demonstrating with members of the Workers Defense League, asked for an appointment with the

Spanish consul, Pelayo García Olay, but was told the consul was unavailable. Nonetheless, Thomas left an invitation for the consul to attend the following meeting in the Freedom House. Despite these efforts, the execution of the underground anarcho-syndicalists took place on March 13 in Barcelona.

Twelve days later, Thomas and Roger Nash Baldwin addressed an audience at a meeting in the Freedom House organized by the SHC, in cooperation with the International League for the Rights of Man, International Association for Democracy and Freedom, Workers Defense League, League for Industrial Democracy, Delegación del Gobierno de Euzkadi, and Republicanos Exiliados en Estados Unidos. Francis Grant, secretary general of the International Association for Democracy and Freedom, was the first to speak, and denounced Franco's mass executions. Robert Alexander, a professor of economics at Rutgers University, reported on his own visit to Spain. Alexander claimed that Franco's repeated executions of union leaders reflected poorly on the moral position of the United States, which engaged in economic agreements with Franco. Baldwin, representing the International League for the Rights of Man, reminded the audience that antifascists in the United States had been fighting against Franco since the outbreak of the Spanish Civil War.[50]

To this effect, González Malo published in *España Libre* a forceful essay entitled "¡Morir de Pie!" (To die on our feet!). He invoked this popular antifascist slogan to remind readers that the fight continued. González Malo ended his article calling for antifascist unity: "Disunited . . . we are encouraging the sad and suicidal role of accomplices and executioners. . . . We must strengthen and focus our sympathy, compassion, condolence, and understanding for all those afflicted by adversity. . . . Let us salute in solidarity with every man who falls fighting for the freedom of the people, of the oppressed classes."[51] For González Malo, this fight was shared with the peoples of Bolivia, Peru, Guatemala, the Dominican Republic, Argentina, Venezuela, or any other country where the people were not free to determine their own destinies.

Two years later, on February 12, 1954, *España Libre* opened its front page with the headline: "Eighteen from the Resistance Sentenced for Life for Distributing Propaganda."[52] This referred to the incident in which ASO members were detained when they were caught circulating ASO bulletins and *España Libre* issues. The SHC sent a telegram to the White House demanding the presence of external observers during the trial, and *España Libre* started a campaign encouraging antifascist allies to fight for the union members. The periodical thanked the people who were already helping ASO, among them Roger E. Baldwin and Norman Thomas.[53] Although these ASO members were given long sentences, they were not executed, which could have happened as a result of the show trials in the Spanish justice system. On April 2, 1954, *España Libre* dedicated its front page to the "terror and repression in Spain," publishing a notice that seventeen resistance fighters had been sentenced for participating in strikes several years before. The article acknowledged Baldwin's achievement in having international observers sent to this trial and encouraging the *New York Times*'s correspondent, Camille M. Cianfarra, to follow the trial in Spain as well.[54] For his contributions, in 1954, Baldwin was awarded an honorary membership in the SHC, along with Norman Thomas and Dwight Macdonald.[55] As a prominent sponsor of *España Libre* throughout the 1960s, Baldwin went on to serve as advisory member to the SHC, as did socialist Robert Alexander.[56]

In the 1960s, González Malo continued to seek Baldwin's help for the ASO.[57] In 1962, he requested that Baldwin provide additional contacts in labor organizations to extend the support that Americans could provide the ASO.[58] In 1962, Baldwin reported on Franco's imprisonments and persecutions in the *España Libre*, and the periodical published Baldwin's formal denunciation written to the United Nations.[59] Additionally, *España Libre* published Baldwin's letters to United Nations Secretary General U Thant. Baldwin denounced Spanish police abuses of union members and Basque and Catalan nationalists.[60] Baldwin bailed anarchist Progreso Alfarache out of a Spanish prison in 1963.[61]

Less publicized, other members defended the clandestine opposition and protested against political imprisonment in *España Libre*. To pursue her political beliefs, Carmen Aldecoa traveled several times to Spain in the 1960s and contacted members of the underground ASO while there. The next year, she chaired the Women's Committee; its successful fundraisers were reviewed in *España Libre* on June 9, 1961, and in February 23, 1962, with a total collection of $1,300 for ASO.[62] From 1961 to 1964, Aldecoa became a member of the International Advisory Committee to help Spanish political prisoners.[63] Additionally, *España Libre* published the reports of other organizations, such as the International Brigades or Aid to Spanish Youth Committee, which traveled to Spain to make inquiries about political prisoners.

Throughout the decades, the SHC sought financial and political support for several alliances of clandestine dissenting groups: the Alianza Nacional de Fuerzas Democráticas (ANFD, Alliance of Democratic Forces) in the 1940s, the Alianza Sindical Española (ASE, Spanish Union Alliance) in the 1950s, and the ASO in the 1960s. In December 1963, Augustin Souchy, a German anarcho-syndicalist and friend of González Malo, visited Spanish anarchists in exile in Paris to inform them about ASO, and asked the International Confederation of Free Trade Unions to help that organization. Spanish Civil War exiles, however, were not united in their support to ASO. Whereas reformist anarchists such as González Malo advocated for political alliances with other exile and opposition groups, Spanish orthodox anarchists exiled in France and Mexico were against inclusion. They felt that coalitional alliances were against anarchist orthodoxy and the precarious and urgent circumstances of the resistance in Spain could make them commit tactical errors.[64] Despite all his efforts on behalf of anarchists, González Malo received several warnings from Spanish anarchist leaders in Paris, who reminded him that he lacked their endorsement to publicly support ASO.[65]

Beyond being newsworthy, the prominent coverage on ASO in *España Libre*, and the coverage about the unfair judicial system in Spain, facilitated González Malo's requests for donations. González Malo sent reports on Spain to several exile and labor networks. As a consequence, the UAW financially and politically supported ASE and ASO over the years.[66] Despite this aid, clandestine resistance groups remained vulnerable under the brutal state repression in Spain. In February 1964, members of the clandestine national committee of CNT in Spain, among them the general secretary of ASO, Francisco Calle Mancilla, were detained. Franco's intelligence network intercepted a phone call between the ASO and an SHC member, Gabriel Javsicas, who was visiting Spain at the time.[67] *España Libre* covered these arrests and González Malo wrote to numerous contacts in the exile community and in the United States to solicit further media attention to the cases. In May 1964, González Malo arranged for ASO to receive $500 from UAW each month.[68] In July 1964, he wrote again to his networks of supporters to deny rumors of communist infiltration in the ASO. However, 1968 marked the end of ASO. Members of the underground opposition were exhausted and terrified after years of prison, torture, and ruthless political persecution. Franco's terror destroyed their will to resist.

González Malo was preoccupied with the future of Spanish anarcho-syndicalism. From Toulouse, anarchist leader Juan Manuel Mateo Molina (Juanel) agreed with him about the possible collapse of the Spanish labor movement after the demise of the ASO.[69] From Marseille, France, anarchist Acracio Bartolomé also wrote to González Malo to express his pessimistic prediction for the labor movement not only due to the political repression but also because of the disunity among popular movements. As he wrote: "I believe that injustice and resentment are the tools of historical development."[70] In June 1965, news of the detentions of CNT members arrived at the offices of *España Libre*. Undercover CNT general secretary Cipriano Damiano González was among those arrested.[71] Years of activism had taken a toll on González Malo's health. In November 1965, Victor Reuther visited him at New York University Hospital and awarded him the United Auto Workers' medal: "In recognition of the great services rendered to the cause of freedom and social justice in the world."[72] However, González Malo's doctor advised him against continuing to engage in any activism or writing, which he only partially agreed to. González Malo died on December 31, 1965. After his death, numerous letters of condolence, appreciation, and notices of donations in his memory were published in *España Libre*.

España Libre, the affiliated associations, the theater groups, the rallies and demonstrations, and mainstream media provided an alternative space of action in the United States where activists practiced their antifascism and anarchism. Although seemingly powerless because of its condition of exile and the uncertain political times in the United States, the SHC carried out extraordinary fundraising, protest, and activism. When Franco came to power, thousands of supporters of the Republic were incarcerated or executed, and their possessions taken away from them and their families. In the United States, the occupation of the public sphere with rallies, demonstrations, antifascist festivals, and antifascist media played a crucial role in raising public awareness about the plight of Spanish refugees and political prisoners. Whereas in Franco's Spain women lost the progressive legal and political rights they had acquired during the Second Republic, in U.S. exile, women, who worked tirelessly in the organization of these public demonstrations of antifascism, were extremely important in maintaining a collective and proletarian identity as well as in building extensive fundraising and solidarity networks to aid political dissenters and prisoners in Spain.

España Libre disseminated information worldwide about political persecution in Franco's Spain (this news even clandestinely reached Spain) while the international press showed scant interest in the execution of political prisoners in Spain. The remaining archive, although only partial, speaks of the urgency and precariousness that marked the SHC's antifascist activism in the United States. Nonetheless, the confederation successfully furthered the cause of its antifascism by organizing fundraisers, protesting on American streets and in American media, and on the pages of *España Libre*. In the following chapters, I describe how the literary expressions published in *España Libre* were an intrinsic and powerful tool of working-class identity, which fueled antifascist activism. Chapter 6 will explore how the periodical provided explicit opportunities to develop a new postwar ethnic identity in the United States through a diverse body of cultural work.

Part Two

Literary Representations and Aesthetics

6

We, the Antifascist People

Those fallen in the Spanish Civil War and those tortured or executed under Franco's rule were focal points of literary representation in *España Libre*. A number of *España Libre* authors presented antifascist mythical figures who subverted the misanthropic fascist representations of progressives and radicals. Alfonso Camín, an anarchist poet, used the Spanish symbol for freedom, Don Quixote, to encourage combative antifascism. Don Quixote, the self-imagined and idealistic knight, still represents today the impossible dream of freedom and justice for all, and was a potent symbol for Hispanic migrants, Spanish Civil War exiles, and radicals. Similarly, the literary knight served as a self-representation of the exile community in Alfonso Vidal i Planas's essays. Félix Martí Ibáñez also referred to the adventurous Spanish icon as the last hope for the antifascist community. These metaphorical discourses illuminated the good fight to readers in expressive and intuitive ways that build upon their deeply held antifascist convictions. With a maternalist approach, anarchist Miguel Giménez Igualada assigned women the role of caregivers in antifascist homes in exile.

In *The Aesthetics of Antifascist Film*, Jennifer L. Barker differentiates two antifascist aesthetic approaches: one that challenges fascist mythmaking with antifascist myths, and another that counters mythmaking itself with documentation, satire, and self-interrogating realism.[1] Along these lines, Martí Ibáñez's depictions of the antifascist community changed from archetypical and traditional modes to new modes of literary representations that accounted for new ways of resistance in exile. Aware of the pernicious effect of master narratives, Martí Ibáñez inspired readers with his vision of a society finally freeing itself of fascism through individual introspection and interpersonal engagement. Other authors documented and poeticized the immigrant life in the United States and provided *España Libre* readers with a developing Spanish American identity in the United States.

Our Dead

Militiamen and Republican leaders who fought in the Spanish Civil War were often featured in *España Libre*. Notably, Francisco Ascaso, from Huesca, exemplified the common worker who participated actively in the anarchist militia. Together with Buenaventura Durruti, Ascaso was one of the most prominent CNT activists during the Spanish Civil War. He died in the assault on the headquarters of the shipyard in Barcelona, on July 20, 1936. Durruti, who died defending Madrid, was portrayed in *España Libre* as an anarchist champion because of his convictions, and as a heroic defender of the Second Republic because of his self-sacrifice.[2] Martí Ibáñez argued that Durruti epitomized not only a war hero but also an anarchist who served humanity by first improving himself.[3] Similarly, public figures of humble origins—prevalent in the Second Republic—garnered front-page news stories in *España Libre*, where their heroic deeds were lauded. General Commander José Miaja Menant joined the Infantry Academy at Toledo when he was eighteen, and four years later he served in the Moroccan War of 1900. By 1932, he had risen to general and defended Madrid during the Spanish Civil War, "while incendiary bombs fell in still-in-flames houses and workers were digging barricades." He was a living testimony to the deeds of workers who defended the capital with their lives.[4] Miaja Menant gave several speeches about the defense of Madrid at New York fundraisers. At his funeral, Colonel Vicente Guarner declared that "General Miaja has entered into history and legend . . . and with him, the noble, joyful and heroic people of Madrid."[5]

From its inception, *España Libre* stressed the common people's heroism, which compelled them to fight in the trenches, die for the homeland, or wander the world. In a 1939 remembrance of the fall of Madrid, General José Asensio Torrado was quoted urging those in attendance to pay tribute to the Spanish people: "the only hero of this conference."[6] In similar terms, the *España Libre* editorial of December 20, 1940, lamented that Spanish workers were consigned to concentration camps or forced to flee their homeland because of their fight against fascism. Noting horrific conditions, the editorial asked why "the law, regulations, religion, racism, did not let [Spaniards] cross borders[;] no one will be able to explain why no one helped the people, subdued with weapons."[7]

Despite their lack of prospects, workers were portrayed as tragic anonymous heroes who still exerted their will. At one fundraiser, in 1940, Antonio Santamaria, the former mayor of El Ferrol, thanked the working-class family who helped him escape Franco's Spain. Their names were not published to keep them safe. While in hiding in their house, the mayor was told by the family that they were aware of the risks they were taking by protecting him: "We know the importance of your presence here; if they find you, they will shoot you and all of us."[8] Similar representations of antifascist workers continued to be published in *España Libre* throughout its history. In 1957, *España Libre* announced that the 60,000 members of the Confedereradas self-defined as workers, as they did at the founding of the confederation twenty years before.[9] Maintaining this tradition of portraying workers as heroic defenders of justice and freedom, the editorial of February 16, 1962, entitled "Nuestros muertos" (Our dead), vindicated these antifascist fighters: "Let us proclaim it loud and clear and with legitimate pride, that [our dead] are the true forgers of a new world governed by equal justice, with bread and freedom for all. A time when access to truth will not be monopolized, nor will it be a class privilege, but a universal possession, in the heart of every studious man, emancipated from prejudices, our dead will have a rightful place."[10]

The SHC commemorated important dates in workers' fight for freedom. Each year, *España Libre* memorialized the Proclamation of the Second Republic (April 14), the people's uprising against the July 18 military coup (July 19), and the Defense of Madrid (November 7).[11] To mark these solemn dates, fundraisers were advertised in *España Libre*, which attracted impressive crowds. The SHC rented sizable theaters and halls, such as the Madison Square Garden or the Manhattan Hall in New York. In the 1940s, these large-scale celebrations included speeches by political leaders and cultural festivities; in the following decades, more humble commemorations were celebrated in Spanish restaurants in Manhattan. *España Libre* extensively covered these events in its pages, and opinion columns elaborated on the significance of these commemorative dates. The periodical also reviewed commemorations celebrated in Mexico and France. Historical commentary provided a sense of continuity and context with the recent cultural and historical past by reviewing the Second Republic's struggle to consolidate a stable alternative to monarchical rule and to move Spanish society toward secularism, empirical scientific inquiry, social democracy, parliamentary government, and a form of industrialization congruous with democratic values and proletarian needs.[12]

Throughout the decades, antifascist heroes beyond militia fighters were not forgotten. The prominent placement in the periodical of the lists of executed dissidents during Franco's rule, usually on its front page, was accompanied by literature dedicated to them. Poet Odón Betanzos Palacios (1926–2007) raised awareness about the extrajudicial executions of dissenters during the Spanish Civil War and Franco's Spain. His own father, the mayor of Rociana del Condado, Huelva, Spain, was executed by Falangists in 1936.[13] Betanzos Palacios dedicated his poem "Manolo Betanzos," published in *España Libre* in June 5, 1964, to his father.[14] The first stanza describes his father's physical and personality traits, the second stanza depicts his execution by firing squad on a desolate country road, and the last stanza describes bloodstains in a fountain. At this violent sight, nature, the moon, and even God trembled.

Following this poetic structure and utilizing these same poetic elements, Betanzos Palacios re-created powerful images in a series of poems dedicated to other executed antifascists: Manuel Barciela, Juan el de la Boeguilla, Antonio María Gómez, Francisco el Arrecio, Manolito Palomo, Virgilio de Encarnación, and José Antonio el Erizo. In his poem dedicated to Manuel Barciela, the element of water invokes his humble origins: "Tenía Manuel Barciela/ la sencillez del agua" (Manuel Barciela was as humble as water).[15] By repeating these literary elements that described his own father's execution, Betanzos Palacios paralleled images with other Spaniards killed by the Francoists, and shared the pain of having a father executed. His poems dramatized the regime's brutal political persecution and dignified the memory of those murdered or vanished without a trace.[16]

Gendered Representations in Exile Literature

The self-representation of the antifascist people was gendered in *España Libre*. Women were often represented in the periodical as the reversal of the modern woman stereotype. One article claimed that Franco's prisons were full of men "of all walks of life and ages, professors, servants, workers, doctors, lawyers, etc. Women were all wives, mothers or sisters of men who had opposed Franco."[17] Stereotypes of women as devoted caregivers populated *España Libre* in the 1940s. In fact, the understanding of women's worth only in relation to men was so ingrained in the exile imaginary that *España Libre* satirist Aurelio Pego concluded that world peace depended on finding Adolf Hitler a girlfriend. In his satirical chronicle, Pego claimed to have found a solution that thwarted Hitler's imperialist threats. Pego assured his readers that Hitler suffered from a peculiar psychosis: he had perverted a man's natural desire for women into a desire for national conquest: "The common man conquers women; Hitler conquers peoples. A man in love rapes a maiden; Hitler violates nations. The common Don Juan drinks too much good wine, promises everlasting love, and violates virgins."[18] In Pego's misogynist narrative, nations become women, who can be lured, raped, and enslaved. Therefore, the antidote to Hitler's expansionist passions is to exchange his object of obsession from nations to women. With equal contempt, Franco, Hitler, and Mussolini were belittled by giving them feminine characteristics in cartoons. In sum, the representation of self-sacrificing wives, crying mothers, abused girlfriends, or feminine men demonstrates that the depiction of antifascist women often embraced traditional domesticity and patriarchal values rather than the modern and radical progressive visions otherwise present in *España Libre*.

Miguel Giménez Igualada (1888–1973) depicted antifascist women as maternal. Originally from Iniesta, Cuenca, Spain, Giménez Igualada, director of the publishing house Nosotros (Valencia), and staff writer for *Al Margen* (Barcelona), survived internment camps in France with the help of SIA. From 1953 to 1963, sometimes under the pen name of Juan de Iniesta, he wrote a series of articles for *España Libre* addressed to women to guide them on their antifascist fight by encouraging them to play a maternal role.[19] These articles reinforced the prevalent subordinate and traditional functions of women. In Giménez Igualada's narrative, women were "daughters, loyal to their parents; women, loyal to their husbands; mothers, loyal to their children; and finally, friends, loyal to their friends."[20] The author exhorted women to be guardians of their exile homes by transforming themselves into "a protected valley, in whose fertile soil your children would blossom in peace and happiness."[21] In 1959, Giménez Igualada published his novel *Los últimos románticos*, which narrates the long courting of a lively woman by a young man. Margarita must "regain" her purity and noble spirit by giving up her social life and submitting to Manuel's control.[22]

In 1960, Giménez Igualada continued to guide women readers on creating a proper exile home by serving her husband and family: "When the husband comes home, it is not necessary to tell him that you were waiting for him with mad anxiety; rather, on the bed, washed and ironed, he finds his pajamas; on the floor the slippers are in formation, as if offering themselves; on the small table, cigarettes at the ready; in the kitchen, soup is cooking, whose aroma arouses his appetite; on the big table, a large bouquet of flowers [delights his eyes]."[23] In exile, women were to cultivate the art of pleasing others, "so that your husband lives in continuous rapture; and, by being good and sweet, making sure your children are always happy."[24] In Giménez Igualada's essays, women were expected to enjoy domestic roles and subject themselves to men. In doing so, women were symbolically creating an exiled antifascist community, and in his view, opposing fascism. Despite these representations and expectations from male writers in the movement, real women clearly did not conform to this representation. Women contributed in extraordinary ways, and the stories of Carmen Aldecoa, Maria Cordellat, Nancy Macdonald, and Mary Reid are examples of how women's refutation of paternalism was essential to the successes of the SHC.

Although most of Giménez Igualada's essays in *España Libre* prescribed antifascist domesticity for women in exile, he published several books about postwar anarchism.[25] In contrast with the maternal approach described in *España Libre*, his books, published in Mexico and away from the scrutiny of the FBI and the Francoist diplomacy in the United States, advocated for anarchist thought and practice, contested propaganda against the movement, and documented his refugee experience. In *Los caminos del hombre: epistolario* (The ways of man: collection of letters, 1961), Giménez Igualada compiled fifty letters written to a fictional friend, Juan, from 1942 to 1960.[26] The letters refuted several negative stereotypes about anarchism. He decided to change the book's original title *Anarquismo* to *Los caminos del hombre*, however, because he was aware of the political climate in which "the word anarchy causes dread."[27] Giménez Igualada denied the assumption that anarchism was violent; instead anarchism was "serene in words and fraternal in actions."[28] Anarchists reject violence because it brings tyranny: "We have learned that violence is insurrection, but that was not and will never be revolutionary . . . because there can be no revolution in the violent act that brings war and carries terror in its heart, because terror ends only in tyranny."[29] In fact, an anarchist is against any sort of domination, Giménez Igualada explained. People become anarchists "when they refuse in their heart to exercise power over any other human creature."[30]

In this respect, Giménez Igualada claimed that anarchism was more than resisting oppression. Anarchism was also a commitment to a harmonious life: "Anarchism, even if it rejects the very concept of government, cannot exist only to critique oppressive forces . . . rather, it must create an ideal life, first in the imagination and then by living it, an ideal that rises above the din of existence, and makes human existence beautiful."[31] Postwar anarchism was strengthened by the power of imagination: "Slowly but surely, progress rather than regression will assert itself." He predicted that "harmony will reign in place of violence, and culture will replace avarice. This human revolution is an anarchist revolution because ethics gives it energy and aesthetics guides it. I love it."[32] Attuned with *España Libre*'s philosophy of the interconnected nature of solidarity and culture, Giménez Igualada highlighted the political importance of the arts.

In a later book, this time entitled *Anarquismo* (1968), Giménez Igualada again responded to the disparagement of anarchism: "To discredit the name of anarchism is to throw away the yearning for improvement and the hope for human harmony. . . . Anarchism is a daring conception of a free life; it is above all attempts to constrain life to a formula."[33] Giménez Igualada defined anarchism as action, but action resulting from introspection: "In the moments of introspection, concentration, meditation, thought; that is to say, in the moments of the depth of life and inner satisfaction and harmony, we all feel capable of acting ethically and beautifully. . . . This deep, vital emotion is what I call anarchist *feeling*, from which derives anarchist *behavior*."[34] Therefore, to Giménez Igualada, the anarchist revolution was an evolving process of introspection and ethical action that would break with all forms of oppression and domination.

Don Quixote

If war heroes were the most common representations of masculinity for working-class antifascism, and women were domesticated in the antifascist representations published in *España Libre*, the quintessential Spanish knight, Don Quixote, came to represent the idealism and mythical quality of the good fight. The literary classic, with its egalitarian Golden Age discourse on freedom, idealism, and individualism, appealed to exiles. Don Quixote personified the self-sacrificing determination for a free world, as foolish as might seem to others; while Sancho represented the popular down-to-earth skepticism that mocked any of Don Quixote's grandiose thoughts.

Alfonso Camín Meana (1890–1982), *España Libre*'s fiercest poet, engaged his readers with this Spanish literary icon. Camín migrated to Cuba in 1905, and wrote for several newspapers, *La Noche*, *Apolo*, and *Diario de la Marina*, for which he covered the First World War.[35] By 1929, he returned to Spain and founded his magazine *Norte* (based in Asturias). When the Spanish Civil War broke out in 1936, Camín left for Cuba and then Mexico. During his Mexican exile, the poet published extensively throughout the Americas. His poems appeared in U.S. Spanish-language and anarchist newspapers—*Cultura Proletaria* (New York), *La Voz* (New York), and *Vía Libre* (New York)—as well as anarchist periodicals of the Spanish Civil War exile, such as *La Novela Española* (Toulouse).[36] Camín visited *España Libre*'s headquarters in February 1940, dressed in his usual black cape and carrying a cane. After that visit, he started publishing antifascist poetry in the periodical with great regularity, most of which has been collected in *Últimos cantos de la guerra* (1948), *Apolos y las rosas* (1951), *Carbones y otros retratos* (1952), *Fantoches* (1954), and *Estafermos* (1956).[37]

With a defiant tone, his poems encouraged violent revolt against fascism. In honor of the Golden Age poet and master satirist Francisco de Quevedo, *España Libre* referred to Camín as the periodical's Quevedo because of his piercing poetic attacks against fascists. Camín's poetry expressed the deep feelings of rage against fascists and their followers. His poem "Otra vez" (Again), published June 15, 1939, advocated for armed struggle: "we need to return to the trenches/ Again we must elevate our verses/ ... we must bleed."[38] The poet warns fascists that the people will not forget and are awaiting their time: "Those who did not hear the bullets/ from Nalón to Naranco/ ... Those who didn't see their wives/ dead at the bottom of the ravine" must know that "Asturias awaits its time/ and so does Spain."[39] Similarly, his poem: "No le temas al mar" (Do not fear the sea), published in *España Libre* in 1952, reminded readers of the power of collective resistance. Metaphorically, the poet advised readers not to dread the sea but the drops, not the king, but the knave, who might rule Spain.[40]

Only a few months later, he published his poem "Evangélica," which proposed violence to empower the people: "When a tyrant is extolled/ and the people suffer and become corrupted,/ there will be no reason nor justice/ like a hand grenade/ ... there is no more reason on earth/ other than a discharge."[41] Camín plays with the several meanings of the word "discharge" in Spanish, which can also mean "to absolve." The poem's title "Evangélica" further reinforces the multiple meanings of the word and incriminates the Spanish Church. The poet encourages people to fire their weapons because the Catholic Church, allied to the fascist powers in Spain, is irrelevant in a world where reason no longer exists.

In 1956, Camín looked for a model to encourage revolt. He asked Quixote to take up his lance again: "I hope Quijano will regain his spear one day."[42] Camín called him Quijano, his common name, instead of calling him Quixote, the one adopted when the literary character imagined himself as a knight. By calling him Quijano, Camín rendered a literary image of powerlessness by painfully signaling that even such a cultural icon of freedom was unable to defeat fascism. The poem hoped for the day Don Quixote would fight again, when idealism rather than practicality once again would reign in the world.

A few years later, in 1958, Camín demanded that poets continue to fight for freedom, "Poet, leave your ivory tower. Come down and fight."[43] Camín criticized those who accommodated to fascist rule: "People who badly applaud their executioner/ ... are like an ox that becomes accustomed to the yoke."[44]

In the poem "Cadenas" (Chains), Camín's disdain was again addressed to those who didn't rebel: "Cannot cause me pain/ enslaved people at ease;/ bark like a wild dog,/ but lick their chains."[45] Besides rage, Camín's poetry also voiced the desolation of witnessing Spain under fascism: "Of pain I will die/ because of my enchained land. That's it. Nothing else can make a rose die."[46] Because of Franco, "so much murderous youth has been achieved."[47] Published in *España Libre* in August 1963, Camín's poem "Camino y Quilla" (Path and keel), expresses the feelings that he and many Spaniards felt in exile: "Eternally loving my land/ if freedom is nowhere where I was born,/ I die in liberty under another sky."[48]

Camín's poetry sometimes re-created the landscape of his homeland of Asturias. Exiles like him "had dreams made of pine trees, sea, and wind."[49] The poet cannot escape his nomadic life: "In vain I want to be a fountain/ with pure water" but "I travel from the hill to the plain/ like overflown river/ or furious hurricane."[50] In his last years, Camín represents himself as part of a Spanish community that has been exiled over the centuries: "From the Sephardics to the Christianized Spain/ you will find, over centuries, wandering and scattered a race worthy of a better luck/ and Spain, all Spain cannot find its way/ roving Don Quixote."[51]

Like Camín, Félix Martí Ibáñez (Cartagena, 1911–New York, 1972) evoked the literary icon of Don Quixote as the last hope for antifascist readers. Martí Ibáñez, an anarchist leader in public health and social services in Catalonia in 1937, fled Spain at the end of the Spanish Civil War and settled in New York. As with Camín, Martí Ibáñez's first essays and short stories in *España Libre* appeared in the 1940s.[52] In similar gendered terms to Giménez Igualada, Martí Ibáñez reminds readers: "Wherever there was an opportunity to charge at the Nazi-Fascist enemy, the errant Spaniard would put aside his sorrow and take up arms. Would not Don Quixote ride his horse in La Mancha, and rescue his Dulcinea, his Spain, from the evildoers who have kidnapped her?"[53] The idealism of Don Quixote represents antifascist Spaniards: "Don Quixote . . . fought against monsters of iron and steel and with his broken spear fell and his blood fertilized the land, now with blossoming poppies that bring hope for a new day . . . and the strength of his idealism will be able to restore an empire of peace and justice."[54]

Another indefatigable contributor was Alfonso Vidal y Planas (1891–1965). Vidal y Planas was a popular author in Madrid before the Spanish Civil War.[55] During the war, Vidal y Planas wrote for *El Sindicalista*, as did Ramón J. Sender, another CNT member. In exile, both wrote for *España Libre*. After escaping Spain, Vidal y Planas lived in New York in the 1940s but eventually moved to

Tijuana to work as a Spanish literature teacher. Vidal y Planas continued to submit antifascist essays and poems to several Spanish-language periodicals in New York, such as *España Libre, Solidaridad Obrera*, and *La Voz*; *La Prensa* in San Antonio, Texas; as well as *El Antifascista, Ariel*, and *La Opinión* in Los Angeles. Vidal y Planas wrote about cinema and the United States, but mostly about the Spanish Civil War, and published articles about anarcho-syndicalists Anselmo Lorenzo, El noi del sucre, or Ángel Pestaña, for instance.

In the sixties, he published the regular *España Libre* column "Luciérnagas" on the topics of Francoism and exile. In one of his columns, published May 4, 1962, Vidal y Planas appealed to the icon of Don Quixote to represent the exile community: "There are two types of Spaniards: us and them. We are those of Don Quixote. They are those of the Cid."[56] The author compared the idealism of Don Quixote with that of the exile community, while employing the imperialistic quality of another well-known knight and the embodiment of Christian Spain, El Cid, to represent Spanish fascist values.

Evolving Exilic Representations

Martí Ibáñez's early texts in *España Libre* were excerpts from his novel about the Spanish Civil War, *Aventura* (Adventure, 1938) that captured the people's heroic response during the war.[57] Martí Ibáñez's most notable work soon moved away from heroic accounts of the war and transitioned to an exilic quality that would mark his literary production in the United States. In his article entitled "La voz de la soledad" (The voice of solitude), published in *España Libre* in April 1940, Martí Ibáñez elaborated on the quintessential theme of exile literature: solitude.[58] However, he did not re-create the nostalgia for the homeland or the isolation of the uprooted, as is customary for the genre. Instead, he found that the profound loneliness felt by exiles was, in fact, a vital opportunity for improving one's perception of the world. Therefore, for Martí Ibáñez, the participation in a transnational antifascist culture in exile stimulated a thought process that reinforced his belief in literature as a tool to enlarge our perception of reality.

Martí Ibáñez's first short story in *España Libre*, "Presagio de Berchtesgaden" (Presage of Berchtesgaden, 1940) expresses such a transformation. The story tells of a premonition Adolf Hitler experiences during a retreat in Berchtesgaden. Hitler is reading a death warrant to Adolfo Walter, a young Jewish author who fought in the Spanish Civil War. Walter had been detained for carrying forbidden books, but when Hitler looks at the young boy, he notices his own reflection in the defiant prisoner's eyes.[59] Hitler orders his guards to take the prisoner away and kill him. Up to this point, "Presagio" echoes the heroic tone of Martí Ibáñez's Spanish Civil War novels, in which common people perform heroic deeds against fascism. However, soon after the encounter, Hitler keeps recalling the incident. Secretly he decides to keep the prisoner alive because he is afraid that the boy has given him the evil eye. Hitler has been affected by the memory of his own angered face reflected in the boy's eyes. "Presagio" counteracts fascist ideology by forcing Hitler to experience reality through the mirrored perspective of himself in the prisoner's eyes. The emotion caused by the vision opens Hitler up to new possibilities of affectively and experimentally understanding reality, even when he does not welcome the experience or the new perspective.

While Hitler is affected by the prisoner's look and reaction, readers experience the story through Hitler's thoughts and feelings. Martí Ibáñez plays with interconnected perspectives to deconstruct a binary logic, which privileges one opposition over the other. Like other anarchist writings, instead of absolutes, the story delivers transitory, ironic, multidirectional adjustments. For this reason, Jesse Cohn likens anarchism to an underground tunnel.[60] It is produced in movement, in physical and metaphysical migrations, for anarchist literature is known for disarticulating representation through a "dialectic of identification and disidentification."[61] In his exile fiction, Martí Ibáñez resisted fascist representation by interconnecting perspectives and, consequently, enlarging perception and consciousness.[62] This accords with Sandra Jeppersen's observation that "anarchist literature has as its task a radical break with conventional perceptions ... extending the limits of the possible."[63]

Such dialectical arrangement is also present in Martí Ibáñez's short story "Episodio en Londres" (Episode in London), serialized in *España Libre* in March 1940.[64] The narrative starts with the description of an English lord preparing for a parliamentary session. His secretary has prepared literary quotes for use in his parliamentary address. The lord likes one of Francis Bacon's observations, "Any strange voice can be the voice of your conscience."[65] Spanish refugee Juan Arnall stands in the parliament's public gallery.[66] In his speech, the English lord argues that England is aiding Spain by helping to restore the monarchy. Juan Arnall shouts out, "¡Mentira! ... ¡traidor!" (Lies! ... traitor!). For creating this commotion, the refugee is asked to leave the premises.[67] "Episodio" repeats the structure of "Presagio." At first, we encounter a worker fighting against incredible odds. However, the heroic mode soon changes into introspection and multiple perspectives. After the incident, the lord has trouble resuming his address: "the speaker is sweating and stumbles over his words ... something had deeply wounded his heart."[68] At that moment, the lord remembers Bacon's phrase, "Any strange voice can be the voice of your conscience." The refugee's cry for help has affected the lord's perception of reality. The climax of the story again showcases self-awareness through others. In this sense, the story re-creates anarchist culture that sees the individual as a product of collective forces.

Barker notes that the trajectory of antifascist aesthetics in the twentieth century becomes an alternate strand of postmodernism: "a postmodern humanism, in which humanism survives the eviscerations of modern fragmentation and fascist dehumanization."[69] With "Episodio," Martí Ibáñez proposes contingent and multiple perspectives as a transformative force to combat complacency with fascist rule. Similarly, "Presagio" counteracts fascist dehumanization with dialectical identification. Engagement with the reader does not rely on the grand action of the protagonists, but on their effect, because characters are forced to reflect on reality through others' eyes and voices—a dialectic embodied in the text itself. As Barker notes: "The realities of repressive politics make the aims of documentation and realistic representation a requirement, but one that is best served by the utilization of dialectical inquiry and modernist and postmodernist strategies in order to avoid simply creating another oppressive master narrative."[70] Martí Ibáñez's anarchist sensibility adapted to exile and proposed individual introspection and engagement with multiple perspectives to combat fascism and avoid reproducing similar oppressive narratives. *España Libre*, as an antifascist periodical, provided an important public venue for the development of postmodern humanist aesthetics. Its editors were visionary in integrating activism and literature that fought for and re-created a world free of fascism.

Encounters with subjugated others in the United States greatly influenced *España Libre*'s authors. Prolific Spanish novelist, essayist, and journalist Ramón J. Sender (1902–1982) perceived border crossers as the key means to rethink freedom after fascism. After serving as a Republican commanding officer during the Spanish Civil War, Sender went into exile first in Mexico and then in the United States. In the United States, Sender was investigated by the FBI from 1943 to 1983 for his contributions to anarchist periodicals, and for his collaborations with the Medical Bureau of the North American Committee to Aid Spanish Democracy and the Exiled Writers' Committee (of the League of American Writers).[71] Sender was an honorary member and an active sponsor of *España Libre* and attended meetings at associations in New York and Los Angeles. He contributed essays on anarchism to *España Libre* and *Dissent* (New York), as well as other Spanish Civil War exile periodicals such as *CNT* (Mexico), *Comunidad Ibérica* (Mexico), and *La Novela Española* (Toulouse). In two similar articles published in 1960 in *España Libre* and *CNT* (Mexico), Sender elaborated on the concept of the "solera fronteriza sublime" (sublime frontier quality) of Spaniards because of their interrelation with other cultures throughout the centuries.[72]

This idea—that border crossings represent both cultural and symbolic acts—appeared again in Sender's *Relatos fronterizos* (Border stories), an anthology of short stories published in 1970. Sender's protagonists are common people who cross all sorts of borders and enact deep understanding of hardships to break free from subjugating ideologies. The stories capture the struggle of Spaniards against fascism, as well as ethnic minorities in the United States fighting against exclusion. For example, a short story tells the tale of peasants crossing the Spanish border with France in the Pyrenees in 1970, who are escaping into France, a story that recalls Sender's own path when he himself escaped fascism in 1939 crossing the same location. In another story, an elderly Mexican woman crosses the U.S.–Mexico border and narrowly escapes the pernicious effects of patriarchy and segregation. In Europe or in the Americas, Sender's protagonists interrogate physical and hermeneutic frontiers as fabrications that attempt to tame them. However, these short stories with transnational themes are not merely invested in demanding justice for the marginalized; rather, they showcase the capacity of the liminal protagonists to foresee freer societies—returning to Sender's coined concept of solera fronteriza sublime. His protagonists achieve extraordinary visions, or sublime frontier qualities from their marginalized positions. On the margins of social and political inclusion, Sender's characters venture to cross geographical and metaphysical frontiers that subjugate them and in doing so they acquire a sublime (although tragic) vision of freedom. Their fight situates them in the margins of society, but Sender finds the definition of freedom precisely in such practice. Influenced by the civil rights movement and building on his post–Spanish Civil War approach to anarchism, Sender interrogated borders as identification systems that create social exclusion.

Evolving Migrant Representations

Edward Said's concept of contrapuntal living delineates political migrants' self-conscious existence, which is articulated in constant and necessary remembrances of the national past—their identity is rooted in their place in history. This articulation of the exile experience evolving into migration literature is expressed in the later texts of the writers-in-exile published in *España Libre*, and it provides a valuable lens for contemplating the broader experience of the SHC members who spent their lives in exile from Spain. As Said points out, while minorities or migrants participate in a certain cultural fluidity and resist unique national identifications, exiles' violent displacement involves simultaneous dimensions that inform each other contrapuntally. The new space and new culture evolve along with the persistence in connecting with the homeland: "For an exile, habits of life, expression or activity in the new environment inevitably occur against the memory of these things in another environment. Thus, both the new and the old environments are vivid, actual, occurring together contrapuntally."[73] Because of the conflict in the homeland, their narrative tension fluctuates between the need for accommodation and the call for resistance. In the last decades of exile, *España Libre* published writers, such as José Castilla Morales, Antonio García Copado, and Alfonso Vidal y Planas, who expressed the workers' experience in U.S. exile as negotiating between two languages and two cultures.

Castilla Morales's exile and migration chronicles run from 1943 until 1961. The pen names he used, El Chico de la Calle (Street kid) and Don Pepe (Average Joe), signaled the humor in them. El Chico referred to his short height and Don Pepe to his common Spanish characteristics. In funny and entertaining ways, his chronicles portrayed colleagues in a personal light in the context of the SHC's national congresses, fundraisers, the premieres of plays, and relations with affiliated organizations. With the telling title of "Bajo Cero" (Below zero), the chronicle published in December 1942 was indeed not only a reference to the winter weather, but also a pun on the difficult financial and political grounds of the grassroots confederation. The chronicle reported how the cold (or the SHC's hardships) showed each member's true character during the Sixth National Congress in El Centro Español, New York. For example, El Chico ironically reported on the attendees: José Asensio telling everyone that the general felt as he was "on summer holidays," while Carmen Aldecoa was patting members as if they were distressed children. El Chico was surprised to find Jesús González Malo unusually temperate and Félix Martí Ibáñez's face red with cold. However, El Chico assured the readers that Alfonso Vidal y Planas's elegance was untouched by the weather. By comically describing the members' personalities alongside reports on the congress, El Chico shared with the community of migrant readers the personal transformations that exile had forced upon them.

El Chico had warm praises for members involved in the fundraising performances and their life-long contributions, which were better understood when examining their ideals as a way of life.[74] Notably, the chronicle to pay tribute to Antonio Martínez, the rehearsal stand-in in his plays, was written in acts to emphasize his life-long dedication to Hispanic and antifascist theater. Act one: Martínez complains that El Chico is mocking him. Act two: interviewer denies the accusation. El Chico cannot laugh at one of the best stand-ins of the Hispanic theater in New York. Act three: El Chico has a collection of all the plays staged by the SHC, and Martínez is always in them. Act four: El Chico asks Martínez to continue his support. El Chico also interviewed active *España Libre*'s contributors and focused in their lives in the United States. In a funny interview with naturist doctor José María Martínez Novella, he depicted Novella in entertaining ways, for instance, as a Tarzan figure living in a Miami Beach house, eating only fruits and vegetables.[75]

In a chronicle published on December 1960 under the pen name of Don Pepe, Castilla Morales paid tribute to founding members who continued to be active in several groups across the United States: the headquarters in New York, the Leales Españoles in Los Angeles, and the Acción Demócrata Española in San Francisco.[76] After remembering those who had passed away, such as Luis Zugadi Garmendia and Pablo de la Torriente Brau, who died in battle in Spain, Don Pepe mentions very active members in 1960 across the country. In New York, there is a long list of names. For example: John Carnero, Agustín Carcagente, Jesús González Malo, Carmen Aldecoa, Alberto Uriarte, Hipólito Cristóbal, Avelino Iglesias, Eduardo Vives, Manuel Dorado, Antonio García Copado, Marita Reid, Carmencita López, the cartoonist Josep Bartolí, and the editor of the English pages John Nicholas Beffel. Also, Don Pepe listed J. M. Martínez Novella in Miami, Aurelio Pego in Puerto Rico, and Juan García Durán in Detroit. In Los Angeles, Don Pepe mentioned several individuals that kept the affiliated organizations alive there: Sabina Zubieta, Antonio Zubieta, José Iborra, Josefina Méndez, Félix Lunar, Baltasar Fernández Cué, Luis Montés, José Rubia Barcia, Gregorio Garay, Frank Eive, and Edith Eive. In San Francisco, Don Pepe mentioned, for example, Javier Benedet, Vicente Benedet, Segundo Eimil, Felipe Osta, and Víctor Rodríguez. Although his description of the community was funny and entertaining, in this particular chronicle, Castilla Morales paid respectful tribute to hard-working members.

However, members were ridiculed for not contributing enough to the antifascist fight and acculturating to a life of comfort and leisure in the United States. Under another pen name, Onuba, Castilla Morales observed Spaniards in New York. The chronicle entitled "De verano" (On summer), published in May 1941, narrated the encounter of Onuba with a Spaniard in a Brooklyn park. The Spaniard reproached Onuba because he was reading news about the European war instead of looking at the shapely women walking in the park. Onuba reasoned that those who called themselves politically neutral, "rather than live, they float" and "in summer you find them everywhere."[77] Written in the first-person plural, the chronicle forced readers to maintain their antifascist stance in contrast to the Spaniard with a buoyant life, empty of political meaning, who was ridiculed in the chronicle by imagining him floating aimlessly into the summer breeze. In his chronicles, Onuba indulged in perilous adventures at the Spanish Consulate on Madison Avenue, singing Spanish Republican songs and thus provoking Francoist officials there, or purposely misinforming them about pro-Republican activities in New York.[78] Nonetheless, his satirical sketches about the consulate and related parties had practical goals: unmasking pro-Franco Spaniards in New York.

An anonymous letter published in *España Libre* criticized El Chico for praising or chastising the community. El Chico responded that Castilla Morales cried over the Spanish tragedy in essays and laughed at Franco with "the popular muse" in plays. Highlighting members' lives in American society allowed them to continue to denounce fascism.[79] Although Castilla Morales's profiles comically described the acculturation or resistance to acculturation of humble and committed antifascists in the United States, he also wrote about their struggles. Under the pen name of Don Pepe, he published a New Year's poem in *España Libre* on January 1, 1954, and dedicated it to contributor Ángel Samblancat Salanova, in exile in Mexico. In the poem, New York was described as a noisy metropolis, "This Babel of iron,/ where the noise rises as shouting to the sky."[80] Despite its unwelcoming quality, the author acknowledged that he was able to condemn Franco without fear in the city. Don Pepe showed both his resistance: "For twenty years I've been here without changing my lifestyle or accent," and his adaptation: "I am a man who lives like an old tree;/ inside deep roots/ outside blossoming foliage."[81] Castilla Morales here describes himself as a tree that had roots in Spain and hopeful foliage blossoming in the United States.

Andalusian poet Antonio García Copado (1914–1991) arrived in the United States in 1958. From 1959 to 1961, García Copado (sometimes under the pen name "Juan del exilio"—John from exile) published a regular column in *España Libre* entitled "Cuénteme usted su vida" (Tell me your life). Like those of Castilla Morales, these interviews recounted the diverse and industrious advancement of members in American society. García Copado mainly featured the experiences of family businesses, especially long-time sponsors of *España Libre*.[82] In one such interview published on December 1959, García Copado interviewed Juan Pliego. As a young boy, Pliego arrived in New York in 1902 with his father and four siblings. At the time, he knew no English—he used to contemplate New York street signs without understanding their meaning—and integration into the new culture was inevitably difficult.[83] Pliego would later work in a tobacco factory and then spend twenty-five years traveling the United States as a tobacco salesman. By 1940, he had saved enough to buy El Cortijo, a vacation home, in Fostertown, Wallkill, New York, which he made into a very successful forty-five-room hotel. At this hotel, he was able to offer the same welcoming Spanish-speaking atmosphere of those vacation villas and boarding houses at which his family first stayed upon their arrival in America when Juan did not yet understand English. In a similar interview published on February 1960, García Copado interviewed another popular member of the community, Galician Jenaro Borines, who immigrated to the United States in 1921. After thirty-seven years of working in a cookie factory, he opened his dream business, the hotel Aldea Borines, where "Spanish kindness" was to be found.[84] These biographies represented the experiences and feelings of exiled workers in the United States.

However, García Copado also published a few poems in *España Libre* that described less happy immigrant experiences in the United States.[85] A couple of poems from December 1959 and January 1960 reflect on New Year's Eve in New York. The poet laments that Spaniards are substituting the Spanish tradition of eating twelve grapes at midnight for good luck with the habit of drinking Coke.[86] The grape culture is juxtaposed with the overpowering U.S. mass industry implied by the reference to the iconic soft drink. In doing so, the poem rejects modern American life and idealizes the homeland's culinary culture. New York is a "Babel condenada" (Doomed Babel) in García Copado's poetry. The city corrals "riadas humanas" (herds of humans) that run back and forth from the factory to their homes.[87] In García Copado's view, the American city strips migrant workers of their heritage and disempowers them through an arduous life. García Copado's poetry replicated the workers' conflicting feelings and represented their personal adjustments while in exile in the United States.

In 1963, Vidal y Planas published *Cirios en los rascacielos y otros poemas* (Candles in skyscrapers and other poems) in which the author expressed his experience as a migrant in New York in the 1940s. He dedicated the book to exiles like himself. *Cirios* employs Spanish signifiers such as church candles, olive trees, and aqueducts to describe New York. Like García Copado, the poet appeases his feelings of psychological displacement and alienation in exile with language reminiscent of Spain's rural landscape. In the poem titled "¡Esta noche va a nevar!" (It is going to snow tonight!), Vidal y Planas depicts snowflakes as stellar olives to be harvested: "Extend blankets, New Yorkers!/ in the parks/ tonight, beautiful and clear/ I am going up to harvest stellar olive trees."[88] The striking conceptualization of snowflakes as cosmic olives emphasizes the climatic and cultural distance the Spanish poet experiences in New York, and how the writer bridges this distance with Spanish elements.[89] Vidal y Planas's poetic and impossible image of harvesting snowflakes as if they were olives illustrates evolving representations of reality for his readers. In similar ways, Vidal y Planas's first perception of New York skyline is evocative of a candle-lit funeral chapel: "Without Spain/ I am dead/ and in the lighted chapel of Yanquilandia I light/ a candle for my soul in each skyscraper."[90] Adapting to a new reality, Vidal y Planas describes New York's skyline with motifs reminiscent of Catholic Spain. One poem, "Mi viña sideral" (My sidereal vineyard), imagines his own death among elements of the Spanish landscape: "When I will die/ I will go to harvest its grapes/ in the slow silver road to the moon/ immensely full/ riding two bullfighters with wings."[91] His poems expressed for *España Libre*'s readers the hybrid language and conceptualization that they use to describe reality in a new land. It is obviously no accident that the subjects of migration and exile are highlighted by *España Libre*. These writings would never have been produced without the readership and community that the periodical and the SHC had created over the years.

Migration and exile are invoked in "La luna llena sobre Manhattan" (Full moon over Manhattan). To Vidal y Planas, the full moon over Manhattan looks like an enormous Spanish bread: "like a generous loaf of white bread / for migrants coming from all over the world."[92] Although the city provides opportunities, it also brings death in another poem in which Vidal y Planas contrasts the Brooklyn Bridge with the Segovia Aqueduct. The poet refers to the bridge as symbol of the metropolis's destructive force that engulfs working class immigrants: "Rivers that fish suicidal trouts/ jumping from bridges!"[93] By juxtaposing the images of suicidal immigrants jumping from the Brooklyn Bridge with the remembrance of the water of the Segovia's aqueduct, Vidal y Planas creates poetic tension between the notions of suicide and life, since an aqueduct was the carrier of life-giving water in the ancient Spanish city of Segovia. In 1965, while suffering from terminal cancer, he published *Mi Guayana gala* (My gala Guayana) and *Las hogueras del ocaso* (The bonfires of twilight), collections of love poems to his wife, poems about his own death, and poems about his nostalgic exile. He dedicated his poetry to other poor exiles like himself in the United States.[94]

In these evolving responses to life in exile, race was surprisingly not a focus of discussion nor of representation in the literature in *España Libre*. The exceptions concerned el Día de la Raza or Columbus Day (October 12). Articles criticized Franco's imperialistic desires and the racist aspects of Spanish fascism. The term *raza* (race) was a charged fascist term as it was employed by Francoist publications to exalt traditional Spain. The invocation of the needs of the raza justified taking away individual and civil rights from Spaniards. In *España Libre*, the term was hardly used, and in opposition to symbolically refer to workers, migrants, or antifascists. For Columbus Day, the Quinteros brothers' zarzuela *La patria chica* (Regional/hometown identity) was often performed to depart from any imperialistic perceptions of the celebration of the day.

Another exception was the commentary on the participation of the Army of Africa on the side of Franco. *España Libre* explained that the subjugated, colonial army was used as cannon fodder and claimed that most Moors and Moroccans knew workers were subjugated too. However, Franco's promise of independence was not mentioned, nor was the fact that the Second Republic did not grant independence to Morocco. When Morocco was about to gain its independence in 1956, contributor Alfonso Ayensa denounced Franco, who, while subjugating Spaniards, considered liberating Moroccans. Ayensa added that he was not defending an outdated colonialism because Spanish exiles were against domination of the peoples of the world and were defenders of peoples' freedom and right to self-determination.[95]

The few confrontations with other ethnic groups concerned rather ideological quibbles, like a given periodical or columnist's Francoist or communist leanings, rather than issues of ethnicity or race. Whether it was to avoid making reference to the fascist connotation of the term *raza*, or in order to not depart from the common ground shared with other ethnic groups in the United States, *España Libre* did not significantly refer to race as a category in its antifascist representations.

As depicted in *España Libre*, the relationship with other ethnicities was one of solidarity. *España Libre* reviewed the other ethnic groups' news and scheduled the confederation's events at times that would not interfere with other groups' events. To improve attendance, commemorations and fundraisers and other events were coordinated among the several ethnic groups to avoid overlapping such occasions. This coordination of dates was explained to readers in *España Libre* and they were encouraged to attend the other groups' events. There was also support for mutual causes. For example, responding to calls of action in *Pueblos Hispanos*, Basque Alberto Uriarte, the SHC's executive secretary, wrote to Governor Nelson Rockefeller on behalf of his organization asking for clemency for Puerto Rican Salvador Agrón in 1962.[96]

España Libre was the SHC's public face that stimulated comradeship and community involvement; equally importantly, it forged a distinctive antifascist identity, one that was relatively autonomous from the representation of the Government of the Second Spanish Republic in exile. Over the decades, *España Libre* evolved literary expressions of exiled, peaceful, proletarian antifascism. In postwar rhetoric, *España Libre* portrayed men as antifascist fighters and women as creators of antifascist domesticity. Some *España Libre* writers built on the powerful symbol of Don Quixote to represent a knight fighting for freedom, and others used a maternalist approach to situate women as opponents of fascism. Giménez Igualada, Aldecoa, González Malo, and Sender published books rearticulating the meaning of anarchism and challenged the Francoist manipulation and erasure of workers' history. Countering the fascist discourse, these authors highlighted workers' heterogeneous cultural and political experience in exile and foresaw subjugated people as crucial actors in societies free of fascism. The sometimes rough-around-the-edges and unedited prose of some of their publications show the deprivations they suffered as exiles. González Malo complained in one of his articles that canonical authors such as Ortega y Gasset had the benefit of being carefully edited, unlike *España Libre* authors such as himself.[97]

Although *España Libre* exposed readers to Spanish Civil War rhetoric and traditional gender perspectives, its literary representations also foreshadowed a more peaceful, inclusive, and intersectional world throughout its decades of publication. Specifically, Martí Ibáñez's short stories changed from a revolutionary focus to one centered on the possibilities of exilic introspection. Distinct from warlike oratory, these stories proposed interpersonal engagement. Even when undesired or transitory, characters' interconnection counteracted fascist dehumanization. José Castilla Morales, Antonio García Copado, and Alfonso Vidal y Planas described the exile experience of workers in the United States through biographical documentation and literary representations based on popular cultural symbols. Their work helped *España Libre* readers to reconcile their own transnational experiences as workers but left aside other categories such as gender and race. Artistic representation was the most revolutionary take on fascism because it enlarged members' comprehension of the significance of their resistance. The following chapters examine in detail some of these literary techniques in theater, chronicles, and cartoons, which Spanish antifascist workers employed to write their own history.

7

Theater—*Género Chico* and Antifascism

In one of Aurelio Pego's satirical sketches, published in *España Libre* on October 3, 1952, Francisco Franco berates Colombian president Laureano Gómez for having made a telling comment: "Do you think, fool, that El Cid Campeador was some sort of Muñoz Seca on horseback? Men who have a historical mission to accomplish neither laugh nor allow jokes to be told."[1] This reference to El Cid evokes the myth of imperial Spain, which was at the core of Spanish fascism. Ramiro Ledesma Ramos, one of the main Spanish fascist ideologues and founder of one of the fascist groups, Juntas de Ofensiva Nacional-Sindicalista (JONS), became convinced that Spain needed to affirm its military and Catholic power and annex Latin America.[2] In Pego's sketch, when instructing a Latin American president on how to be seriously commanding, Franco cites El Cid as a symbol of Catholic imperialism. El Cid, a medieval Spanish warrior, was known for his victories on the battlefield against the Moors. In Pego's sketch, Franco affirms that El Cid is a cultural reference to the greatness of Spain; he cannot be compared with Pedro Muñoz Seca, a popular playwright who combined comedy and farce during the Second Republic. Muñoz Seca's humorous skits belonged to a popular stage dating back to Lope de Rueda and Miguel de Cervantes that manifested in the *género chico* (minor or popular genre) during the Second Republic. With the reference to these two historical figures, Pego's satirical chronicle contrasts fascist Spain with a republican and popular one.

Figure 9. Mary Reid and Dr. J. M. Martínez, surrounded by regular SHC performers. Félix Martí Ibáñez is seated next to Reid, front row, fifth from left. Courtesy of José Nieto and Brandeis Special Collections.

The SHC's stage productions built on this tradition of the 1920s and 1930s; they comprised satiric dramatizations, comedies of manners, and light operas.[3] Numerous U.S. Spanish-language periodicals reviewed the plays performed by actors and organizations under the aegis of Sociedades Hispanas in the 1920s and 1930s. These same organizations and actors joined to fight fascism during the Spanish Civil War and helped publish *España Libre*. From thirty plays per year in the 1940s to the fifteen per year in the later decades on average, plays attracted numerous participants and raised thousands of dollars across the United States in the affiliated organizations and with traveling troupes. In particular, plays in New York, Pennsylvania, and Virginia were extremely popular.

Although antifascist play scripts were not published in *España Libre*, performances were advertised and reviewed in *España Libre*, as well as in other Spanish-language periodicals, and provide valuable information about their plots, characters, settings, and costumes. The periodical's intensive coverage and members' participation in performances promoted attendance and thus collection of funds. These semi-professional fundraisers became sophisticated cultural events that included theater, vaudeville shows, dinners, lotteries, and dances. They took place at the social halls of constituent organizations or in nearby rented theaters. This chapter examines popular plays that represented Spanish customs and color. The humor and lyricism of popular genres reinvented the privations of exile into an aesthetic experience of self-representation and political action. The original antifascist plays, in particular those of José Castilla Morales, and the directorial and acting artistry of Mary Reid were essential elements of their theatrical success.

Popular Theater

The vitality of the SHC's theater in the United States mirrored its popularity in the 1920s and 1930s in Spain.[4] At the turn of the twentieth century, popular theater was the chief public entertainment of the working class, with an average of one thousand performances each month in Madrid alone in the 1920s.[5] Works of the género chico (popular, farcical genre) were performed most often. These were noted for their sharp-witted action, skilled dialogues, verbal humor, and working-class characters. The genre dominated the commercial stage with its *sainetes* (one-act plays with or without music that featured workers as characters), operettas and *revistas* (musical comedies dealing with current events and social problems), and *juguetes cómicos* and *astracanes* (farcical and absurd comedies). These functioned as humorous subversive ruptures of the Spanish canonical theater. The género chico was a bridge between the traditional classical genres and the avant-garde of the twentieth century and used humor to highlight the social injustices common people faced. Undoubtedly, the genre, with authors like Carlos Arniches (1866–1943), who humorously deployed puns on the popular usage of Spanish, encapsulated the artistic sensibility of workers with colloquial speech and farcical approaches to reality.[6]

Before the Spanish Civil War, the género chico, the *esperpento* (the grotesque), and the absurd dominated the Spanish stage and constituted parodic and critical responses to the politically convulsive era.[7] The fool, one of the most salient figures of Spanish popular theater, censured the institutional values that have confined common people since the sixteenth century, and still survives on in the Hispanic world.[8] The plays performed at the SHC's fundraisers drew on the same stock characters found in the género chico to fuel resistance to those in power at the time, such as Spanish fascists and western democratic elites indifferent to the fate of Spanish democracy. The fool mimicked and parodied not only fascists but also the inefficiency of ruling elites everywhere.

Popular theater, with its humor and lyricism, also provided members with effective ways to fundraise for the victims of fascism. Musical operettas or zarzuelas, which celebrated regional customs, frequently appeared on stage. This popular Spanish lyric genre alternates spoken word and musical numbers. Zarzuelas had been favored by workers and anarchist associations in Spain and the United States since the turn of the twentieth century.[9] Following this tradition, Castilla Morales wrote two original zarzuelas, *Arrosalina* and *Los Perdigones*, which were popular and very much applauded in 1948 fundraisers. Esteban Roig composed the music.[10]

For members, *sainetes*, another lyrical genre, evoked nostalgia for the optimistic and revolutionary working class of the 1930s. *Sainetes* were humorous musical farces with stereotyped characters and exaggerated situations that represented "the ruined and corrupt aristocracy; the booming, snobbish, petty bourgeoisie desperate to mingle with the aristocracy; and the poor but happy working class, which exuded local color."[11] The SHC often staged the *sainetes*, *entremeses*, and *comedias de costumbres* (comedies of customs) of Serafín Álvarez Quintero (1871–1938) and Joaquín Álvarez Quintero (1873–1944).[12] Other popular authors included Carlos Arniches and Joaquín Dicenta. The common people's expressions, jokes, *tertulias* (chats), and lore were the most important aspect of these plays. In her research on humorous Spanish theater, Rakhel Villamil-Acera contrasts the picturesque *costumbrismo* of the Quintero brothers with the poetic refinement of García Lorca's representation of Andalusia to examine why the Quintero brothers' theater was popular in Madrid at the turn of the twentieth century.[13] Undoubtedly, their theater provided a nostalgic space for urban working classes who had migrated from the countryside, and their light comedy invigorated popular representations of Andalusia.[14] The Quintero brothers' plays were as popular in exile as they had been in workers' associations in pre–Civil War Spain. Their witty humor constructed a liberating take on life and nostalgia for past times felt in exile. The Quinteros' theater portrayed common people in inquisitive and playful enjoyment in contrast to the rigid, pompous, and vacuous myths of fascist power and racial perfection.

The *astracán* of Pedro Muñoz Seca (1879–1936) was another popular genre on the SHC's stage. Like other genres the organization produced, it too had been popular in pre–Civil War Spain.[15] Astracán was a multiform genre that combined *sainete*, comedy, and farce, and distanced theatrical performance from realism.[16] The parodic and comedic nature of the genre suited the exile audience ready for liberating deconstructions of the weightiness of canonical dramas. Muñoz Seca's play *Un drama de Calderón* (1919), with the collaboration of Pedro Pérez Fernández, was performed on March 1940 at the New York's Centro Español, and on November 1942 at the city's Palm Garden.[17] The play, which is simultaneously a tribute to and a parody of Pedro Calderón de la Barca's baroque honor dramas, exemplifies the astracán genre that informed the SHC's stage.[18] With exaggerated characters, the complicated plot develops through a series of entertaining misunderstandings. Mary, a modern American woman from Washington, D.C., likes to read detective novels and dreams of passionate escapades with her Spanish husband, Jorge Manrique, who prefers a tranquil existence. Mary flirts with every man she sees, while her husband pretends to be oblivious. Through a series of mix-ups, when her husband comes home, two of her current admirers hide underneath the bed. One of them convinces the other that they would be better off pretending they were actually in the house to commit theft, thus distracting the husband and allowing their escape.[19] Although Mary agrees to their plot, because she wants to bring passion to her marriage by making her husband jealous, she nonetheless tells her husband that two men were pursuing her. However, her husband, who has overheard all the conversations, is unconcerned, and pretends to be asleep to avoid having to deal with all the commotion.

The hilarious plot gives a critical perspective to gender and national stereotypes, employing comic relief to lessen the tensions between the audience's national and exile identities. Whereas in Calderón de la Barca's canonical plays, men are characteristically jealous and justify their crimes of passion, Muñoz Seca's *Un drama de Calderón* subverts the archetype of the macho Spanish husband with a character that cannot care less about his wife's flirting with other men.[20] While Calderón de la Barca's characters adhere to conventional understandings of religion and honor, Muñoz Seca's characters transform such orthodox dogma by inventing new plots inside the author's plot. *Un drama de Calderón* proves that life can be as illogical and absurd as an astracán and invites the public to explore and enjoy life's absurdities.[21]

Popular genres such as the astracán did more than cultivate Spanish popular culture and raise funds against fascism; they nurtured an absurd, even surrealist interpretation of life, transforming canonical expectations for popular tastes. The play had the unconscious appeal of subverting a tradition that, in exile, was deceptive and illusory. On stage, the astracán genre rejected the desiccated cultural rigidity enforced in fascist Spain while it also criticized American women's independence and "loose morals." The astracan's absurdity created a means of escaping the political and personal hardships of exile for antifascist workers.

Original Antifascist Plays

The SHC also performed original antifascist plays written by its members.[22] José Castilla Morales's (1893—1961) playwriting developed within Hispanic and anarchist circles of New York. When he arrived in New York in the 1920s,

Hispanic popular theater was at its height in the city. Plays were performed weekly in workers' and migrants' diverse political, social, and cultural associations.[23] Castilla Morales became an active member of the Centro Instructivo y Recreativo (Cultural and Recreational Center), a cultural association in Brooklyn that served as a meeting place for Spanish, Italian, and American anarchists and labor activists. It hosted the newsroom of anarchist periodical *Solidaridad* and a bookstore, The Road to Freedom. In the center, Castilla Morales met Ignacio Zugadi Garmendia, who was a painter and an actor for the Roca-Mondragón theatrical company.

Castilla Morales and Zugadi Garmendia associated themselves with the Ateneo Hispano (Hispanic Athenaeum) to distance themselves from the continuous fights between the staff writers of the anarchist periodicals *Cultura Obrera* and *Cultura Proletaria*.[24] On Saturdays at the Ateneo Hispano, amateur actors performed a drama, a comedy, and a zarzuela. Summer meetings were celebrated at Annandale Naturist Hispanic Society, where picnics, excursions, and dances strengthened bonds between members. To financially support the launch in 1934 of the Ateneo's periodical *Ateneo*, Castilla Morales wrote an original play, *La aparición de Ateneo* (The Athenaeum's appearance).[25] Performed on February 17, 1934, the play included two acts and six *cuadros* (skits).[26] Jiménez Colón composed the music for the play. In October 1934, the Ateneo Hispano organized a series of events to protest the Second Republic's repression of the miners' strike in Asturias. For one event, Castilla Morales wrote an *apropósito* (topical one-act play), *La verdad de los presos* (The prisoners' truth), which was a success on the Ateneo stage.[27] Ateneo's actors would eventually also perform for SHC plays.[28]

The SHC's theater continued the anarchist tradition of using drama as a means for disseminating anarchist perspectives and organizing mutual aid. As was customary in other anarchist exile communities in France and Latin America, antifascist productions were more than fundraisers; they functioned as spaces of activism and community support in the dissociative experience of exile in the United States.[29] Castilla Morales's antifascist plays continued this legacy of didactic and political playwriting that fulfilled multiple roles: it provided a meeting place for workers, satisfying their social needs, and functioned as a catalyst for political consciousness. Rather than a commodity for cultural consumption, Castilla Morales's plays were participatory political protests that deconstructed Spanish fascism and its consequences for the antifascist audience.

The announcements and reviews in *España Libre* provide significant insights into the most commonly recurring characteristics of Castilla Morales's antifascist plays.[30] They were composed of a few *actos* (skits) or theatrical vignettes, usually set in the United States. Workers were protagonists who enlisted in pro-Republic forces during the Spanish Civil War, sang revolutionary songs, and were concerned about fellow Spaniards under Franco's rule. Castilla Morales created stock characters who stirred workers to become politically active. Undoubtedly, his anarchist aesthetics intersected with Spanish-language folk theater in the United States, which to this day holds a long tradition of dramatizing exploitation and Americanization. In this respect, Castilla Morales's theater shared the social goals of Chicano Luis Valdes's El Teatro Campesino as well as Federico García Lorca's Teatro Universitario La Barraca in Spain. Castilla Morales's plays dignified the exiled workers' fight against fascism by making them protagonists.[31] The inclusion of a humorous take on American characters made the plots funny and allowed the audience to release the anxiety of exile by mocking the host country.

Castilla Morales's *La madre española*, staged for the first time in March 1941 in the Palm Garden, New York, had two acts and twelve skits. One of these acts, "¡Ay, Carmela!" staged the tragedy of two married Spanish refugees in the United States.[32] Their farcical tribulations surely provoked self-conscious laughter among the audience. Another act, "Vecinas, vecinas aquí está el cartero" (Neighbors, neighbors, the postman is here), is about an American postman reading letters to illiterate refugees in Galician and Italian, their languages of origin. The expressive scene depicts their migrant life as antifascist refugees in the United States. To add humor, the postman mispronounces these languages. Humor enhances the many facets of the scene: the vulnerability of the illiterate, the vitality of the working class, and the possibilities of cross-ethnic solidarity. Comedy restores community in exile. The political efficacy of Castilla Morales's flippant humor is based on its capacity to appropriate power: the parody does not focus on the suffering of the victims of fascism but on the possibilities of solidarity in the United States. Both acts, ¡Ay, Carmela! and "Vecinas, vecinas aquí está el cartero," built on Ramón del Valle-Inclán's *esperpento*, a theatrical technique that radically distorts tragedy until it becomes humorous. The technique helped Castilla overturn melodramatic representations of antifascist refugees and transformed antifascist exile into an empowering farce.

Castilla Morales's most celebrated play, *La República no ha muerto* (The Republic is not dead), first staged in April 1941, exemplifies his stock characters. For the occasion, Castilla Morales acted as master of ceremonies, Esteban Roig composed the music for the play, and Catalan artist Miguel Mingot designed the set. The *acto* (skit) "Spanish Colony" is set in a landing field in New York where Uncle Sam is confronted by several regional stereotypes of Spain, who accuse him of not aiding pro-Republic forces, and force him to fly above Spain to witness Franco's atrocities. The heroic but also farcical deed of folkloric workers confronting Uncle Sam and making him fantastically fly across the stage revealed both the actuality and the potentiality of the historical moment. Jesse Cohn, examining anarchist literature, claims that it tests the limit of symbolic representation because it includes both what reality is and what it should be, discovering the ideal within the real.[33] Castilla Morales's audience affectively identified with the historical reality while enjoying ludic engagement with the unreal proposition that allowed them to laugh at Uncle Sam, who was unmasked as morally inferior.[34] The histrionic flying stage trick served as comic self-empowerment under the constraints of exile. In other words, humor resisted realistic representation and proposed a ludic enjoyment of the unreal.

Other members also wrote antifascist plays. Like Castilla Morales, they wrote humorous popular genres, often juguetes cómicos, which were brief, fast-paced acts that mixed music and drama. Numerous comedic misunderstandings provoked and entertained the audience.[35] Manuel Sugrañés, a successful producer in Barcelona, helped by the SHC to migrate to New York, was another active member.[36] The Falangists executed his wife, one of his sons died in Barcelona, and the other died in a camp in France.[37] He wrote *Paco, Benito y Adolfo: ¿Cuál de los tres es más golfo?* (Franco, Benito, and Adolf: Who is the biggest scoundrel?) in 1941. The three-skit parody adapted José Zorrilla's classic play Don Juan Tenorio to mock fascists.[38] That same year, Sugrañés's *El paraíso fascista* (The fascist paradise) mocked fascism by dramatizing the escape from Madrid of three comedians by dressing up as a priest, an Italian, and an American dancer. The stock characters clearly incriminated the Church, Benito Mussolini, and the United States for their sympathy for Franco. In addition, Luis Garagarza, secretary of the Grupo Vasco in New York, wrote three antifascist plays, *El fascismo en Vizcaya* (1937), *Cosas que pasan* (1942), and *Andanzas de un curita* (1943). Recovering the traces left behind by the active members of the theater unveils not only the silenced history of political persecution that these refugees endured but also their response to it. The writing and performing of the plays (not only on their opening dates but throughout the years) kicked their antifascism into social art that denounced the injustices they had suffered and alerted the world about fascist Spain.

Marita Reijal, Marita Ríos, or Mary Reid (1895, Gibraltar, Spain–1980s, place unknown) was crucial in the success of the SHC's stage. Nicolás Kanellos claims that Reid was "responsible for the survival of Spanish-language drama in New York during the Depression and World War II."[39] Reid, whose father was English and mother Spanish, made her New York stage debut with the Compañía de Teatro Español (Spanish Theater Company). She also toured with Fortunio Bonanova's Lyric Theater Company in 1921. Discussing the popular Hispanic stage in New York, Janet L. Sturman highlights Reid's stardom in the 1920s and 1930s: "Many impresarios organized their productions less around repertoire than around a celebrity with box-office attraction. One regularly appearing headliner, Marita Reid, served as both stage star, director, and playwright for over three decades."[40] At the time, directors, actors, and impresarios from Spain were well regarded in the Hispanic theater.[41] In the 1950s and 1960s, Reid performed in some English-language plays on Broadway and television. She also had a part in the movie *Crowded Paradise*, produced in Puerto Rico.[42] Reid mentored other Latina performers such as Tina Ramirez, director of Ballet Hispánico.

Reid played in professional circuits and mutual aid societies of Spaniards, Cubans, and Puerto Ricans.[43] She performed in a variety of genres, ranging from drama to zarzuela. Reid was one of the founders of Centro Andaluz and became one of the most important actresses in the Ateneo Hispano. Before the Spanish Civil War, she formed her own company, Compañía Marita Reid, which was featured in the reviews of the New York periodical *La Prensa* about the popular plays in the city's Centro Andaluz, Unión Benéfica Española, and Centro Social Venezolano. In 1936, Reid became a member of the Committee de Fiestas (Fundraisers Committee) of the SHC. In the next two decades she performed, directed plays, and acted as master of ceremonies in hundreds of antifascist fundraisers.

Reid, a star of Spanish drama in New York, revived the género chico in the United States while it declined in Spain due to the Francoist censorship. Her dedication to theater and to antifascism created a culture of participation in solidarity with the victims of fascism. She staged numerous Spanish popular plays that celebrated working-class identity, directed original farcical plays that denounced fascism, and raised funds for those suffering in Franco's Spain. Many of the plays she directed featured strong women. In this respect, Reid followed the steps of the first woman film director in Spain, Rosario Pi (1899–1967), who introduced an independent woman in the folkloristic zarzuela film *El gato montés* (1935) that already "encompasses a certain degree of self-consciousness and modernity in the way in which it relates to traditional motives and clichés."[44] For her commitment, Reid was called the dame of the Spanish theater. Most telling, she was a powerful proletarian champion against Spanish fascism.

At one event in Casa Galicia in 1957, Reid thanked the SHC for promoting popular Spanish theater because in exile, "many Spaniards, who left their land very young, learned to know and love the Spain they left behind. And they learned it through the comedies, dramas and *sainetes*, written by us, and represented in this society."[45] For her continuous commitment to antifascism, Reid was awarded the Medal of Dama de la Orden de la Liberación in 1957 by the Government of the Second Spanish Republic in exile.[46] Aurelio Pego demanded a big "Olé" (Bravo) for the "primera reina republicana" (first Republican queen) in one of his columns published in *España Libre* in 1958.[47] In an earlier chronicle, Pego claimed that: "To talk about Spanish theater in New York is to talk about Mary Reid."[48] The columnist concluded: "Franco has in Mary Reid a formidable enemy."[49] Reid was a loyal donor to the SHC until it dissolved in 1977. Unfortunately, her antifascist contributions have not yet gained the broad recognition that other Spanish actresses in exile have achieved, such as Maria Casares in France and Margarita Xirgu in Latin America.

Like Reid, other members contributed to the organization of theatrical productions, raising funds while at the same time advancing their artistic careers. The 1930s reviews on Consuelo Moreno noted her inexperience on stage but she

Figure 10. Unidentified SHC play. Reid in the center is wearing a long-sleeve white blouse. Courtesy of José Nieto Ruiz and Brandeis Special Collections.

became popular in New York's professional Hispanic theaters after performing in theatrical fundraisers.[50] In the 1940s and 1950s, she became a local celebrity of the vibrant Hispanic Broadway scene. She even moved to Hollywood for a short time in 1944.[51] Similarly, Carmen López opened a dance studio in New York after her dancing performances in fundraisers.[52]

The numerous reviews and articles published in *España Libre* and other Spanish-language periodicals disclose the hybrid nature of the performances in the SHC's productions—which mixed grotesque and satirical sketches with transnational references, parodied canonical drama, evoked the nostalgia of popular plays and dances, and blurred the distinctions between popular and high musicals in operettas and zarzuelas—and redefined multiple popular dramatic responses to fascism in exile. In operatic terms, members did not perform with the affected heaviness of a Wagnerian tenor. Instead, members adapted and performed género chico plays and sang zarzuelas with lighthearted agility. Such vocal flexibility embodies the Spanish workers' antifascist culture, which flourished in the United States. The absurd created a liberating artistic universe for members. Superlatively, Muñoz Seca's *Un drama de Calderón* parodied the Spanish canon with absurd plots for the delight of the politicized audience, who surely appreciated the dialectical tension of an astracán: a surrealist displacement from Spanish canonical tradition that was both ratified and redefined in exile. In *La República no ha muerto*, absurdity challenges antifascist representation. It cannot be contested because it is clearly artificial. Humor transformed the tragedy of exile into empowering farcical action.

Theater was extremely successful in community building and fundraising from the founding of the SHC. Reviews in *España Libre* show the hands-on activism of SHC members. With clever and subversive humor, plays raised funds for the Spanish victims of fascism, and became a tool to increase solidarity of exiled Spanish workers. Fundraising performances engaged with Spanish theatrical tradition through their renewal and adaptation to exile. Género chico plays were peopled with American and immigrant characters, which allowed the audience to reflect on its antifascist fight and its emerging ethnic identity in the United States. Ridiculing an Uncle Sam, who was indifferent to fascism in Spain, and mocking the liberated American Mary, who stereotyped the sexuality of Spanish men, brought humorous transgressions to the stage. The formal characteristics of Castilla Morales's plays grew from a long tradition of anarchist farce, which subverted power while it instructed workers on the political issues of the day. The SHC's theater intersected not only with anarchist legacies but also with a well-established popular and Hispanic theatrical scene in New

York. In fact, theatrical fundraising was successful because it built upon such a vibrant Latino theatrical culture.

Marked by parodic self-representation, the popular dramaturgical genres and anarchist aesthetics did not contest fascist rhetoric of power and mythic perfection with antifascist myths. Instead, antifascist theater ridiculed fascist narratives with comedy and farce. Humor was the most important literary technique of the SHC's antifascism. It avoided re-creating another dogmatic movement that reproduced fascistic worldviews like those they were fighting. Humor kept antifascism full of life and open to possibilities. The SHC's antifascism was not nihilistic but vigorous; it was not nostalgic about a radical past but was instead able to laugh at itself. The periodical's very name claimed playful antifascist strategies of resistance under Franco's Spain. When forced to repeat the Spanish fascist motto "Spain: One, Great, and Free," antifascists shout only two words: "Spain: Free" and transformed the fascist motto of a glorious imperial Spain into a free Spain. The following chapters show other humorous approaches to resistance.

8

Aurelio Pego, Antifascist Satirical Chronicler

Satirists were central contributors to print protest in *España Libre*. Their writings transformed the antifascist experience into a full narrative voice.[1] Unlike Italian Fascism and German Nazism, Spanish fascism survived the Second World War and continued until the death of Franco. *España Libre*'s contributors such as Aurelio Pego fought such fascistization of Spain. Specifically, his provocative chronicles fueled members' antifascist sentiment by boldly mocking the mythical representation of the Caudillo. The satirist also ridiculed the myth of imperial Spain and viciously parodied Spanish National Catholicism. In later years, Pego's more spirited chronicles lampooned Americans and Spanish exiles for their inability to end Franco's rule. While Spanish fascists romanticized violence and death as cleansing agents that would wash away a corrupt democracy and bring about a national rebirth, Pego's caustic humor revealed the actual effects of fascist power and political repression.[2]

The Chronicle as a Genre

Since Miguel de Cervantes, the Spanish literary genre *crónica* has vividly described places, historical events, and local social customs. In the nineteenth century, José Mariano de Larra initiated modern Spanish journalism with his innovative use of satire in his chronicles.[3] With a brisk narrative rhythm and sharp humor, Larra engaged his readers and transformed the *costumbrista* tradition (crónicas of social customs that instructed the newspaper's readership in etiquette) into an artistic and aesthetic instrument of political and social protest.[4] Humor put critical distance between reality and the satirist's humorous take on it. In the United States, Spanish-language chronicles have been "rife with local color and inspired by oral lore of the immigrants."[5] Pego masterfully employed the techniques of the crónica toward his goal by re-creating popular expressions, proverbs, colloquial language, dialogues, linguistic puns, and scenes in *tertulias de café* (café gatherings). Also, Pego created alter egos of himself. The satirist shared with *España Libre* readers his militant antifascism and made them laugh with his double meanings mocking the pillars of Spanish fascism. In contrast with the often-lively humor of Latino cronistas, Aurelio Pego derided fascism with caustic undertones. As a counternarrative of the nonviolent protest of *España Libre*, Pego wrote bold sketches asking for the assassination of Franco.

Aurelio Pego

As a prolific author and a staunch anti-Francoist, Pego joined the staff of *España Libre* in 1940. His antifascist satirical columns ran in every edition until the paper closed in 1977. In fact, Pego's employer once told a FBI agent that Pego would fall asleep at his desk because he spent so much time writing anti-Francoist literature.[6] The writer's exhaustion was not surprising because he published hundreds of satirical skits in *España Libre* and other Spanish Civil War exile periodicals, besides writing commissioned opinion columns for numerous newspapers in the Hispanic world, including the United States. Pego knew he was being watched by the FBI and shared his apprehensions with General Secretary Manuel Dorado. However, Pego argued that there was no reason to be scared or less willing to organize, attend fundraisers and commemorations, or write for *España Libre*: "I've said it over and over that the FBI knows the SHC perfectly and I know I've been investigated and approved by the FBI."[7] Under the FBI's suspicious watch, Pego constructed rhetorical bombs that lambasted Spanish fascism, American diplomatic relations with Franco, and the Western democracies' indifference toward liberating Spain. We must examine fascist Spain before we explore Pego's humor.

Fascist Spain

Although international monetary organizations imposed economic liberalization in the late 1950s and made of Spain a collaborator in the war against communism, the essential elements of Spanish fascism never disappeared and political repression never decreased, particularly against workers' organizations. In fact, the regime institutionalized fascist political culture through the Movimiento Nacional, influential until the death of Francisco Franco. Recent scholarship considers core fascist characteristics as the basic components of Francoist Spain.[8] Franco's Spain showed three clusters of characteristics that define a fascist state. First, Franco's Movimiento Nacional focused on social cleansing, creating a national feeling of state of emergency, and vertical obedience. Second, Franco's display of force and power generated a culture of war and a cult of the Movimiento's heroes. Third, violence, terror, and a state of emergency became effective mechanisms for the nazification of the state.[9] According to Ángel Viñas: "The simultaneous and permanent combination of these features has never been found in any other political system in the Western world that was not also fascist."[10]

After the war, Franco continued his project of the social cleansing of dissenters. From 1939 to 1952, between 20,000 and 50,000 citizens were executed in a deliberate and continuous elimination campaign. At one point in 1941 the jails held 280,000 political inmates, while hundreds of thousands suffered legal and extralegal persecution.[11] However, the irregular forms of execution during the dictatorship make it difficult to arrive at a definitive figure.[12] As a full-fledged exemplar of fascism, Franco's social cleansing mechanisms involved incarceration, forced labor in concentration camps, extrajudicial execution, and subsequent disposal in mass burial sites.[13] Until the end of the dictatorship, violence and death were deemed necessary for the renewal of the nation.[14]

Wanting to emulate other fascist regimes, Franco "massively intervened in the economy, regulating both trade and the supply system. He also manipulated markets, imposed import substitution, and forced industrialization."[15] Franco sought economic independence through self-sufficiency, which was unachievable in rational economic terms, but it propped up his nationalist goals. This approach was inspired by the Nazis' militarized economic discipline.[16] The result was poverty and starvation, which caused great suffering and limited the population's resistance to terror.[17] Franco not only physically closed borders, but also censored communications, mass media, and public events, which greatly limited Spaniards' access to information. Delegates from the government attended all social and cultural events, assessing and controlling what was done and said in these gatherings. The Spanish population felt constantly watched.

Spanish fascists believed in the unity, uniqueness, and perfection of the Spanish nation.[18] The ubiquitous Francoist slogan, "España: Una, Grande y Libre" (Spain: One, Great, and Free), summarized the myth of militarized, Catholic, and grand *españolidad*, free of subversives. The regime's propaganda represented

Franco as the charismatic, bold leader who saved Spain from the leftist radicalism.[19] Franco was the ultimate source of law and constantly presented to the population as the leader chosen by God for the renewed grandeur and glory of Spain.[20] Franco's image as a military commander, "El Generalissimo," permeated Spanish public spaces with grandiose monuments. The fascist salute, an imitation of the Nazi salute, was required on numerous public occasions, even when simply going to watch a film in a cinema. The regime's ubiquitous propaganda, termed NODO (Noticiario y Documentales/News and Documentaries), infused cinemas and television. It lauded Franco and the fascist Movimiento.

These techniques of repression and the use of state bureaucratic channels by traditional patronage networks subdued the Spanish population into obedience. Rather than being channeled by the Falange, fascist influence was a component of the state itself.[21] While Nazi Sondergerichte (Special Tribunals) were created in Germany in public (a law was put into place on March 21, 1933, for example), in Spain, the state terror was institutionalized in secret. As Viñas notes: "Much of this legislation was in breach even of the 'legal' standards set by Franco. Ministerial decisions arbitrarily modified the sentences passed on prisoners convicted by the military courts."[22] Right up to the end of the regime in the 1970s, multiple declarations of a state of war were used to exert unlimited control over the population.[23] Paul Preston has termed the speed and scale of social and economic repression "the politics of revenge."[24] Passive acceptance became the norm among Spaniards, who were just trying to survive.[25] Finally in the 1960s and 1970s, younger technocrats eventually ended the economic chaos of the previous two decades and Spain experienced an economic boom.[26]

Pego Mocks Franco

Pego humorously attacked Franco and Franco's Spain on many levels. He mocked the adjectives "idyllic and paternal" employed by José María Pemán, a Spanish journalist, to praise Franco's regime. Pego claimed that, when reading the piece, he "went back to reading the last adjective . . . criminal. But no, it's paternal."[27] By rereading Pemán's last adjective (paternal) and offering an alternative (criminal), Pego entertained the thought that Pemán must have accidentally used the wrong adjective, since one could only describe the regime by the adjective "criminal."

Responding to a propagandistic photograph of Franco catching a tuna weighing 710 pounds, Pego referred to him in another *España Libre* crónica as "the matador." Matador is a synonym for *torero* (bullfighter), the prototypical representation of masculine bravado, an image promoted by Spanish fascism. However, Pego referred to the literal meaning of the word, "killer," to be more accurate: "He killed in Morocco, killed in Spain, kills now in the sea and has killed Spaniards for twenty years. An impressive record... his passion for murder will live on throughout time as: Francisco Franco, the Great Matador of Spain."[28] By wittily paralleling fishing to bullfighting, Pego exposed the propaganda representation of Franco as master fisherman. Instead, his crónica in *España Libre* claimed that Franco should better be memorialized as a vicious murderer.[29]

In his satirical chronicle, "Sí señor, un ejemplo" (Yes sir, an example), Pego ridiculed a speech by Franco in which the dictator claimed that Spain was an example to the world of a model state. Pego agreed with Franco, but perhaps for somewhat different reasons: the Spanish state, Pego wrote, was an example of cruelty, sadism, barbarism, repugnance, hatred, and mistrust, a perverse model, a malevolent example of a state.[30] In "El valiente generalísimo tiene miedo" (The brave Generalissimo is fearful), the *España Libre* satirist scornfully wondered why the Caudillo feels he needed bodyguards: "If he is convinced, as he seems to be from his speeches, that he has done so much good for Spain and its people, why is he afraid to fraternize with them, the very people who owe him so much, so far as he is concerned?"[31]

Pego's satiric attack against the Caudillo became even more venomous when exposing the regime's civil rights infringements. According to Ferran Gallego, Franco's Spain "was one of the most prominent examples of fascism: capable of exerting violence against its own population" with a war of extermination against "subversive citizens."[32] In *España Libre*, Pego again turned Spanish fascism on its head: instead of Franco killing people, the people ought to murder Franco. In "Querido odiado" (Dear hated one), the author questioned the depth of the people's hatred of Franco: "It is a trivial and useless hatred, hatred as harmless as a water gun."[33] In "Cómo se puede hacer caer a Franco" (How to make Franco fall), Pego played with the symbolic or literal meaning of the verb *caer* (fall) and asks for someone to "finish off" the dictator. Such a person "must have certain essential qualities: real guts and a sincere contempt for life itself."[34]

Disappointed that Spaniards were taking too long to overthrow the Caudillo, Pego thought that one option was to militarize the many rats of Madrid.[35] The substitution of combative rats for Spaniards emphasized the meaning of rat as an insult—to be a traitor—and was directed at both the dictator and at the passivity of many Spaniards. In "¿A qué esperar más?" (What are we waiting for?), Pego again shamed Spaniards for not having murdered Franco, and reminded them: "This general does not hesitate to resort to violence, and he provoked a dreadful civil war ... thus, what goes around comes around."[36] Pego encouraged Spaniards in another crónica "anímense" (Give it a shot!).[37] Poking fun at the dictator and asking *España Libre* readers to assassinate him deflated the propagandistic representations of Franco as the mythic and indestructible savior of Spain.[38]

Franco was just as enamored of gaudy military parades as were the other fascist leaders. However, in Spain's case, Franco celebrated his victory over his own population in a civil war for the forty years of the regime. The constant displays of victory during his regime extended to the names of streets, plazas, schools, hospitals, and monuments to remind Spaniards of the Movimiento leaders.[39] At the same time, however, the bodies of those who fought for the Republic were buried in mass graves or otherwise disappeared. Even today their families are still looking for their unidentified bodies. Pego was compelled to point out that Franco's state terrorized the Spanish people with little pageantry. After yet another of the innumerable military parades celebrating the victory of the fascists, Pego asked: "Whose victory?" (La victoria ... ¿de quién?)."[40] The only thing that Franco had to declare victory over was the freedom of the Spanish people: "General Franco's Spain is the only nation that annually celebrates the murder of thousands and thousands of fellow citizens in a civil war ... the victory of revenge, the victory of rancor, the victory of impiety, the victory of avaricious militarism."[41] The satirist regarded the soldiers and their awe-inspiring weaponry, ostentatiously marching past the onlookers, as a visible manifestation of Franco's central message: "Watch out, Spaniards, if you rise against me, I will crush you like cockroaches."[42] His brazen statements exposed the fascist terror that frightened Spaniards into submission.

Pego Mocks the Francoist Economy

As a typical fascist state, Franco's Spain adopted state capitalism. The results were disastrous: during the post–Civil War famine, from 1939 to 1945, approximately 200,000 Spaniards died of hunger.[43] Although there was enough food to feed the population, much of it was diverted to the black market, leaving little to be rationed out to ordinary citizens. Antonio Cazorla Sánchez attributes this disaster to the "corruption, racial and class prejudice, and economic ignorance" that characterized the regime.[44] For decades, Aurelio Pego harped on the hunger and poverty characteristic of Franco's Spain. In "Contigo hasta sin pan ni cebolla" (With you, even without bread and onions), Pego mocked a speech by the Spanish foreign minister reciting the regime's platitudes. The minister, Martín Artajo, assured his audience that he had been faithful "to the dictates of race . . . feared God, revered the nation, served justice, and loved the Spanish people."[45] To deconstruct Artajo's formulaic string of vapid fascist platitudes, Pego played with the meaning of the Spanish proverb, "contigo con pan y cebolla" (with you, bread and onions are enough), making it a negative in the title for his chronicle. The Spanish saying is used to express the idea that love is stronger than material needs; thus, love allows us to endure a hard life, even one in which we would have only bread and onions. Because of the rampant poverty under Franco's rule, Pego applied irony to assume that Artajo had referred to the love described in the popular saying. Instead of meaning: "your love makes a life of poverty bearable," Pego turned the saying on its head: "Franco's love brings only unbearable poverty." In other words, using sarcastic logic, the extreme poverty must measure the purity of the dictator's love for his people: "And because of this pure love the Spanish people are all skin and bones."[46] Building on the proverb, the satiric representation challenged the minister's assertion of the regime's "love for the people" and opened a new, paradoxical meaning for love: poverty for the people.[47]

Pego Mocks National Catholicism

A series of Pego's chronicles mocked the Spanish fascists' fanatical belief in the uniqueness of Catholic Spain, otherwise known as "National Catholicism." This theological innovation was a pillar of the Francoist regime. According to National Catholicism, Franco was Caudillo by the grace of God. In his chronicle, "Misa cantada y champaña" (Canticle mass and champagne), the author described a Mass attended by pro-Franco residents in Puerto Rico. The service was to commemorate July 18, the date Franco's military revolt began. Pego imagined the congregation thanking God for permitting the "ecclesiastics and Falangists coming to power," and staining Spain with the blood of the people. Pego thought that the soul of the congregants would be better served by asking God's forgiveness for what Franco had done to Spain.[48] Parodying the sacrament of Catholic confession, the satirist made evident the "unholy" alliance between the Church and a murderous state. Fascists' sins were so grave that not even God himself could pardon them. Evoking the deity in another crónica, Pego responded to one of Franco's speeches in which the dictator claimed that Spaniards now lived a better life. Perhaps so, sneered Pego but "they also die better, they die in massive numbers." Returning to the religious imagery so beloved by the regime, Pego assured Franco that "God will reward you. God or Satan."[49]

In his chronicle "Curas motorizados" (Motorized priests), Pego mocked Franco's obsequious clergy by suggesting they be provided with Italian Vespas, "for... if revolutionary agitation arose again in Spain, all those motorized priests could make great recruits for the army. They could form a new Panther division, and each scooter could be equipped with automatic machine guns.... Perhaps the rattle of the Priest's machine guns would be sacredly transubstantiated from 'tac-tac-tac-tac' to 'to-hell-with-you-may-God-for-gi-ve-you-Vi-va-Fran-co.'"[50] Pego portrayed a powerfully grotesque image of pro-Franco priests fighting for the Caudillo and condemning to hell all of those who fought for liberty.

In "¿Veinte años más? ¡Qué optimista!" (Twenty more years? What an optimist!), Pego referred to another of the Franco's recurrent themes: that Spain's future was inevitably bright, since he had returned the country to the Catholic fold, under his benign protection.[51] Pego played with the Spanish word *fe* that means both "faith" and "confidence." He imagined how Spaniards must have acted, upon hearing these words: "People began to search their pockets and every corner at home of their houses to try to find the elusive confidence that the dictator had purportedly returned to them. It was nowhere to be found."[52] The comic pun visualized the image of Spanish people looking for confidence instead of religious faith. In other words, the linguistic pun reversed the religious scene and encouraged Spaniards, once more, to look for the strength to kill Franco instead of searching for spiritual guidance.

Pego Mocks Americans

After the fall of the Axis powers, the Caudillo transformed his fascination with Adolf Hitler and Benito Mussolini into the commodification of Spain with affordable tourist packages, commercial filmmaking, and a workforce eager to work at any wage rate. Franco's reputation as a fanatical anticommunist now endeared him to the Americans, who acquired the right (at a suitable annual rent) to establish military bases in the country.[53] Pego unmasked Franco's commercial maneuverings in his chronicle "Los garantizadores del porvenir" (The guarantors of the future). The crónica imagined at length a Falange meeting in Madrid. The text ends with a final twist: "And the shameful United States, its hypocrisy now revealed to the whole word, have chained their democracy to an unequivocally fascist country, which they prop up with their precious dollars."[54] The object of the political attack was not merely the Falangist movement in Spain but the commercial relations of the United States with Spain. Readers, observing from their comfortable position in the United States Pego's rendering of a fascist meeting in Spain, were briskly awoken to the fact that, as taxpayers, they were supporting fascism.

Indignation and righteousness marked Pego's satiric crónicas that shamed pro-Franco Americans. In "Don Patricio y su cabeza" (Mr. Patrick's head), he scornfully poked fun at Nevada senator Patrick Anthony McCarran, who defended Franco as a bulwark against communism. With his tax money propping up the Spanish economy in return for the privilege of renting military bases in Spain, Pego felt even more entitled to confront the dictator: "Look, little Caudillo, don't tell me your usual lies. My tax money is providing you with the opportunity to tyrannize the Spanish people. And if I have to pay up, I have the right to bawl about it now and then. Harassing you is the only pleasure I can get from the taxes I pay to keep you afloat."[55] Pego continued to mock American commercial relations with Franco's Spain in "¿Tuberculos propagandistas?" (Propagandist tubers?). In April 1952, Spanish potatoes exported to the United States were checked by the Agriculture Department for the potato-root eelworm upon arrival. Pego recommended the inspectors to skip such arduous job, since "we all know the current state of moral and economic putrefaction in Spain; everything is rotten to the core."[56]

In these chronicles, Pego's expressed his perplexity over the United States' political and commercial support of the regime. In "Dos caras que resultan caras" (Double dealings that turn out to be expensive), Pego reprimanded the United States for its immorality in having friendly diplomatic relations with Franco. When the United States invited the Spanish secretary of foreign affairs to visit Washington, Pego protested, "Isn't the United States supposed to be the Defenders of the Free World? Well, start proving it by helping free people from totalitarian subjugation, instead of becoming a cozy ally of their repressive dictator; besides being hideous, it's indecent."[57] With the expressive title of "El cornúpeto de Washington" (The cuckold of Washington), Pego caustically criticized the U.S. government's incapacity to acknowledge the conditions under which Spaniards were living:

> To State Department and Pentagon officials, Spain apparently seems to be like some kind of "ghost town," like those little deserted towns in Arizona or Oregon were once booming mining metropolises ... and today they are dead cities, without inhabitants. ... What I mean is this: U.S. officials have no doubt seen Spaniards in Spain, but seem oblivious to the fact that they are, in fact, flesh and blood people—or, should I say, bony people with a bit of flesh on them—and not just ghosts, phantoms, or corporeal spirits.[58]

With the reference to skinny ghosts, Pego ridiculed the U.S. government, which was focused on the benefits of picking up another anticommunist ally and unable to empathize with the suffering of the Spanish people. His multilayered irony was quickly understood by antifascist readers to whom the phantasmagoric description painfully reminded them of their hungry or murdered relatives and friends.

With the presence of the United States Naval Forces in the Mediterranean and finally with the establishment of American military bases in Spain in 1953, Pego imagined extravagantly funny situations in several crónicas.[59] He considered that the Caudillo would wind up being annoyed at the presence of hardworking and smiling American soldiers in Spain, those "hundreds of young and smiling Americans who will build roads, tracks, ramps and docks."[60] For they would, no doubt, laugh at Spain's backwardness under Franco, "[they] will invade the bars of nearby cities and laugh their heads off at medieval life around them, which they believed only existed in movies."[61] Tourism brought Americans to Spain; however, Pego predicted many complications arising from their visits: Spaniards were going so hungry that they might even cook and eat the fat American tourists.[62]

Pego did not limit sarcasm to the actions of his adopted homeland: he criticized international institutions for their indifference to the brutality of the regime. The *España Libre* chronicler scoffed at UNESCO (United Nations Educational, Scientific, and Cultural Organization) for admitting Spain as a member in 1952. Pego played with the spelling of UNESCO, which is similar to the Spanish word for despicable (*asco*): "Many, when they read UNESCO, believe it was a printing error of the words UN ASCO [despicable one]."[63]

Pego Mocks Exiles

Pego even mocked his own readers for their response toward conditions in Spain. Incisively, the author poked fun at their idealized memory of the Second Republic; after all, it "was a typical Spanish Republic; in other words, we all tried to understand each other but couldn't. . . . We celebrate [in exile] some ideal republic, a republic of lovers, because each time we commemorate its anniversary . . . we remember the republic we dreamt about, but which never existed."[64] This crónica, entitled "Una república de enamorados" (A republic of lovers), belonged to a series that castigated exiles for their inability to effect real social change. In "El no comer como arma política" (The hunger strike as a political weapon), Pego humorously derided a proposal to launch a hunger strike as a form of antifascist protest. Addressing whomever came up with the idea, Pego lamented: "I fear, dear friend, that your idea will not have any impact. Hunger as a political weapon would not exactly incite our exiled leaders. I've seen some of them eat . . . I can testify that they would prefer to perish of indigestion rather than hunger."[65] Pointing to the comfortable life of some exiled politicians, the satirist attributed their passionate antifascist speeches not to their political fervor but to the many calories they had ingested, "Our exiled leaders of Spanish republicanism . . . continue to feast at banquets. . . . The only advantage from gorging themselves is that it helps them deliver their fiery speeches."[66] In "La heroica emigración republicana" (The heroic republican emigration), Pego responded to the speech of Julio Just in Paris in July 1953. Just, who was serving as the president of the Government of the Second Republic in exile, admonished Dwight Eisenhower, the U.S. president at the time, that Franco's Spain should not be allowed to join NATO because the repressive regime that governed Spain was an affront to the heroic deeds of the Spanish people who died fighting fascism or were now in exile. Thinking about the exile community, Pego reconsidered such heroic attributes: "I don't seem to recall what heroic deeds to overthrow the Franco regime they have accomplished? I mean, apart from recovering from the gastric feat of drinking up to six cups of coffee during their long discussions about Franco."[67]

Pego thought exile in the United States had become much too comfortable for his comrades. To prove it, he "transcribed" a conversation he supposedly overheard in Puerto Rico. Two enthusiastic exiled Spaniards discuss the need for a revolutionary action in Spain. One suggests: "Let's plan [the revolution] in the nicely air-conditioned restaurant at the airport."[68] Mockingly, Pego taunted those in exile in American-style comfort, who avoided the gritty work of freeing Spain. In another chronicle, he used irony again to recommend his readers to buy a new cushion to fight Franco: "What do you intend to do about the Spanish Question? Apparently, your idea of confronting Franco is to buy a new chair to sit in so you're comfortable while you watch events in Spain."[69]

In "Señora, mi esperanza está en usted" (Ma'am, my hope is in you), Pego lost hope in the ability of men to overthrow the regime; his last hope was that women would rise up and fight for freedom. To him, they embodied moral authority that men lacked. Pego provides domestic examples in his chronicle— "Have you seen most men when they're dealing with children? . . . . Men are clumsy and poor parents: all they do is mess up the stomachs of kids by giving them candy or make them behave with a cruel spanking." Pego adds, "What fools!"[70]

Although the author included himself as part of the community he satirized, his bitter attitude distressed some *España Libre* readers. Indeed, successful satire demands that the audience finds the author's means of conveying his wit to be funny. Some thought Pego was too irreverent, or too critical of the exiles' impotence in their ability to overthrow the Franco regime. *España Libre* editors received letters of complaint about Pego's invectives against Spaniards.

However, he addressed them with more sarcasm. In "¿A quién echamos la culpa?" (Who's to blame?), Pego cited one letter complaining of his mockery of brave Spaniards, who had fought in the trenches against fascism. The satirist replied succinctly: "Oh, really? You talk about the great Spanish people. There are thirty million of them, but just one man controlling them, as if they were thirty million puppets."[71] This chronicle shows his unapologetic antifascism.

Antifascist Roque Barca

In the late 1950s, Pego created a fictional character, Roque Barca, who was an adventurous resistance fighter who infiltrated Spain.[72] Pego described Barca as "an anti-Francoist disguised as a Francoist in the middle of Madrid or Barcelona, [who] in the name of Franco and the Falange performs devastating work for both."[73] In creating Barca, Pego made use of a prototypical character of satirical crónicas: the simpleton or the fool. This stock character has mocked the ruling elite since the Middle Ages and still stays strong today in Hispanic literature. Building on this tradition, Barca, with his apparently innocent appearance, was an undetected saboteur in Spain, "because he's an insignificant man (and thus, naturally he gets along with officials in Madrid), nobody pays attention to him. His apparent commonness conceals him . . . yet he is effective because fear is the only free thing in Spain. . . . At a recent Falangist meeting, Roque Barca spread the word that downtown Madrid was going to be bombed that night. How does he know? Roque always says that someone told him . . . nerves are frayed in Madrid because of his rumors."[74]

Barca created a lot of confusion with several mischievous acts in "La confusión también ayuda" (Confusion also helps). During Franco's visit to Barcelona in June 1960, Barca was very active, because he was "a lone saboteur, plump and short, shaved and rosy-cheeked, with a rather distinguished appearance. He devoted himself to sowing confusion, which is not an ineffective method for anti-Francoists."[75] In the story, Barca was introduced to the minister of the interior, General Alonso Vega, and told him a rumor he heard about some revolutionaries who were masquerading as police officers. And there was another rumor that communist provocateurs had mined the entrance to Barcelona's port to blow up the *Galicia*: "Fascists were facing chaos by land and sea. Barca ruined Franco's visit since the Caudillo was too scared to deliver his sensational speech."[76] Similarly, in "No hay que dejarlo tranquilo" (We should not leave him be), Barca unleashed some juvenile gags, setting off firecrackers and setting fire to a restaurant's kitchen while Franco was visiting some town. Simply put: "Franco's security is on edge."[77]

The endearing Barca never felt intimidated. Once Pego supposedly received a postcard from him, when he was ostensibly in Seville organizing a "brigada pasiva" (passive brigade) against the regime: "The only obligation of the members of this passive brigade was ... to do nothing. There won't be enough prisons or concentration camps for the regime to lock up all the indolent Spaniards on a sit-down strike."[78] One year, on the day Franco's coup was commemorated (July 18), Barca spread the rumor that Franco was terribly ill.[79] A year later, Barca invented the existence of a new clandestine political party.[80] With his mundane, at times even ludicrous determination, Barca exposed the pretended bravado of Spanish fascists who were on edge because of him.

As the Franco regime declined in the late 1960s and 1970s, Pego's satire became more self-assured. When Spanish students revolted against the dictatorship in 1968, Pego sarcastically alerted Franco to be careful: "Think of your followers, who get upset fearing life without their Caudillo—they can't lead a normal life if they do not know who their leader is. . . . Tomorrow they might wake up and have no Caudillo. They'll feel like their heads were cut off."[81] In the last decades of Franco's rule, *España Libre* published Pego's most lighthearted satires. In "Una dictadura gastada" (A worn-out dictatorship), Pego thought Franco looked old and tired: "Franco, there is a way to feel young again, just do what the tourists do: pack your bags and leave."[82] In these two examples, the menacing tone addressed to a weakened dictator is quite evident.

The viciously insightful humor of Pego's long-running chronicles in *España Libre* greatly appealed to many readers because it encouraged their will to resist fascism. Satire does not reconcile the reader with reality, nor does provide them with a solution; instead it proclaims "the urgency of change."[83] Pego's double meanings did exactly that: they conveyed a tragic truth of civil rights infringements in Spain. With such unsettling irony, readers were shocked into remembering the Spaniards still suffering under Franco's terror. Pego's puns, popular sayings, and wit not only vindicated the militant antifascism of the common people as espoused by the SHC, but also exposed the exiles' powerlessness to overthrow Franco's regime. Indeed, his satirical chronicles satisfied several narrative needs for members, who had been forced into exile by a dictator who terrorized their homeland. Yet, they seemed unable to affect events in Spain. They needed more than moral edification; they craved comic relief and community, and Pego's sarcasm provided both. Pego not only galvanized political protest through his provocative and biting style but also constructed a comedy of manners: Americans and exiles were humorously scolded for their comfortable relationship with Franco.

Roque Barca, Pego's histrionic fictional alter ego, disrupted fascism in Spain, unlike the actual exiles who read his work while comfortably sitting in their favorite American café. Paradoxically, Pego's chronicles were textual similes of those long exile *café tertulias* that Pego mocked when he imagined exiles forever criticizing Franco and Americans, inevitably over never-ending cups of coffee. Certainly, his witty remarks and his dynamic, humorous dialogues transported readers to such tertulia atmosphere, re-created on the page for the transnational reach of *España Libre*. Barca, a buffoon, acted with cold effectiveness while the exiled leaders occupied themselves enjoying America's charms and dreaming of an idealized future for Spain. Although, many SHC members and *España Libre* writers were devoted to the exile community abroad and the resistance in Spain, Pego scorned the broader membership for accommodating to a life of exile. Barca served multiple functions: as a joker or a *pícaro*, he celebrated the literary tradition of the people; he symbolized the antifascist fight they felt in their hearts; and he provoked a self-conscious laughter that evidenced the reality of their limitations in the fight against oppression. Contesting Spanish fascist terror, humor was an empowering tool that energized members and countered their downfall to victimization and embitterment. Pego's sharp satire transformed the exile condition into a laughable, and thus livable, experience.

9

Damned Cartoons! Workers' Identity and Resistance

On April 5, 1940, *España Libre* published a cartoon by an unidentified artist that featured Francisco Franco as a flabbergasted construction worker.[1] The cartoon pictures Spain destroyed after the Civil War, and a swastika is presented as the marker of this destruction. The "Franco-worker" is shown as being at a loss for how to reconstruct the country. This one-panel cartoon was a response to the celebrations being held in Spain on the first anniversary of Franco's conquest of the country, and it showed a very different perspective than the one pushed by Franco's regime in Spain, where the idea of reconstruction was part of its national mythmaking. Consistent with fascist ideology in Italy and Germany, one of the central myths of Spanish fascism was redemption, something that would be achieved through the sacrifice of life for the glory of the nation. According to Javier Rodrigo: "Destruction was a precondition for reconstruction, since the national community could only emerge 'through violence itself.' ... [As] in Germany and Italy, post-war Spain constructed a sacralizing and absorbing rhetoric that elevated violence and death to a mystical experience. This was coherent with a ... regenerated nation [that] had to demonstrate its vitality through aggression."[2]

Several years earlier, General Millán Astray, one of the Francoist rebels, publicly performed such a fascist ritualization at the University of Salamanca on October 12, 1936, during the events celebrating Columbus Day. That day, the rector Miguel de Unamuno opened his remarks at one of the sessions with a critique of Franco's forces and pronounced his famous words "vencer no es convencer" (to defeat is not to convince). In response, Millán Astray shouted to the assembly: "¡Muera la intelectualidad traidora!" (Death to traitorous intellectuality!) along with "¡Abajo los intelectuales!" (Down with the intellectuals!) and "¡Viva la muerte!" (Long live death!).[3] The caption for the cartoon with the Franco-worker that appeared in *España Libre*—"Es más fácil destruir que construir" (It's easier to destroy that to build)—contrasts these Spanish fascist values with those of the common people. The implication of this editorial cartoon is that workers are a constructive force who built the Second Republic and fought for liberty during the Spanish Civil War—while fascists, who now must rebuild the country, are depicted as a destructive force that lacked the skills necessary to do so.

This cartoon's publication—with its condemnation of fascism and its celebration of proletarian values—illustrates the role of graphic art in *España Libre*. To maintain the vital role of graphic art in *España Libre*, the periodical published both originals and reprints from celebrated cartoonists and accepted anonymous submissions. This chapter explores the graphic art attacking fascism and re-creating working-class identity that appeared in the periodical, specifically focusing on the cartoons of Sergio Aragonés and Josep Bartolí Guiu. As visual discursive spaces, cartoons ratified the emotions of a transnational antifascist and proletarian community and asked readers to think collectively about the need for solidarity and protection of the working-class culture in exile and under fascism.

Taking into account the FBI and Franco's agents' watch on *España Libre*, these editorial cartoons were a courageous feat. In the context of the Cold War—when "few progressive organizations survived the postwar years of inquisition and innuendo, government investigations and congressional backlash against the labor movement"[4]—the SHC's ongoing resistance through times of harsh repression in Spain and political tension in the United States highlights the extraordinary tenacity of the SHC, its newspaper *España Libre*, and cartoonists such as Aragonés and Bartolí Guiu.

Most illustrations published in *España Libre* were single-panel pantomimes, silent cartoons that made no use of dialogue balloons or any text except perhaps for a title or caption. The picture then stands as a puzzle that demands the reader's active engagement. In other words, the reader must ultimately interpret its meaning. The meaning of purely pictorial humor is activated in the reader's mind. Significant artistic skill is necessary to synthesize all the elements of the cartoon using visual language. However, the use of visual abstraction transcends the barriers confronting textual language, which made of cartoons an excellent transnational antifascist communication tool in *España Libre*.

Transnational Cartoons

Before the Second World War, single-panel cartoons in *España Libre* responded to the events of the Spanish Civil War, and then, after the war, to the events taking place in Franco's fascist Spain. There were numerous unsigned cartoons and a good number of drawings signed with pen names, such as Pum, Roberto [Roberto Gómez], Couto, and Rocue. A substantial number of pantomimes from other Spanish Civil War exile periodicals and magazines were reprinted in *España Libre*, among them Julián Gamoneda. During the Second World War, it was also customary to reprint cartoons from American and European cartoonists such as Fritz Behrendt (*Het Parool*, Amsterdam), Edmond Duffy (*Baltimore Sun*), Bill Mauldin (*St. Louis Post-Dispatch/Chicago Tribune*), Bruce Alexander Russell (*Los Angeles Times*), Fred Seibel (*Richmond Times Dispatch*), Burt Thomas (*Detroit News*), and George Whitelaw (*Daily Herald*, London). In the 1950s, 1960s, and 1970s, cartoonists Chumy Chúmez (Jose María González Castrillo), Jerano Colina, Forges (Antonio Fraguas de Pablo), Alfredo Monrós, Jaume Perich Escala, Francisco Rivero Gil, Ángel Antonio Mingote Barrachina, Pepoti, Ramón, Antonio "Toño" Salazar, and Cesar were often featured.

Cartoons did much more than alleviate the terror felt under fascism and in exile. The fervent opposition of *España Libre* to fascism was developed in pictorial strategies that mocked the mythical pretensions of Spanish fascism. The irreverent repositioning of paradigms assuaged readers' fears during the Spanish Civil War and during the dictatorship afterward. For example, in an editorial cartoon published on February 7, 1941, a religious theme attempts to deconstruct the myth of Hitler that his followers sought to create.[5] In the cartoon, Hitler's posture recalls the crucifixion of Jesus, leading readers to relate the Christian notion of salvation brought by the Crucifixion of Jesus Christ to the alleged redemption promised to Germans by Nazi propaganda. Hitler holds an elevated position. His bloody extended hands express the regenerative power of violence. However, the ironic caption, "El Ángel de la Paz" (The angel of peace) questions these fascist myths. "El Ángel de la Paz" refers to the monument with the same name (Friedensengel) erected in Munich in 1899 to commemorate twenty-five years of peace after the Franco-Prussian War of 1870–71. Whereas the monument projects angelical wings that symbolize hope, protection, and spiritual comfort, the "guardian angel" in this cartoon has the angular metallic wings of a bomber airplane, decorated with swastikas that signify war and fascism. His "congregation" is a sea of skulls. As a messianic leader, Hitler does not bring peace and prosperity to his people but rather their very destruction. If angels deliver salvation to those who listen, the one-panel pantomime shows that the fascists only deliver death. Visual wit disrupted ways of seeing by boldly repositioning sacred and fascist myths.

Misogynistic Drawings

Some cartoons built on gender stereotypes to attack Franco. The Second Republic (1931–1939) extended civil rights to women, and was perceived by some as men's loss of patriarchal privilege. Under the Spanish Constitution of 1931, which gave birth to the Second Republic, women could vote and stand for parliament. Social reforms, including liberal divorce laws, enhanced their civil and employment rights. The conservative sectors of society interpreted the progressive reforms enacted by the Republic as a crisis of traditional Spanish identity. The sexual identity of progressive men was questioned because the Republic had opened public spaces for women. Franco's propaganda often accused the Republicans of "unmanliness" and emphasized Franco's virility by presenting him as a sportsman and hunter.

Following the same misogynist logic, antifascist cartoons used feminine images to belittle Franco, Hitler, and Mussolini. In 1940, Gamoneda's cartoon that illustrated the *España Libre* article "El Spanish House" denounced the presence of Spanish fascists in New York by depicting four fascist agents striking feminine poses and wearing high heels, all meant to denigrate them.[6] Another of his cartoons portrayed Franco, feminine in appearance, next to the Army of Africa, a swastika, and a football, references to the ways Franco conquered people's will during the war and under his rule.[7] A third cartoon showed the effeminate dictator with long eyelashes, wearing lipstick and holding a rose.[8] In a similar vein, in "Último número" (Last show), Franco was represented as a female juggler who is walking a tightrope wearing high heels.[9] The Falangist arrows he is holding in one hand are symbols of the fascist ideology he embraced to gain power. His leggings are "made in USA" to signify his alliance with the United States in the fight against communism. Franco is also holding a crown, symbolically referring to his holding up Juan Carlos de Borbón as the future king, who was expected to support the regime's values. However, the caption, "Último número," and the act of walking a tightrope connoted Franco's dangerous balancing of alliances to remain in power.

Cartoons that employed femininity as a means to disgrace enemies also ridiculed the National-Flamenquismo, a nationalistic agenda of the regime that appropriated flamenco culture.[10] In a cartoon entitled "Por bulerías" (For flamenco singing and dancing), drawn by an artist named "Fryer" and reprinted from the *Excélsior* (Mexico), Franco is portrayed as a female flamenco dancer who is dancing to a tune played by Uncle Sam, who has been transformed into a flamenco guitarist.[11] The caption calls Franco "Bien pagá" (Well-paid), alluding to the famous *copla* song (folksong) by Miguel de Molina, which tells the story of a prostitute in love with a client. The client reminds the prostitute that she cannot expect romantic love from him because she has exchanged her sexual favors for money. The drawing refers to the Pact of Madrid, signed by the United States and Spain on September 1953, which permitted the United States to construct and use air and naval bases in Spanish territory, while the United States pledged to furnish economic and military aid to Spain.

Similarly, the cartoon "Españolada," published on December 25, 1959, and signed by "Roberto," revisited the same theme. *Españolada* is a pejorative term used to refer to Spanish musical comedy films produced in the 1930s and 1940s, also called *folclóricas*, portraying Andalusian and Roma and Sinti performers of flamenco. These popular films exoticized and appropriated Andalusia, flamenco, Sinti and Roma culture, and toreros. In the cartoon, Franco is dressed as a flamenco dancer and dances to President Dwight D. Eisenhower's music.[12] Cartoons like "Españolada" feminized fascists and Franco to make them appear as ludicrous, posturing, and vain characters. This form of comic attack evinces the era's deeply rooted patriarchal paradigms. Attributing traditional feminine qualities to Franco, Mussolini, and Hitler was in fact a common humorous attack by cartoonists during the Second World War.[13]

Response to Imperial Spain and Catholic Nationalism

Franco's propaganda portrayed the Spanish Civil War as a crusade to reestablish Spain's Catholic and imperial past. To highlight these ideological goals, Franco's coat of arms displayed the yoke and arrows of those supreme Catholic monarchs, Ferdinand and Isabella. Franco was also referred to as the "Caudillo de la Hispanidad" (Leader of the Hispanic Culture). The imperial aspirations of the dictator were to be realized by his Consejo de Hispanidad (Hispanic Council), established on November 2, 1940, with the objective of luring Latin America back into the Spanish orbit and exporting fascism. Responding to this event, a one-panel illustration, published in *España Libre* on January 17, 1941, depicts an audience composed of stock characters who represent the supporters of the Consejo de Hispanidad: the Church, the Army of Africa, bullfighters (who signify the traditions appropriated by the regime), the Spanish elite, and the Civil Guards. They are listening with rapt attention to a parrot whose speech balloon depicts a caravel (a ship like the one used by Christopher Columbus to reach the New World or pirates sailing the "Spanish Main"). The caption, "He aquí el eje espiritual del Hispanicismo" (This is the spiritual axis of Hispanidad), equates the ship, an iconic representation of colonization, to a pirate's ship and a parrot as the speaker of the Hispanidad.[14] The cognitive dissonance produced by a parrot addressing the stock characters provides a humorous intersection of meanings.[15] The visual depiction debunks the myth of Spanish Empire by implying that the El Consejo de Hispanidad was committing acts of piracy, such as attempting to fascistize Latin America, an affront of similar proportions to its past colonization.

According to National Catholicism, a cornerstone of Francoist ideology, Franco was Caudillo by the grace of God. Under such divinely sanctioned rule, Franco had reinstituted the traditional Catholic values of the nation and the family, which had been undermined by the Second Republic. The regime used every opportunity to hammer home this point, lending ammunition for parody in *España Libre*. In one cartoon, in time for Christmas 1959, cartoonists played upon the Catholic Church's support of Francoism. In December of that year, President Eisenhower had visited Spain to underscore the alliance with the United States in the fight against communism. In a cartoon published December 1959 and authored by "Pepoti," Franco is hosting a dinner party for President Eisenhower. The caption for the cartoon reads: "He Is Giving a Party for the Leader of the Free World."[16] The festive tableware, candles, and champagne visually signify the Christmas season. Franco is busy getting the table ready; a set of keys is hanging from his pocket. The extravagant Christmas dinner party held for Eisenhower during his Good Will Tour is juxtaposed to drawings of Spanish prisons overcrowded with dissenters. Ironically positioned in the dining room as family portraits, these images of prisoners overlooking Eisenhower's jolly visit denounce the repressive judicial system that included torture and execution of political dissenters, which had started as early as April 1, 1939.[17] Not only does the cartoon make visible the repressiveness of the Spanish regime, it also emphasizes that the "Leader of the Free World" is enjoying a Christmas reception hosted by Franco, a cruel dictator who holds the keys to the Spanish people's freedom.

On November 4, 1960, a pantomime authored by "Ramón" addresses the same issue. In the scene, Franco is depicted as a lamb. Both the Franco-lamb character and a priest are looking away while a Civil Guard is executing a civilian by strangulation. A caption recites the biblical verse, "Y paz en la Tierra a los hombres de buena voluntad" (Peace on Earth to Men of Good Will), which asks believers to accept Jesus as their savior and celebrate the peace brought by the Lamb of God.[18] However, bold and dark brushstrokes of the cartoon emphasize the menacing and destructive power of National Catholicism, which allied the Church with the regime in its horrific purge of dissenters.

Response to Political Persecutions

Beyond deconstructing fascist myths, cartoons in *España Libre* evidenced the workers' resistance to fascism and aimed at encouraging solidarity. In the 1960s and 1970s, *España Libre* published a number of cartoons by Josep Bartolí Guiu (1910–1995) that illustrated the periodical's working-class ethos during the last two decades of the periodical. Upon Franco's victory in the Spanish Civil War, this Catalan cartoonist had fled into exile into France where he escaped a French refugee/prison camp and the Gestapo. Eventually making his way to Latin America, Bartolí Guiu lived in Mexico after the Second World War and developed a close friendship with Frida Kahlo. Later, after moving to the United States, he drew for *Holiday* magazine, and was part of the 10th Street group, along with Willem de Kooning, Franz Kline, Jackson Pollock, and Mark Rothko. In 1973, he was awarded the Mark Rothko Award.[19]

In addition to celebrating workers, Bartolí Guiu's cartoons in *España Libre* were strongly anti-Franco. In a one-panel drawing, published on March 18, 1960, Franco is characterized as a vicious and idle butcher who is holding a knife while he looks away, smiling. The Falange emblem is drawn on his counter, and Spain hangs on a hook as a dismembered body.[20] The abhorrent view of a slaughtered human body epitomizes the fascist violence exerted against the people. Moreover, the sinister stillness of the scene contrasts with the usual hustle of a market stall where industrious merchants sell nutritious food and chat with customers. Thus, the disparaging parody of this market scene contrasts Francoist stagnation and horror with working-class vitality.[21]

Several cartoonists published in *España Libre* raised awareness of the political persecution of dissenters in Spain. Before the Spanish Civil War, socialist Francisco Rivero Gil (1899–1972) had published cartoons in mainstream Spanish newspapers. Once in exile in France, and later the Dominican Republic, Colombia, and Mexico, the caricaturist corresponded with González Malo and sent his drawings to *España Libre* for publication.[22] In one example of his work, his one-panel pantomime of June 17, 1960, elegantly depicts with clean strokes the endurance of incarcerated political prisoners. The three labor leaders portrayed in the cartoon show clear signs of exhaustion: ragged clothes and thin, wrecked bodies.[23] However, the drawing also depicts their moral fortitude as one of the prisoners holds his head high, an action that visually translates as an unbreakable determination of the workers not to give up in their efforts to win freedom for all.

Similarly, Bartolí Guiu's cartoon published in *España Libre* on October 21, 1960, "Esto sí está estabilizado en España" (This has been established in Spain), reported on the long prison sentences given to labor leaders. The cartoon depicts a chained political prisoner, his clothes ragged, and his beard unshaven. The man looks exhausted: his eyes show dark circles and his arms drop by his sides, symbolizing defeat. However, his fists are still tight and his chin is slightly held up high, signs of his quiet, lingering resistance and inner strength in the face of adversity.[24] Bartolí Guiu's depicts the people's endurance under fascism with a sophisticated and subtle style.

Drawing Worker's Resistance

Sergio Aragonés (Castellón, Spain, 1937–) published seventy original cartoons in the periodical, most of which illustrated the deeds of the labor resistance. His cartoons were part of *España Libre*'s documentation of workers' history and its coverage of the underground labor opposition in Spain. Aragonés was a child during the Spanish Civil War. His family fled to France because they were affiliated with the UGT and they very aware that Franco's brutality was especially pronounced against labor unionists. However, because of the Nazi occupation of France, they were forced to escape once again, this time to Mexico. In 1962, now an adult, Sergio Aragonés moved to New York.[25] Through the Spanish Civil War exile network, Aragonés's family contacted González Malo, and until the latter's death in 1965, Aragonés served as the editorial cartoonist and a contributing editor to *España Libre*.[26]

In weekly meetings, González Malo summarized the news sent to him by the Spanish underground resistance, and Aragonés would translate it into cartoons with a subversive visual wit to be published on the front page of *España Libre*.[27] Aragonés's cartoons reinforced the antifascist culture of the periodical, something that influenced Aragonés in turn and that would have a major transformative impact on the young artist, planting the seeds of a life-long condemnation of a fascist worldview.[28] His artistic work in *Mad* magazine continued to reject fascist ideas about conformity, persecution, and exclusion, ideas that he regarded as central elements of fascism. Instead, "Marginals," his long-running feature in *Mad* magazine, invited readers to think critically about established values, empathize with others, and laugh at their own faults.[29]

On September 4, 1964, one of Aragonés's cartoons reported on the long prison sentences given to Francisco Calle, José Cases, and Mariano Pascual for being the leaders of the underground Spanish workers union, the ASO. It features an allegorical figure that represents the workers of the world reading a front-page headline "Guilty."[30] The cartoon provided a mirror experience for *España Libre* readers, who were reading about their ASO comrades imprisoned in Spain. The aesthetic experience interwove working-class and antifascist resistance. Comrades in Spain were facing state terror while comrades abroad fought for their rights. Aragonés re-created this transnational proletarian identity by drawing a worker, whose head is an earth globe, shedding a tear. The image is reminiscent of Popeye the Sailor Man or Rosie the Riveter for its iconic potential and reveals how Aragonés's artistry was nurtured in his transnational experiences.[31] As a child in Mexico, he had access to European cartoonists through the Spanish exile community, as well as to American caricaturists. Cartoons such as "Guilty" not only strengthened collective identity and political efficacy, but also provided readers with an affective experience where they could understand that emotions they might be feeling were also shared by other exiles, as other literary genres of *España Libre* did. An allegorical worker crying over the long prison sentences of his comrades, as in "Guilty," was an open door to a multitude of emotions for readers: sadness, rage, courage, and righteousness.

As a resistance artist, Aragonés preserved hope for a free Spain and brightened the spirits of his desolate readers. In another of his cartoons, published on January 1, 1964, Aragonés drew an imprisoned man who represents public opinion in Spain. The man is bound and guarded by a distracted Civil Guard. A small child holds a blanket that has 1964 written on it. The child tiptoes toward the bound man with a pair of scissors in his hand, ready to set the man free. To exiles abroad and the underground readers in Spain, the cartoon conceptualized revolution. Aragonés's visual wit transformed subjection into rebellion. The subjection of a population requires constant surveillance, and the cartoon claims that the resistance is ready for that moment when that surveillance fails. Most importantly, the infant in this cartoon signifies the new generation of freedom fighters; the protagonist has lost the iconic 1930s virile masculinity and menacing antifascist fist. In 1964, revolution is nonviolent, rather joyous, and almost imperceptible in its action (symbolized by the tiptoeing of the child). The nurturing aspects of the new revolutionary movements are emphasized by the warmth of the baby's blanket, which invokes the solidarity necessary for social change. Therefore, the cartoon visually translates the belief in a new free world as the result of joyous rebellion and affective solidarity with others. Also, the cartoon explores the threshold where freedom happens: when an inquisitive and playful attitude to life interrogates power and authority, central tenets of the antifascist culture in which Aragonés grew up.

Other Aragonés cartoons showed how the clandestine workers' alliance undermined the dictatorship. In the first cartoon of the series presented, April 14—the date that commemorates the Second Republic—has been painted on a wall in Spain; in the second, the name of the two labor unions, UGT and

CNT, are written on the sleeves of two hands, which are simultaneously in a handshake and strangling the dictator.[32] From New York, *España Libre* cartoons informed world readers about the role of the socialist and anarchist unions in the fight for freedom in Spain.

España Libre's cartoons also evidenced the strength of Spanish workers' identity in exile. Members and writers transformed the bleak conditions of exile in the United States into a culture of solidarity and cooperation. Their exile experience was not a voyage into isolation; rather, members coalesced into a print community that denounced fascism and forged solidarity with the underground labor opposition in Spain. Bartolí Guiu captures the conflicting emotions of exile in his cartoon "Libertad."[33] On a ship, two Spaniards are fleeing Spain and sailing toward freedom. Their flag is "Libertad" (Freedom), and Bartolí Guiu draws the two men with similar postures and identical facial expressions. Repetition of images in cartoons is a method of sparking recognition. Here it visually re-creates the Spaniards' friendship in despair. The visual narrative depicts the pain of exile as much as it describes comradeship.

The transnational submissions of cartoons as well as the international circulation of *España Libre* suggests that graphic art not only responded to Spanish politics but was also in communication with transnational popular cultures, which embraced cartoons as part of their affective and aesthetic practices. Graphic art succinctly and universally communicated the threat of fascism, transcending language barriers. Inquisitive comic art fostered awareness of the dangers of fascism and articulated resistance against it in defense of freedom. Wit in religious-themed cartoons deconstructed fascist mythmaking and helped readers critically analyze politics in Europe. Responding to global politics during the Cold War, cartoons condemned the United States' diplomatic relations with Francoist Spain. At the expense of women, misogynist art mocked fascists and humor relieved the dissociative experience of exile.

Workers were portrayed as a constructive societal force versus the destructive impetus of fascism. When Aragonés translated the reports of the Spanish underground dissidents into visual language on the front-page of *España Libre*, he perceptively counteracted the Franco regime's propaganda; his cartoons raised awareness of the plight of Spanish refugees and exiles, who were escaping political persecution and torture. The notion of masculine heroism that made anarchism appealing to workers during the Spanish Civil War transformed into playful commitment in present possibilities in exile. Workers' strength was represented by their capacity to reflect on the events while caring for each other after the defeat in the Spanish Civil War. Bartolí Guiu's art informed a collective working-class consciousness and empowered readers to be politically aware and active against the political persecution of Spanish dissenters. Most importantly, exile cartoons constructed working-class identity even as Franco systematically attempted to destroy it in Spain.

During Franco's rule, a countercultural resistance to fascist myths was based on an inquisitive playfulness as well as a joyous and affective engagement with others, setting *España Libre* readers free from fascist ideas of society. The abundant and high-quality artwork in *España Libre* challenged fascist myths and preserved proletarian identity in exile. Compared with the rough-and-ready vitriol in Aurelio Pego's satiric crónicas, caricaturists attacked fascism with polished and precise strokes that advanced, nevertheless, a piercing and painful understanding of the plight of Spanish people. In the conclusion, I explore the legacy of the SHC's antifascism, anarchism, and exile in the United States.

Conclusion

The SHC's Antifascist Legacy

Workers and radical networks are elusive historical subjects. Their horizontal functioning escapes academic research trained to concentrate on a few relevant historical figures.[1] The story of Spanish immigrants is one such cases of invisibility. Imprecise official figures, clandestine channels of migration, and lack of national distinctions between Spanish-speaking migrants have hampered the study of peninsular immigration to the United States.[2] Additionally, interpreting primary sources has challenged scholars and archivists not fluent in Spanish and workers' antifascist literature has escaped the attention of American scholars. Finally, the more accessible papers from the exiled elite have brought academics to conclude that Spanish exiles in the United States were a small number of key politicians and intellectuals housed in top American universities. Therefore, the body of research on the Spanish Civil War exodus has focused on Mexico and France, the two countries that hosted larger numbers of fleeing Spaniards. *Fighting Fascist Spain* counters the erasure of common people from social history and literature and shows how intellectual and political ideas are transferred and transformed collectively "from below." This study reconstitutes a lost legacy and examines authors and texts never before studied.

Through *España Libre*, this book has explored the formation of the Sociedades Hispanas Confederadas, its structure, its participation in antifascism and anarchism, and its evolution through the years. Although the SHC built on existing working-class community organizations and practices, it remained culturally and politically independent. The anarchists' capacity to ally with progressive and statist groups against fascism did not impact their bottom-up organizational approach. Executive members gained their positions by devoting endless hours to the organization and by making inclusion their rule.[3] Protest and direct action occurred on the streets with boycotts, demonstrations, and public support to victims. Workers' protest was also visible on the pages of their paper, with its coverage of solidarity and the publication of political thought, subversive cartoons, literature, humor, and theatre. The underlying premise of this work is that the SHC's antifascist solidarity was rooted in a realm shaped by this complex web of political and cultural heritages that Spanish immigrants brought with them and were further reinforced by allies in the United States, which in turn built local and transnational antifascist communities. Likewise, *España Libre*'s proletarian culture was fashioned by the legacy of prior anarchist, anarcho-syndicalist, socialist, and exile networks. The SHC had a clear transnational consciousness: old migrants and new exiles coalesced in overlapping communities that were linked to similar networks in other countries.

On the occasion of the Second Spanish Republic Government in exile granting the SHC the liberation medal, Félix Martí Ibáñez published in *España Libre* the many ways in which the SHC advanced antifascist work. He described the SHC being "a forum and barn, settlement and refuge for all of us, and its place of honor in the vanguard of the militant global forces for freedom and democracy for all, and for dignity and integrity of men."[4] In other words, the SHC provided exiles a free space to settle, to receive aid, and to create a better world. The periodical published sporadic contributions as long as they endorse a world free of fascism and totalitarianism. Martí Ibáñez added that the SHC "always embraced the indomitable concept that the good fight was not over... its example of determination, loyalty, and altruism has been our inspiration and has spurred us to action."[5] Although Allies defeated fascism elsewhere in Europe, the SHC claimed that Spain remained fascist until 1977. As long as fascism ruled in Spain, *España Libre* wrote history from below and re-created proletarian communities, which politically and culturally resisted fascism. In other words, for *España Libre* antifascism remained a significant, participatory, and transnational political philosophy for Spanish exiles in the United States.

SHC members established local and international networks linking likeminded people that overlapped exile, ethnic, radical, labor, progressive, and personal networks established in the United States. *España Libre* became the active hub of transnational antifascism. The ability of the SHC to interact with all diverse support groups proves that the historical figures recovered in this book were as politically flexible as they were committed to an antifascist and free future. Despite its coalitional tactics and community-building strategies in exile, the SHC and its periodical never divorced from the working-class political and cultural legacies. In fact, these legacies were invigorated in exile. In the United States, Spaniards have remained relatively hidden in immigration and radical historiography, but *España Libre* proves their integration into unions and workers' associations in the United States.

España Libre, as the organ of the SHC, was a site of political and cultural production. The writings published in the periodical were essential for helping Spanish exiles adapt to life in the United States. The identity of the SHC's members was built around their antifascist exile, on memory, and on prefigurative politics which they expressed in *España Libre*, and which, in turn created a tight-knit community. By inviting its readers to contribute to the periodical, editors erased boundaries between its writers and readers. *España Libre*—along with the affiliated associations, theater groups, rallies, and demonstrations— provided public spaces of protest and solidarity in the United States where members could live their antifascism, anarchism, and socialism.

España Libre also reveals an unknown but long-standing dimension of antifascist and anarchist culture in the United States. Its radical and vanguard activist work functioned on many interconnected layers: mutual aid, collective action, self-empowerment, self-management, and cultural production. All of these helped achieve solidarity and aided numerous victims of the Spanish Civil War and Franco's Spain: refugees, prisoners, and the underground resistance. In this respect, the SHC moved from radical politics marked by the Spanish revolution to collective action based on print culture, solidarity, and transnational networks of action. The way this print culture developed and survived in the periodical demonstrates the diversity among its workers, their organizational skills, and their innovative adaptation to exile. In the United States and abroad, the SHC's ties to radical, progressive, and liberal groups facilitated the circulation of news, solidarity, culture, and thought. Consequently, the published issues of *España Libre* now represent an archive of progressive and radical American and Spanish history written in a collaborative and creative fashion.

España Libre's investment in social change was directed not toward the United States but toward Spain through its highly organized transnational networks, which were instrumental in providing solidarity to refuges and exiles, as well as the underground resistance in Spain. Despite the variety of radical and progressive perspectives the periodical published, a common mission and solidarity for victims of fascism was always present. This did not mean that sharp disagreements, conflicts, or mutual recriminations never arose. Nonetheless, members generally did not allow themselves to waste time, resources, and energies in unproductive political diatribes. The editors and executive members saw themselves as facilitators of an exile public press focused on fighting fascism and helping its victims. In addition to their work at the periodical, this mission was carried out by speaking at public meetings, rallies, and cultural fundraisers. The need to stay focused on the brutal events and fascist repression in Spain did not allow time for political infighting or hurt feelings. There was only time to focus on putting their talents to use for the cause of justice and freedom.

Fighting Fascist Spain recovers the stories of a number of individuals who led the SHC. In this regard, this book connects some of the major figures of the Spanish Civil War exile with lesser-known actors, making their contributions more visible. However, these lesser-known individuals did not work in isolation; many workers served their constituent organizations throughout the years of *España Libre*'s publication, not only in the editing and printing but also in organizing the fundraisers that sustained it. The SHC was an inclusive horizontal organization, with regular assemblies and yearly congresses where every member could vote on decisions and elect editors. The main editors and contributors of its periodical were conscious of the liberating and consciousness-raising potential of continuing acts of resistance. The editors operated transnationally and reached antifascists globally. *España Libre* facilitated the global circulation of antifascist texts, plays, and thought among workers.

España Libre, as an exile periodical, was the most important connecting point for members of the organization, providing a bridge across ideological differences. It facilitated extraordinary solidarity, which in turn fostered deep interpersonal social ties. Among the many people who helped people fleeing Spain, Ernest Fleischman, Maria Cordellat, and González Malo saved many lives. These individuals exemplify the relentless and multifaceted efforts to support refugees abroad and dissenters in Spain. *España Libre* published about members who occupied social centers, popular theaters, streets, work spaces, and the mainstream media with their cultural products to conceptualize an antifascist society. Helping refugees was part of a political strategy in exile to continue radical and progressive cultures abroad. In other words, *España Libre* was the antifascist workers' prime institution that allowed for members to assist in fundraisers, rallies, conferences, demonstrations, assemblies, and congresses—and then published reviews of such efforts. The periodical also occupied a transnational public media space and sustained a global network of solidarity and antifascism.

Although not always explicit, gender and racial hierarchies were present in *España Libre*. For example, the confederation did not always include women as executive members and contributors. Numerous elements in the operation of the periodical also testify to this patriarchal culture. Men monopolized business meetings, organized committees, and edited *España Libre*, which occasionally published misogynist literature. Despite the patriarchal relations, women members organized sophisticated cultural fundraisers and held important roles at different times in the organization. Over the years of exile, the periodical's history, however, showed no significant evolution in its patriarchal culture. Its lack of acknowledgment of race issues also remained a constant, except to connect fascism and racism. In general, the migrants' and exiles' response to fascism showed a complex pan-Hispanic identity in which the *patria chica* and local kinship—as well as class identity—proved to be stronghold against fascism. All SHC members retained roots to the region of Spain from which they came, and these roots—often connected through villages—became part of the friendship and kinship networks that framed their connections to the global antifascist movement for freedom and justice for workers in Spain. While nationality was somewhat contested with these local affinities, race and gender remained unchallenged in the periodical.

There are interlocking aspects that define *España Libre*'s cultural and political identity: its self-educated workers, its anarchist adaptability to exile, its transnational ties, its organized solidarity, and its transformative culture and humor. *España Libre* underscores the multifaceted ways in which members enacted anarchism in exile through print culture, literature, theater, cartoons, and anarchist thought. The thirty-eight years of sustained publication, the numerous literary works published in *España Libre*, and the hundreds of plays performed by the members show that literature for and by workers meant much to readers and members. In fact, editors, contributors, and readers adapted in exile and created their postwar identity through a diverse body of cultural work in *España Libre*. The SHC cannot be understood adequately in terms of a political coalition alone but rather in the transformative roles that culture—in the forms of graphic art, cartoons, literature, and theater—had for members in their fight against fascism. Artistic expression was one of the most revolutionary means of fighting fascism because it enlarged members' comprehension of their reality and the significance of resistance. Antifascism and anarchism resisted obliteration for more than three decades anchored not only in *España Libre*'s dissemination of uncensored news and calls to action, but also in its capacity to reestablish culture abroad.

España Libre's authors cultivated a rich set of tools that interrogated the way fascist power operates. They lived and practiced empathy, solidarity, introspection, and engagement with others for a peaceful and free society. José

Castilla Morales, Antonio García Copado, and Alfonso Vidal y Planas portrayed the migrant experience of workers in the United States with biographical and literary representations that built on popular concepts to help readers made sense their transnational experiences. Challenging general assumptions on immigrants and exiles, these works had a notable impact beyond just the SHC, as attested by the numerous publications of some of these authors and artists in other periodicals, magazines, and books. In *España Libre*, in essays, fiction, and poetry, workers were the narrative center around which the story developed. It was history and culture by and for workers.

España Libre's antifascism was aesthetically vigorous. Popular and original antifascist plays with workers as protagonists allowed the audience to reflect on their new ethnic identity in the United States. Humor on the stage was an empowering tool that energized members and helped them resist feelings of victimization and embitterment. In other words, exile for the SHC was not merely a feeling of nostalgia about a radical past. Rather, it was an ongoing antifascist fight able to laugh at itself in a new context. The notion of masculine heroism that made anarchism appealing to workers during the Spanish Civil War was transformed into farcical approaches to revolution. Original works of antifascist theater shows the literary, aesthetic, and playful richness of this culture.

Fiction in *España Libre* helped inspire healing, empowerment, and engagement within the antifascist struggle. Anger, sarcasm, and irony were used to attack fascists while satire was used to undermine fascism's logic of power. Humor was the most important element within this literary antifascism because it helped construct an antifascist culture that avoided the reproduction of dogmatism—such as the kind that had led to the very deadly fascistic worldviews that *España Libre* was resisting. Aurelio Pego's puns and wit celebrated the popular and militant antifascism of the SHC but also criticized exiles for their inability to free Spain. His irony and satire kept antifascism full of self-criticism. Workers engaged with political graphic art and cartoons whose sharp irony and critiques helped dispel the cognitive dissonance that people experience when living under fascism and exile. Likewise, exile cartoons helped construct working-class identity in exile that was no longer visually represented in the combativeness that had made anarchism appealing to workers during the Spanish Civil War, but rather employed a rhetoric of playfulness to present possibilities of social change. Bartolí Guiu used elegant and compassionate art to reverse the dehumanization of fascism, and like him, other cartoonists sought to inspire ideas of interdependence and shared struggles among Spanish exiles. The humor and empathy employed in the graphic art published in *España Libre* was directed to making members and readers aware of the infinite possibilities present in every given moment, even in periods of extreme repression.

España Libre's achievements are also the result of the everyday attention to its anarchist values of equality, freedom, peace, prefigurative politics, and an ethical congruence of means and ends. The Spanish anarchists in exile in the United States have been largely forgotten and the movement's legacy misrepresented by fascist and Cold War discourses. Whereas Spanish anarchism is generally depicted as defeated after the Spanish Civil War, *España Libre* shows that anarchism lived on in the work of the SHC. When the anarchist movement was decimated in Spain after decades of brutal political repression, like other ethnic anarchist groups in the United States, the Spanish anarchist movement did not disappear; instead, it remained operational in the transnational networks of exile and in the United States. In addition to its work focusing on solidarity and denouncing fascism, the SHC also devoted time to safeguarding anarchist thought and practice against the efforts by Spanish fascism to eradicate it.

In exile in the United States, anarchist members used the relative freedom of the U.S. legal framework and civic institutions to exercise mutual support and solidarity. They based their practice on occupying of the public space with demonstrations, theater, and fundraisers. Their continuous fundraising and solidarity consolidated the interdependence of resistance groups. They empowered workers in exile with grassroots activism and print protest, expressed through their own confederation, the SHC, and its periodical *España Libre*. Poetry, short stories, theater, chronicles, and cartoons playfully subverted fascism and foresaw a free future for comrades. The SHC nurtured an adaptable, vibrant, and collective strength able to fight fascism and continued to conceive social revolution within the limits of exile in the United States, with subversive strategies that culturally empowered workers.

Although neither *España Libre* nor the SHC was merely devoted to anarchism, documenting, vindicating, and reformulating anarchism and anarcho-syndicalism in exile became one of the most important goals for some *España Libre*'s authors. In order to help place *España Libre*'s work into the broader intellectual and political thought of the nineteenth and twentieth centuries, this book has also explored in detail the key intellectual and political investigations of many notable individuals among the SHC's and *España Libre*'s network, including González Malo, Carmen Aldecoa, Félix Martí Ibáñez, and Ramón J. Sender. They developed their approaches to anarchism based on their war and postwar experiences.

Kenyon Zimmer has described anarchism in the early twentieth century as "a movement of movements, worldwide in scale but composed of overlapping groups and networks loosely demarcated by characteristics such as location, language, and nationality."⁶ Such capacity for flexibility and adaption continued after the Spanish Civil War. Anarchists were not anchored to the past. Instead, they innovatively adapted to the postwar political context. Benjamin J. Pauli names this postwar new perspective "benevolent statism," which forced anarchists in Britain and in the United States to rearticulate their thought and practice into what has been called "practical" (Ruth Kinna) or "new" anarchism (Pauli).⁷ This adaptation came about because, at the time, states were favorably perceived for their "massive mobilization of centralized power" in their response to the fascist threat.⁸

In her search for an affirmative political project that went beyond just the pain of exile and antifascism, Carmen Aldecoa researched and wrote on the broad political legacies of anarchist transnational journalism extending back in the nineteenth century. In *Del sentir y pensar: Libro primero* (Of feeling and thinking: Book one, 1957), Aldecoa sought to preserve the history of labor print culture that was being systematically erased by Franco's censors. Aldecoa successfully showed how print culture and literature contributed to the transnational education of workers and highlighted the contributions of labor activism to society at large. By recovering labor print culture and literature, Aldecoa demonstrated anarchism's long-term impact in the education of workers and society at large. She proved how the anarchist press was the main organ for circulation of ideas in pre–civil war Spain.

Miguel Giménez Igualada wrote several books against the vilification suffered by the anarchist movement under the Franco dictatorship and in the United States during the McCarthy years. Giménez Igualada sought in his writing to undo stereotyped perceptions of anarchism as terrorism and to restate instead the values of cooperation, egalitarianism, and peace. He defended anarchism while cognizant that it was perceived in a negative light during the American Red Scare and the Cold War. Jesús González Malo's epistolary work maintained transnational dialogues on the development of anarcho-syndicalism within Spanish exile circles and the underground resistance in Spain. His clandestine correspondence discloses his postwar tactics to strengthen labor movements, embracing coalitions as a strategy of generating collective and inclusive practice and thought from below. Aware that repression in Spain was undermining the political role of workers, González Malo contested fascist, elitist, and orthodox approaches that limited workers' access to the political forefront. In an effort to find common ground, González Malo, in his writings, sought out the intersections between anarchism and the humanist liberal tradition. Giménez Igualada and González Malo both reinforced the idea that anarchism was a lifestyle rather than a dogmatic doctrine. By integrating diverse political approaches in his discussion of popular sovereignty, González Malo questioned the elitist representation of workers and examined the pervasive force of dominant ideologies that created an elitist depiction of popular movements. He vehemently rejected the prevailing discourse that suggested workers were unruly. Instead, he effectively counterbalanced it by providing evidence of their long history of leadership and organizational skills. González Malo reinforced the need to liberate people from dogma and instead foster their individualism, while encouraging dialogue between peoples and ideologies.

Inspired by his exilic experiences in the southwestern United States, Ramón J. Sender elaborated on the meaning of borders and freedom in *Relatos fronterizos* (1970), a collection of short stories that fictionalized liminal border-crossers in their re-creation of freedom, a key concept in anarchism. Although it is generally accepted that Franco's fascism destroyed Spanish anarchism, exiles nevertheless evolved their thought and practice in host countries. More importantly, however, these authors innovated their practices beyond the constraints of exile and antifascism. The American experience provided Sender with opportunities to examine how physical and psychological borders limit individual and collective freedoms. Aware of the consequences of transgressing established norms, Sender created fictional liminal characters who exercised both autonomy and solidarity. In a more postmodern perspective, Sender's protagonists in *Relatos fronterizos* represented the later twentieth-century freedom fighters, concerned with topics of fascist subjugation still relevant today. *España Libre* and the SHC remained a central fulcrum in the intellectual, political, and activist work of all of the thinkers and writers recovered in this book, dedicated to the evolution of anarchist thought in the United States exile.

The later intellectual trajectories of some of these exiles show that the development of their anarchist ideas was inexorably linked not only to legacies of revolution in Spain but also to their adaptation in the United States. For example, Sergio Aragonés transferred his tongue-in-cheek critical take on the fascist myths of power, perfection, and regenerative death in *España Libre* to the representation of American life in *Mad* magazine by demythologizing similar totalitarian tendencies in democratic societies. *España Libre*'s counterculture permeated Aragonés's artistic development in the United States. His "Marginals" in *Mad* magazine constantly challenge fascist views of reality that impose the foundational myths of power, perfection, and regenerative destruction. Instead, Aragonés's work proposes an inquisitive and playful attitude to life—valuing diversity and acknowledging fun.[9] Likewise, Martí Ibáñez transferred his anarchist utopian thinking to the magical short stories for the medical magazine he founded, *MD*.[10] In this respect, these artistic and political ideals were influential in ways similar to how anarchist civil and peaceful disobedience influenced mass movements in the United States of the 1960s, as proven in Andy Cornell's *Unruly Equality: U.S. Anarchism in the Twentieth Century* (2016).

In their writings, Martí Ibáñez and Sender investigated the ways people occupy different subject positions as a result of repressive state power. Anarchists innovated and adapted to the fight against fascism. In exile, anarchists affiliated with the SHC did not seek violent insurrection against the state, but spontaneous prefiguration of a free society enacted by everyday acts of mass organizing, cooperation, and cultural transformation. Instead of eliminating the idea of revolution, exiles integrated their revolutionary principles into everyday life during the Cold War in the United States. In this regard, *España Libre* details the transfers among ideologies that tend to be represented as mutually exclusive. Moving toward a postmodern approach, revolution was exercised by inclusion rather than through a violent contest of political power. *España Libre* not only professed postwar Spanish anarchism's distinctiveness but also demonstrated its endurance and malleability as a political and cultural ideology in the United States until it ceased publication in 1977.

The SHC's exemplary solidarity, voluntary collective action, self-governance, and artistic flourishing addressed one of the most revolutionary questions facing fascism: how to care for others in a postwar society? Although the SHC was led by anarchists, the confederation was inclusive in terms of political progressiveness because of the focus on the antifascist struggle. The robust body of documents produced by members that were addressed to a diverse readership—documents that now serve as primary sources of their history, including correspondence, minutes, essays, leaflets, proceedings, essays, and literature in *España Libre*—proves their flexible militancy and horizontal organizing. In exile, anarchism continued to oppose any form of coercive authority and privilege while favoring social and economic equality for all people, something that kept the SHC strong throughout its existence.

As the stories and documents that I discuss in this book have shown, workers contributed to building an antifascist movement in America. In reading one of the first publications about the Spanish Civil War exile in the United States, Castilla Morales lamented the erasure of the SHC, and consequently of workers, from this historiography. The SHC's executive members suspected that democracy would soon forget their progressive contributions. This perception is stated repeatedly in the periodical. For example, an article in *España Libre*'s November 2, 1962, issue states, "As militant democrats and anarchists, we reaffirm ourselves as enemies of all dictatorships and, for freedom, we will pay the required price."[11] And they did. Their humanitarian, political, and cultural bottom-up approaches and contributions have not been fully acknowledged in Spanish Civil War exile or antifascist literature until now. Democracy in Spain and America owe much to the antifascists who fought for justice and freedom. The history of the SHC's cooperative and cultural activism is increasingly relevant when thinking about current debates about global fascist-inspired political movements. *España Libre*'s careful documentation of the politics and culture of workers shows a preoccupation with how to represent heterogeneity. Significantly, this awareness of master narratives displayed in literary antifascism has remained a permanent influence for contemporary theory and literature. The periodical's uncompromising critique of fascist power and violence—and the SHC's everyday and evolving practice of resistance—has produced a key legacy, and it is a legacy that offers needed lessons for how to avoid societies where fascism can be reproduced and normalized. Members created a culture of solidarity, critical introspection, engagement with others, and an experience of joy that would leave a long-lasting impact on the world well beyond the era of the SHC. Popular joy as a form of resistance vindicated a fascist-free society. Such a self-aware movement away from violence grounded modes of resistance in exile. The cultural values espoused by *España Libre* continue to challenge repressive assumptions on popular movements and foster peaceful and free societies. The story of unbreakable disobedience through joyful dissent is a powerful counter-example to repressive fascist movements.

Appendix A
SHC-Affiliated Associations

Acción Demócrata Española, Crockett, California
Acción Demócrata Española, Pittsburg, California
Acción Demócrata Española, Sacramento, California
Acción Democrática Española, San Francisco, California
Agrupación A.M.A., New York, New York
Agrupación Amigos de Azaña, New York, New York
Agrupación Antifascista Ibérica, Detroit, Michigan
Agrupación de Mujeres Antifascistas, Bronx, New York, New York
Agrupación Leales Españoles, Los Angeles, California
Agrupación Obrera Hispana, Bronx, New York, New York
Agrupación Socialista Española, New York, New York
Alianza Obrera Española, New York, New York
Amigos de la Democracia, Lorain, Ohio
Amigos de Sociedades Hispanas Confederadas, Panama
Artistas Unidos, New York, New York
Artistic Group *España Libre*, New York, New York
Ateneo de Educación Social, Newark, New Jersey
Ateneo Español, New York, New York
Ateneo Hispano, Bethlehem, Pennsylvania
Ateneo Hispano, Brooklyn, New York, New York
Ateneo Hispano Americano, White Plains, New York
B. Durruti #4778 I.W.O., Mount Carmel, New York, New York

Appendix A

Casa de Galicia, New York, New York
Casa de la República, The Philippines
Centro Andaluz, Brooklyn, New York, New York
Centro Asturiano, New York, New York
Centro de Estudios Sociales, White Plains, New York
Centro de Instrucción y Recreo de Bergondo y sus contornos, New York, New York
Centro Español, Gary, Indiana
Centro Español, Paterson, New Jersey
Centro Español de Beneficencia, New Kensington, Pennsylvania
Centro Galicia, New York, New York
Centro Hispano Americano, Bridgeport, New York
Centro Hispano Progresivo, Wilkes-Barre, Pennsylvania
Centro Montañés, New York, New York
Centro Vasco-Americano, New York, New York
Círculo de Trabajadores, Brooklyn, New York, New York
Círculo Valenciano, New York, New York
Club Acacia, New York, New York
Club Amigos de España, Cleveland, Ohio
Club Coruña, New York, New York
Club Cubano Julio Antonio Mella, New York, New York
Club Cultural y Recreativo Español, Queens, New York, New York
Club Demócrata, Stockton, California
Club Demócrata Español, San Leandro, California
Club España, New York, New York
Club Español, Barre, Vermont
Club Femenino Español, Massillon, Ohio
Club Hispano Portugués, Paterson, New Jersey
Club Ibérico Benéfico, San Leandro, California
Club Masónico Sol de la Fraternidad, New York, New York
Club Obrero Español, New York, New York
Club Portugués Nova Aurora, Mount Vernon, New York
Club Pro Libertad Española, New York, New York
Comisión de Damas del Comité Antifascista Español, Elizabeth, New Jersey
Comité Antifascista, Canton, Ohio
Comité Antifascista, Lackawanna, New York
Comité Antifascista, McKeesport, Pennsylvania
Comité Antifascista, Scarsdale, New York
Comité Antifascista Español, Elizabethport, New Jersey
Comité Català Antifeixista, New York, New York
Comité Centro Cultural Español, New Britain, Connecticut
Comité de Ansonia, Ansonia, Connecticut
Comité de Ayuda, Pawtucket, Rhode Island

SHC-Affiliated Associations

Comité de Ayuda a España, Danbury, Connecticut
Comité de Ayuda a España Leal, Canton, Ohio
Comité de Ayuda a los Niños del Pueblo Español, Tampico, México
Comité de Damas de la Alianza Obrera Española, New York, New York
Comité de East St. Louis, East St. Louis, Illinois
Comité de la Sociedad de Beneficencia, New Kensington, Pennsylvania
Comité de Montpelier, Montpelier, Vermont
Comité de Patterson, Patterson, New Jersey
Comité de Perth Amboy, Perth Amboy, New Jersey
Comité de Unificación Hispana, New York, New York
Comité Español de Ayuda a España, East St. Louis, Illinois
Comité Español de Ayuda a los Refugiados, Saint Louis, Missouri
Comité Español, Bethlehem, Pennsylvania
Comité Español, Staten Island, New York
Comité Femenino, Astoria, Queens, New York
Comité Femenino, Niagara Falls, New York
Comité Femenino, Schenectady, New York
Comité Femenino, White Plains, New York
Comité Femenino Auxiliar del S.A. Club, Bayonne, New Jersey
Comité Femenino de Ayuda a España, East St. Louis, Illinois
Comité Femenino de Brooklyn, Brooklyn, New York, New York
Comité Femenino Vasco, New York, New York
Comité Hispano de la Local 89 de Cocineros, New York, New York
Comité Portugués pro Democracia Española, Somerville, Massachusetts
Comité pro Ayuda a España, Wharton, West Virginia
Comité pro Cruz Roja Española, New York, New York
Comité pro Democracia Española, Jersey City, New Jersey
Comité pro Democracia Española, New York, New York
Comité pro Democracia Española, Niagara Falls, New York
Comité pro Víctimas Sociales, New York, New York
Comité SHC, Amsterdam, New York
Comité Solidaridad (IWW), New York, New York
Comité Unido, Paterson, New Jersey
Compañeros Antifascistas, Bryten, California
Damas Auxiliares del Spanish American Citizens Club, Bayonne, New Jersey
Fraternidad Universal, Newark, New Jersey
Frente Popular, Brooklyn, New York, New York
Frente Popular, Carolina, West Virginia
Frente Popular, Donora, Pennsylvania
Frente Popular, Rome, New York
Frente Popular, Weirton, West Virginia
Frente Popular Antifascista Gallego, Newark, New Jersey

Appendix A

Frente Popular Antifascista Gallego, New York, New York
Frente Popular de Queens, New York
Frente Popular Español, Fairmont, West Virginia
Frente Popular Hispano Americano, Fairmont, West Virginia
Galicia Social Club, New York, New York
Grupo 19 de julio, Marcus Hook, Pennsylvania
Grupo Amantes de la Libertad, Miami, Arizona
Grupo Antifascista, Bronx, New York, New York
Grupo Antifascista, Lillybrook, West Virginia
Grupo Antifascista Español, Bridgeport, Connecticut
Grupo Antifascista Español de Nemacolin, Pennsylvania
Grupo Antorcha, New York, New York
Grupo Artístico Miaja, New York, New York
Grupo Artístico Pérez Galdós, New York, New York
Grupo de españoles de New Brunswick, New Brunswick, New Jersey
Grupo Democrático Español, Westfield, Massachusetts
Grupo *España Libre*, New York, New York
Grupo Español, East Gulf, West Virginia
Grupo Español, Raysal, West Virginia
Grupo Español Amigos de Azaña, New York, New York
Grupo Español Antifascista, Passaic, New Jersey
Grupo Femenino, Raysal, West Virginia
Grupo Leonés, New York, New York
Grupo Liberal Demócrata Español, Loomis, California
El Grupo Libertario, San Francisco, California
Grupo Lister, Philadelphia, Pennsylvania
Grupo Salmerón, Brooklyn, New York, New York
Grupo Solidaridad, New York, New York
Grupo Tierra, New York, New York
Grupo Valenciano, New York, New York
Grupo Vasco, New York, New York
Grupos Libertarios, Annadale, Staten Island, New York
Hispanos Unidos, Detroit, Michigan
Hispanos Unidos, Newark, New Jersey
Izquierda Republicana, New York, New York
Junta de Cultura Española, Tampa, Florida
Juventudes Escolares Españolas del Bronx, Bronx, New York, New York
Juventudes Españolas de América, New York, New York
Juventudes Españolas de Brooklyn, Brooklyn, New York, New York
Juventudes Españolas del East Side, New York, New York
Juventudes Gallegas, New York, New York
Juventudes Libertarias Españolas, New York, New York

SHC-Affiliated Associations

Liga Democrática Española de Canadá, Montreal, Canada
Lista n. 25 Café "Aires de Terra," New York, New York
Logia Hispano América, New York, New York
Logia Lealtad Española, New York, New York
Muros y Sus Contornos, Newark, New Jersey
Mutualista Obrera Mexicana, New York, New York
New England Committee for the Defense of Spanish Democracy, Boston, Massachusetts
Plus Ultra Democratic Club, Bayonne, New Jersey
Pro Democracia Española, San Juan, Puerto Rico
Ramal de la IWO, Beckley, West Virginia
Sada y Sus Contornos, New York, New York
S.A. Iberia, Detroit, Michigan
Social Group 19th of July, New York, New York
Sociedad Benéfica, Donora, Pennsylvania
Sociedad de Socorros Mutuos La Nacional / Spanish Benevolent Society / Centro Español / Sociedad Española de Beneficiencia, New York, New York
Sociedad Española de Beneficencia, Chicago, Illinois
Sociedad Española de Beneficencia Mutua, Los Angeles, California
Sociedad Fraternal Hispano Americana, Philadelphia, Pennsylvania
Sociedad Naturista Hispana, Annadale, Staten Island, New York
Sociedad Popular Antifascista, Donora, Pennsylvania
Solidaridad Internacional Antifascista, Winters, California
Spanish American Citizens Club, Bayonne, New Jersey
Spanish American Citizens Club, Queens, New York, New York
Spanish American Citizens Club, Yonkers, New York
Spanish American Social and Political Club, New York, New York
Spanish American Social Club, White Plains, New York
Spanish American Women Club, Niagara Falls, New York
Spanish Democratic Action, Crockett, Texas
Spanish Democratic Action, Fresno, California
Spanish Group, Island Park, New York
Spanish Socialismo Group, New York, New York
Spanish Welfare Association, Lackawanna, New York
Teatro del Pueblo de New York, New York, New York
Unidad Gallega, New York, New York
Unión de Cocineros Local 89, New York, New York
United Committee to Aid Spanish People, Paterson, New Jersey

Appendix B
Supporting Networks and Individuals

Government of the Second Spanish Republic in Exile. The Government of the Second Spanish Republic continued to be active in exile after the victory of Francisco Franco's forces in the Spanish Civil War and existed until the restoration of democracy in Spain in 1977. However, the United States did not recognize it.

Confederación National del Trabajo (CNT). The Spanish anarchist National Confederation of Labor was outlawed during Francisco Franco's dictatorship. Nonetheless, it continued working clandestinely inside Spain and conducted further activities from exile. There was a major split among members: those in favor of collaborating with the Government of the Second Spanish Republic in exile and those opposing collaboration. The SHC did cooperate with the government-in-exile but remained an independent organization.

Unión General de Trabajadores (UGT). The Spanish national socialist union continued its operations in exile and clandestinely in Spain.

Partit Obrer d'Unificació Marxista (POUM). *España Libre's* editors in the 1960s and 1970s were members of the Workers' Party of Marxist Unification. With its leader, Julián Gorkin, also in exile, they united forces with liberal and monarchic opponents to Franco toward democratization in Spain.

American unions. The International Ladies' Garment Workers' Union (ILGWU), the Industrial Workers of the World (IWW), the United Automobile Workers (UAW) and the American Federation of Labor and Congress of Industrial Organizations (AFL-CIO) regularly supported the antifascist periodical with small donations.

Roger Nash Baldwin. One of the founders of the American Civil Liberties Union, Baldwin was a sponsor of *España Libre*, and an advisory member of the SHC. He worked to have international observers sent to watch trials of unionists in Franco's Spain.

David Dubinsky and Jay Lovestone. With the American Federation of Labor (AFL), they worked closely with the SHC in politically and economically supporting the clandestine unions in Franco's Spain.

Victor Reuter. With his brother Walter, he led the Congress of Industrial Organizations (CIO), and worked closely with the SHC in politically and economically supporting the clandestine unions in Franco's Spain.

Rudolf Rocker. German anarchist intellectual who gave several antifascist speeches at the SHC's rallies and fundraisers. Rocker and his wife, Milly Witcop, developed a close friendship with Jesús González Malo and his wife, Carmen Aldecoa. Rocker was awarded honorary membership to the SHC.

Norman Thomas. A leading U.S. socialist and founder and executive director of the American Civil Liberties Union, Thomas was an honorary member of the SHC. He focused international attention on the execution of dissenters in Franco's Spain.

Appendix C
Sporadic Contributors, Writers, and Reprinted Authors

Aguilar, Mario
Aláiz, Felipe
Albar, Manuel
Albornoz Limiana, Álvaro de
Alegría, Ángela P.
Alerta, Juan
Alonso, Daniel
Alonso, Manuel
Altolaguirre, Manuel
Álvarez, Agustín
Álvarez, Santiago
Andrade Moscoso, Raúl
Andrade Rodríguez, Juan
Antoñanzas, Mateo
Arce, Gustavo
Arciniega, Rosa
Arciniegas, Germán
Asensio Torrado, José
Avecilla, Ceferino R.
Ayensa, Alfonso
Baeza Flores, Alberto
Barradas, Julio A.
Barrera, Claudio

Bejarano, José Miguel
Bernardo, Federico
Bonet, Pedro
Bookchin, Murray
Braña, Manuel
Bua Rivas, Benito
Cabezas, Felipe A.
Cabezas, Juan Antonio
Carpio, Campio
Castro, José
Castrovido, Roberto
Clariana, Bernardo
Climent, Juan B.
Cuatrecasas, Juan
Descortes, Donoso
De Solza R., Juan José
Durán, Manuel
Eive, Frank
Esplà Rizo, Carlos
Fernández, Víctor
Fernández Escobés, Antonio
Foix, Pere
Frola, Francisco

Garay, Gregorio
García, Pepín
García de Riu, Lorena
García Fernández, Adolfo
Gayol, José
Gómez, Abreu
González, Ceferino
González, Josemilio
González López, Emilio
Gredos, Juan de
Groenwald, H.
Guillot Muñoz, Gervasio
Gutiérrez, Avelino
Herrera, D.
Iglesias, Eduardo
Iglesias, Enrique
Iglesias Suárez, Ignacio
Jackson, Gabriel
Junquera, Manuel
Just, Julio
Kippmann, Walter
Latcham, Ricardo A.
Lazaro, Ángel
Llano, Manuel A.
Lucea, Olegario
Mallo, Jerónimo
Mangada Rosenorn, Julio
Marichal, Juan
Marroquin Rojas, Clemente
Martín, Cristina
Martínez Barrio, Diego
Miaja Menant, José
Millares Vázquez, Manuel
Miqueli González, Violeta
Miró, Fidel
Mistral, Silvia
Montane de las Manateras, Pedro (pseud.)
Montaner, Carlos Alberto
Montseny, Federica
Moral, Armando del
Morayta, Miguel
Moreno, Jorge
Moreno Rojas, Juan F.
Mori, Arturo
Mowrer, Richard
Navarro, Lázaro
Negrín López, Juan
Ontañon, Eduardo de
Orive Alonso, Mario
Osorio Tafall, Bibiano Fernández
Ossorio Gallardo, Ángel
Palacio, Solano
Palencia, Isabel de
Palmer, Sebastián
Palou, Guillermo
Papsila, Esteban M.
Pareja, José
Peirats Valls, José
Pellerano, Alfredo B.
Penichet, Antonio
Pérez, José
Poza Juncal, Hernán
Pradera, Daniel R.
Prado Rodríguez, Jesús
Prieto Tuero, Indalecio
Puyol Albéniz, José María
Río, Ángel del
Río, Benigno del
Ríos Urruti, Fernando de los
Rodríguez Aldave, Alfonso
Rodríguez Barbeito, Andrés
Rodríguez Pérez, José
Rojo, V.
Ruibarry, J. M.
Saborit, Andrés
Saenz, Vicente
Sánchez-Albornoz, Claudio
Sánchez Saornil, Lucia
Sanjurjo, José
Santa Cruz, Miguel de
Santillán, Diego Abad de
Sarrate Laplana, Roberto
Sellarés, Pedro
Sol, Vicente

Solano, Wilebaldo
Solano Palacio, Fernando
Soloni, Félix
Somoza Silva, Lázaro
Suárez, Andrés
Suárez Solís, Rafael
Supervía, Rafael
Szulc, Tad
Torres Campaña, M.
Toryho, Jacinto

Uslar-Pietri, Arturo
Valera Aparicio, Fernando
Vázquez Gayoso, Jesús
Vázquez Humasque, Adolfo
Villa, Antonio de la
Viñuales Farina, Mariano
Winchell, Walter
Zozaya, Antonio
Zugadi Garmendia, Ignacio

Appendix D
Aided Refugees and Political Prisoners

This partial list is compiled from the documents and letters in the ELC and JGMP archives.

Abad de Santillán, Diego
Abadia Mauri, Aurelio
Abiz, Emilio
Abril, Margarita
Acker, Leon
Aguado González, Enrique
Aguardo Echevarría, Mariano
Aguilera, Salvador
Albornoz, Álvaro
Aldana, N.
Alonso Falero, Antonio
Álvarez, Ángel
Álvarez, Antonio
Álvarez, Bernardo
Álvarez, Fernando
Álvarez, Valentín, and family
Álvarez Díaz, Joaquín
Álvarez Fernández, Antonio
Arguelles, M.
Astero, Manuel
Barbadilla, Ángel
Barbás, Aurelio
Bargados, Andrés
Barrero, Francisco
Barreiro, Armando, and family
Bartolomé Álamo, Jesús
Bidoganiz, Santos
Blanco, Monpart
Boix, Antonio
Bolinches, Rosario
Bonturi, Bruno
Bravo Yáñez, Lola
Cabrera, Agustín
Cabrera Hernández, Agustín
Cajtak, Joseph
Calucci, Cesare
Cañas, Ángel, and family
Canencia, Arturo
Carreras, Bruno
Carreras Villanueva, J., and family

Cervero, Eduardo
Cistare Gularons, Antonio
Cobo, Antonio
Colmer, Wenceslao
Colorrio, Santiago
Cores, Bernardo
Costa, Jaime
Costela González, Manuel
Cristóbal, Samuel
Croza Cabrera, Agustín
Darvesi, Eduardo
Degoniz Valle, José Luis
De la Vega, J.
Del Olivo, F.
Del Roal, Carmen
Deus, Modesto
Díaz, Fernando
Díaz, José, and family
Díaz, Mariano
Díaz, Pablo
Díaz, Serino
Diego, Cayetano
Diego, Francisco
Domínguez, Miguel
Domínguez Campos, Alfonso
Echavarría, Juan
Echevarría Imaz, Máximo
Elexpe Arce, Víctor
Ezquizabal, Eduardo
Fernández, José
Fernández, Marcial
Fernández, S.
Fernández Gamarra, León
Fernández Herrador, José
Fernández Machín, Ramón
Fernández Rodríguez, Manuel
Figueras, Ricardo
Galeani, J.
García, Antonio
García, Faustino
García, José Iñigo
García, Raymond

García Álvarez, Emilio
García de Riu, Lorena
García García, Francisco
García Larrea, Ramón
García Oliver, Juan
García Polanco, Bernabé
García Ruiz, A.
García Soco, Ricardo
Gelabert, Andrés
Gil, Pino
Giráldez, Manuel
Godoy, Juan
Goicochea, Luis
Gómez, Diego
Gómez, Isabel
Gómez, Mario
Gómez García, J.
González, Emilio
González, José
González, Manuel
Guisado, Nemesio
Guerrero, Eduardo
Gutiérrez Álvarez, Jesús
Guzmán, Jaime
Guzmán, José
Helmick, Rudolf
Hernández, Artemio
Hormandoria, Cristóbal
Iglesias, Avelino
Iglesias Alonso, Remedios
Iturriaga, Zacarias
Jiménez Nortez, Ginés
Katnich, Ivan
La Torres, Antonio
Lago Martínez, Bernabé
Lagrava, Pedro
Lechuga, Horna
Lecumperi, José
Lecuona, Carmen
Llaneras, Jaime
Llinares, Tomas
Lobón, Francisco

Lopategui, Norberto G.
López, César
López, Diego
López, Raimundo
López Becerra, A.
López Becerra, Anastasio
López Fernández, Manuel
López Moyano, Juan
López Novello, Higinio
López Parrando, Pilar
Lozoya, Virgilio
Luigi, Bonino
Luigo García, José
Luis Alba, José
Luis Alba, Octavio
Malave, Alberto
Malave, Luz María
Manrique, P.
Martí Ibáñez, Félix
Martín, Eustaquio
Martín, Restituto
Martínez, Encarnación
Martínez Alvez, Francisco
Martínez Cofino, Rafael
Martínez Iglesias, Domingo Joaquín
Martínez Mislata, Miguel
Martínez Vila, Luis
Medina Fernández, Enrique
Medrano Castillo, Juan
Menéndez, Emilio
Menéndez, Luis
Migoya de la Llana, José
Migoya Iglesias, Acacia
Migoya Iglesias, Josefina
Mingorance, Juan E. Domingo
Minuit, Peter
Miramontes, Luís
Mojón Vázquez, Ramón
Montero, Jesús C.
Montero, José M.
Montes, Julio
Moragues, Antonio

Mora Puigcerver, Ignacia
Moreno, Enriqueta
Múgica Arbelca, Juan
Muñiz, José
Nazareth, Mario A.
Nieto Ruiz, José
Orgaz, Eduardo
Osorio Iglesias, Benjamín
Oviedo, M.
Palma, E.
Pan, Antonio
Pareja, Francisco
Peguir, Irene
Pérez, José
Pérez, Ramón
Pérez, Saturnino
Pérez, Varela
Pérez Alzubide, José
Pérez Martin, José
Pérez Pérez, Emilio
Perramón Mora, José
Perramón Mora, Roberto
Peterson, Hans
Piñeiro, Luis
Porto, Rosendo L.
Prego Vieiro, José
Prieto, Martín
Reggiani, Antonio
Reyes Ramos, Juan
Rico, José
Rico, Víctor
Rodenas, Ramón
Rodríguez, Ocasio
Rodríguez, Víctor
Rodríguez Boti
Rodríguez Tecla, Vicente
Rodríguez Urbina, Félix
Romeo, Aurelio
Romo, E.
Ruis, Juan
Ruiz Gómez, Ramón
Ruiz, (sisters)

Sáez, G.
Salinas, Félix
Sánchez, Emilio
Sánchez, Miguel
Sánchez Frade, Alfonso
Sanmartín, Antonio
Santamaría, A.
Segura Golmayo, Vicente
Silvestrini, Humberto
Socas, Ricardo G.
Souto, Arturo
Spielman, Samuel
Stiuvenburg, John
Suárez García, Manuel
Suárez Picallo, Ramón
Suárez Suarez, Manuel

Tafall, Osorio
Talarico, Luiggi
Tallón, Josefa
Tineo, Enrique
Torhyo, Jacinto
Trivelli, Bartolome
Unanue, Eladio
Vidal, Guillermo
Vidal y Planas, Alfonso
Viegas Vaz, José
Viejo, Máximo, and spouse
Viesea, Luis
Vila, Luis M.
Wetting, Enrique
Zarraga, Jesús
Zvirblys, Domas

Appendix E
Popular Plays and Zarzuelas Produced by the SHC, 1939–1977

Abatí, Joaquín, *Entre doctores* (1892)
Álvarez Quintero, Serafín, and Joaquín Álvarez Quintero, *El amor en el teatro* (1908)
———, *Amores y amoríos* (1908)
———, *Así se escribe la historia* (1917)
———, *El chiquillo* (1899)
———, *Los chorros del oro* (1906)
———, *Doña hormiga* (1930)
———, *Malvaloca* (1912)
———, *La media naranja* (1903)
———, *Morritos* (1906)
———, *El nuevo servidor* (1905)
———, *El ojito derecho* (1897)
———, *La patria chica* (1907)
———, *La puebla de las mujeres* (1912)
———, *Lo que hablan las mujeres* (1932)
———, *Solico en el mundo* (1911)
Arniches, Carlos, *La cara de Dios* (1899)
———, *Los caciques* (1920)
———, *Las estrellas* (1911)
———, *La venganza de la Petra; o, Donde las dan las toman* (1917)
Aza, Vital, *Robo en el despoblado* (1898)
———, *El sueño dorado* (1890)

Benavente, Jacinto, *Los intereses creados* (1907)
Calvacho, Carlos, *Para mentir, las mujeres* (1880)
Carreño, Anselmo C., Luis Fernández de Sevilla, Reveriano Soutullo, and Juan Vert, *La del Soto del Parral* (1927)
Cervantes Saavedra, Miguel de, *Los habladores* (1881)
De Echegaray, José, and Esteban Roig, *De mala raza* (1921)
Dicenta, Joaquín, *Juan José* (1895)
Esteso y López de Haro, Luis, *Monomanía torera* (1915)
Estremera, José, *La cuerda floja* (1894)
Fernández Ardavín, Luis, *Doña Diabla* (1925)
Flores, Ricardo, and Vicente Peydró, *Las carceleras* (1904)
Garcia Álvarez, Enrique, and Fernando Luque, *La tragedia de la viña o el que no come la diña* (1920)
García Lorca, Federico, *Mariana de Pineda* (1927)
———, *La zapatera prodigiosa* (1930)
Gavault, Paul, *Tía Ramona* (1917)
Gil y Luengo, Constantino, and Julián Romea, *El teniente cura* (1914)
Gómez, Alonso, and Pedro Muñoz Seca, *El contrabando* (1905)
González de Iribarren, José, *La partida de ajedrez* (1878)
González del Castillo, Emilio, *Las leandras* (1931)
Jackson Cortés, Eduardo, ¡*Quién fuera libre!* (1891)
Jackson Veyán, José, *La tonta de capirote* (1896)
———, *Una limosna por dios* (1914)
Larra, Luis de, *La trapera* (1902)
Linares Becerra, Luis, Juan Bautista Pont, and Gerónimo Giménez, *El cuento del dragón* (1912)
Lope de Vega, Félix, *Fuenteovejuna* (1619)
Lucio, Celso, et al., *Marcha de Cádiz* (1902)
Lustonó, Eduardo, *Basta de suegros* (1875)
Mata, Pedro, *En la boca del lobo* (1922)
Morera y Valls, Francisco, et al., *Justicia catalana* (1887)
Muñoz Seca, Pedro, and Pedro Pérez Fernández, *Coba fina* (1917)
———, *Un drama de Calderón* (1921)
Navarro, Calixo, and Javier Govantes de Lamadrid, *La tela de araña* (1882)
Paradas, Enrique, and Joaquín Jiménez, *Las corsarias* (1919)
Penella Moreno, *La niña de los besos* (1911)
Pérez Capo, Felipe, *La vena de plata* (1916)
Pérez Galdós, Benito, *Doña Perfecta* (1876)
Pina Domínguez, Mariano, and Ángel Rubio, *Ya somos tres* (1880)
Ramos Carrión, Miguel, *La criatura* (1920).
———, *La muela de juicio* (1902)
———, *La real gana* (1915)

Ramos Carrión, Miguel, and Vital Aza, *Robo en el despoblado* (1898)
Ramos Martín, Antonio, *El sexo débil* (1927)
Ramos Martín, Antonio, and Jacinto Guerrero, *Los gavilanes* (1924)
Saco del Valle y Flores, Arturo, et al., *El túnel* (1905)
Selles, Eugenio, *El rayo verde* (1905)
Sorozábal, Pablo, Emilio González del Castillo, and Manuel Martí Alonso, *Katiuska* (1931)
Thomas, Brandon, *La tía de Carlos* (1892)
Torrado, Adolfo, *Una gallega en Nueva York* (1946)
Torrado, Adolfo, and Leandro Navarro, *Los pellizcos* (1934)
Unzandizaga, José María, *Las golondrinas* (1913)
———, *La llama* (1918)

Appendix F
Original Antifascist and Exile Plays, 1937–1950

Information, often incomplete, has been compiled from reviews and articles published in U.S. Spanish-language periodicals.

Original Plays	Opening Dates (Approx.)	Director/Group/Actors and Roles	Further Details
Ignacio Zugadi Garmendia, ¡Milicianos al frente! (Militia to the front) Prologue and epilogue by José Castilla Morales	Ateneo Hispano, New York Sept. 26, 1936	José Ferrer, Luis Zugadi Garmendia, Leonor Lucas, Julián Benedet, Francisco Huerta, Rosita Flores, Enrique González, Ana Barrios, Delfín Fernández, Alfredo Alegría, Lola Amato Prompter: Antonio Martínez	Humorous and tragic dialogues about the Spanish Civil War Prologue: In the mountains of Guadarrama, near Madrid, a militiaman enunciates the reasons why he is defending the Second Republic. In a working-class barrio in Madrid, Casimiro and Don Atilano are reading about the war in the paper. Don Atilano thinks is not fair that people must fight in the trenches for a republic. Instead, people should fight to have the state dismantled. Women think only fascists stay home and read the paper. Leocadia takes a rifle and tells men they are cowards for not fighting for democracy. When women are about to enroll in the militia to defend Madrid, men join them too. The script has survived and can be found in the Recovering the U.S. Hispanic Literary Heritage project, University of Houston.
José Castilla Morales, with music by Leopoldo González, Ensayos breves de teatro popular Includes ¡Abajo Franco! (Down with Franco) and Rebeldía (Rebelliousness)	Mar. 28, 1937	Mary Reid, Julián Benedet, José Arana, Gregorio Garay	In ¡Abajo Franco!, a Spanish working-class married couple argue in New York. The man is an antifascist, but his wife claims that he acts superior toward her. They reconcile with a revolutionary song. In Rebeldía, a militiaman says goodbye to his girlfriend in Madrid. Ends with a revolutionary song. The script has survived and can be found in the Recovering the U.S. Hispanic Literary Heritage project, University of Houston.
Sebastián Recio, El pueblo mártir (The suffering people)	June 20, 1937	Director: Mary Reid Sociedad "Calpe América" María Trujillo, L. Artas, M. Trujillo, P. Hoyos, M. Palomares	
Mary Reid, Sor Piedad (Sister Piedad)	June 20, 1937		A wounded militiaman and a nun are executed. She was serving as a spy for the Republicans among the rebels.
Nicola Brunori, Suora Estrella (Sister Estrella)	Manhattan Lyceum, New York, June 6, 1937	Juventud Libertaria Hijas de España Miguel Pérez, Ana María, Maestro Vizcaíno, Anita Rabal	Farce about fascist Italy and Spain

Original Plays	Opening Dates (Approx.)	Director/Group/Actors and Roles	Further Details
Luis Garagarza, *El fascismo en Vizcaya* (Fascism in Vizcaya)	Webster Hall, New York, Oct. 24, 1937	Grupo Vasco	
José Paniagua Anaya, *Desolación* (Desolation)	Centro Hispano Americano, Pittsburg, California, Nov. 9, 1937	Carmen Sánchez, Josefina Sánchez Aja, Daniel Sánchez Aja, Jaime Díaz, Lydia Díaz, Maria Singh, Victoriano Luciano, Antonio E. González, Ida Bernardi, Eulogita Ribas, Rafael Morillas, Ramón Bernardi	Josefina Sánchez sings the song "Agapito." Her character symbolizes the common Spaniard who has migrated to the United States.
Ignacio Zugadi Garmendia, *Huelga en el Puerto* (Strike in the docks)	Transport Hall, New York, Dec. 5, 1937	Grupo Ateneo Hispano	
José Blanco, *El Mensajero* (The messenger)	Canton, Ohio, May 13, 1938	Comité Antifascista Español	Dramatic one-act
José Blanco, *Entre Actos* (Between acts)	Canton, Ohio, May 13, 1938	Comité Antifascista Español	Comic one-act
Ignacio Zugadi Garmendia, *Volvieron los bárbaros* (The return of the barbarians)	Centro Español, New York, Nov. 1939	El Teatro del Pueblo Leonor Lucas, Mary Reid, Carmen Novo, Julián Benedet, Vicente Cordellat, Víctor Fernández, José Ferrer, Vicente Roca, Delfín Fernández, Gregorio Garay, Alejandro Díaz, José Moscardo	
Leopoldo González, *El cigarillo* (The cigarette)	Manhattan Center, Oct. 2, 1938		
Leopoldo González, *La cocina antifascista* (The antifascist kitchen)	Hunts Point Palace, Bronx, New York, Apr. 1940	Las Juventudes Españolas Variety shows by Estela y Papo, Cesar Tapia y Maclovia, Los Ojedas, Don Casanova, Joe Iglesias, Miss Hony Jodson, Gloria Ripaldi y Josefina Terenti, Roberto Rodriguez y Josefina Menendez Baritone: Arturo Cortes Speakers: Pedro Villa Fernández and Valeriano Calderón Music: Esteban Roig Orchestra	*Juguete cómico* (farce) mocking fascism

Original Plays	Opening Dates (Approx.)	Director/Group/Actors and Roles	Further Details
Sebastián Recio, *España Unida* (United Spain)	Centro Español, New York, Mar. 17, 1940	Compañía de Mary Reid, Grupo Leonés Mary Reid, Luis Orta, Alejandro Ellul, Juanito López, Pepe Iche, Gregorio Garay, Manuel Mena	Short play that explained how political ideas and regionalisms do not help the antifascist cause but when the people from Madrid, Galicia, Andalusia, Basque Country, Catalonia, and Valencia agree, Spain can be saved from fascism.
Ignacio Zugadi Garmendia, *El drama eterno* (The eternal drama)	Manhattan Center, New York, Jul. 19, 1940	Leonor Lucas, Chicha Fernández, José Argibay, Rafael Rueda, Cesareo Llano, Ramón Quesada, José Quesada, Gregorio Garay, Francisco Barroso	Two-act farce with music by Leopoldo González[1] Juan E. Domingo Mingorance and Miguel Mingot decorated the set.
Manuel Sugrañés, *Asturias la indomable* (Asturias the indomitable)	Manhattan Center, New York, Oct. 1940	Victoria Martínez, Isabel Vento, Elsa Sierra, María Trujillo, Elena Becerra, Josefina Mulinelli, Esperanza Orta, Josefina Amor, Rosa and Josefina Marijuan, Olivia Fernández, Josefina and Kay Gandarillas, Juan Triguera, Antonio Rueda, Manuel Junquera	*Cuadro simbólico* (symbolic tableau vivant) The set was painted by Juan E. Domingo Mingorance. Gregory Garay sang an antifascist hymn.
Manuel Sugrañés, *Paco, Benito y Adolfo: ¿Cuál de los tres es más golfo?* (Franco, Mussolini, and Hitler: Who is the biggest scoundrel?)	Palm Garden, New York, Jan. 1941	Mary Rei: English girl Ignacio Zugadi: Garmendia: Hitler Isabelita Zugadi: Dead child Coto Fueyo: Commander Sebastian Palme: Benito Mussolini Carlos Blanc: Uncle Sam with Rafael Molina, Teresita Neal, Leonor Lucas, Carmen Novo, Flora Restoy, Isabelita Zugadi, F. Coto Fueyo, Alejandro Eliul, José Arigibay, José Amorós, Rafael Rueda, Vicente Roca, Gregorio Garay	Four-act skit, parody of *Don Juan Tenorio* In the act "Objetivos militares" (Military objectives), children who had been killed by Nazi bombs confront Hitler. He becomes terrified and regrets not having killed all the children in the world. Juan E. Domingo Mingorance painted the set.

Original Plays	Opening Dates (Approx.)	Director/Group/Actors and Roles	Further Details
Grupo Salmerón, *Noche de Ronda* (Serenading night), *Los hombres* (Men)	Feb. 9. 1941	Grupo Salmerón, Grupo España Libre Rafael Rueda: Drunk man María Trujillo, Manuel Trujillo, Miguel Morales, Sebastián Palmer, Carmencita López, Yuyita Concheiro, Sylvia Concheiro, Gloria Ripalda, pequeña Minerva, Elenita Trujillo, Fay Torrens, Juanito López, and Francisco Portolés Variety shows by Currito y Coral Piano: Maria Cordellat MC: José Argibay	Comic dialogue
José Castilla Morales, *La madre española* (The Spanish mother)	Palm Garden, New York, Mar. 1941	Carmen Novo, Ignacio Zugadi Garmendia, José Argibay, Mary Reid, Elenita Trujillo	Comic-dramatic entr'acte in two acts with twelve more acts. The topical two-act comic play dramatized the Spanish community in New York and their daily tribulations, including their listening to the SHC's radio broadcast. Main acts: In "Esta noche no hay cena" (There is no dinner tonight), an aristocratic family in Madrid cannot get used to the food rationing in Spain. "La campanillera" (Andalusian singer and dancer of religious songs); "La canción castellana" (The Castillian song); "Trágala, trágala," (Swallow it); "Ay, Carmela, Ay Carmela" (Oh Carmela); "Vecinas, vecinas, aquí está el cartero," (Neighbors, neighbors, the postman is here). In this act, letters are read in Galician and in Italian. A symbolic vignette represents "La jota" (Spanish folk dance) Other acts: "La raza eterna" (The eternal race); "La copla española" (Spanish folk song); "Cascabeles" (bells). In "La tristeza de Andalucía" (Andalusian sadness), an Andalusian woman sings the sadness of seeing Andalusia without flowers after the war. "Epílogo" (Epilogue) "La madre Española" (The Spanish mother).

Original Plays	Opening Dates (Approx.)	Director/Group/Actors and Roles	Further Details
José Castilla Morales, ¡Ay Carmela!	Bridgeport, CT, Mar. 1941	Carmen Novo, Ignacio Zugadi Garmendia	
José Castilla Morales, La República no ha muerto (The Republic is not dead) Music by Esteban Roig	Manhattan Center, New York, Apr. 13, 1941	Mary Reid, Carmiña Novo, Pepita Gil, Angelita Comallonga, Flora Restoy, Teresita Neal, Eusebia Fernández, Carlos Blanch, Esperanza Orta, Alberto Uriarte, Gregory Garay, Ignacio Arrién, Segunda Arrién, Isabel Garay, Santiago Lezcano, Yuyita Concheiro, Gloria Ripalda, P. Coto Fueyo, Celso Gil, José Argibay, Pepe Fernández, Elvira Fernández, Alejandro Ellul, Rafael Rueda, Antonio Rueda, Vicente Cordellat, J. Quiles, José Dimas, Toni Portolés, Leo Ferrer, Luis Orta, Pepita Gil Invited speaker: Alfonso Vidal y Planas Prompters: Antonio Martínez and José Morros	Acts: "Prólogo" (Prologue) "Los romeros de la Albonica" (The pilgrim from Albonica) "Nobleza asturiana" (Asturian nobility) "Cuando el indiano volvió" (When the Spaniard-American returned) "Sublevación de la Pilarica" (The mutiny of the Pilarica) "La Santa Espina" (Catalan song) "La botica iluminada" (Visionary remedy) "El corte del farruco" (The migrant's cut) (farruco = migrant from Galicia or Asturias) "La colonia Española" (The Spanish community abroad) "El Palleter" (Vicente Doménech) Epílogo: "¡Apoteosis!" (Epilogue: Apotheosis!) Miguel Mingot decorated the set.
José Castilla Morales, La panadera asturiana (The Asturian baker)	Webster Hall, New York, Oct. 1941	Mary Reid: Manuela Julian Benet: Young gentleman Ray Miqueli: The father Alejandro Díaz: A miner Edelmiro Borrás: Lieutenant with Carmen Novo, Flora Restoy	About the miners' strikes in Asturias, Spain, in Oct. 1934. A maid is dishonored when her child is not recognized by the father, a young gentleman. She moves to a little town where she becomes an admired single mother and the town's baker.
José Castilla Morales, Andalucía	Bridgeport, CT, Oct. 1941		This might be the stand-alone act "Tristeza de Andalucía" from the play La Madre española (1941)
Manuel Sugrañés, El paraíso fascista (The fascist paradise)	Oct. 31, 1941, Nov. 9, 1941		Apropósito (a topical one-act play) In a hostel in Madrid, comedians hide from Falangists, who are following them. They disguise themselves as a priest, an Italian, and an American dancer in order to escape the fascist forces. The disguises are meant to criticize the Church, the Italian Fascists for their intervention in the Spanish Civil War, and the Americans for not helping the Republic.

Original Plays	Opening Dates (Approx.)	Director/Group/Actors and Roles	Further Details
Luis Garagarza, *Cosas que pueden pasar* (Things that might happen)	Palm Garden, New York, Mar. 6, 1942	Director: José Ferrer Angelita Camallonga, Elenita Trujillo, Flora Restoy, José Ferrer, Joaquín López, Alejandro Díaz, Carlos Puga, José Argibay, Rafael Rueda, Celso Gil, Sebastián Palmer, Juanito Rueda Prompter: Antonio Martinez	Comedy in three acts. The first act foresees the establishment of fascism in the world. In the second act, the Spanish Republican Government saves Spaniards from being lynched by dictators. In the third act, fascist Spaniards living in USA show what they would do if fascism wins.
Manuel Sugrañes, *Knock-out*	St. Georges Hall, May 1942	Lolita Gote, Eduardo López	*Juguete cómico* (one-act farce)
José Castilla Morales, *Octubre Asturiano* (Asturian October)	Ateneo Hispano, New York, Sept. 1942	Flora Restoy	Workers have occupied a stately mansion in the midst of the miners' strike of 1934. These characters voice the people's needs and desires and fight to the end knowing that they will die for their cause.
José Argibay, *Tragedia espiritual* (Spiritual tragedy)	Ateneo Hispano, New York, Feb. 13, 1943		Introspective play about the author's emotions
Luis Garagarza, *Andadas de un curita* (A priest's old ways)	Webster Hall, New York, Feb. 1943	Several affiliated committees Juan Manuel Perez: Father Amador Isabel Arazomena: Priest's housekeeper José Argibay: Sacristan Rafael Rueda: Marquis Sebastián Palmer: Manager Prompter: Antonio Martinez	Set in Vizcaya. A priest tries to be more modern and ends up allowing dancing parties for the parishioners. In one scene, Italian Fascists get their faces slapped with freshly caught fish. A review noted that the Webster Hall was full to capacity, and funds raised stopped two deportations and bought tickets for these refugees to travel to visa-granting Mexico. Funds also helped get medicines, and to pay for other visas for Latin American countries and for refugees detained on Ellis Island.
José Castilla Morales, *Esta noche no hay cena* (There is no dinner tonight)	Palm Garden, New York, Mar. 1943		Stand-alone act from his play *La madre Española*
José Argibay, *El testamento del muerto* (The will of the dead)	Palm Garden, New York, Feb. 1943, Mar. 1943	Grupo Antifascista del Bronx Isabel Arozamena, Nelly Rodríguez, Carmencita López, Consuelo Moreno, Elena Trujillo, Pequeña Minerva, Carmencita López, Nelly Rodríguez Prompter: Antonio Martinez	Set in Madrid, a well-off family cannot get used to the rationing in the city after the Spanish Civil War. Comic *sainete* (musical farce)

Original Plays	Opening Dates (Approx.)	Director/Group/Actors and Roles	Further Details
José Castilla Morales, *Severo, Severino y Severiana*	Palm Garden, New York, May 1943	Artistic Director: Luis Miralles Stage Director: Julián Benedet Carmen Novo: Severiana Julián Benedet: Professor Carlos Blanc: Young gentleman Jerónimo Monfort: Dubious character Pepita Gil: Naïve young lady Flora Restoy: Carefree lady Enrique Miret: Don Hilarión Prompter: Antonio Martínez MC: José Argibay	Farce with seven characters: a sullen maid called Features Severiana, a traditional professor, a free-spending Casanova, a dubious character, a young lady, a bored lady, and an extravagant character
Ignacio Zugadi Garmendia, *Hombres y Mujeres* (Men and women)	Palm Garden, New York, Oct. 1943	Centro Asturiano New York Leonor Lucas, Julián Benedet, Ignacio Zugdi, Isabelita Zugadi, Carmina Hourrutinier, Nelly Santigosa, Maria Trujillo, Angela Alegría, Linda Goñi, Francisco Huerta, Vicente Cordellat, Sebastián Palmer, Mateo Antoñanza, Delfín Fernández, Alejandro Díaz, Amor Villar, Manuel de la Nuez	Comedy in three acts about politicians of an imaginary country. The play shows their ambitions and contradictions.
José Castilla Morales, *La villa immortal* (The immortal city) Music by Esteban Roig	Palm Garden, New York, Nov. 1943	Ángela Alegría: Ms. Josefa Rafael Rueda: Nemesio Aida Perlata: Natalia Carmita Hourruitiner: Venancia J. Manuel Pérez: Platino Miguel Morales: Responsible person Sebastián Palmer: Mr. Barraguet María del Carmen Gómez: Rosita la Macarena Enrique Miret: Mr. Wells Carmencita López: Pisa Bonito Edelmiro Borrás: Albino Blanco Julio Minguillón: Manolo Flora Restoy: Ms. Eulogia Epilogue read by Félix Martí Ibáñez	Two-act comedy-drama about the fall of Madrid to the rebel forces during the Spanish Civil War. The clients of a hostel in the city exemplify different Spanish stereotypes.

Original Plays	Opening Dates (Approx.)	Director/Group/Actors and Roles	Further Details
Sebastian Palmer, *La España peregrina* (Migrant Spain)	Casa Galicia, New York, Mar. 1944	Mary Reid, Ángela Alegría	Six-act tragedy about Spanish refugees in Santo Domingo.
Soria, *La escuela moderna* (The Modern School)	Escuela Española, New York, Mar. 1945	Director: M. Porto Students from the Esteban Roig School Prompter: M. López MC: Sebastian Palmer	
José Castilla Morales, *Alarma en el ministerio* (Alarm in the administration) Prologue and Epilogue by Sebastian Palmer	Webster Hall, New York, Oct. 7, 1945		Comic play
José Castilla Morales, *¡Salud y átomo!* (Good health and atoms!)	Palm Garden, New York, Dec. 1945	Carmen Novo	Funny play with a complicated plot about eccentric characters in a newsroom
José Castilla Morales, *La familia de Don Cristóbal* (Don Christopher's family)	Webster Hall, New York, Oct. 1946	Lola Restoy, Marita Reid, Nina Zabal	Columbus arrives in the Americas.
José Castilla Morales, *Puente y camino* (Bridge and path)	Palm Garden, New York, Feb. 1947	Flora Restoy: Olegaria Grace Flecha: Grace Flecha Carmen Novo: Adela José Argibay: Don Andrés Angel King: The doctor Celso Gil: Lucio Rafael Rueda: Picio Juan M. Pérez: The patient Prompter: Antonio Martínez	Comedy in three acts. Funny short dialogues, many scenes on and off stage.

Original Plays	Opening Dates (Approx.)	Director/Group/Actors and Roles	Further Details
José Castilla Morales, *El abanico de abril* (The April's fan) Music by Bernabé Solís	Manhattan Center, New York, Mar. 1947	María Trujillo, Flora Restoy, Grace Flecha, Carmen Alvarez, Florentino Ferro, J. Manuel Pérez, Rafael Rueda, Gregorio Garay Soprano: Aída Peralta Baritone: Alfonso Ibars Prompter: Antonio Martínez Scene painter: Vicente Roca	Lyric musical Romance and patriotism in the Second Spanish Republic Fourteen acts: "La dama madura" (The seasoned lady) "El lenguaje del abanico" (The language of the fan) "Las lavanderas del Tajo" (The laundresses of the Tajo River) "La canción del refugiado" (The song of the refugee) "Los barqueros del Ebro" (The boatmen of the Ebro River) "Carta de España" (Letter from Spain) "Frasquito El Evacuao" (Frasquito the Relocated) "La canción del camión" (The truck song) "Conspiración" (Conspiracy) "Nobleza Vasca" (Basque honor) "Tolerancia" (Tolerance) "No Pasa Nada" (It's fine) "Fantasía" (Fantasy) "Cita a Medianoche" (Midnight date) "El Morado" (Purple) "Apoteosis" (Apotheosis) The "Song of the Refugee" was partially reproduced in *EL*: "I am the refugee/ That is not fearful/ And rambles/ Singing his song/ And even if the world/ Does not care about my suffering/ I open horizons/ And I do not care/ Because I bear in my body/ The marks of a warrior/ A warrior for liberty/ I can fight at war/ I can work for peace!²
José Castilla Morales, *El tantán de la resistencia* (The tomtom of the resistance) Music by Esteban Roig	Palm Garden, New York, Oct. 1947	María Trujillo, Aída Peralta, Grace Flecha, Flora Restoy	*Sainete* (musical farce) in one act set in a community courtyard in Madrid in 1947. It mocks Francisco Franco's regime.

Original Plays	Opening Dates (Approx.)	Director/Group/Actors and Roles	Further Details
José Castilla Morales, *Cita a media noche* (Midnight date)			Lusitania and Aironot meet at midnight in Portugal and talk about Lusitania's neighbor, Carmen de Iberia, who has been harassed by a man. Aironot says his friends have come to help her. Each male character represents a country that wants Carmen, who represents Spain. Carmen does not want to be a sell-out. The script has survived and was published in *EL*, Dec. 29, 1947.
José Castilla Morales, *Arrosalina* Music by Esteban Roig	Palm Garden, New York, Feb. 1948	La Nati, Anita de Plama, Encarna, Mari Cruz, Grace Flecha, María Cordellat, Lola Bravo, María Trujillo, Lolita Álvarez, Flora Restoy, Leoncio, Alejandro Díaz	Zarzuela
José Castilla Morales, *Los perdigones* (The partridge chicks) Music by Esteban Roig	Livingston Hall, New York, Feb. 1948	Mary Reid: Marquess of Aguria Flora Restoy: Pepa the Gypsy Anita de Palma: Rosarillo Nina Zabal: Natalia María Trujillo: Juanilla Vicente Cordellat: Chupipilla Ray Miqueli: Alfredo Francisco Portolés: Lieutenant Gregorio Garay: Perico Prompter: Antonio Martínez	Zarzuela about Andalusian customs, set in a country house in Andalusia. Alfred, the son of the marquis, is in love with María del Carmen, daughter of a worker. The marchioness and the house staff help the lovers. Alfred is accused of belonging to a resistance organization. It includes an elegy for Federico García Lorca.
José Castilla Morales, *¡Ay qué tíos!* (Alas, what dudes!)	Dec. 12, 1948	Marita Reid, Race Flecha, Dorita Miqueli, Flora Restoy, Nina Zabal, María Trujillo, Carmen Flecha	*Juguete cómico* (farce) in two acts
José Castilla Morales, *Con permiso del señor* (With permission of our lord and master)	Feb. 12, 1950	Teresita Osta, Dorita Miqueli, Nina Zabal	

Appendix G
Regular Speakers and Performers, 1937–1977, and Their Roles

Speakers

Allen, Jay
Alonso, Daniel
Álvarez del Vayo, Julio
Arenas, Jesús
Asensio Torrado, José
Baldwin, Roger Nash
Barski, Edward
Bergamín, José
Browder, Earl
Calderón, Valeriano
Cannon, Walter B.
Castilla Morales, José
Castro, José
Curran, Joe
De Albornoz, Álvaro
De la Villa, Antonio
De los Ríos, Fernando
De los Ríos, Laura
Enters, Angna
Fernández Sánchez, Leonardo
Ferrer Sanmartí, Sol
García Lorca, Francisco
González, Ernestina
González, Gloria
González López, Emilio
González Peña, Ramón
Granell, Eugenio Fernández
Enjuto Ferran, Federico
Issac, Stanley M.
Laderer, Emil
Lobo, Rev. Leocadio
López Reyes, José
Lore, Ludwig
Marcantonio, Vito
Marcelino, Domingo
Martí Ibáñez, Félix
Martínez Barrio, Diego
Maurín Julià, Joaquim
McConnell, Francis J.
Meana, Carmen
Miaja Menant, José
Negrín y López, Juan
Norman, Thomas
O'Flanagan, Reverent

Osorio Tafall, Bibiano
Palmer, Sebastian
Pérez, Providencia
Poza Juncal, Hernán
Preteceille, Ojiere
Quitanilla, Luis
Reid, Mary
Reissig, Reverent Herman Frederick
Rocker, Rudolf
Rodríguez Castelao, Alfonso Daniel
Ruiz Vilaplana, Antonio
Sender, Ramón J.
Saenz, Vicente
Suarez Picallo, Ramón
Soto, Luis
Thomas, Norman
Toryho, Jacinto
Torres, Domingo
Valenti, Girolamo
Villa Fernández, Pedro
Wagner, Robert
Zimmerman, Charles
Zugadi Garmendia, Ignacio

Performers

Alegría, Ángela (actress)
Alonso, María (actress)
Alonso, Martín (guitarist)
Alonso, Ruth (singer)
Álvarez, Aida (dancer, La Conga Cabaret)
Álvarez, Carmencita (dancer)
Amor, Esperanza (actress)
Antoñanzas, Mateo (actor)
Argibay, José (actor/comic)
Arozamena, Isabel (actress)
Arrién, Ignacio (actor)
Artes, Dora (tango singer)
Arvizu, Juan (singer)
Atidiello, Ramón S. (actor)
Avellanet, Adolfo Puerto Rican guitarist
Avellanet, Inés, Puerto Rican guitarist

Baliño, Vicente (conductor)
Barrios, Ana (actress)
Belmonte, Gloria (dancer)
Benedet, Julian (actor)
Betancourt, Leticia (actress)
Blanch, Carlos (actor)
Boizan, Julieta (dancer, piano player)
Borrás, Eldemiro (actor)
Bravo, Lola (dancer)
Brizee, Mary (singer)
Cairo, Bello (pianist)
Capo, Bobbi (singer)
Capobianco, Mr. (pianist)
Cardoza, Mildred (dancer)
Casanova, Don (singer)
Ceballos, Eutimio (actor)
Comallonga, Angelita (actress)
Comallonga, Pepita (actress)
Concheiro, Silvia (dancer)
Concheiro, Yuyita (dancer)
Cordellat, Maria (pianist, actress, teacher)
Cordellat, Vicente (singer)
Córdoba, Arturo de (actor)
Cortés, Arturo (singer)
Coto, Mike (actor)
Coto Fueyo, P. (unknown)
Coto Fueyo, Violeta (actress)
Currito y Coral (dancers)
De la Nuez, Manolito Jr. (actor)
De Torre, Emilio (band conductor)
Díaz, Alejandro (actor)
Dimas, José {role?}
Divar, Julia (singer)
Domínguez, Tomás (actor)
Elica, Flora (actress)
Ellul, Alejandro (actor)
Estela y Papo (band conductors)
Falcón, Rafael (actor)
Fernández, Anita (singer)
Fernández, Carmen (actress)
Fernández, Chicha (actress)
Fernández, Delfín (actor)

Regular Speakers and Performers, 1937–1977, and Their Roles

Fernández, Elvira (dancer)
Fernández, Eusebia
Fernández, Pepe y la Rancherita (flamenco dancers)
Fernández, Víctor (actor)
Ferrer, Leo (actor)
Flores, Mariquita (dancer)
Furniz, Zoilaluz (singer)
Garay, Alberto (actor)
Garay, Gregorio (singer)
Garay, Isabel (actress)
García, José (guitarist)
Gil, Celso (actor)
Gil, Pepita (actress)
Gómez, María del Carmen (singer)
Gómez, Vicente (guitarist)
Goñi, Linda (dancer)
González, Gloria (singer)
González, Violeta (actress)
Gracia, Julieta (dancer)
Hermanitos del Villar (dancers)
Hoyo, Paco (actor)
Huerta, Francisco (actor)
Iche, Pepe (actor)
Iglesias, Joe (reciter)
Johnson, Ho (dancer)
Jonson, Hony (dancer)
Junquera, Manuel (actor)
La Gitanilla (singer)
La Mora y Moyano de Córdoba (dancers)
La pequeña Minerva (flamenco dancer)
Larzabal, Caridad (actriz)
Lasanta, Manuel (actor)
Lazabal, Caridad (actress)
Lezcano, Santiago (actor)
Lima, Alberto de (singer)
Llano, Cesáreo (actor)
Lolita y Juneda (dancers)
López, Carmencita (dancer and singer)
López, Juanito (singer)
Los Chilenos (dancers)
Los hermanos Elías (dancers)
Los Ojedas (dancers, Cabaret Casino Cubano)
Lucas, Leonor (actress)
Maestro Violino (musician)
Mandret, Luís (actor)
Maria Berta, Frances Irizarry and Valenti (tango singer and guitarist)
Mariluz (actress)
Mariquita (actress)
Martínez, Antonio (prompter)
Martínez, Victoria (soprano)
Mena, Manuel (actor)
Ménendez, Josefina "La Galleguita" (dancer)
Mihail, Lillian (dancer)
Mingorance, Juan E. Domingo (scene painter)
Mingot, Miguel (scene designer)
Minguillón, Julio (singer)
Miquel, Agustín (singer)
Miralles, Luis (prompter)
Monfort, Jeronimo (actor)
Montero, Dorita (dancer)
Morales, Celia (dancer)
Morales, Miguel (actor)
Moreno, Consuelo (singer)
Moreno, Miguel (flamenco singer)
Muñoz, Armanda (actor)
Muñoz, Felipe (singer)
Neal, Teresita (soprano)
Novo, Carmen (actress)
Orta, Esperanza (actress)
Orta, Luis (actor)
Ortega, José (actor)
Osta, Teresita (dancer)
Palacios, Gloria (dancer)
Palmer, Sebastián (actor)
Pérez, Juan Manuel (actor)
Portoles, Antonio (singer)
Portoles, Francisco (Frank) (singer)
Pumar, A. (prompter)
Quesada, José (actor)

Quesada, Ramón (actor)
Rabal, Anita (singer)
Ramona y Manolo (dancers)
Rapsilas, Esteban M. (actor)
Reid, Mary (actress)
Restoy, Flora (actress)
Ripaldi, Gloria (dancer)
Rodríguez, Antonio (guitarist)
Rodríguez, Johnny (musician)
Rodríguez, Nellie (actress)
Rodríguez, Roberto (dancer)
Roig, Esteban, and the Happy Boys (band)
Rosy, Cony (actress)
Rueda, Antonio (actor)
Rueda, José (actor)
Rueda, Rafael (actor)
Ruíz, Betty (dancer)
Ruíz, Lolita (flamenco dancer)
Ruíz, Maclovia (dancer, Cuban Cabaret Casino Havana-Madrid)
Sánchez, Abelardo (pianist)
Santigosa, Nelly (singer)
Saro, Juan José (singer)
Sarro, Pina (singer)
Segui, Arturito (flamenco dancer)
Selgas, Celestino (prompter)
Soler, Domingo (actor)
Sommovigo, Oddonne (musician)
Suárez, José (actor)
Tacón, Francisco (actor)
Tain, Antonio (conductor of band Club Madrid)
Tapia, Cesar (dancer, Cuban Cabaret Casino Havana-Madrid)
Terenti, Josefina (dancer)
Teresiya de Triana and the malagueño (flamenco dancers)
Torrens, Fay (dancer)
Torres, Manuel (pianist)
Trujillo, Elena "La Malagueñita" (dancer)
Trujillo, Manuel (actor)
Trujillo, María (actress)
Uriarte, Alberto (actor)
Urrutinier, Carmen (actress)
Usoz, Adolfo (accordionist)
Valiente, Gloria (singer)
Villarino, Geronimo (guitarist)
Villasuso, Asunción G. (singer)
Zayas, Victoria (actress)
Zugadi Garmendia, Ignacio (actor)
Zugadi, Isabelita (actress)

Notes

Introduction: The SHC's Opposition to Spanish Fascism

1. Although scholars have provided approximate numbers of Spanish migrants and exiles to the United States, statistics do not always account for undocumented workers and refugees. See Rueda Hernanz, *La emigración contemporánea de españoles a Estados Unidos, 1820–1950*; Rueda Hernanz, "El asociacionismo de los españoles en los EE.UU. en los siglos XIX y XX"; and Varela-Lago, "Conquerors, Immigrants, Exiles."

2. It was first called Comité Antifascista Español. The separation from the Communist membership also prompted the change of the organization's publication's name from *Frente Popular* (1936–1939) to *España Libre* in Nov. 1939.

3. Arenas, "Cómo se inició la ayuda en Nueva York," *CNT* (México), July 19, 1944. The numerous Hispanic workers' societies had unsuccessfully tried to confederate in 1929 ("De nuestros lectores," *La Prensa* [New York City], Mar. 29, 1929). In 1937, the strict neutrality laws compelled the affiliation of these organizations into a confederation in order to provide the government with detailed information about aid sent to Spain. Also, antifascist committees from firmly established migrant organizations (ethnic, mutual aid, regional, cultural) affiliated with the SHC.

4. Summer meetings were celebrated at the nudist Sociedad Naturista Hispana in Annadale, Staten Island, where excursions and dances enhanced fraternity among Hispanics (Don Pepe, "59 Henry Street," *EL*, Feb. 3, 1961; Don Pepe, "59 Henry Street," *EL*, Apr. 7, 1961). In 1942, *España Libre*'s newsroom moved to 231 West 18th Street.

5. Don Pepe, "59 Henry Street," *EL*, Feb. 17, 1961.

6. After the classic historiography centered on nations, fascism has been investigated in comparative studies to nuance the uniqueness of each national case. Most recently,

transnational approaches focus on cross-border interactions and exchanges. For example, scholars are documenting Fascist Italy's attempts to establish a Spanish fascist nation through the creation of a state party, a charismatic leader, a single union, and a single militia. See Gallego and Morente, "The Peculiarities of Spanish Fascism," in *The Last Survivor*, 1–35.

7. Gallego and Morente, "The Peculiarities of Spanish Fascism," 15.

8. Gallego and Morente, "The Peculiarities of Spanish Fascism," 15–17.

9. Albanese and del Hierro, *Transnational Fascism in the Twentieth Century*, 162.

10. Bauerkämper and Rossoliński-Liebe, *Fascism without Borders*; Albanese and del Hierro, *Transnational Fascism in the Twentieth Century*; Rodrigo, *La guerra fascista*; Costa Pinto and Kallis, *Rethinking Fascism and Dictatorship in Europe*.

11. Albanese and del Hierro, *Transnational Fascism in the Twentieth Century*, 165.

12. See Freeman, *Working-Class New York*, 18.

13. Vega and Iglesias, *Memoirs of Bernardo Vega*, 191. Although the literature on American volunteers who went to Spain is prolific, new research on U.S. anarchists will bring more information about their participation in the Spanish Civil War. See Zimmer, "The Other Volunteers," 19–52.

14. "Pablo de la Torriente Brau: Lecturas," *Frente Popular*, Sept. 30, 1937; "Luis Zugadi," *EL*, Mar. 1, 1940.

15. "Luis Zugadi," *Frente Popular*, Mar. 11, 1938.

16. "Luis Zugadi," *Cultura Proletaria*, Mar. 19, 1938. Other SHC members killed in action were Plácido Rodríguez and Avelino González Mallada.

17. "Matías de la Rosa," *EL*, Apr. 2, 1965.

18. In New York, he also founded the Sociedad Naturista Hispana in Annadale, Staten Island ("Rogelio Fernández, In Memoriam," *EL*, May–June 1969).

19. Similarly, the vice consul of the Second Spanish Republic in Panama, Manrique Iglesias Alvar, moved to New York in 1938, where he wrote for *Selecciones*, *Life*, and *Newsweek*. He was a generous donor to the SHC's causes and did not miss any fundraiser, sometimes even acting as master of ceremonies.

20. "Notas de duelo," *EL*, Jan. 12, 1945.

21. García Copado, "Cuénteme usted su vida," *EL*, Mar. 4, 1960.

22. García Copado, "Cuénteme usted su vida," *EL*, Dec. 25, 1959.

23. However, some small businesses were pro-Franco and their owners showed their support to fascist Spain by publishing their views in pro-Francoist periodicals in the United States, among them Benito C. Collada, owner of "El Chico" nightclub. For a full list of Francoist publications and businesses in the United States, see Chase, *Falange*, 211, 234; and Rey García, *Stars for Spain*.

24. De Pereda, *Windmills in Brooklyn*, 28.

25. Vega and Iglesias, *Memoirs of Bernardo Vega*, 107.

26. Colón, *Pioneros puertorriqueños*, 43–45.

27. Other popular villas for the antifascist community were La Toja (Staten Island), Hotel Escorial (Asbury Park, NJ), Villa Ideal (Walden, NY), Villa Nueva (Plattekill, NY), Hotel Hollywood (Highmount, NY), La Granja (Allaben, NY), Villa Victoria (Plattekill, NY), and Valencia (Ramapo, NY).

Notes to Introduction

28. Rafael Guastavino, Vicente Martínez Ybor, José Francisco Navarro, and Manuel Rionda are other well-known Spanish immpresarios and entrepreneurs of the time. Valencian architect Guastavino (1842–1908) designed the vaults for the Grand Central Station, Carnegie Hall, the old Penn Station, the Metropolitan Museum of Art, the Plaza and Baltimore hotels, and the Cathedral of Saint John the Divine. See Cabezas, *La ciutat vertical*; Loren, *Texturas y pliegues de una nación*. In addition, some wealthy Spaniards are credited with having financed the construction of Catholic churches and cathedrals in the United States. These include Martínez Ybor, Navarro, Rionda, Juan Cebrián, Eusebio Molera, Susan Dominguez, Gregorio del Amo, Mrs. Micaela H. de Alba, and Manuela and María de Barril. Asturian Manuel Rionda built his family's sugar empire and partnered with the Czarnikow-Rionda Company in 1896, one of the most prominent sugar broker corporations of its time. Similarly, José Francisco Navarro founded "six of the most important companies in the United States and built the first co-op apartment buildings in Manhattan in 1883" (Varela-Lago, "Conquerors, Immigrants, Exiles," 29–30, 217–223).

29. They were escaping labor unrest in Cuba. The acquisition eventually became Ybor City.

30. "Digna posición de un director de un diario estadounidense," *EL*, Jan. 30, 1953. Also see Varela-Lago, "'We Had to Help,'" 36–56; and Varela-Lago, "'No Pasarán,'" 5–35.

31. "Miguel Alonso," *EL*, Mar. 6, 1953.

32. Qtd in Marco, "States of War: 'Being Civilian' in 1940s Spain," in *Interrogating Francoism*, ed. Graham, 162.

33. Viñas, "Natural Alliances," in *Interrogating Francoism*, ed. Graham, 149.

34. Gallego and Morente, "The Peculiarities of Spanish Fascism," 4.

35. Gallego and Morente, "The Peculiarities of Spanish Fascism," 22.

36. Payne, *Fascism in Spain, 1923–1977*, 363; Rodríguez Barreira, "The Many Heads of the Hydra," 702.

37. Payne, *Fascism in Spain*, 477.

38. Indeed, fascist historiography can be a contentious field. Other scholars define fascism as a reaction to the First World War and the Versailles Treaty, which excludes Spain, country that was not involved in those historical changes. Davis and Lynch, *The Routledge Companion to Fascism and the Far Right*, 95.

39. Casanova and Preston, *Anarchism, the Republic, and Civil War in Spain*, 206.

40. Casanova and Preston, *Anarchism, the Republic, and Civil War in Spain*, 206.

41. See appendix A for a list of the affiliated societies. The Sociedades Hispanas Confederadas was translated as "Confederated Spanish Societies of the United States" in *España Libre* but also as "Spanish Societies Confederated to Aid Spain" in affiliation certificates. Although I offer the alternative translation "Confederation of Hispanic Societies," the shortened "Confederadas" was the term more often used by members.

42. "Cultura Nazi," *EL*, Apr. 12, 1940.

43. Villar Mingo, "Hombres de la resistencia," *EL*, Oct. 21, 1960. Before the Spanish Civil War, Villar Mingo was the editor of the anarchist periodicals *Solidaridad Obrera* (Barcelona), *CNT* (Madrid), *Fragua Social* (Valencia), and *La Protesta* (Buenos Aires).

44. González Malo, "De la tragedia Ibérica," *EL*, Jan. 5, 1940.

45. Following *España Libre*'s usage, I employ the term "Spanish fascism" to broadly refer to the fascist characteristics of the Franco regime.

46. McClennen, *The Dialectics of Exile*, 1, 32.

47. McClennen, *The Dialectics of Exile*, 32.

48. McClennen, *The Dialectics of Exile*, ix, 63.

49. McClennen, *The Dialectics of Exile*, 32.

50. Molina, *El movimiento clandestino en España*.

51. At the time, many Spanish maritime workers carried out seafaring activities in the main port cities of the United States, New York, Boston, and Baltimore. See Fernández Bieito, "Migración y sindicalismo," 113–135.

52. J. Edgar Hoover, Letter to SAC Baltimore, Nov. 7, 1942, Jesús González Malo, FBI Case 100-HQ-105493, NARA.

53. See Navarro Navarro's *Ateneos y grupos ácratas* (2002); McClennen, *The Dialectics of Exile* (2004); Navarro Navarro, *A la revolución por la cultura* (2004); Goyens, *Beer and Revolution* (2007, 2014); Ward, *Trinity of Passion* (2007); Bencivenni, *Italian Immigrant Radical Culture* (2011); Barker, *The Aesthetics of Antifascist Film* (2013); Tomchuk, *Transnational Radicals* (2015); and Zimmer, *Immigrants against the State* (2015).

54. See Cohn, *Underground Passages*.

55. See Yaross Lee, *Twain's Brand* and Camfield, *Necessary Madness*.

56. Although centered on Italian migration, the closest of these works is Guglielmo's *Living the Revolution*.

57. See Chabrán, "Spaniards" (1987); 152–190; Sánchez-Albornoz, ed., *Españoles hacia América* (1988); Rueda, *La emigración contemporánea de españoles a Estados Unidos, 1820–1950* (1993); Varela-Lago, "Conquerors, Immigrants, Exiles" (2008); Faber and Martínez Carazo, eds., *Contra el olvido* (2009); Fernández and Argeo, *Invisible Immigrants* (2014); Cancilla Martinelli and Valera-Lago, eds., *Hidden Out in the Open* (2018); and Castañeda and Feu, *Writing Revolution* (2019). Also see Amo and Shelby, *La obra impresa de los intelectuales españoles en América, 1936–1945* (1950).

58. See Rey García, *Stars for Spain* (1997); Requena and Sepúlveda Losa, *Las Brigadas Internacionales* (2003); Smith, *American Relief Aid and the Spanish Civil War* (2013); and Carroll and Fernández, *Facing Fascism* (2017).

59. See Avrich's *The Modern School Movement*, 327–328.

60. Vials, "Fight against War and Fascism and the Origins of Antifascism in US Culture," 309–321.

61. The international success of Martí Ibáñez's *MD* magazines constituted a public affront to the Francoist diplomacy. At the time, Franco was trying to enhance Spain's status in Latin America by establishing contacts with professional elites (Brydan, *Franco's Internationalists*, 120–121, 124–125).

62. A review of the dictionaries and edited volumes published by the Spanish Civil War literary exile research group (Grupo de Estudios del Exilio Literario, GEXEL) or the ones published by the Recovering the U.S. Hispanic Literary Heritage (RUSHLH) shows the integration of politics and culture in exile. In anarchist studies, Marcella Bencivenni and Jesse

Cohn particularly have highlighted the intrinsic role of culture in generating anarchist politics. Bencivenni, *Italian Immigrant Radical Culture* (2011); Cohn, *Underground Passages* (2015).

63. Lorde, *A Burst of Light*, 131.

64. Spaniards rearticulated anarchism in exile in ways like those described by Cornell, "A New Anarchism Emerges," 105–132; and Pauli, "The New Anarchism in Britain and the US," 134–155.

65. El Chico de la Calle [José Castilla Morales], "No son todos los que están," *EL*, July 20, 1950.

66. El Chico de la Calle [José Castilla Morales], "No son todos los que están."

Chapter 1. Transnational Networks of Support

1. Actas Sociedades Hispanas Confederadas, Sept. 19, 1961, ELC.

2. "Grata visita," *EL*, Oct. 6, 1961.

3. Among other factors, the new hemispheric reach with the opening of the Panama Canal increased interest in Spanish courses at universities at the time. See James D. Fernández, "Longfellow's Law: The Place of Spain and Latin America in US Hispanism, circa 1915," in *Spain in America: The Origins of Hispanism in the United States*, ed. Richard L. Kagan (Urbana: University of Illinois, 2002), 122–141.

4. Del Río attended events with his wife, Puerto Rican author Amelia Agostini del Río. Del Río also wrote for *Ibérica* (New York, 1953–1974), a magazine edited by exile politician Victoria Kent and philanthropist Louise Crane.

5. For example, noted politician and academic Fernando de los Ríos had a precarious visa status that affected his employment. His salary at the New School for Social Research was not enough to sustain his family and he had to be financially helped by his brother. See Muñoz-Rojas, *Poco a poco os hablaré de todo*. According to Claus-Dieter Krohn, a New School scholar salary in 1939, "when scholars from all over Europe sought refuge[,] ... sank to less than $650" (Krohn, *Intellectuals in Exile*. trans., 29).

6. Víctor Alba, a regular contributor to *España Libre*, suggested that González Malo contact William Ebenstein (Princeton University), Robert J. Alexander (Rutgers University), Arthur P. Whitaker (University of Pennsylvania), Neal Buhler (Institute for Labor Research, New York), Germán Arciniegas (Colombian ambassador to Italy), Víctor Raúl Haya de la Torre, and Julián Gorkín (Cuadernos del Congreso por la Libertad de la Cultura, Paris). Víctor Alba, Letter to Alberto Uriarte and González Malo, Oct. 15, 1961, ELC.

7. See Kanellos and Martell, *Hispanic Periodicals in the United States*.

8. Despite the support, there were some minor disputes over the years on topics of antifascism and communism. For a review of pro-Republic newspapers see Kanellos and Martell, *Hispanic Periodicals in the United States*; and Rey García, *Stars for Spain*.

9. Del Moral was a regular contributor to *La Opinión* (Los Angeles); most surely this article was a reprint. Armando Del Moral, "De visita con las estrellas," *La Prensa* (San Antonio), May 2, 1957.

10. Aragonés, Interview by author, Jan. 7, 2014.

11. See Kanellos, "Spanish-Language Anarchist Periodicals in Early Twentieth-Century United States," 59–84; and Chabrán, "Spaniards," 151–189. At the turn of the twentieth

century, Spanish anarchists considered New York to be a desirable destination for exiles. Spaniards mainly emigrated from Barcelona and Galicia (Íñiguez, *Esbozo de una enciclopedia histórica del anarquismo español*, 177–178, 182, 206–207).

12. Nieto Ruiz, interview by author, Nov. 8, 2013.

13. Molina Mateo was jailed in 1946 for his service as secretary of the National Committee of the National Confederation of Labor (CNT) and the National Alliance of Democratic Forces (ANFD). Released in 1952, he went into exile in Toulouse (Zwy Aldouby, Letter to Jesús González Malo, May 4, 1964, JGMP).

14. "La ayuda a España, o un vivero de aprovechados," *Cultura Proletaria*, Sept. 18, 1937; "¡Basta de Farsas!" *Cultura Proletaria*, July 24, 1937.

15. Zugadi, "Contestando a un editorial de 'Cultura Proletaria,'" *Frente Popular*, Aug. 10, 1937. ; Montse Feu, "España Libre (1939-1977)" (PhD. Diss., University of Houston, 2011, 39-51).

16. Arenas Ruiz, "Hombres de Sociedades Hispanas Confederadas," *EL*, Dec. 7, 1962.

17. "Mosaico," *Via Libre*, May 1, 1940.

18. El Chico de la Calle [Castilla Morales], "Gente Conocida: Salvador Espí," *EL*, Aug. 13, 1943. Furthermore, recent publications acknowledge the connected hubs of Hispanic anarchists. See Shaffer's *Black Flag Boricuas* (2013); Streeby's *Radical Sensations* (2013); Meléndez Badillo's *Voces libertarias* (2013); Lomnitz's *The Return of Comrade Ricardo Flores Magnón* (2014); Nicolás Kanellos's "Spanish-Language Anarchist Periodicals in Early Twentieth-Century United States" (2014), 59–84; Sueiro Seoane's "Inmigrantes y anarquistas españoles en EEUU (1890–1920)" (2014); Baer's *Anarchist Immigrants in Spain and Argentina* (2015); Feu's *Jesús González Malo: Correspondencia* (2016); Castañeda's "'Those Were Times of Propaganda and Struggle'" (2017).

19. Anarchist communities in the United States had a long-established culture of theatrical fundraisers for prisoners. The pages of Spanish-language newspapers reviewed many original and popular plays regularly performed by workers' associations as early as the 1910s and 1920s.

20. Bekken and Martín Revellado, "Spanish Seamen, the IWW, and Maritime Syndicalism, 1902–1940," in *Writing Revolution*, ed. Castañeda and Feu, 103–118.

21. Avilés Farré and Herrerín López, *El nacimiento del terrorismo en Occidente*, 176.

22. Numerous Wobblies volunteered to fight in Spain and were either killed or wounded there. See White, "'The Cause of the Workers Who Are Fighting in Spain Is Yours,'" 212–227.

23. For example, "IWW Committee Opposing Franco," *EL*, Feb. 10, 1950; "Importantes resoluciones adoptó el su congreso la Amalgamated Clothing Workers," *EL*, June 9, 1950.

24. "En Montreal," *El*, May 6, 1960.

25. "Juan Bacofra," *EL*, July 20, 1962.

26. Feu, ed., *Jesús González Malo: Correspondencia*, 199.

27. Marcos C. Mari, Letter to Aurelio Pego, Aug. 29, 1967; Esteban Torres, Letter to SHC, Oct. 5, 1966; Esteban Torres, Letter to SHC, Nov. 3, 1966; Esteban Torres, Letter to SHC, Feb. 3, 1976, all ELC.

28. An announcement about the $1,000 donation was published in *EL* on Jan. 3, 1964, and another donation of $2,000 was announced on the May 7 issue of 1965. The UAW

continued to support *España Libre* even after the death of Victor Reuther, director of International Affairs of the UAW. Carcagente, Letter to Aurelio Pego, July 1, 1970, ELC.

29. ILGWU, Letter to SHC, Oct. 18, 1963, ELC; Gonzalez Malo, Letter to David Dubinsky, Oct. 31, 1963, ELC.

30. "Remiten $500 a la UGT," *EL*, Nov. 30, 1951.

31. See Avrich, *The Modern School Movement*.

32. Avrich, *The Modern School Movement*, 122, 172.

33. Vega and Iglesias, *Memoirs of Bernardo Vega*, 34. At the time, Maximiliano Olay was the U.S. representative of the Spanish National Confederation of Labor, CNT.

34. Avrich, *The Modern School Movement*, 327–328.

35. "Propaganda antifascista en América: La S.I.A. de los Estados Unidos organizó una cena de Despedida a nuestros compañeros del Moral y Martí Ibáñez," *Solidaridad Obrera* (Barcelona), Dec. 14, 1938.

36. "Gran Mitin," *EL*, May 1, 1942; "Ateneo Hispano," *EL*, Feb. 19, 1945.

37. "Miembros distinguidos," *EL*, Apr. 16, 1954.

38. "The One World Award Committee, Inc.," *EL*, May 19, 1950.

39. The SHC organized the event in cooperation with International League for the Rights of Man, International Association for Democracy and Freedom, Workers Defense League, League for Industrial Democracy, Delegación del Gobierno de Euzkadi, and Republicanos Exiliados en Estados Unidos ("Gran Acto," *EL*, Mar. 21, 1952, ELC).

40. Baldwin asked Secretary-General U Thant to act on the human rights violations occurring in Spain. Juan Papanek, executive president of the International League for the Rights of Man also signed the letter (Roger Baldwin, "La Liga Internacional de los Derechos del Hombre protesta," *EL*, Dec. 4, 1964).

41. Baldwin assisted several liberal and radical organizations. See Robert C. Cottrell, *Roger Nash Baldwin* (New York: Columbia University Press, 2000).

42. Jesús de Galíndez disappeared in New York after his involvement in the campaigns against General Rafael Leónidas Trujillo Molina, the Dominican dictator.

43. Agustin Carcagente, Telegraph to Harry Rappaport, Mar. 20, 1970, ELC.

44. See Avrich, *The Modern School Movement*, 319.

45. "El funeral de Carlo Tresca," *EL*, Jan. 22, 1943.

46. "Arando en el mar," *EL*, May 2, 1947.

47. Norman Thomas, Letter to Jesús González Malo, Dec. 31, 1953, ELC. For more on union relations between the United States and Spain during the Franco regime, see Rodríguez Jiménez, "Trade Unionism and Spain–US Political Relations, 1945–1953," 96–124; Rodríguez Jiménez and Hosoda, "Convidados de piedra o promotores del cambio?" 37–60; and Rodríguez Jiménez, "La AFL-CIO y el sindicalismo español, 1953–1971," 863–892.

48. "Brillante conferencia en La Nacional," *EL*, Sept. 26, 1952.

Chapter 2. *España Libre*, the Antifascist Periodical

1. "El nuevo embajador de los Estados Unidos en España," *EL*, Feb. 8, 1952.

2. Piqueras and Sanz, "Introduction," in *A Social History of Spanish Labour*, ed. Piqueras and Sanz, 14.

3. "Actas y acuerdos tomados en el sexto congreso nacional de SHC," *EL*, Jan. 8, 1943.

4. For this reason, a proposal of giving more votes or privileges to groups with more members or to those who collected more funds was voted against during the Third National Congress, convened in New York in 1939. The rationale behind this decision was to avoid rivalries among groups that would encourage members to help one group and not another. As long as a given affiliated group collected a minimum of $300 in donations per year, it had the same rights and duties of any associated group. "Breve Reseña Histórico-Política de Nuestra Organización," ELC.

5. Figures stated in *España Libre*: "Statement of Ownership, Management and Circulation," *EL*, Oct. 9, 1953; Oct. 7, 1955; Oct. 20, 1961; Mar. 5, 1965; Sept. 3, 1965; Sept. 10, 1967; Sept.–Oct. 1969; Sept.–Oct. 1970; Sept.–Oct. 1971; Sept.–Oct. 1972; Aug.–Dec. 1973; Aug.–Oct. 1974; Oct.–Dec. 1975; Oct. 1976. Also, figures were given by José Nieto Ruiz, telephone interview by author, Mar. 29, 2014; Jesús González Malo, Letter to Josep Buiria, Jan. 6, 1965, JGMP; González Malo, Letter to Carlos Esplá, Sept. 20, 1964, JGMP.

6. Comité Antifascista Español de los Estados Unidos de Norte América and Sociedades Hispanas Confederadas de los Estados Unidos de Norte América, *España Libre* (Brooklyn, NY: Comité Antifascista Español de los Estados Unidos, 1939–1977).

7. In the 1940s, José Castilla Morales, Andrés Rodríguez Barbeito, and Sebastian Palmer received compensation for their dedication to *España Libre* and the SHC but there were complaints and monetary compensation was discontinued (Account Sheets, ELC).

8. In New York, such enterprises were El Moderno (luncheonette), El Siglo (bookstore), La Valenciana (clothing store), Café Montero, Casa Piqueras (clothing store), El Ebro (restaurant), Café Alambra, Café Mirador, J. E. Bar, Barbería Martínez (barbershop), Oviedo (restaurant).

9. Rita Hayworth, born Margarita Carmen Cansino, was the daughter of Eduardo Cansino, who immigrated to the United States from Andalusia, Spain, in the 1910s.

10. The letterhead that circulated in 1962 featured list of sponsors in this order: Víctor Alba, Alvaro de Albornoz,* Carmen Aldecoa, Robert Alexander, Bruno Alonso, Roger N. Baldwin, Albert Camus,* Pablo Casals, Giuseppe Chiostergi, Marín Civera, Ernest Davies, Enrique de Francisco,* Ángel del Río,* Salvador de Madariaga, Federico de Onís, Albert Einstein,* Carlos Esplà, H. William Fitelson, Francisco García Lorca, Gloria Giner de los Ríos, Harry Girvertz, Joe Glazer, Félix Gordón Ordás, Eugenio F. Granell, Frances Grant, Patrick E. Groman, Donald Harrington, Edouard Herriot,* Sidney Hook, Andrés Iduarte, Murray Kempton, Hans Kohn, Dwight Macdonald, Nancy Macdonald, Arthur Macdowell, José Martel, Diego Martínez Barrios, Lucio Martínez Gil,* Joaquín Maurín, Cipriano Mera, Luis Monguio, A. J. Muste, Tomás Navarro Tomás, Maurice Orbach, Rodolfo Pacciardi, Jim Peck, Rose Pesotta, Eugene Claudius Petit, Paul Ramadier, A. Philip Randolph, Sir Herbert Read, Herman F. Reissig, Victor Reuther, Elmer Rice, Serafino Romuladi, Rudolf Rocker,* José Rubia Barcia, Andrés Saborit, Federico Sánchez Guerra, Ramón J. Sender, Ignazio Silone, Fernando Valera, Nilita Vientós Gastón, George Woodcock. *Deceased.

11. Jesús González Malo, Letter to President Lázaro Cárdenas, Nov. 3, 1953, ELC.

Notes to Chapter 2

12. Manuel Dorado and Jesús González Malo, Letter to Albert Einstein, Apr. 19, 1954, ELC.

13. Published in *España Libre* on Apr. 23, 1954, distinguished members were listed in this order: Diego Martínez Barrios, Álvaro de Albornoz, Bruno Alonso, Roger Baldwin, Albert Camus, Pablo Casals, Marin Civeran, Luise Crane, Guiseppe Chiostergi, Albert Einstein, Carlos Esplá, Enrique de Francisco, Waldo Frank, Félix Gordón Ordás, Frances Grant, Edouard Herriot, Victoria Kent, Murray Kempton, Asociación Liberal Española, México, Nancy Macdonald, Dwight Macdonald, José Martel, Lucio Martínez Gil, Cipriano Mera, A. J. Muste, Liga de Mutilados e Inválidos de la Guerra de España, Tomás Navarro Tomás, Federico de Onís, Maurice Orbach, Mario de Orive, Rodolfo Pacciardi, Rose Pessota, Eugene Claudius Petit, Paul Ramadier, Herbert Read, Herman F. Reissig, Authur Schlesinger Jr., Ramón J. Sender, Norman Thomas, Fernando Valera, George Woodcock.

14. During the Spanish Civil War, Castro served also as secretary of the Committee of Aid (Comisión de Abastos).

15. Book offerings were limited to the conditions of the antifascist exile, focused on fundraising. The authors most often featured in the 1940s were Azorín, Pío Baroja, Camillo Beneri, Vicente Blasco Ibáñez, Antonio de Carlo, John Dos Passos, Luigi Fabbri, Francesc Ferrer i Guardia, Waldo Frank, Rómulo Gallegos, José Garcia Pradas, Henry George, Julián Gorkin, Juan Ramón Jiménez, Victoria Kent, Peter Kropotkin, Gaston Leval, Anselmo Lorenzo, Gregorio Marañon, Ricardo Mella, Federica Montseny, Max Nettlau, Friedrich Nietzsche, Maximiliano Olay, George Orwell, Federico de Onís, José Ortega y Gasset, Pierre-Joseph Proudhon, Santiago Ramón y Cajal, Eugen Relgis, Rudolf Rocker, José Enrique Rodó, Helmut Ruediger, Ángel Samblancat, Diego Abad de Santillán, Arthur Schopenhauer, Upon Sinclair, Agustin Souchy, Henry D. Thoreau, Ernst Toller, Jacinto Toryho, Miguel de Unamuno, Adrián del Valle, Mariano Viñuales, Emile Zola, and Stefan Zweig.

16. During Vives's library service, authors most often featured were Claude G. Bowers, Alfonso Camín, Marín Civera, Guillermo Cotto Thorner, Fernando de los Ríos, Salvador de Madariaga, Isabel de Palencia, Pere Foix, Jesús González Malo, Julián Gorkin, Maxim Gorky, Francisco Largo Caballero, Felipe León, Avro Manhattan, Emmett McLoughlin, José Martí, Emmett McLoughlin, Fidel Miró, Federica Montseny, Roque Nieto Peña, Jim Peck, José Peirats, Eugen Relgis, Vicente Sáenz, George Seldes, Ramón J. Sender. Agustin Souchy, Pedro Vallina, and Stefan Zweig.

17. During Nieto Ruiz's library service, authors most often featured were Víctor Alba, Azorín, Pío Baroja, Alonso Camín Meana, Miguel de Cervantes, Albert Ellis, Luigi Fabbri, León Felipe, Pere Foix, José García Pradas, Manuel González Prada, Mariano José de Larra, Gregorio Marañon, Ricardo Mella, Max Netlau, Odón Betanzos Palacios, George Orwell, Eugenio Relgis, Rudolf Rocker, José Rubia Barcia, Vicente Sáenz, Ramón J. Sender, Agustín Souchy, Miguel de Unamuno, and Stefan Zweig.

18. As with many other small merchants, Esteban Roig supported *España Libre* by running regular advertisements. Additionally, his band, the Happy Boys, played at most fundraisers.

19. Several letters between the SHC's executive members and Esteban Roig as well as with Victoria Kent document these exchanges. ELC.

20. Books were also donated to Spanish Refugee Aid, which send them to refugees and exiles in France. Miguel R. Ortiz, Letter to Nancy Macdonald, July 31, 1963, ELC.

21. Jesús González Malo, Letter to Josep Peirtas, Apr. 10, 1961, in Feu, ed., *Jesús González Malo: Correspondencia*, 166.

22. Lunar, *A cielo abierto*, 17, 34.

23. "He sufrido todas las injusticias de que no he podido librarme. Nunca acepté ninguna" (Lunar, *A cielo abierto*, 181).

24. Lunar, *A cielo abierto*, 55–111.

25. Lunar, *A cielo abierto*, 98–169.

26. For more on Jim Peck and his work with Macdonald, see Andrew Cornell, *Unruly Equality: U.S. Anarchism in the Twentieth Century* (Oakland: University of California Press, 2016).

27. "Baldwin Honored by International League of the Rights of Man," *EL*, Jan.–Feb. 1969.

28. "Mutual Aid League Marks Fifty Years," *EL*, Mar.–Apr. 1970.

29. John Nicholas Beffel, Letter to Nancy Macdonald, June 26, 1962, ELC; George Selder, Letter to John Nicholas Beffel, May 1, 1960, ELC.

30. John Nicholas Beffel, Letter to Jesús González Malo, Oct. 31, 1963, ELC.

31. Spanish Refugee Aid Records, TAM 326.

32. "Rose Pesotta," *EL*, Jan. 1, 1966.

33. Molina Mateo was jailed in 1946 for his service as secretary of the National Committee of the National Confederation of Labor (CNT) and the National Alliance of Democratic Forces (ANFD). Released in 1952, he settled in Toulouse. Zwy Aldouby, Letter to Jesús González Malo, May 4, 1964, JGMP (unprocessed collection at the time of visit).

34. See Quentin James Reynolds, Ephraim Katz, and Zwy Aldouby, *Minister of Death: The Adolf Eichmann Story* (New York: Viking Press, 1960); and Jerrold Ballinger and Zwy Aldouby, *The Shattered Silence: The Eli Cohen Affair* (New York: Coward, 1971); https://www.cia.gov/library/readingroom/docs/DEGRELLE,%20LEON_0041.pdf.

35. "¡Por un nuevo 14 de abril!" *EL*, May 7, 1965.

36. See list of sporadic contributors in appendix C.

37. This section recovers long-run contributions in approximate chronological order. Regular antifascist writers, essayists, poets, and cartoonists, who assiduously infused *EL* with combative political protest and literature, are examined in further detail in later chapters.

38. National Catholicism was a fundamental ideological support to the Spanish regime and advocated that Franco was Caudillo "por la gracia de Dios" (by the grace of God). See Amor y Vázquez, "Recuperaciones," 9–26.

39. "Explicación necesaria," Editorial, *EL*, Mar. 21, 1941. Some these columns were collected in Albornoz Limiana's book *Páginas del destierro* (1941).

40. Juan Picador y Picadillo, "Confesiones de Juan Picador y Picadillo," *EL*, Oct. 4, 1940.

41. Aurelio Pego, "*Polvo y Camino,*" *EL*, Sept. 10, 1970.

42. Tavera, *Solidaridad Obrera*, 59; Marin, *Anarquistas*, 242.

43. The book also collects essays published in *La Opinión* (Los Angeles), *Le Socialiste* (Paris), and *Pueblo* (Havana).

44. Ordaz Romay, "Características del exilio español en Estados Unidos," 245.

45. Amo and Shelby, *La obra impresa de los intelectuales españoles en América*, 103.

46. June Namias, "Andrés Aragón: After the Death of Spain," in *First Generation: In the Words of Twentieth-Century American Immigrants* (Urbana: University of Illinois Press, 1978), 92–101.

47. Glondys, "The Idea of Europe, Transnational Networks, and Spanish Anti-Totalitarian Mobilisation," 203–220.

48. See Feu, ed., *Jesús González Malo: Correspondencia*, 31, 52, 71, 199, 205.

49. Later Pere Pagès taught political science at the University of Kansas, the American University, and Kent State University, in Ohio.

50. "Víctor Alba agasajado," *EL*, July 5, 1957.

51. Rivera García, "Regeneracionismo, socialismo y escepticismo en Luis Araquistáin," *ARBOR Ciencia, Pensamiento y Cultura* (Sept.–Oct. 2009): 1019–1034.

52. Preston, *Salvador de Madariaga*, 5.

53. "Explicación necesaria."

54. *Cuadernos* was financed by the CIA through the Congress for Cultural Freedom (CCF), an anticommunist advocacy group founded in 1950. See Glondys, *La Guerra Fría cultural y el exilio republican español.*

55. Gorkin, "Mañana," *EL*, Mar.–Apr. 1966.

56. González Malo, "Carta abierta a Don Salvador de Madariaga," *Comunidad Ibérica* Sept.–Oct. 1964.

57. Madariaga elaborated on his regenerating notion of an elite organic democracy in *The Genius of Spain* (1923), *Englishmen, Frenchmen, and Spaniards* (1928), and *Anarquía o jerarquía (Anarchy or hierarchy, 1936)*. See Preston, *Salvador de Madariaga*; and Caminals, "Salvador de Madariaga and National Character."

58. Granell, "El campo de la lucha por la libertad ha vuelto a establecerse en España," *EL*, May–June 1977.

Chapter 3. *España Libre* and Its Editors

1. Aurelio Pego, Letter to Jesús González Malo, Mar. 25, 1964, ELC.

2. There were other pro-Republic newspapers: *España Libre*'s predecessor *Frente Popular* (1937–1939), as well as *Spanish Revolution* (1936–1937), *Spanish News Digest* (1937), *North American Committee to Aid Spanish Democracy Bulletin* (1937), *Spanish Labor Bulletin* (1936–1939), *Catalonia* (1938), *Catalonian Correspondence* (1937–1939), *News of Spain* (1938–1939), *Democracy Marches* (1939), *Spanish Information* (1946–1947), *Ambos Mundos* (1946), and *Ibérica* (1953–1974). Spanish refugee and SHC member Enrique Ungría directed the cultural magazine *Ecos* in 1947, which regularly announced the SHC's cultural fundraisers. In Washington, D.C., there was *Bulletin: Washington Friends of Spanish*

Democracy (1939) and in Los Angles, *El Antifascista* (1938–1939) and *Ariel* (1939). Hispanic newspapers also covered the Spanish Civil War and the Franco's dictatorship from progressive perspectives and radical: *La Prensa* (1913–1963), *Cultura Proletaria* (1927–1959), and *La Voz* (1937–1939). However, none maintained an exclusive focus on Franco's Spain for thirty-eight years. Edited by noted Spanish socialist Victoria Kent, *Ibérica* (1953–1974) was the other long-run periodical. While *España Libre*'s main leaders were anarchists, Kent leaned ideologically toward republicanism. Other exile cultural and regional centers also published short-run magazines, for instance, *Ressó*, from the Catalan Center of New York, edited by Sofía A. Alberti. For more on pro-Republic newspapers see Kanellos and Martell, *Hispanic Periodicals in the United States*; and Rey Garcia, *Stars for Spain*.

3. "Frente a los traidores," *EL*, Aug. 9, 1940.

4. Gabriel Roca, "Hacia la meta," *Luz*, Feb. 5, 1938; Jesús Arenas, "Cómo se inició la ayuda en Nueva York," *CNT* (México), July 19, 1944; Jesús Arenas, "Hombres de Sociedades Hispanas Confederadas," *EL*, Dec. 7, 1962.

5. Influenced by communist politics, *Frente Popular*'s literature is not part of this study, which focuses on *España Libre*.

6. "Lo que debe ser el órgano de SHC," Editorial, *EL*, Nov. 24, 1939.

7. "Movimiento Obrero," *Frente Popular*, Nov. 30, 1937.

8. "Insistiendo," Editorial, *EL*, Feb. 12, 1943.

9. See recent and emerging scholarship, e.g. Brydan, *Franco's Internationalists* (2019), on the broader Spanish involvement with the Nazi New Order.

10. Félix Martí Ibáñez, "Flores sobre la tumba del Duce que agoniza," *EL*, June 18, 1943.

11. "Franco omnipotente," *EL*, June 13, 1947.

12. Aurelio Pego, "Protesta en nombre de dos difuntos," *EL*, Feb. 2, 1945.

13. "Diario de la Marina," *Frente Popular*, May 1, 1937. Chase also documents this news in *Falange*.

14. "¡Qué papelazo estáis haciendo señores profesores!" *EL*, June 25, 1948.

15. Gallego, *El evangélio fascista*, 571; Santiánez, *Topographies of Fascism*, 168–176.

16. "Continuación del informe del tercer congreso nacional," *EL*, Feb. 2, 1949; Antonio Penichet, "La España conquistadora y la España por conquistar," *EL*, Dec. 29, 1939. Such allegations were also made by Chase in *Falange*. The author traced the creation of the council to Wilhelm von Faupel, the Hitler-appointed chief of the Ibero-American Institute of Berlin in 1934.

17. De los Ríos, "Nazi Infiltration in Ibero-America,"389–409. Also see, on eugenic programs intended to "purify" the body politic of Spain from the 1930s onward, Turda and Gillette, *Latin Eugenics in Comparative Perspective*, 111.

18. "Larga y difícil tarea," Editorial, *EL*, Jan. 12, 1940.

19. Chase, *Falange*, 210.

20. There are numerous publications on the role of the United States in the Spanish Civil War. Recently, Andreu Espasa, *Estados Unidos en la Guerra Civil Española*, accounts in detail for the geopolitical reasons behind the U.S. nonintervention in Spain.

21. Their service was recognized in several of the interviews published by El Chico de la Calle [Castilla Morales].

22. "El 19 de Julio celebrado con el entusiasmo de siempre," *EL*, July 23, 1943.

23. De Albornoz Limiana, "La federación Latina," *EL*, May 28, 1943.

24. "Concertaron un ACUERDO las dos GRANDES SINDICALES Españolas," *EL*, Jan. 8, 1943.

25. "¿Cuál es la situación jurídica de los españoles?" *EL*, Aug. 30, 1940; "Sin patria, pero con dignidad," Editorial, *EL*, Dec. 20, 1940.

26. This was a common practice among anarchist newspapers in exile and with limited funds.

27. Articles by Carmen Aldecoa, Jesús González Malo, Félix Martí Ibáñez, Eugenio Fernández Granell, Aurelio Pego, Rudolf Rocker, and Agustin Souchy.

28. Rarely was U.S. news discussed in the paper, and then only when in relation with Spain. However, the Vietnam War was an exception, particularly among anticommunist contributors such as Salvador de Madariaga and Ramón J. Sender, who defended the war effort as a necessary evil.

29. Aurelio Pego, "Veinticinco años de paz," *EL*, Mar. 6, 1964.

30. Jobaga, "¿25 años de paz o 25 años de rencor?" *EL*, Aug. 7, 1964.

31. Glondys has written about the role of these intellectuals in exile in the democratization of Spain. They exerted great influence in the process toward a democratic Spain from within the international organizations they worked for. See Glondys, *La Guerra Fría*; and Glondys, "The Idea of Europe, Transnational Networks and Spanish Anti-Totalitarian Mobilisation," 203–220.

32. Aurelio Pego, "El último bistec on Pedro," *EL*, Apr. 2, 1954.

33. Onuba [José Castilla Morales], "Trabajador anónimo," *EL*, Apr. 18, 1941. The other prompter who served the SHC for many years was Luis Miralles. His wife was an active member of the Association of Antifascist Women.

34. Dates for Iglesias and Díez are unknown (Abelardo Iglesias, "Retales de una vida: Uno menos," *EL*, Mar.–Apr. 1966; "Un hombre ejemplar," *EL*, Oct. 6, 1961).

35. "Teresa Puig," *EL*, July 6, 1962; "Un hombre ejemplar."

36. In the winter activities 1933–34, the Puerto Rican League (Liga Puertorriqueña) announced Castilla Morales's conference "Socialismo, Comunismo y Anarquismo: Sus diferencias y su interpretación" (Socialism, communism, and anarchism: Differences and interpretations) at the Grupo Eugenio Maria de Hostos, affiliated group with the Liga Puertorriqueña in New York on Mar. 6 and 18, 1934. "Advertisements," Jesús Colón Collection, Organizational Activities, Feb. 2, 1933, APHHC.

37. His pen names were El Chico de la Calle, Onuba, and Don Pepe.

38. "Castilla de vacaciones," *EL*, Aug. 25, 1950.

39. He worked as a self-employed publicist and as Spanish manager for a chemical laboratory in New York.

40. Gregorio Garay, "Un espíritu de titán: José Castilla," *EL*, Oct. 20, 1961.

41. His obituary does not specify the exact years that he served as president ("D. José Carnero," *EL*, May–June 1975).

42. Alonso was another decidedly active member: he fundraised for clothes for refugees, drove members of the Government of the Second Spanish Republic in exile during

their visits to the city, served as administrator in several positions for *España Libre* and the SHC, and organized fundraisers. El Chico de la Calle [Castilla Morales], "Gente conocida: Manolo el Pontevedrino," *EL*, May 28, 1943.

43. Casanova and Preston, *Anarchism, the Republic, and Civil War in Spain*, 123.

44. Pego also was employed at the Office of War Information in New York from 1942 to 1943 (Aurelio Pego, FBI case 1242376-001, NARA). In 1933, he published *Como ovejas descarraidas* (Madrid: Javier Morata, 1933), a manuscript of humorous and poetic chronicles about his migrant experience in New York.

45. Pego published with *Ecos de Nueva York* (New York), *Época* (San Antonio), *Hablemos del Hogar Moderno* (New York), *El Heraldo de México* (Los Angeles), *Nueva Democracia* (New York), *La Prensa* (New York), *La Prensa* (San Antonio), and *Tribuna Hispana* (New York) among others. In Spain, his reprints and originals were regularly featured in *Ahora: Diario Gráfico* (Madrid), *Diario de Valencia* (Valencia), *La Gaceta Literaria* (Madrid), *Popular Film* (Barcelona), *La Prensa* (Tenerife), and *El Sur* (Córdoba), and *La Vanguardia* (Barcelona).

46. "Pego, reelecto Presidente," *EL*, May 30, 1952.

47. "Carteristas honorarios," *CNT* (México), Feb. 1959.

48. "La despedida de Pego," *EL*, July 18, 1952.

49. Pego, Letter to Ortiz, Dec. 11, 1965, ELC.

50. Pego, "El General desconocido a quien todos conocían," *EL*, Mar. 17, 1961.

51. In May 1933, González Malo was named president of the Sociedad de Trabajadores del Muelle, Santander ("Actividades sindicales," *La Región*, May 3, 1933). He oversaw the mixed militia and organized the evacuation when Santander fell to the rebels in August 29, 1937. Also see Alexander, *The Anarchists in the Spanish Civil War*; and Solla Gutiérrez, *Una efímera autonomía*, 18, 22.

52. González Malo wrote to Consuelo Trueba in Cuba, who contacted anarchist José García, her brother-in-law, who lived in Bridgeport, Connecticut. Both sent money for his passage to the Americas (Jesús González Malo, FBI Case 100-HQ-105493, NARA). Like other members, his arrival to New York City was marked with difficulties but also was made possible through the anarchist networks' solidarity. From Cuba, González Malo's friend Mosés Gómez sent $825 to France for passages to Cuba for González Malo and Carmen Aldecoa. Spanish exile José Rubia Barcia invited Aldecoa to be on the faculty of La Escuela Libre in Havana. González Malo traveled to the United States under the Spanish immigration quota on Sept. 30, 1940. Upon his arrival, he worked as dishwasher at several restaurants to save enough money to pay for Aldecoa's passage. Later he worked as machinist for several companies of the city, and Aldecoa taught Spanish at New York University (Feu, ed., *Jesús González Malo: Correspondencia*, 161).

53. Confederadas Minutes, Jan. 15, 1954, ELC.

54. For example, González Malo asked essays from anarchists Federico Arcos in Windsor, Canada, and Jacinto Toryho, who had moved to Buenos Aires, Argentina.

55. Joaquín Maurín Julià, "Palabras de despedida," *EL*, Jan. 1966, supplement. González Malo had asked for essays from anarchists Federico Arcos in Windsor, Canada, and Jacinto Toryho, who had moved to Buenos Aires, Argentina.

56. In 1969, Nieto Ruiz founded Iberama publishing and published Ramón J. Sender's *Nocturno de los 14* (1969) and reprinted Max Nettlau's *Miguel Bakunin's La Internacional y la Alianza en España (1868–1973)* (1971), among other works. Nieto Ruiz is now working on four bibliographies: *Bibliografía de la II República Española (1931–1939); Bibliografía de la intervención extranjera y las Brigadas Internacionales en la Guerra Civil Española, 1936–1939; Derrotados, exiliados, transterrados de la Guerra Civil española: Bilbliografía del exilio español, 1936–1975;* and *Bibliografía del regimen Franquista (1939–1975).*

57. Feu, ed., *Jesús González Malo: Correspondencia,* 26.

58. Feu, ed., *Jesús González Malo: Correspondencia,* 174.

59. González Malo, Letter to Manuel Martínez Feduchy, Sept. 23, 1960, JGMP.

60. Almost twenty years later, in 1964, González Malo received news that some of these members were released from prison. Feu, ed., *Jesús González Malo: Correspondencia,* 50.

61. González Malo, FBI Case 100-HQ-105493, J. Edgar Hoover to SAC Baltimore, Nov. 7, 1942, NARA.

62. *La guerra en España: ¡Basta!* (1938), *Carta abierta a la comarcal montañesa* (1947), *Dictamen sobre modalidades constructivas del sindicalismo revolucionario* (1947), *La incorporación de las masas* (1952), *Por los fueros del anarcosindicalismo: Contra "políticos y puritanos"* (1956), and *Raíz y trascendencia del anarquismo español* (1963).

63. González Malo, *La incorporación de las masas,* 76.

64. Jesús González Malo, "Un concepto equívoco: El de la pluralidad syndical," *EL,* May 7, 1965.

65. Jesús González Malo, "La labor de los sindicatos II," *Solidaridad Obrera* (Mexico), Jan.1, 1943, NARA.

66. Jesús González Malo, "Crónica de Nueva York. ¿Qué es el 65?" *CNT* (Mexico), June 1957; Jesús González Malo, "Destellos optimistas," *EL* (Toulouse), Jan. 19, 1958.

67. Jesús González Malo, "Rectificaciones de fondo y forma," *Comunidad Ibérica,* Sept.–Oct. 1963, 28–31.

68. Jesús González Malo, Letter to Carlos Esplá, Aug. 8, 1964 (Feu, ed., *Jesús González Malo: Correspondencia,* 242–247).

69. Jesús González Malo, "Socialismo humanista," *EL,* May 15, 1959.

70. Elías Díaz, "Estudio preliminar," in de los Ríos, *El sentido humanista del socialismo,* 7–59, xv, xvii, 9.

71. De los Ríos, *El sentido humanista del socialismo,* 83.

72. Jesús González Malo, "Del carácter español: Individualismo y anarquísmo," *EL* (Paris), Apr. 8, 1956.

73. Sumner, *Dwight Macdonald and the Politics Circle,* 4.

74. Kaiser, "Partial Affinities" 124.

75. Shatz, ed., *The Essential Works of Anarchism,* 393–394.

76. González Malo, "Una vida ejemplar: Rodolfo Rocker," *EL,* Sept. 19, 1958.

77. "Precursores de la libertad: Fermín Salvochea en su 114 aniversario (De un folleto de R. Rocker)," *EL,* Mar. 17, 1956.

78. On the mutual influence of Rocker and Spanish anarchists see Hofmann, "Rudolf Rocker y el anarquismo hispano," 151–162.

79. In 1955, he sent Rocker Renée Lamberet's *Mouvements obvriers et socialisted, L'Espagne*, and told him there were volumes about Italy, England, Germany, and the United States (Jesús González Malo, Letter to Rocker, Feb. 12, 1955, JGMP). Later that year, Rocker sent González Malo Martinez Ruiz's *Notas sociales* and Ricardo Mella's *Los sucesos de Jerez*.

80. González Malo, *La incorporación de las masas*, 419, 524; "La labor de los sindicatos," *Solidaridad Obrera* (Mexico), Mar. 6, 1943.

81. Ramón J. Sender, "Sobre federalism," *Comunidad Ibérica*, May–June 1964.

82. Knowing about Rocker's 1910 book in Yiddish about Francesc Ferrer i Guardia's educational principles, González Malo sent Rocker a letter to inform him that Ferrer's daughter was at the University of Buffalo writing about her father's legacy and that he had given her Rocker's address. Rudolf Rocker, *Francisko Ferrer: Un di fraye ertsihung fun der yugend* (London: Arbayter Fraynd, 1910); and Jesús González Malo, Letter to Rudolf Rocker, Dec. 12, 1954, JGMP.

83. Rudolf Rocker, Letter to Jesús González Malo, Aug. 17, 1946, JGMP.

84. Jesús González Malo, Letter to Rudolf Rocker, Apr. 21, 1956, JGMP.

85. Jesús González Malo, "Una vida ejemplar."

86. Fermín Rocker, "In Memoriam: J. González González Malo," *EL*, May 6, 1966.

87. González Malo, *La incorporación de las masas*, 10, 41, 217, 435; Jesús González Malo, "Rectificaciones de fondo y forma," *Comunidad Ibérica*, Sept.–Oct. 1963.

88. Jesús González Malo, "No caben disyuntivas," *EL* (Paris), July 15, 1956.

89. Jesús González Malo, "Una vida ejemplar: Rodolfo Rocker," *EL*, Sept. 19, 1958.

90. Mella, qtd. in Jesús González Malo, *Del carácter español: Individualismo y anarquismo*, 9, JGMP.

91. Mariano Viñuales, "*La incorporación de las masas*," *Solidaridad Obrera* (Paris), May 9, 1953.

92. He published them in *EL* (Toulouse and Paris) between Nov. 1955 and Apr. 1956.

93. Jesús González Malo, "Por una economía libertaria VI," *EL* (Paris), May 29, 1955.

94. Jesús González Malo, "Somos revolucionarios," *CNT* (Mexico), Jan. 1, 1956.

95. González Malo, "Somos revolucionarios."

96. Jesús González Malo, "Socialismo humanista," *EL* (Toulouse), May 3, 1959.

97. Jesús González Malo, "Con el mismo espíritu," *CNT* (Paris), Aug. 6, 1961.

98. Carmen Aldecoa, Letter to Alberto Uriarte, Mar. 12, 1966, ELC.

99. Avelino Hernández, "Relieves del exilio: Carmen Aldecoa," *EL* (Toulouse), Oct. 27, 1957.

100. The name of the camp is not mentioned in the FBI report consulted (FBI case 100-HQ-105-493).

101. Víctor Fuentes, "Carmen Aldecoa," email message, Mar. 6, 2010.

102. "La conmemoración del 14 de abril," *EL*, Apr. 23, 1954.

103. Aldecoa published papers from two conferences about the Spanish labor movement given at Columbia University in 1952 and 1956. Aldecoa was not able to write the second and third volume for health reasons (Jesús González Malo, Letter to Romulo, Jan. 9, 1965, JGMP). Not collected in this volume are her signed essays in exile periodicals such as *El correo de Asturias* (Buenos Aires, 1941), and *¡Ayuda!* (Cuba, 1937).

104. Aldecoa, *Del sentir y pensar*, 115.
105. Aldecoa, *Del sentir y pensar*, 118.
106. Aldecoa, *Del sentir y pensar*, 120.
107. Aldecoa, *Del sentir y pensar*, 127.
108. Aldecoa, *Del sentir y pensar*, 125–126.
109. Aldecoa, *Del sentir y pensar*, 126, 132.
110. Jesús González Malo, "Socialismo Humanista IX," *EL* (Toulouse), Aug. 23, 1959.
111. For example, José Peirats, G. Brandes, Han Ryner, Andrián del Valle, Federica Montseny, Federico Urales Bakunin, Kropotkin, Netlau, Rocker, Proudhon, Anselmo Lorenzo, Fermín Salvochea, José Prat, Ricardo Mella, José Sánchez Rosa, Isaac Puente, Diego Abad de Santillán, Manuel González Prada, Eduardo de Guzmán, José Peirats, Antonio García Birlán, Higinio Noja Ruiz, Marx, Kautsky, Deville, Engels, Pablo Iglesias, Miguel Aquina, Lluria Iruretagoyena, Juan José Morato, Vigil Montoto, Francisco Largo Caballero, Julián Besteiro, Lucio Martínez Gil, and Luis Romero Solano.
112. Aldecoa, *Del sentir y pensar*, 170–183.
113. She mentions Calleja, Sampere, Renacimiento, Cenit, Minerva, Zeus, and Casa Maucci (Aldecoa, *Del sentir y pensar*, 150).
114. Aldecoa, *Del sentir y pensar*, 34, 35.
115. Aldecoa, *Del sentir y pensar*, 55.
116. Ortiz had assisted González Malo.
117. *"España Libre* restablece su formato y su actitud," *EL*, Mar.–Apr. 1, 1966.
118. Caudet, *Correspondencia*, 32; Clavería, *Maurín: De Huesca a Nueva York: La revolución interrumpida* (Sariñena, Spain: Editorial Salvador Trallero, 2010), 139; Jeanne Maurín, *Cómo se salvó Joaquín Maurín: Recuerdos y testimonies* (Madrid: Júcar, 1979).
119. Clavería, *Maurín*, 134–137; qtd. in Caudet, *Correspondencia*, 33; Max Eastman of the *Reader's Digest* also wrote a letter on his behalf (Joaquín Julià Maurín, FBI case DOCID32527774, NARA). In addition, Costa Rican president José Figueres named Maurín Julià a Costa Rican press delegate to the UN, which also helped to avoid his deportation in the McCarthy era (Caudet, *Correspondencia*, 39; Clavería, *Maurín*, 141).
120. Maurín Julià noticed that feature articles in most Latin American newspapers at the time were translations from U.S. columnists and decided to start a journalistic agency that offered such articles. He then contacted newspapers and submitted articles first using several pseudonyms and signing his work with invented names for Latino journalists until he hired more writers. By 1954, ALA worked with thirty-five newspapers in Latin America. In the United States, ALA sold articles to *El Diario de Nueva York*, *Temas* (New York), *La Prensa* (San Antonio), and *La Opinión* (Los Angeles). ALA grew to syndicate authors such as Ramón Sender, Raúl Andrade, Miguel Ángel Asturias, Alfonso Reyes, Germán Arciniegas, Waldo Frank, José Vasconcelos, Ramón Gómez de la Serna, and Arturo Uslar-Pietri. See Caudet, *Correspondencia*, 13, 46, 178; Víctor Alba, "Los refugiados españoles en la prensa francesa (1945–1947)," in *Emigración y exilio: Españoles en Francia, 1936–1946*, ed. Josefina Cuesta Bustillo and Benito Bermejo Sánchez (Madrid: Eudema, 1996), 146. Other exiled Spanish intellectuals also contributed, including Luis Araquistáin and Salvador Madariaga. See Bonsón Aventín, *Joaquín Maurín, 1896–1973: El impulso moral*

de hacer política (Huesca, Spain: Diputación de Huesca, Instituto de Estudios Altoaragoneses, 1995), 367; Caudet, *Correspondencia*, 33; Roy, *Maurín als Estats Unis* (Barcelona: Centre d'Estudis Internacionals, University of Barcelona, 1989), 3.

121. For a comparison on editions see, Joel Sans Molas, "'Hacia la Segunda Revolucion' de Joaquim Muarín i l'Octubre del 1934," *Miscel.lànea* IX (2011): 195–218.

122. Maurín Julià also wrote about the Cold War, the spread of communism in Latin America, and the student revolts in Spain. Some of these articles were later incorporated in his books.

123. See Eugenio Fernández Granell, *Correspondencia con sus camaradas del P.O.U.M. (1936–1999)* (Santiago de Compostela, Spain: Fundación Granell, 2009); and Eugenio Fernández Granell, *Ensayos, encuentros y invenciones*, ed. César Antonio Molina (Madrid: Huerga y Fierro Editores, 1998).

124. Ordaz Romay, "Características del exilio español," 273; Granell, *Ensayos, encuentros y invenciones*, 277–286.

125. Ordaz Romay, "Características del exilio español," 291–301.

126. Ordaz Romay, "Características del exilio español," 305; Eugenio Granell Foundation, http://www.fundacion-granell.org/historia_fundacion/index.php?lang=3.

127. Granell employed several pseudonyms, among them E. M. Fernández; I.T. (Indio Tupinamba); Fernández; X.Y.Z.; E.L.; and L.L. (María Pita, Fundación Eugenio Granell, email to author, Dec. 16, 2019).

128. González Malo, *La incorporación de las masas*, 435; González Malo, "Socialismo humanista," *EL*, May 15, 1959, CRL; "Socialismo humanista," *EL*, Aug. 21, 1959, CRL.

129. González Malo, "Un concepto equívoco."

Chapter 4. The Struggle against Deportations

1. Un refugiado, "Hacia América a bordo del Washington," *EL*, Nov. 24, 1939.
2. "Grupo Antifascista del Bronx," *EL*, Jan. 1, 1943.
3. "Crimen y complicidad," Editorial, *EL*, Jan. 21, 1948.
4. "Crimen y complicidad."
5. The ILGWU extended a similar invitation, to which Largo Caballero responded in the same manner ("Como piensan nuestros refugiados," *EL*, June 21, 1940).
6. Thomas would also participate in the SHC's demonstrations in front of the Spanish Consulate and the United Nations in New York City.
7. Other organizations and individuals mobilized their resources to bring international attention to Largo Caballero. See Arostegui, *Largo Caballero*; "Recuerdo a Marcelino Domingo," *EL*, May 15, 1959.
8. See Francisco Largo Caballero, *Mis recuerdos: Cartas a un amigo* (Mexico City: Ediciones Unidas, 1976), 264.
9. "Recuerdo a Marcelino Domingo." The article also noted that Largo Caballero had started his political involvement as a union construction worker.
10. "En la 'libre' America," *Solidaridad Obrera* (Paris), Oct. 22, 1949.

Notes to Chapter 4

11. González Malo, *La incorporación de las masas*, 325.

12. "Nuestras actividades," *EL*, Oct. 10, 1956.

13. In 1999, de Dios Unanue's *El caso Galíndez: Los vascos en los servicios de inteligencia en Estados Unidos* (Taffalla, Spain: Txalaparta Argitaletxea, 1999) was published posthumously. De Dios was murdered in 1992 by Colombian drug traffickers in the United States because of his antidrug crusading in *Cambio XXI* and *Crimen*.

14. Krohn, *Intellectuals in Exile*, 2. For deportation of anarchists in the 1910 and 1920s, see Zimmer, "The Voyage of the *Buford*," 132–163.

15. Krohn, *Intellectuals in Exile*, 26.

16. Mexico, Panama, Guatemala, Venezuela, Poland, Czechoslovakia, Hungary, Yugoslavia, Romania, and Albania maintained diplomatic relations with the Second Spanish Republic in exile. See Yossi Shain, ed., *Governments-in-Exile in Contemporary World Politics* (New York: Routledge, 1991), 152.

17. "Los refugiados en Africa," *EL*, June 25, 1943.

18. "Libertados los últimos prisioneros politicos del norte de África," *EL*, July 2, 1943.

19. "Sandrán en breve," *EL*, Nov. 26, 1943.

20. "Hay centenares de españoles presos en Rusia," *EL*, Feb. 20, 1948; "Reconstrucción económica de España," *EL*, Apr. 16, 1948.

21. "Paradero de personas: Río Tinto," *EL*, July 9, 1943.

22. "Se desea saber," *EL*, June 27, 1947.

23. The SHC's papers have numerous and similar records, albeit unspecific, about aid sent to Spain. The poor housekeeping speaks of the SHC's limited resources, and none could be devoted to curate its archive. Clavijo Ledesma, "La política sobre la población refugiada durant la guerra civil, 1936–1939," 211; "De nuestras sociedades y comités," *EL*, Nov. 30, 1937, 11.

24. "Informe de Tesoreria," ELC. Two ambulances were sent in the *Normandia* with the help of the Medical Bureau. Further data on aid during the Spanish Civil War can be found in the predecessor periodical *Frente Popular*, which is not part of this study.

25. "Report," ELC.

26. Compiled from several documents in ELC.

27. "Primera lista de refugiados del Ipanema que llega a SHC," *Frente Popular*, June 2, 1939; "El Ipanema," *Frente Popular*, July 7, 1939.

28. José Castro, Letter to M. José Gómez, undated, ELC; "Memorandum giving some highlights of this organization's history," ELC.

29. Summary from several documents in ELC.

30. "Memorandum giving some highlights of this organization's history," ELC.

31. García Oliver, *El eco de los pasos*, 522, 537.

32. Prego Vieiro was director of the periodical *Solidaridad* in La Coruña, Spain. Once in Mexico, he served as chief editor of newspaper *CNT*.

33. "Balance general de cuentas," *EL*, July 23, 1942.

34. Nancy Macdonald was the manager of the periodical *Partisan Review*, while Dwight Macdonald, her husband, was its editor-in-chief. Through their editorial work for the

Partisan Review and *Politics*, the Macdonalds greatly influenced New York City's intellectual and political commentary. See Linz, "Una respuesta de intelectuales norteamericanos al exilio español," 43–55. Macdonald, *Homage to the Spanish Exiles*, 129.

35. Nancy Macdonald, Letter to John Carnero, Nov. 3, 1961, SRA, TAM.

36. Later more lawyers joined Ernest Fleischman: John González Moscoso, Maximino González, Edith Lowenstein, Charles O. Porter, Enrique Ramos, and Jesse L. Rosenberg offered their services pro bono as counsels for Spanish refugees.

37. For instance, lawyer Charles Sternberg (International Rescue Committee) denied help to some petitions of help because they were not recognized as antifascist refugees by the SHC. Carmen Cordellat, Letter to Stenberg, Apr. 11, 1948, ELC.

38. Nancy Macdonald, Letter to Carmen Aldecoa, Sept. 16, 1961, ELC.

39. SHC, Letter to Nancy Macdonald, July 8, 1961, ELC.

40. Information summarized from several letters. Nancy Macdonald, María Isabel Aldecoa, SIA, TAM).

41. Although Ana Estan Frias had worked as a seamstress, her employers had neglected to pay her Social Security taxes (Margaret Childers, Letter to Ms. Guerrero, Oct. 2, 1985; Nancy Macdonald, María Isabel Aldecoa, SIA, TAM).

42. Linz, "Una respuesta de intelectuales norteamericanos al exilio español," 46.

43. Macdonald, *Homage to the Spanish Exiles*.

44. El Chico de la calle, "Impresiones del tercer congreso de SHC," *EL*, Dec. 5, 1941.

45. Similarly, González Malo sent funds to pay Sirio del Solar Romero's passage to Panamá. Jesús González Malo, FBI Case 100-HQ-105493, NARA.

46. However, some were not published at the request of refugees or their families.

47. The cost of passages was $1,509. Other costs, which included clothes, food, passports, and legal fees, were $1,004 ("Cuentas claras," *EL*, Feb. 2, 1945).

48. Eight detainees were helped ("Refugiados USA Ellis Island," *EL*, Jan. 31, 1947).

49. Four passages were paid ("Refugados Ellis Island y USA," *EL*, Mar. 28, 1947.)

50. Sometimes the published information was intentionally partial to protect refugees and their families. Unfortunately, the quality of some of the periodicals where these notices are published make these notices partially or completely illegible.

51. Ten refugees were relocated in Venezuela ("Salieron más refugiados para Venezuela," *EL*, Sept. 12, 1947).

52. Six refugees were relocated to Venezuela ("Salen para Venezuela," *EL*, June 4, 1948).

53. González Malo and Uriarte, Letter to Feduchy, Mar. 27, 1961, JGMP.

54. "Otra demonstración de la tragedia," *EL*, Sept. 26, 1947.

55. "México les concede asilo," *La Prensa*, July 30, 1958.

56. González Moscoso was a Freemason and member of the lodge La Universal. He was a second-generation Spanish American, his parents having migrated from Mera, La Coruña, Spain, to New York.

57. "During his thirty years with the New York law firm of Delson & Gordon, Mr. Fleischman represented the United Federation of Teachers and the Social Service Employees Union in New York. He was active in civil rights causes and defended several

political figures from abroad who faced deportation" ("Ernest Fleischman," Obituary, *New York Times*, Sept. 30, 1987).

58. See Carlos García Santa Cecilia and Montse Feu, "José Nieto, Last Exile from the Francisco Franco Dictatorship, CNT Militant, Found Refuge in New York." https://www.fronterad.com/wp-content/img/nr0274/jose-nieto-english.pdf. Translation of García Santa Cecilia and Feu, "José Nieto, último exiliado del franquismo, militante de la CNT, hizo de Nueva York su refugio."

59. Murray Kempton, "The Refugee," *New York Post*, Nov. 30, 1962.

60. Nieto Ruiz, who was given a visa to stay in the United States, was the first and possibly the only Spanish Civil War refugee to obtain political asylum in the United States. José Nieto Ruiz, Interview by author, Nov. 8, 2013. See García Santa Cecilia and Feu, "José Nieto, Last Exile from the Francisco Franco Dictatorship." Although Fleischman's sons knew of their father's pro bono work, they were not aware of the extent to which Fleischman successfully defended many potential deportees. Fleischman's sons remembered their father's efforts to social justice: "He kept a personal portfolio of refugees, union organizers, civil rights activists, and other 'little' clients who could not afford the defense that our father provided them. Most of it was thankless work, thankless except for the few individuals who my father could protect. To hear all these years later, that he saved so many lives is deeply moving for us" (John Fleischman, email to author, Dec. 10, 2013).

61. Jesse L. Rosenberg, "Radio Address," *EL*, May 2, 1941.

62. Rosenberg, "Radio Address."

63. Rosenberg, "Radio Address."

64. Ernest Fleischman, Letter to SHC, Sept. 14, 1968, ELC.

65. Several letters, ELC.

66. Shum illustrated Samblancat's novel about anarchists in Barcelona, *La ascensión de María Magdalena: Novela de los bajos fondos barceloneses* (1927).

67. Cordellat also supported fundraisers by playing the piano while her husband Vicente sang for antifascist audiences. Her husband was an active member of the Izquierda Republicana affiliated association in New York.

68. Immigration and Naturalization Service, Letter to SHC, Dec. 29, 1944, ELC.

69. Deogracias Rojo arrived in New York in 1920 (Koldo San Sebastián, email to author, Sept. 27, 2013). In 1925, he also donated to a collection organized by *La Prensa* (New York) to send money to an ill Spaniard ("Español enviado enfermo a España," *La Prensa*, Apr. 30, 1925).

70. The remaining archive contains some of her letters from 1944 to 1949, which provide more glimpses of her role in preventing deportations. In May 1948, Cordellat asked Jesús Vázquez Gayoso, the Spanish Republic consul in Caracas, Venezuela, for resident visas for several detainees in Ellis Island: Ramón Fernández Machín, Ramón Mojón Vazquez, Francisco García García, Ricardo García Soco, and A. López Becerra; and for families in France of José Migoya de la Llana, Remedios Iglesias Alonso, Acacia Migoya Iglesias, Josefina Migoya Iglesias, as well as Antonio Pan García, still in Spain. Pan García arrived in Venezuela soon afterward. In the same letter, she asked for a visa for Ramón Mojón Vázquez. In July

1948, Cordellat contacted the Federal Reformatory in Petersburg, Virginia, asking for the release of José Pérez Alzubide, Víctor Elexpe Arce, Alfonso Domínguez Campos, Vicente Rodríguez Techa, Manuel Costela González, and Félix Rodríguez Urbina because she had obtained visas for them. On another occasion, in Nov. 1948, she also obtained funds from the IRRC to help Miguel Martínez Mislata, José Luís Degonia Valle, and Alfonso Sánchez Frade. Maria Cordellat, Letter to C. Sternberg, International Relief and Rescue Committee, Apr. 8, 1948. Maria Cordellat, Letter to C. O. Nicholson, Nov. 9, 1948. (Other information has been summarized from several letters and documents, ELC.)

71. Cordellat requested visas for José Lecumperi and Antonio García, both detained for the violation of the Stowaway Act. In October 1948, she processed a report for Alexandre Herculano Salgado and Alfonso Sánchez Prades and asked Dr. J. Vázquez Gayoso for visas for Jesús Zarraga, Joaquín Álvarez Díaz, and Bernabé Lago Martínez, all of them stowaways detained in Ellis Island. In Nov. 1948, she thanked Vázquez Gayoso for the resident visa for Jesús Zarraga Camarigua and asked for new visas for detained Spaniards in Ellis Island: Ramón Ruiz Gómez, Fernando Álvarez, and Emilio Pérez Pérez (Maria Cordellat, Letter to Dr. Jesús Vázquez Gayoso, Nov. 26, 1948, ELC).

72. Enrique Aguado-González, Juan Medrano-Castillo, and José Viegas Vaz arrived on the SS *Sarpedon* from Spain; Francisco Pareja and Aurelio Abadia Mauri on the *Peter Minuit* from Belgium; Benjamin Osorio Iglesias and Mariano Aguardo Echevaria arrived as stowaways in the SS *Kern Hills*. Several letters, ELC.

73. United States Department of Justice, Letter to Cordellat, Oct. 27, 1948, ELC.

74. Federal Correctional Institution, Danbury, Letter to Maria Cordellat, Mar. 1948, ELC.

75. Maria Cordellat, Letter to C. O. Nicholson, Federal Reformatory, Petersburg, Va., Nov. 9, 1948.

76. Maria Cordellat, Letter to Immigration and Naturalization Service, Boston, Feb. 17, 1949, ELC.

77. Juan J. Carrasco, Letter to Maria Cordellat, Apr. 17, 1948, ELC.

78. Aurelio Pego, "Una heroina y unos desagradecidos," *EL*, Nov. 4, 1948.

79. Immigration and Naturalization Service of Portland, Oregon, Letter to Maria Cordellat, Jan. 20, 1949; Maria Cordellat, Letter to Immigration and Naturalization Service of Portland, Oregon, Jan. 20, 1949, ELC.

80. Diego was a stowaway in a ship from Santander. Jesús Revaque Garea, a Spanish Civil War exile in Mexico, taught workers in the Santander Dock Workers Union before the war.

81. Jesús González Malo, Letter to Jesús Vázquez Gayoso, Apr. 23, 1948, in Feu, ed., *Jesús González Malo: Correspondencia*, 64.

82. Jesús González Malo, Letter to Indalecio Prieto, Mar. 18, 1961, JGMP. Several weeks later, González Malo invited him to speak at the rallies taking place in New York to stop deportations of sailors.

83. González Malo, Uriarte, and Carnero, Letter to Feduchy, Mar. 27, 1961, JGMP.

84. SHC, Letter to Manuel Martínez Feduchy, Nov. 28, 1960, ELC

85. SHC, Letter to Manuel Martínez Feduchy, Mar. 14, 1961, ELC.
86. Announcement, *EL*, Sept. 20, 1962.
87. González Malo, Letter to William Fitelson, Oct. 16, 1961, ELC; SHC, Letter to ILGWU, Feb. 14, 1963, ELC; SHC, Letter to the International League for the Rights of Men, Nov. 17, 1959, ELC.
88. SHC Minutes, Jan. 15, 1954, ELC.
89. González Malo, Letter to Luís Montés, Apr. 29, 1963, ELC. Grant also recommended Jim Peck for the position of editor of the English pages of *España Libre*.
90. When the *Stockholm* collided with the *Andrea Doria* on July 25, 1956, the anarchist García Polanco helped rescue several people, including Linda Morgan, the daughter of Edward P. Morgan, a radio announcer for the ABC Network. Her stepfather, Camille Cianfarra, a *New York Times* reporter, also was on the *Andrea Doria*. Despite his fleeting recognition by the American press as a hero, García Polanco was accused of subversive activities once established in Canada (Tania Long, "Canada May Oust Hero of Disaster: A Seaman in Andrea Doria Collision Faces Deportation," *New York Times*, Nov. 26, 1963). Also, Javier Benedet, secretary of Acción Demócrata de San Francisco, an affiliated association, wrote regularly for SIA's biweekly Antifascista (Los Angeles, 1937–1939).
91. See appendix D for a partial list of refugees and prisoners helped by the SHC.
92. Joaquín Maurín Julià, "Palabras de despedida," *EL*, Jan. 1966, Supplement. There were some reservations among members about attending the ceremony because the United States never granted refugee status to Spaniards. Without a consensus, Alberto Uriarte attended with some members of the Spanish community in New York (José Nieto Ruiz, interview by author, Nov. 8, 2013).

Chapter 5. Solidarity for Political Prisoners

1. "En el entierro de Puig la policía disuelve la multitud," *EL*, May–June 1974.
2. Pérez, "Fascist Models and Literary Subversion," 73–87. For more on Franco's repression of political prisoners, see Anderson and del Arco Blanco, eds., *Mass Killings and Violence in Spain*.
3. Molina, *El movimiento clandestino en España*.
4. I have traced 700 fundraisers from November 1939 to 1977.
5. See photographs of demonstrations in figs. 4 to 7.
6. "Piquetes frente al consulado de Francia en Nueva York," *EL*, Mar. 22, 1940; "Nuestra protesta," *EL*, Jan. 8, 1960; "SHC logra otro triunfo," *EL*, May 6, 1960; "El piquete," *EL*, Apr. 21, 1961; "Gran entusiasmo en nuestro acto de afirmación democrática," *EL*, Nov. 17, 1961; "Cisma en Nueva York: En torno al doce de octubre," *EL*, Nov. 6, 1964.
7. Varela-Lago, "Conquerors, Immigrants, Exiles," 283.
8. "¡Boicot a los productos fascistas!" *Frente Popular*, Oct. 27, 1939.
9. The authors of the article were Armiña Banyan, María Bringa, Alba Castilla (daughter of José Castilla Morales), Celeste Cesuraga, Rosa Cesuraga, Josefina Gil, Dolores Llull, Blanca Machado, Amparo Miralles, Peggy Reyes, Emilia Rodríguez, Enriqueta Romeo,

Josefina Sánchez, and Ana Santana (Banyan et al., "Seamos conscientes ¡Boicot a los productos!" *EL*, Dec. 22, 1939).

10. Violeta Miqueli González, "Distintas clases de antifascistas," *EL*, Mar. 15, 1940.

11. Miqueli González, "Distintas clases de antifascistas."

12. "España, nosotros y los fascistas," *EL*, Dec. 15, 1939.

13. "Boicot. ¡A la lucha!" *Frente Popular*, Jan. 6, 1939.

14. "El festival homenaje a Madrid culminó en un éxito sorprendente," *EL*, Nov. 24, 1939.

15. During the Spanish Civil War, Mingorance fought with another SHC member, Luis Zugadi, in Madrid. At the end of the war, he crossed the French border with other refugees. In 1940, Mingorance arrived in New York, but moved to Mexico in 1944. In the 1950s, he moved to Monterrey and taught painting there. Zugadi died in battle in Spain.

16. "Éxodo," *EL*, Mar. 22, 1940.

17. "Dolores Bouveta," *EL*, Oct. 21, 1953.

18. "Agrupación Leales Españoles," *EL*, Aug. 28, 1942.

19. For this study, I have considered the twenty-one events carried out from November to December 1939, after *Frente Popular* changed its name to *España Libre* to reflect its independence from communist influence.

20. The Spanish Civil War was in fact the result of the people's resistance to a military coup, which planned for a "rapid alzamiento, or rising, to be followed by a military directory like that established in 1933"; however, "they had not counted on the strength of working-class resistance" (Preston, *The Spanish Holocaust*, 102)

21. This was the case of the rally celebrated in the Manhattan Center on Jan. 8, 1940 ("Camaradas delegados," *EL*, Jan. 12, 1940).

22. Federico García Lorca's brother, Francisco Garcia Lorca, and Lorca's niece, Laura García Lorca, performed in two theatrical events in 1944. Fernando de los Ríos, who served as the Second Republic ambassador to the United States from 1936 to 1939, gave sixteen speeches for the SHC.

23. The younger members of AMA were photographed in *España Libre*. One photograph's caption included the names of the young women standing (left to right), Enriqueta Romeo, Josefina Sánchez, Peggy Reyes, Blanca Macado, Celeste Gosuraga, Josefina Gil, and María Bringa; and sitting (left to right) Armina Banyan, Ana Santana, Evelyn Rodríguez, Alba Castilla, Dolores Lull, Rose Gesuraga, and Amparo Miralles ("Juventudes de AMA," *EL*, Feb. 16, 1940).

24. Its president in 1941 was Antonia Pujol, and its representatives at assemblies that year were María Machado and Teresa Castilla. Flora Restoy, as well as Dolores Dorado, wife of executive member Manuel Dorado, also led the group. Pujol, a Majorcan woman, also cooked for AMA fundraising dinners.

25. "Agrupación Leales Españoles," *EL*, Aug. 28, 1942.

26. "Una prueba elocuente," *EL*, Mar. 1, 1940.

27. "Obituario: Flora Restoy," *EL*, July 24, 1959.

28. "Gran Picnic," *EL*, June 11, 1943.

29. "Agrupación Leales Españoles," *EL*, Aug. 13, 1943.

30. However, fifty-three fundraising activities were held in 1958.
31. "¡Vigorización!" Editorial, *EL*, Apr. 17, 1953.
32. "El efecto de nuestra despedida," Editorial, *EL*, Nov. 18, 1955.
33. "Breve Reseña Histórico-Política de Nuestra Organización," ELC.
34. Colón, *Pioneros puertorriqueños en Nueva York*, 242.
35. "Gran función pro radio del programa de SHC," *EL*, Feb. 21, 1941.
36. "La muerte de la abuela," *EL*, Oct. 29, 1943.
37. Neira Vilas and Montero, "A cultura galega en Buenos Aires: 1950–1960," 9–52.
38. "Silencio bochornoso," *EL*, Jan. 5, 1940.
39. "Radiado por La voz de las Sociedades Confederadas," May 30, 1942, ELC.
40. "Velada en el Ateneo," *EL*, Feb. 12, 1943.
41. His brother Antonio Martínez Novella, an anarchist who rallied with Juan López and Pestaña in the 1930s, authored several books on social issues, and died in prison in Francoist Spain (Iñiguez, *Esbozo de una enciclopedia histórica del anarquismo español*, 388).
42. *La medicina en su triple aspecto* (1922) and *Man in Nature and Behavior* (1951).
43. *España Libre* mentions, for example, politicians and government officials like Congressman Philip J. Philbin of Massachusetts; Ambassador Carlton J. Hayes; Mr. Richard Arens, secretary, House Un-American Activities Committee, Washington, DC; Senator J. Glenn Beall of Maryland; the Honorable Andrew H. Berding, assistant secretary of the U.S. Department of State.
44. Herrerín López, *La CNT durante el franquismo*, 92.
45. "Doble monstruosidad," *EL*, Oct. 25, 1940.
46. Confederated Spanish Societies, "Release for Publication," Sept. 14, 1961.
47. José Nieto Ruiz, telephone interview by author, Nov. 8, 2013.
48. The executed were Catalan union members Pedro Adrover Fons, José Pérez Pedrero, Santiago Amir Gruanas, Gines Urrea Peña, and Jorge Pons Argiles ("Fueron ejecutados cinco hombres de la Resistencia," *EL*, Mar. 21, 1952).
49. "Gran Acto," *EL*, Mar. 21, 1952; "Importante el Mitin de Protesta contra las ejecuciones en España," *EL*, Mar. 28, 1952.
50. Maurice Orbach, "Report on Franco-Spain," *EL*, Feb. 5, 1954.
51. González Malo, "¡Morir de pie!" *EL*, Mar. 21, 1952.
52. "Condenan a 18 de la Resistencia por acción de propaganda," *EL*, Feb. 12, 1954.
53. Other personalities mentioned were Jay Lovestone, George Delaney, Waldo Frank, Dwight Macdonald, and Victor Reuther ("Una mujer y nueve hombres a presidio," *EL*, Feb. 26, 1954).
54. "Juzgan en Vitoria a 17 hombres de la resistencia," *EL*, Apr. 2, 1954. The same front page denounced the torture of nineteen Freemasons in Madrid's provincial prison. They were sentenced up to thirty years because Freemasonry was prohibited under Franco's rule. The article asks American Freemasons to help free their brothers.
55. "Miembros distinguidos," *EL*, Apr. 16, 1954.
56. Robert J. Alexander was also an advisory member of *Ibérica*.

57. González Malo, Letter to Roger Baldwin, Apr. 27, 1960. JGMP; "La Santa Alianza," *EL*, Dec. 15, 1961.
58. González Malo, Letter to Roger Baldwin, May 4, 1962, JGMP.
59. "Facts of Sadism in Spain for U.N.," *EL*, Jan. 19, 1962; "Death Penalty Sought for Student in Spain," *EL*, Oct. 5, 1962.
60. Ján Papánek, chairman of the International League for the Rights of Man, also signed the letter (Roger Baldwin, "La Liga Internacional de los Derechos del Hombre protesta," *EL*, Dec. 4, 1964; Baldwin, "Pro-Presos," *EL*, Feb. 16, 1962).
61. Alfarache, who served under the Catalan and Spanish governments during the Spanish Civil War, fled to Mexico but clandestinely returned to Spain to represent the CNT. In 1947, he was arrested for his involvement with the underground ANFD.
62. "Un éxito completo," *EL* June 16, 1961; "Gran entusiasmo en nuestro acto de afirmación democrática," *EL*, Nov. 17, 1961.
63. The other council members were Robert Alexander, Ángel del Río, Eugenio Granell, Joaquín Maurín, Francisco Ayala, and Víctor Alba.
64. Herrerín López, *La CNT durante el franquismo*, 415.
65. Herrerín López, *La CNT durante el franquismo*, 292.
66. His papers show that, from 1937 to his death in 1965, he wrote at least four thousand letters to more than two hundred correspondents in thirty-three different cities. See Feu, ed., *Jesús González Malo: Correspondencia*.
67. Melquiades Robert, Letter to González Malo and Aldecoa, Feb. 24, 1964, JGMP.
68. For more on union relations between the United States and Spain during the Franco regime see Rodríguez Jiménez, "Trade Unionism and Spain–US Political Relations, 1945–1953," 96–124; Rodríguez Jiménez and Hosoda, "Convidados de Piedra o promotores del cambio?," 37–60; and Rodríguez Jiménez, "La AFL-CIO y el sindicalismo español, 1953–1971," 863–892.
69. Feu, ed., *Jesús González Malo: Correspondencia*, 55.
70. Acracio Bartolomé, Letter to Jesús González Malo, Feb. 10, 1965, JGMP.
71. However, he escaped into France soon afterward (Feu, ed., *Jesús González Malo: Correspondencia*, 55).
72. "El Sindicato del Automóvil le otorga medalla a Jesús González Malo," *EL*, Dec. 10, 1965.

Chapter 6. We, the Antifascist People

1. Barker, *The Aesthetics of Antifascist Film*, 17–18.
2. "Anarchist Leader Is Killed in Madrid," *New York Times*, Nov. 21, 1936.
3. Félix Martí Ibáñez, "Mi concepto del héroe," *EL*, Aug. 30, 1940.
4. Associated Press, "Deaths in Raid Put at 200: Rebel Planes Rain Bombs in Madrid," *New York Times*, Nov. 9, 1936.
5. V. Rico, "Miaja, como símbolo," *EL*, Feb. 21, 1958.
6. José Asensio, "Al pueblo madrileño en la gesta heroica de su resistencia," *EL*, Nov. 17, 1939.

Notes to Chapter 6

7. "Sin patria, pero con dignidad," Editorial, *EL*, Dec. 20, 1940.
8. "Lo que dijo el alcalde del Ferrol," *EL*, Feb. 23, 1940.
9. "Nuestras actividades," *EL*, Nov. 20, 1957.
10. "Nuestros muertos," Editorial, *EL*, Feb. 16, 1962.
11. The Asturian miners' strike of 1934 was also commemorated.
12. Scott Eastman, "Nationalism," in *Iberia and the Americas: Culture, Politics, and History*, vol. 3, ed. Will Kaufman (Santa Barbara, CA: ABC-CLIO, 2006), 759–766.
13. Odón Betanzos Palacios, "Éxito de unas obras poéticas," *EL*, Nov. 20, 1953.
14. Betanzos Palacios, "Manolo Betanzos," *EL*, June 5, 1964.
15. Betanzos Palacios, "Manuel Barciela," *EL*, Mar. 6, 1964.
16. Because of his own family experience, executions and incarceration for political beliefs were important marks in Betanzos Palacios's pieces in *España Libre* but also in his other published works. In 1975, he wrote the introduction to Patricio Escobar's *Las sacas*, which denounced the civil rights infringements in Franco's prisons. Besides his poetry and his commitment to protest against Franco's terror, Betanzos Palacios served as vice secretary of the SHC in 1964 and 1965, founded the literary periodical *Mensaje de Nueva York* in 1969, and was a founder of the North American Academy of the Spanish Language in 1973.
17. "Horrible espectáculo ofrece España después de un año de 'victoria,'" *EL*, May 10, 1940.
18. Aurelio Pego, "Hay que buscarle novia a Hitler," *EL*, Sept. 20, 1940. My research on the periodical's gendered representation was initially published in Feu, "Transnational Working-Class Women's Activism in New York's Confederated Hispanic Societies," 187–208.
19. The maternalist strategy was not uncommon in antifascism. See Yusta Rodrigo, "Género y antifascismo en España, de la II República a la Guerra Fría," 227–247; and Eley, *Forging Democracy*, 296.
20. Miguel Giménez Igualada, "Lealtad," *EL*, May 5, 1961.
21. Giménez Igualada, "Tierra de Sembradura," *EL*, Nov. 4, 1960.
22. Giménez Igualada, *Los últimos románticos*.
23. Giménez Igualada, "La frase amorosa," *EL*, Mar. 4, 1960.
24. Giménez Igualada, "Vida sencilla," *EL*, Sept. 2, 1960.
25. *El niño y la escuela* (1942), *Más allá del dolor* (1946), *Rutas de luz* (1949), *Los últimos románticos* (1959), *Los caminos del hombre: epistolario* (1961), *Salmos* (1965); *Bondad* (1965); *Lobos en España: Estudio político-religioso* (1967); *Anarquismo* (1968), *Stirner* (1968).
26. In exile print culture, the name "Juan" was a code word for any Spaniard.
27. Giménez Igualada, *Los caminos del hombre: epistolario*, 13.
28. Giménez Igualada, *Los caminos del hombre: epistolario*, 11.
29. Giménez Igualada, *Los caminos del hombre: epistolario*, 85.
30. Giménez Igualada, *Los caminos del hombre: epistolario*, 11.
31. Giménez Igualada, *Los caminos del hombre: epistolario*, 29.
32. Giménez Igualada, *Los caminos del hombre: epistolario*, 82–83.

33. Giménez Igualada, *Anarquismo*, 27.
34. Giménez Igualada, *Anarquismo*, 39.
35. Camín also fought under Pancho Villa in the Mexican Revolution (Iñíguez, *Esbozo*, 115).
36. Camín also wrote for *Las Novedades* (New York), *Gráfico* (New York), *La Prensa* (San Antonio), *Evolución* (Laredo, Texas), and *El Cronista del Valle* (Brownsville, Texas).
37. Camín was the author of more than twenty books of poetry and one of the earlier promoters of Afro-Cuban poetry. He contributed with some of his own Caribbean-themed poetry to *España Libre*. He also published some essays and short stories.
38. Camín, "Otra vez," *EL*, June 15, 1939.
39. Camín, "En el prado del Rayán," *EL*, Sept. 28, 1950.
40. Camín, "No le temas al mar," *EL*, July 4, 1952.
41. Camín, "Evangélica," *EL*, Sept. 19, 1952.
42. Camín, "Mater Dolorosa," *EL*, Mar. 17, 1956.
43. Camín, "Poeta," *EL*, May 16, 1958.
44. Camín, "Yugo," *EL*, Oct. 4, 1957.
45. Camín, "Cadenas," *EL*, Sept. 21, 1962.
46. Camín, "La muerte de la rosa," *EL*, Sept. 15, 1961.
47. Camín, "Barca florecida," *EL*, Feb. 23, 1940.
48. Camín, "Camino y quilla," *EL*, Aug. 2, 1963.
49. Camín, "A los gallegos de pino mar y viento," *EL*, Jan. 2, 1940.
50. Camín, "Lucha," *EL*, Oct. 15, 1949.
51. Camín, "Éxodo," *EL*, June 12, 1959.
52. Martí Ibáñez also published in other anarchist periodicals of the Spanish Civil War exile such as *La Novela Española* (Toulouse).
53. Martí Ibáñez, "El rescoldo de la hoguera," *EL*, Jan. 15, 1943.
54. Martí Ibáñez, "Perfiles de Hidalgo," *EL*, Oct. 10, 1947, 3.
55. The playwright Muñoz Seca helped him adapt his celebrated novel *Santa Isabel de Ceres* (1926) as a play for the popular stage (Javier Barreiro, "Los bestsellers de la bohemia Española," *Boletín Hispánico Helvético* 10 [Oct. 2007]: 90).
56. Vidal y Planas, "Luciérnagas," *EL*, May 4, 1962.
57. Félix Martí Ibáñez, "Cuaderno de bitácora: Julio," *EL*, July 19, 1940.
58. Martí Ibáñez, "Cuaderno de bitácora: La voz de la soledad," *EL*, Apr. 26, 1940.
59. He might be refering to antifascist author Adolf Walter Freund (Martí Ibáñez, "Presagio," *EL*, Feb. 16, 1940).
60. Cohn, *Underground Passages*, 391.
61. Cohn, *Anarchism and the Crisis of Representation*, 177.
62. This analysis originally appeared in Feu, "'Transatlantic Trenches' in Spanish Civil War Journalism," 53–78. Also see Feu, "Anarchist Aesthetics in Félix Martí Ibáñez's 'The Star Hunt,'" 35–48.
63. Jeppersen, "Becoming Anarchist,"189–213, 201.
64. Martí Ibáñez, "Cuaderno de bitácora: Episodio en Londres," *EL*, Mar. 15, 1940; Martí Ibáñez, "Cuaderno de bitácora: Episodio en Londres," *EL*, Mar. 22, 1940.

65. Martí Ibáñez, "Cuaderno de bitácora: Episodio en Londres," *EL*, Mar. 15, 1940.

66. Arnall had a small print shop in Spain until bombs destroyed it and killed his family. After he joined the Republican army, Juan would sit in his trench at night and remember his print shop and the bloody dust where his wife died. After the war, Quakers helped him to get to London and work in a Quaker's print shop.

67. Martí Ibáñez, "Cuaderno de bitácora: Episodio en Londres," *EL*, Mar. 22, 1940.

68. Martí Ibáñez, "Cuaderno de bitácora: Episodio en Londres."

69. Barker, *The Aesthetics of Antifascist Film*, 25.

70. Barker, *The Aesthetics of Antifascist Film*, 26.

71. Ordaz Romay, "Características del exilio español en Estados Unidos," 265.

72. González Malo and other exiles shared this belief. The concept of *convivencia* (coexistence) among cultures and religions in Spain has marked many Spaniards' mythical self-representation (Sender, "Montesquieu y el español 'fronterizo,'" *CNT* (México), May–June 1960; Sender, "El español 'fronterizo,'" *EL*, June 17, 1960).

73. Said, *Reflections on Exile and Other Essays*, 71, 186.

74. Castilla Morales interviewed the antifascist Vicente Roca, who performed on the stage and often prepared the set and continued to contribute weekly to antifascist causes (El Chico de la calle, "Visita invernal al campo naturista de Annadale," *EL*, Jan. 22, 1960). Similarly, Castilla Morales featured Carmen Novo, who performed in many plays and was working at a radio station (El Chico de la calle, "Gente conocida: Nuestra Carmiña," *EL*, Apr. 1, 1960). El Chico visited Antonio García Vallín, who spoke at many fundraisers and always donated to fundraisers. El Chico asked him for a donation during his interview (El Chico de la calle, "¡Buenos días, don Antonio!" *EL*, Mar. 18, 1960). Finally, El Chico divided his interview with Antonio Martínez, the stage prompter, into four acts, and in the last one he requested a donation (El Chico de la calle, "Gente conocida: Tragicomedia," *EL*, Apr. 15, 1960).

75. El Chico de la calle, "El hombre niquelado que vive en Miami," *EL*, Sept. 17, 1943.

76. Don Pepe, "Para nosotros . . . ," *EL*, Dec. 16, 1960.

77. Onuba, "De verano," *EL*, May 30, 1941.

78. "Fielato consular," *EL*, Feb. 2, 1940; "El retrato de miaja," *EL*, Mar. 1, 1940.

79. "Réplica a una carta," *EL*, Feb. 19, 1960.

80. Don Pepe, "Revisando las noticias," *EL*, Jan. 1, 1954.

81. Don Pepe, "Revisando las noticias."

82. He interviewed Juan Pliego (El Cortijo) and Jerano Borines (Aldea Borines), owners of popular vacation resorts and also interviewed the owners of popular restaurants in New York, all of whom were prominent sponsors of the SHC; Domingo González (Restaurante Ebro), Pepe González (Café Madrid), Manuel Montero (United Café), Antonio Sánchez Castilla (Restaurante Castilla), and Carlos Suárez (La Bilbaína). Similarly, García Copado wrote the history of other business owners such as Aurelio Rodríguez Fernández, who managed the Fernández Bilingual Institute. On another occasion, García Copado featured Venezuelan Juan González Hernández, who served the exile community as host (under the name Mario de Lara) of Spanish-language programs broadcast by WHOM radio. García Copado also interviewed José

Adurez (who was originally from Santander) and worked in various restaurants around New York. García Copado also interviewed Cándido Villa and José González, both from Pontevedra, who worked in agriculture.

83. Juan Pliego's family had lived two years in Mexico and Cuba before arriving in New York (García Copado, *EL*, Dec. 4, 1959).

84. García Copado, "Cuénteme usted su vida," *EL*, Feb. 19, 1960. See also Ismael Martinez Jr., *Las Villas of Plattekill and Ulster County* (Charleston, SC: Arcadia Publishing, 2016).

85. García Copado was the author of several books of poetry, short stories, novels, and plays. His collection of poems dedicated to Juan Ramón Jimenez, *Canción del amor imposible* (1959), received an honorable mention in the Certamen Literario Internacional del Círculo de Escritores y Poetas Iberoamericanos de Nueva York in 1958.

86. Antonio García Copado, "Elegía de fin de año," *EL*, Jan. 8, 1960; García Copado, "Las doce uvas de la ausencia," *EL*, Dec. 25, 1959; Montse Feu, "España Libre (1939–1977)" (PhD diss., University of Houston, 2011), 39–51.

87. García Copado, "Elegía de fin de año."

88. Blankets are used to harvest and carry olives. Vidal y Planas, "¡Esta noche va a nevar!" in *Cirios en los rascacielos y otros poemas* (Tijuana, Mexico: Litográfica de Baja California, 1963), 23.

89. Olives are harvested by shaking the tree's branches and making the fruit fall into a blanket in what could be seen as a rain of olives.

90. Vidal y Planas, "Cirios en los rascacielos," 20.

91. Vidal y Planas, "Mi viña sidereal," 74.

92. Vidal y Planas, "La luna llena sobre Manhattan," 29.

93. Vidal y Planas, "La luna llena sobre Manhattan," 25. Alirio Díaz Guerra was the first Latino author to exploit the symbolic potential of the New York's landmark in his novel *Lucas Guevara* (1914). After unfortunate tribulations in the unwelcoming city, the immigrant protagonist commits suicide by jumping from the bridge.

94. Vidal y Planas, "Las hogueras del ocaso," *EL*, July 2, 1965.

95. Alfonso Ayensa, "Los suicidas y desleales manejos del franquismo en África del Norte," *EL*, Sept. 16, 1955.

96. Agrón was charged with the murder of two teenagers in a notorious gang fight in 1959. For more on Agrón see Eric C. Schneider, *Vampires, Dragons, and Egyptian Kings: Youth Gangs in Postwar New York* (Princeton, NJ: Princeton University Press, 1999) and Piri Thomas, *Down These Mean Streets* (New York: Knopf, 1967).

97. González Malo, "Sender dolorido: Unamuno malparado," *EL* (Paris), Mar. 11, 1956.

Chapter 7. Theater—*Género Chico* and Antifascism

1. Aurelio Pego, "Colombia sobre el tapete de Franco," *EL*, Oct. 3, 1952.

2. Payne, *Fascism in Spain*, 56, 127.

3. See appendix E of popular plays frequently performed by the SHC.

4. Only a few canonical plays were performed by the SHC. When a canonical play was staged, it was inevitably paired with comedic or musical acts.

5. María Francisca Vilches de Frutos and Dru Dougherty, "La escena madrileña entre 1900 y 1936: Apuntes para una historia del teatro representado," *Anales de la Literatura Española Contemporánea* 17, no. 1/3 (1992): 75–86.

6. Villamil-Acera, "La construcción del diálogo teatral en el teatro cómico español," 2, 48, 77–79. See also Fuentes, *La marcha al pueblo de las letras españolas*; Dougherty, "The Commercial Stage, 1900–1936," 579–594, 579; and López Campillo, "Vanguardia burguesa y cultura anarquista en la *Revista Blanca* (1923–1936)," 237–242.

7. See appendix E list of popular plays frequently performed at fundraisers.

8. See Kanellos, *A History of Hispanic Theatre in the United States*; Mendez Montesinos, *The Ingenious Simpleton*; Sturman, *Zarzuela: Spanish Operetta, American Stage*.

9. Marin, *Anarquistas*, 183.

10. Unfortunately, *España Libre* announcements and reviews of these zarzuelas do not provide more information about their plots.

11. Nancy J. Membrez, "La (re)invención," 78, qtd. in Villamil-Acera, "La construcción del diálogo teatral en el teatro cómico español," 74.

12. The comedia was a full-length drama in several acts and staged with an expensive set. Entremeses and sainetes were brief entr'acts. For more on Quintero brothers' plays see Mariano de Paco, *El teatro de los hermanos Álvarez Quintero* (Murcia, Spain: Editum, 2010).

13. Villamil-Acera, "La construcción del diálogo teatral en el teatro cómico español," 104.

14. Federico de Onís, "Preface," *Contemporary Spanish Texts* (D. C. Heath and Company, 1926), iii–xviii, xiv.

15. The género chico was also popular in anarchist and exile enclaves in France and Latin America.

16. Cantos Casenave and Romero Ferrer, *Pedro Muñoz Seca y el teatro de humor contemporáneo*, 67; Villamil-Acera, "La construcción del diálogo teatral en el teatro cómico español," 120, 132.

17. Performed by Centro Español, Agrupación Socialista Española, and Grupo Vasco. Director: Antonio de la Villa. During the Spanish Civil War, Muñoz Seca was detained by anarcho-syndicalists in Barcelona, then imprisoned in Madrid for his monarchical and religious beliefs. Communists killed him not long thereafter.

18. The eccentric modern two-act farce parodied two genres: the Spanish honor drama such as Calderón de la Barca's *La venganza de don Mendo*, and detective novels.

19. Dougherty and Vilches, "La escena madrileña," 100. The reader will note the resonance between Mary's fascination with crime novels and the illusory crime plotted by Mary's two admirers.

20. Spanish critic and author Azorín lauded Muñoz Seca's capacity to rebel against classical realism and melodrama (Villamil-Acera, "La construcción del diálogo teatral en el teatro cómico español," 127).

21. Villamil-Acera, "La construcción del diálogo teatral en el teatro cómico español," 14.

22. See appendix F with more details of these recovered antifascist plays.

23. The Hispanic press reviewed these performances (these reviews have facilitated the description of many of these plays in appendixes F and G).

24. Don Pepe [José Castilla Morales], "59 Henry Street," *EL*, Jan. 6, 1961.

25. The *Ateneo*'s mission was to educate workers, disseminate anarchist and syndicalist ideas, and inform readers about other anarchist groups and their political meetings and conferences. The magazine published contributions from Spain and Buenos Aires.

26. Castilla Morales would later publish satiric poems in *España Libre* under the pseudonym Lirón. Most poems were published in a collection entitled *Bombas de mano* (1938). See Amor y Vázquez, "Recuperaciones," 9–26.

27. Don Pepe [José Castilla Morales], "59 Henry Street," *EL*, Mar. 17, 1961.

28. For example, Julian Benedet, Delfín Fernández, José Ferrer, Pepita Gil, Feliciano Huerta, Leonor Lucas, Carmen Novo, Marita Reid, Vicente Roca, Lola Rodríguez, Carmelita Rodríguez "La Monterito," and brothers Luis and Ignacio Zugadi Garmendia ("Nuestro teatro: La aparición del Ateneo," *Ateneo*, Apr. 21, 1934). See appendix G for a list of regular performers.

29. See Vigil, "El teatro en los medios libertarios del exilio," 449–464; Litvak, *Musa Libertaria*; Soriano and Madrid, *Bibliografía del anarquismo en España*.

30. Often, Antonio de la Villa wrote the reviews. The journalist for *Ahora* (Madrid) was exiled in New York and served as secretary of fundraising activities in the 1940s.

31. Despite the obvious literary calling, Castilla Morales had a pragmatic reason to write original plays: the Society of Spanish Authors claimed copyright for each Spanish play represented at the fundraisers. Castilla refused to pay to an administration under Franco's rule ("Festivales de SHC," *EL*, Editorial, Apr. 2, 1948).

32. Possibly, Castilla Morales was adapting José Sanchis Sinisterra's ¡*Ay, Carmela!* (1940), also about two traveling players, Carmela and Paulino, during the Spanish Civil War. Please see my examination of Castilla Morales's plays in Feu, "José Castilla Morales y España Libre," 87–104.

33. Cohn, *Anarchism and the Crisis of Representation*, 57–60.

34. Other Latino comic plays of the era featured a parodic Uncle Sam character.

35. See appendix F that documents a total of thirty-four antifascist plays written by a handful of members.

36. In Barcelona, Sugrañés had been a successful producer, adapting foreign models to the Spanish stage. Dougherty, "The Commercial Stage, 1900–1936," 582.

37. "Manuel Sugrañes," *EL*, Aug. 6, 1943.

38. For other Juan Tenorio adaptations in Spanish Civil War literature, see Lonsdale, "Don Juan in Exile," 95–106.

39. Kanellos, "Marita Reid," 613–614. Also see Elisa de la Roche, ¡*Teatro Hispano! Three Major New York Companies* (New York: Garland Publishing, 1995), 6.

40. Sturman, *Zarzuela*, 63.

41. Kanellos, *A History of Hispanic Theatre*, 199.

42. Kanellos, "Marita Reid," 613–614; "Marita Reid le da la mano a Shakespeare y a Cervantes," *EL*, Feb. 5, 1954; "Marita Reid en el cine," *EL*, June 25, 1954.

43. She was married to José Tavira, an ex-torero and theatrical impresario in New York.

44. Pi adapted the original text of the Paramount version, *Tiger Love* (1924) directed by George Melford. Juan A. Tarancon, Elena Oliete-Aldea, and Beatriz Oria, *Global Genres*,

Local Films: The Transnational Dimension of Spanish Cinema (New York: Bloomsbury Academic, 2015), 24.

45. "Sentidas palabras de Mary reid agradeciendo el homenaje," *EL*, June 7, 1957.
46. "Recuerdo de la defensa de Madrid y del octubre asturiano," *EL*, Dec. 6, 1957.
47. Aurelio Pego, "Dedicación lejana," *EL*, Aug. 1, 1958.
48. Aurelio Pego, "Actriz del pueblo," *EL*, Feb. 27, 1948.
49. Aurelio Pego, "Actriz del pueblo."
50. G. Celonio, "Revoltillo farandulero," *Gráfico*, Feb. 22, 1930. In 1937, Moreno was contacted by Franco's agents in New York who asked her to work as a spy for them. She was offered as reward the protection of her family in Madrid, but she refused to spy ("Ecos de Broadway," *Ecos de Nueva York*, July 18, 1954).
51. "Consuelo está por allá," *EL*, May 5, 1944.
52. "¡Gloriosa resistencia!" *EL*, Oct. 16, 1959.

Chapter 8. Aurelio Pego, Antifascist Satirical Chronicler

1. Some authors such as Onuba (José Castilla Morales) penned sketches and Lirón (Adolfo Jiménez Colón) composed poetry.
2. On fascist violence in Spain see Armengou and Belis, *Els nens perduts del franquisme*; Rodrigo, *Cautivos: Campos de concentración en la España franquista, 1936-1947*; Rodrigo, "Fascism and Violence in Spain;" Jerez-Farran and Amago, eds., *Unearthing Franco's Legacy. Mass Graves and the Recovery of Historical Memory in Spain*; Ferrán and Hilbink, eds., *Legacies of violence in Contemporary Spain*.
3. Mauro Muñiz, *Larra* (Madrid: Epesa, 1969), 89.
4. Ángel Estévez Molinero, "Relaciones entre literatura y periodismo: Implicaciones históricas (y en páginas interiores, Larra, Galdós y Umbral)," *Epos* 14 (1998): 258; Susan Kirkpatrick and Marta Eguía, trans., *Larra: El laberinto inextricable de un romántico liberal* (Madrid: Editorial Gredos, 1977), 7.
5. Kanellos, "*Cronistas* and Satire in Early Twentieth Century Hispanic Newspapers," 9.
6. The manager at William R. Warner Division of W. Hudnut, Inc., discussion with FBI informant (Aurelio Pego, FBI case 1242376-001, NARA).
7. Aurelio Pego, Letter to SHC, Apr. 8, 1953, ELC.
8. Gallego, "Fascistization and Fascism," 159–181, 165.
9. Óscar Rodríguez Barreira, "The Many Heads of the Hydra: Local Parafascism in Spain and Europe, 1936–50," *Journal of Contemporary History* 49, no. 4 (2014): 725.
10. Viñas, "Natural Alliances: The Impact of Nazism and Fascism on Franco's Domestic Policies," in *Interrogating Francoism*, ed. Graham, 153.
11. Antonio Cazorla Sánchez, *Fear and Progress: Ordinary Lives in Franco's Spain, 1939–1975* (Malden, MA: Wiley-Blackwell, 2010), 8.
12. Jorge Marco, "States of War: 'Being Civilian' in 1940s Spain," in *Interrogating Francoism*, ed. Graham, 162; Julián Casanova, "Dismembering Francoism: What Is at Stake in Spain's Memory Wars?" in *Interrogating Francoism*, ed. Graham, 206.
13. Rodrigo, "Fascism and Violence in Spain," 188, 192.

Notes to Chapter 8

14. Rodrigo, "Fascism and Violence in Spain," 188.

15. Cazorla Sánchez, *Fear and Progress*, 6.

16. Viñas, "Natural Alliances," 154, 150.

17. In 1952, the government somehow liberalized the economy and "dropped several of its most dysfunctional and irrational policies" (Cazorla Sánchez, *Fear and Progress*, 6). Although the liberalization of trade achieved some of the highest levels of growth in the world economy (after two decades of autarky), it also unleashed "stark inequalities, high levels of poverty, and political repression" (Brydan, *Franco's Internationalists*, 170).

18. Payne, *Fascism in Spain*, 13, 91.

19. For more on the epic and mythical representations of Franco, see Ignacio Fontes and Manuel A. Menéndez, *El parlamento de papel: Las revistas españolas en la transición democrática* (Madrid: Asociación de la Prensa de Madrid, 2004).

20. Viñas, "Natural Alliances," 153; Gallego, "Fascistization and Fascism," 170. On the mythical construction of fascism see Zira Box, *España, año cero: La construcción simbólica del franquismo* (Madrid: Alianza Editorial, 2010); and Roger Griffin, *The Nature of Fascism* (New York: Routledge, 1991).

21. Viñas, "Natural Alliances," 154.

22. Viñas, "Natural Alliances," 150.

23. Viñas, "Natural Alliances," 153.

24. Preston, *The Politics of Revenge*; Preston, *The Spanish Holocaust*.

25. Barreira, "The Many Heads of the Hydra," 725.

26. Cazorla Sánchez, *Fear and Progress*, 6–9; also see Javier Rodrigo, *Hasta la raíz: Violencia durante la Guerra Civil y la dictadura franquista* (Madrid: Alianza, 2008).

27. Pego, "Le dedica un articulito a Franco," *EL*, Feb. 2, 1962.

28. Pego, "Ahora mata peces," *EL*, Oct. 21, 1955.

29. Pego, "El decreto del miedo," *EL*, Dec. 2, 1960.

30. Pego, "Sí señor, un ejemplo," *EL*, Oct. 4, 1963.

31. Pego, "El valiente generalísimo tiene miedo," *EL*, Dec. 7, 1956.

32. Gallego, "Fascistization and Fascism," 173.

33. Pego, "Querido odiado," *EL* (Paris), Oct. 19, 1948.

34. Pego, "Cómo se puede hacer caer a Franco," *EL*, Feb. 19, 1960.

35. Pego, "¿Acabarán de verdad con todas las ratas?" *EL*, May 6, 1966.

36. Pego, "¿A qué esperar más?" *EL*, Apr. 19, 1957.

37. Pego, "Desafíos tontos, no," *EL*, Oct. 19, 1962.

38. For more on the mythical representations of Franco, see Fontes and Menéndez, *El parlamento de papel*.

39. Casanova, "Dismembering Francoism," 204; Nil Santiáñez. *Topographies of Fascism: Habitus, Space, and Writing in Twentieth-Century Spain* (Toronto: University of Toronto Press, 2013).

40. Pego, "La victoria . . . ¿de quién?" *EL*, May 7, 1973.

41. Pego, "La victoria . . .

42. Pego, "La victoria . . .

43. Cazorla Sánchez, *Fear and Progress*, 6, 10; Viñas, "Natural Alliances," 150.
44. Cazorla Sánchez, *Fear and Progress*, 9–11.
45. Qtd. in Pego, "Contigo hasta sin pan ni cebolla," *EL*, Oct. 31, 1952.
46. Pego, "Contigo hasta sin pan ni cebolla."
47. The skilled satirist Pego exposes fascist redefinitions of language. For similar phenomenon in Nazi Germany, see Victor Klemperer's masterpiece, *Lingua Tertii Imperii: Notizbuch eines Philologen* (1947), which examines linguistic contortion.
48. Pego, "Misa cantada y champaña," *EL*, Aug. 7, 1953.
49. Pego, "Viven mejor y mueren major," *EL*, Mar. 6, 1959.
50. Pego, "Curas motorizados," *EL*, May 4, 1956.
51. Pego, "¿Veinte años más? ¡Qué optimista!" *EL*, Dec. 4, 1959.
52. Pego, "¿Veinte años más? ¡Qué optimista!"
53. See Preston, *El gran manipulador*; Neal Rosendorf, *Franco Sells Spain to America: Hollywood, Tourism, and Public Relations as Postwar Spanish Soft Power* (New York: Palgrave Macmillan, 2014).
54. Pego, "Los garantizadores del porvenir," *EL*, Nov. 13, 1953.
55. Pego, "Don Patricio y su cabeza," *EL*, May 23, 1952.
56. Pego, "¿Tubérculos propagandistas?" *EL*, Apr. 11, 1952.
57. Pego, "Dos caras que resultan caras," *EL*, Feb. 17, 1956.
58. Pego, "El cornúpeto de Washington," *EL*, Sept. 25, 1953.
59. Pego, "¡La flota sexta a la vista!" *EL*, Jan. 4, 1952.
60. Pego, "El gracioso peligro yanqui," *EL*, Oct. 24 1952.
61. Pego, "El gracioso peligro yanqui."
62. Pego, "Vinieron las lluvias y los turistas," *EL*, Oct. 10, 1952.
63. Pego, "Precio de admisión," *EL*, Dec. 5, 1952.
64. Pego "Una república de enamorados," *EL*, Apr. 12, 1940.
65. Pego, "El no comer como arma política," *EL*, Jan. 25, 1952.
66. Pego, "¡Pobrecitos de nosotros!" *EL*, May 22, 1953, 2.
67. Pego, "La heroica emigración republicana," *EL*, July 17, 1953.
68. Pego, "Un instrumento de accion revolucionaria," *EL*, Sept. 26, 1952.
69. Pego, "Le va a crecer Chepa," *EL*, Jan. 2, 1953.
70. Pego, "Señora, mi esperanza está en usted," *EL*, July 11, 1952.
71. Pego, "A quién echamos la culpa?" *EL*, Aug. 18, 1961.
72. With a slight change in spelling, Pego might be honoring the historical memory of Roque Barcia Martí, a nineteenth-century republican author and thinker.
73. Pego, "La sotana de Hierro," *EL*, June 7, 1957.
74. Pego, "Roque siembra el miedo," *EL*, Jan. 2, 1959.
75. Pego, "La confusión también ayuda," *EL*, June 3, 1960.
76. Pego, "La confusión también ayuda."
77. Pego, "No hay que dejarlo tranquilo," *EL*, Nov. 1, 1957.
78. Pego, "La brigada pasiva," *EL*, Mar. 21, 1958.
79. Pego, "La glándula misteriosa," *EL*, July 18, 1958.

80. Pego, "Una sigla de doble filo," *EL*, Apr. 3, 1959.
81. Pego, "En busca de Franco II," *EL*, May 3, 1968.
82. Pego, "Una dictadura gastada," *EL*, Dec. 7, 1962.
83. Charles A. Knight, *The Literature of Satire* (Cambridge: Cambridge University Press, 2004), 114.

Chapter 9. Damned Cartoons! Workers' Identity and Resistance

1. "Aniversario de 'la Victoria,'" *EL*, Apr. 5, 1940. The cartoon was published again on the front page of the issue dated Jan. 17, 1941.
2. Rodrigo, "Fascism and Violence in Spain," 187. For a comparison with the phenomenon of sacralization in Fascist Italy, see Emilio Gentile, *The Sacralization of Politics in Fascist Italy* (Cambridge, MA: Harvard University Press, 1996).
3. About the event see Carlos Rojas, *¡Muera la inteligencia! ¡Viva la muerte! Salamanca 1936, Unamuno y Millán Astray frente a frente* (Barcelona: Planeta, 1995); Luis Portillo, "Unamuno's Last Lecture," in *The Golden Horizon*, ed. Cyril Connolly (New York: New York University Press, 1955), 397–403.
4. Orleck, *Common Sense and a Little Fire*, 257.
5. The author has not been identified. It was reprinted on Nov. 4, 1941.
6. "El Spanish House y los pipiolis de la Falange," *EL*, Sept. 4, 1940. Part of my research on the use of feminine stereotypes in antifascist humorous attack was initially published in Feu, "Transnational Working-Class Women's Activism in New York's Confederated Hispanic Societies (1939–1977)," 187–208. Gamoneda published *¡Guerra al Fascismo!*, a collection of his cartoons, in Mexico in 1939.
7. *EL*, Sept. 3, 1965. For the uses of football as propaganda under the regime, see Alejandro Quiroga, "Spanish Fury: Football and National Identities under Franco," *European History Quarterly* 45, no. 3 (July 2015): 506–529.
8. *EL*, Apr. 19, 1940.
9. "Último número," *EL*, Feb. 5, 1960.
10. On National-Flamenquismo, see Marion Winrow Hart, "La Nación Flamenca: The Influence of Flamenco on Spanish Nationalism" (PhD diss., University of California at Irvine, 2013).
11. Fryer, "Por bulerías," *EL*, Oct. 16, 1953.
12. Roberto [Roberto Gómez], "Españolada," *EL*, Dec. 25, 1959.
13. See Bencivenni, *Italian Immigrant Radical Culture*; García-Guirao, "Para matar a Franco (de risa)," 274–313; and Aranzazu Sarría Buil, "Sátira y caricatura desde el exilio," 77–97.
14. "Noticia gráfica," Cartoon, *EL*, Jan. 17, 1941.
15. For more on cognitive studies of humor, see Gregg Camfield, "Some Reflections on the Bitter-Sweet Comedy of Neuro-Criticism," *Studies in American Humor* 3, no. 29 (2014): 1–12.
16. Pepoti, "He Is Giving a Party for the Leader of the Free World," *EL*, Dec. 4, 1959.
17. Preston, *The Spanish Holocaust*, 616.
18. Ramón, "Y paz en la Tierra," *EL*, Nov. 4, 1960.

19. Bartolí Guiu also illustrated the regular "Columna de honor" (Honorary column) with portraits. He published in the exile newspaper *Ibérica* (New York City), edited by Spanish Civil War exile politician Victoria Kent. See Parcerises, ed., *Josep Bartolí*; and Jaume Cañameras, *Conversa amb Bartolí*.

20. Bartolí Guiu, Cartoon, *EL*, Mar. 18, 1960.

21. Under the perspective of the health benefits of humor, my earlier research on Bartolí Guiu and some of these drawings is published in Feu, "Aesthetically Resilient: Josep Bartolí Guiu's Political Cartoons in *España Libre*," 73–90.

22. While in exile, Rivero Gil also published in several Latin American newspapers. See Suothard, "Francisco Rivero Gil," 380–405; and Southard, "Rivero Gil's 'Aleluyas de la defensa de Euzkadi,'" 1–19.

23. Francisco Rivero Gil, "Ilusiones de Franco," *EL*, June 17, 1960.

24. Bartolí Guiu, "Esto sí está estabilizado en España," *EL*, Oct. 21, 1960.

25. Sergio Aragonés, telephone interview by author, Dec. 27, 2013.

26. Aragonés occasionally served as spokesman in the SHC as he did on Apr. 5, 1963, when full-day activities were scheduled to commemorate the Second Spanish Republic in exile. At noon, there was a demonstration in front of the Spanish tourist office at 485 Madison Avenue in New York. The demonstrators' posters included Aragonés's drawings denouncing fascism in Spain. Members of the American Socialist Party, the Social Democratic Federation, the Libertarian League, the Liberation Group, the Workers Defense League, and the Young People's Socialist League joined the demonstration. Later, Aragonés acted as the master of ceremonies at a benefit at the Hispanic society La Nacional. A professor of Spanish at Hunter College, Emilio González López, gave a speech during the event and several performers volunteered to entertain the audience to raise funds for political prisoners in Spain. "Confederated Spanish Societies," *EL*, July 5, 1963.

27. My earlier research on Aragonés and some images of his cartoons can be found at Feu, "Sergio Aragonés Marginalizes Francoism in *España Libre* (NEW YORK)," 127–144.

28. He soon landed his first contract with *Mad* magazine. Aragonés is the creator of the bestseller comic heroes Groo the Wanderer and Boogeyman, among others. He has received seven awards from the National Cartoonist Society, including the prestigious Reuben Award (1996), multiple Harvey and Eisner Awards, the Saló de Barcelona Award (1995), the Schulz Award (1999), the Shazam Award (1972), the Adamson Award (1985), and the La Plumilla de Plata Award (2003), among others.

29. See Feu, "Antifascist Laughter in the Margins," 71–111.

30. Aragonés, Cartoon, *EL*, Sept. 4, 1964.

31. During the Spanish Civil War, anarchists adopted Popeye as their mascot for his working-class identity. Hochschild, *Spain in Our Hearts*, 54.

32. Aragonés, telephone interview by author, 2013; Aragonés, Cartoon, *EL*, Apr. 5, 1963; Aragonés, Cartoon, *EL*, July 5, 1963.

33. The caption reads "The truth is that, with this flag, we will find no port" ("La verdad es que, con esta bandera, no hallaremos un puerto") (Bartolí Guiu, "Libertad," *EL*, Feb. 3, 1961).

Conclusion: The SHC's Antifascist Legacy

1. For the construction of social history from below, see Bantman, "The Militant Go-Between," 274–287; Turcato, *Making Sense of Anarchism*, 47; Hoyt, "Methods for Tracing Radical Networks," 75–106; Cohn, *Underground Passages*.

2. Although scholars have provided approximate numbers of Spanish migrants and exiles to the United States, statistics do not account for undocumented workers and refugees.

3. With the exception of Stalinist, totalitarian, and elitist perspectives.

4. "Adhesión del Dr. Félix Martí Ibáñez," *EL*, Feb. 17, 1950.

5. "Adhesión del Dr. Félix Martí Ibáñez."

6. Zimmer, *Immigrants against the State*, 4.

7. Kinna, *Anarchism: A Beginner's Guide*, 246; Pauli, "The New Anarchism in Britain and the US," 134.

8. Pauli, "The New Anarchism in Britain and the US," 134–135.

9. See Feu, "Antifascist Laughter in the Margins," 71–111.

10. See the anarchist influences in Feu, "'Transatlantic Trenches' in Spanish Civil War Journalism."

11. Executive committee, "Por la libertad, cualquier precio," *EL*, Nov. 2, 1962.

Appendix F. Original Antifascist and Exile Plays, 1937–1950

1. Leopoldo González was the composer of the famous antifascist song "No pasarán" ("They Shall Not Pass"), sung at fundraisers and adopted in battlefields in Spain. González also composed several songs played at fundraisers: "Miaja," "España en llamas" (Spain in flames), "19 de Julio," "Abajo Franco" (Down with Franco), "Rebeldía" (Rebellion), "Miliciano" (Militiaman), "Cigarrillos" (Cigarettes), and "Marinero Leal" (Loyal sailor).

2. "Yo soy el refugiado / que no teme a la vida / y va por los caminos / lanzando su cantar / Y aunque nada le importe / al mundo mi sufrir / voy abriendo horizontes / y nada me importa a mí. / Que llevo en mi cuerpo / marcadas las huellas / huellas del guerrero / de la Libertad / ¡Yo sé pelear en la guerra ! / ¡Yo sé trabajar en la paz! ("Ateneo Hispano," *EL*, Apr. 4, 1947).

Bibliography

Archives

APHHC	Arte Público Hispanic Historical Collection Database (EBSCO)
BNC	Biblioteca Nacional de Catalunya, Barcelona
CRAI	Pavelló de la República CRAI, University of Barcelona
CRL	Center for Research Libraries Database
ELC	*España Libre* Collection, Robert D. Farber University Archives and Special Collections, Brandeis University
HAN	Hispanic American Newspapers Database (Readex)
JGMP	Jesús González Malo's Papers, Robert D. Farber University Archives and Special Collections, Brandeis University
LOC	Library of Congress, Washington, DC
NARA	National Archives and Records Administration
PH	Prensa Histórica Database
PHN	ProQuest Historical Newspapers Database
RUSHLH	Recovering the U.S. Hispanic Literary Heritage, University of Houston
TAM	Tamiment Library and Robert F. Wagner Labor Archives, New York University

Interviews and Email Communication

Aragonés Domenech, Sergio. Telephone interviews (2013–2018).
Fleischman, Max. Telephone and email interviews (December 2013).

Fuentes, Víctor. Email messages (2010–2018).
Nieto Ruiz, José. Email messages and interviews (2011–2018).
San Sebastián, Koldo. Email messages (2013–2018).

Periodicals

Ariel (Los Angeles)
CNT (México)
CNT (Paris)
Comunidad Ibérica (México)
Cultura Proletaria (New York)
Ecos de Nueva York (New York)
El Antifascista (Los Angeles)
El Heraldo de México (Los Angeles)
Época (San Antonio)
España Libre (New York), or *EL*
España Libre (Paris)
España Libre (Toulouse)
Frente Popular (New York)
Hablemos del Hogar Moderno (New York)
Ibérica (New York)
La Opinión (Los Angeles)
La Prensa (New York)
La Prensa (San Antonio)
La Voz (New York)
Nueva Democracia (New York)
Solidaridad Obrera (Paris)
Via Libre (New York)

Published Sources

Albanese, Matteo, and Pablo del Hierro. *Transnational Fascism in the Twentieth Century: Spain, Italy, and the Global Neo-Fascist Network*. London: Bloomsbury, 2016.

Alexander, Robert J. *The Anarchists in the Spanish Civil War*, vol. 2. London: Janus Publishing Company, 1999.

Aldecoa, Carmen. Del sentir y pensar: Libro primero. Mexico City: Bartomeu Costa Amic, 1957.

Alted Vigil, Alicia. "El teatro en los medios libertarios del exilio." In *El exilio libertario español de 1939*, vol. 2, edited by Aznar Soler, 449–464. Bellatera, Spain: Gexel, 1998.

Amo, Julián, and Charmion Shelby. *La obra impresa de los intelectuales españoles en América, 1936–1945*. Stanford, CA: Stanford University Press, 1950.

Amor y Vázquez, José. "Recuperaciones: Antifranquismo neoyorquino: Las Sociedades Hispanas Confederadas y sus *Bombas de mano*." *Letras Peninsulares* 11, no. 1 (Spring 1998): 9–26.

Bibliography

Anderson, Peter, and Miguel Ángel del Arco Blanco, eds. *Mass Killings and Violence in Spain, 1936-1952: Grappling with the Past.* New York: Routledge, 2014.

Armengou, Montserrat, and Ricard Belis. *Els nens perduts del franquisme.* Barcelona: Catalanfilms & tv: 2002.

Arostegui, Julio. *Largo Caballero: El tesón y la quimera.* Barcelona: Debate, 2013.

Avilés Farré, Juan, and Ángel Herrerín López. *El nacimiento del terrorismo en Occidente: Anarquía, nihilismo y violencia revolucionaria.* Madrid: Siglo XX, 2008.

Avrich, Paul. *The Modern School Movement: Anarchism and Education in the United States.* Edinburgh: AK Press, 2006.

Baer, James. *Anarchist Immigrants in Spain and Argentina.* Urbana: University of Illinois Press, 2015.

Bantman, Constance. "The Militant Go-Between: Émile Pouget's Transnational Propaganda, 1880-1914." *Labour History Review* 74, no. 3 (Dec. 2009): 274-287.

Barker, Jennifer Lynde. *The Aesthetics of Antifascist Film: Radical Projection.* New York: Routledge, 2013.

Bauerkämper, Arnd, and Grzegorz Rossoliński-Liebe. *Fascism without Borders: Transnational Connections and Cooperation between Movements and Regimes in Europe from 1918 to 1945.* New York: Berghahn, 2017.

Bencivenni, Marcella. *Italian Immigrant Radical Culture: The Idealism of the Sovversivi in the United States, 1890-1940.* New York: New York University Press, 2011.

Brydan, David. *Franco's Internationalists: Social Experts and Spain's Search for Legitimacy.* Oxford: Oxford University Press, 2019.

Cabezas, Bea. *La ciutat vertical.* Barcelona: Columna, 2011.

Camfield, Gregg. *Necessary Madness: The Humor of Domesticity in Nineteenth-Century American Literature.* New York: Oxford University Press, 1997.

Cañameras, Jaume. *Conversa amb Bartolí.* Montserrat: Publicacions de l'Abadia de Montserrat, 1990.

Cancilla Martinelli, Phylis, and Ana Valera-Lago, eds. *Hidden Out in the Open: Spanish Migration to the United States (1875-1930).* Boulder: University Press of Colorado, 2018.

Cantos Casenave, Marieta, and Alberto Romero Ferrer. *Pedro Muñoz Seca y el teatro de humor contemporáneo (1898-1936).* Cádiz, Spain: University of Cádiz, 1998.

Carroll, Peter N., and James D. Fernández. *Facing Fascism: New York and the Spanish Civil War.* New York: Museum of the City of New York, 2007.

Casanova, Julián, and Paul Preston. *Anarchism, the Republic, and Civil War in Spain, 1931-1939.* London: Routledge, 2005.

Castañeda, Chris. "'Those Were Times of Propaganda and Struggle': El Despertar and Brooklyn's Spanish Anarchists, 1890-1905." In *Radical Gotham: Anarchism in New York City from Schwab's Saloon to Occupy Wall Street,* edited by Tom Goyens, 77-99. Champaign: University of Illinois Press, 2017.

Castañeda, Chris, and Montse Feu. *Writing Revolution: Hispanic Anarchist Print Culture and the United States.* Urbana: University of Illinois Press, 2019.

Caudet, Francisco, ed. *Correspondencia Ramón J. Sender-Joaquín Maurín (1952-1973).* Madrid: Ediciones de la Torre, 1995.

Chabrán, Rafael. "Spaniards." In *The Immigrant Labor Press in North America, 1840s–1970s: An Annotated Bibliography.* Vol. 3, *Migrants from Southern and Western Europe*, edited by Dirk Hoerder, 151–189. Westport, CT: Greenwood Press, 1987.

Chase, Allan. *Falange: The Axis Secret Army in the Americas.* New York: G. P. Putnam's Sons, 1943.

Cohn, Jesse. *Anarchism and the Crisis of Representation: Hermeneutics, Aesthetics, Politics.* Selinsgrove, PA: Susquehanna University Press, 2006.

———. *Underground Passages: Anarchist Resistance Culture, 1848–2011.* Oakland, CA: AK Press, 2015.

Colón, Joaquín. *Pioneros puertorriqueños en Nueva York, 1917–1947.* Houston: Arte Público Press, 2002.

Cornell, Andrew. "A New Anarchism Emerges, 1940–1954." *Journal for the Study of Radicalism* 5, no. 1 (2011): 105–132.

———. *Unruly Equality: U.S. Anarchism in the Twentieth Century.* Berkeley: University of California Press, 2016.

Costa Pinto, Antonio, and Aristotle Kallis. *Rethinking Fascism and Dictatorship in Europe.* New York: Palgrave Macmillan, 2014.

Davis, Peter, and Derek Lynch. *The Routledge Companion to Fascism and the Far Right.* London: Routledge, 2002.

De los Ríos, Fernando. "Nazi Infiltration in Ibero-America." *Social Research* 7, no. 1.4 (1940): 389–409.

———. *El sentido humanista del socialismo.* Edited by Elías Díaz. Madrid: Ediciones Castalia, 1976.

Dougherty, Dru. "The Commercial Stage, 1900–1936." In *The Cambridge History of Spanish Literature*, edited by David T. Gies, 579–594. Cambridge: Cambridge University Press, 2004.

Eley, Geoff. *Forging Democracy: The History of the Left in Europe, 1850–2000.* New York: Oxford University Press, 2002.

Espasa, Andreu. *Estados Unidos en la Guerra Civil Española.* Madrid: Catarata, 2017.

Faber, Sebastiaan, and Cristina Martínez Carazo, eds. *Contra el olvido: El exilio español en Estados Unidos.* Alcalá de Henares, Spain: Instituto Franklin de Estudio Norteamericanos, Universityof Alcalá, 2009.

Fernández, James D., and Luis Argeo. *Invisible Immigrants: Spaniards in the US (1868–1945).* Village Station, NY: White Stone Ridge, 2014.

Fernández Bieito, Alonso. "Migración y sindicalismo: Marineros y anarquistas españoles en Nueva York (1902–1930)." *Historia Social* 54 (2006): 113–135.

Ferrán, Ofelia and Lisa Hilbink, eds., *Legacies of violence in Contemporary Spain.* New York: Routledge, 2017.

Feu, Montse. "Aesthetically Resilient: Josep Bartolí Guiu's Political Cartoons in *España Libre* (1939–1977 NYC), a Spanish Civil War Exile Newspaper." In *The Body, Subject and Subjected: The Representation of the Body Itself, Illness, Injury, Treatment, and Death in Spain and Indigenous and Hispanic American Art and Literature*, edited by Debra D. Andrist, 73–90. Eastbourne, UK: Sussex Academic Press, 2016.

———. "Anarchist Aesthetics in Félix Martí Ibáñez's 'The Star Hunt.'" *Cuadernos de Aldeeu* 30 (Spring 2016): 35–48.

———. Antifascist Laughter in the Margins: Sergio Aragonés's *Mad Marginals*." *Cuadernos de Aldeeu* 31 (Spring 2017): 71–111.

———. "José Castilla Morales y España Libre (1939–1977): Sátira contra la dictadura de Francisco Franco desde Henry Street, Brooklyn." *Migraciones & Exilios, Cuadernos AEMIC* 14 (2014): 87–104.

———. "Sergio Aragonés Marginalizes Francoism in *España Libre* (NEW YORK)." *Camino Real*, Alcalá de Henares: Instituto Franklin–UAH 7, no. 10 (2015): 127–144, https://www.academia.edu/18779049/_Sergio_Aragonés_Marginalizes_Francoism_in_España_Libre_NYC_Camino_Real.Alcalá_de_Henares_Instituto_Franklin-_UAH_7_10_2015_127-144.

———. "'Transatlantic Trenches' in Spanish Civil War Journalism: Félix Martí Ibáñez and the Exile Newspaper *España Libre* (Free Spain, New York 1939–1977)." *Journal for the Study of Radicalism* 10, no. 2 (Fall 2016): 53–78.

———. "Transnational Working-Class Women's Activism in New York's Confederated Hispanic Societies (1939–1977)." In *Feminism and Migration: Cross-Cultural Engagements*, edited by Glenda Bonifacio, 187–208. New York: Springer, 2012.

———, ed. *Jesús González Malo: Correspondencia personal y política de un anarcosindicalista exiliado (1950–1965)*. Santander, Spain: University of Cantabria, 2016.

Freeman, Joshua B. *Working-Class New York*. New York: New Press, 2000.

Fuentes, Victor. *La marcha al pueblo de las letras españolas, 1917–1936*. Madrid: Ediciones de la Torre, 1980.

Gallego, Ferran. *El evangélio fascista: La formación de la cultural política del franquismo (1930–1950)*. Barcelona: Crítica, 2014.

———. "Fascistization and Fascism: Spanish Dynamics in a European Process." *International Journal of Iberian Studies* 25, no. 3 (2012): 159–181.

Gallego, Ferran, and Francisco Morente. *The Last Survivor: Cultural and Social Projects Underlying Spanish Fascism, 1931–1975*. Brighton, UK: Sussex Academic Press, 2017.

García-Guirao, Pedro. "Para matar a Franco (de risa): El periódico ácrata y los usos del humor gráfico." In *Exilio e identidad en el mundo hispánico: Reflexiones y representaciones*, edited by Beatriz Caballero Rodríguez, Laura Fernández López, and Tim Bowron, 274–313. Alicante, Spain: Biblioteca Virtual Miguel de Cervantes, 2012.

García Oliver, Juan. *El eco de los pasos*. Paris: Ruedo Ibérico, 1978.

García Santa Cecilia, Carlos, and Montse Feu. "José Nieto, último exiliado del franquismo, militante de la CNT, hizo de Nueva York su refugio." *Fronterad*, February 20–26, 2015. http://www.fronterad.com/?q=jose-nieto-ultimo-exiliado-franquismo-militante-cnt-hizo-nueva-york-su-refugio.

Giménez Igualada, Miguel. *Anarquismo*. Mexico City: B. Costa-Amic, 1968.

———. *Los caminos del hombre epistolario*. Mexico City: B. Costa-Amic, 1961.

———. *Los últimos románticos*. Mexico City: B. Costa-Amic, 1959.

Glondys, Olga. *La Guerra Fría cultural y el exilio republican español: Cuadernos del Congreso por la Libertad de la Cultura (1953–1965)*. Madrid: CSIC, 2012.

———. "The Idea of Europe, Transnational Networks, and Spanish Anti-Totalitarian Mobilisation (1939–1977)." In *The Last Survivor: Cultural and Social Projects Underlying Spanish Fascism, 1931–1975*, edited by Ferran Gallego and Francisco Morente, 203–220. Brighton, UK: Sussex Academic Press, 2017.

González Malo, Jesús. *La incorporación de las masas*. Buenos Aires: Editorial Americalee, 1952.

Goyens, Tom. *Beer and Revolution: The German Anarchist Movement in New York City, 1880–1914*. Urbana: University of Illinois Press, 2007, 2014.

Graham, Helen, ed. *Interrogating Francoism: History and Dictatorship in Twentieth-Century Spain*. London: Bloomsbury, 2016.

Greene, Julie. *The Canal Builders: Making America's Empire at the Panama Canal*. New York: Penguin Books, 2009.

Guglielmo, Jennifer. *Living the Revolution: Italian Women's Resistance and Radicalism in New York City, 1880–1945*. Chapel Hill: University of North Carolina Press, 2010.

Herrerín López, Ángel. *La CNT durante el franquismo: Clandestinidad y exilio (1939–1975)*. Madrid: Siglo XXI, 2004.

Hochschild, Adam. *Spain in Our Hearts: Americans in the Spanish Civil War, 1936–1939*. Boston: Houghton Mifflin Harcourt, 2016.

Hofmann, Bert. "Rudolf Rocker y el anarquismo hispano." In *El anarquismo español y sus tradiciones culturales*, edited by Bert Hormann, Pere Joan i Tous, and Manfred Tietz, 151–162. Madrid: Iberoamericana, 1995.

Hoyt, Andrew. "Methods for Tracing Radical Networks: Mapping the Print Culture and Propagandists of the Sovversivi." In *Without Borders or Limits: An Interdisciplinary Approach to Anarchist Studies*, edited by Jorell A. Meléndez Badillo and Nathan Jun, 75–106. Newcastle upon Tyne, UK: Cambridge Scholars Publishing, 2013.

Íñiguez, Miguel. *Esbozo de una enciclopedia histórica del anarquismo español*. Madrid: Fundación de Estudios Libertarios Anselmo Lorenzo, 2001.

Jeppersen, Sandra. "Becoming Anarchist: The Function of Anarchist Literature." *Anarchist Developments in Cultural Studies* 2: *Art and Anarchy* (2011): 189–213.

Jerez-Farran, Carlos, and Samuel Amago, eds. *Unearthing Franco's Legacy: Mass Graves and the Recovery of Historical Memory in Spain*. Notre Dame IN: Notre Dame University Press, 2010.

Kanellos, Nicolás. "Marita Reid." In *Latinas in the United States: A Historical Encyclopedia*, edited by Vicki Ruíz and Virginia Sánchez Korrol, 613–614. Bloomington: Indiana University Press, 2006.

———. "Spanish-Language Anarchist Periodicals in Early Twentieth-Century United States." In *Protest on the Page: Essays on Print and the Culture of Dissidence since 1865*, edited by James L. Baughman, Jennifer Ratner-Rosenhagen, and James P. Danky, 59–84. Madison: University of Wisconsin Press, 2014.

Kanellos, Nicolás, and Helvetia Martell. *Hispanic Periodicals in the United States: Origins to 1960: A Brief History and Comprehensive Bibliography*. Houston: Arte Público Press, 2000.

Kinna, Ruth. *Anarchism: A Beginner's Guide*. Oxford: Oneworld Publications, 2005.

Krohn, Claus-Dieter. *Intellectuals in Exile: Refugee Scholars and the New School for Social Research*. Translated by Rita and Robert Kimber. Amherst: University of Massachusetts Press, 1993.

Laforcade, Geoffroy de, and Kirwin Shaffer, eds. *In Defiance of Boundaries: Anarchism in Latin American History*. Gainesville: University Press of Florida, 2015.

Linz, Juan J. "Una respuesta de intelectuales norteamericanos al exilio español." In *La oposición al régimen de Franco*, edited by Javier Tusell Gómez, Alicia Alted Vigil, and Abdón Mateos López, 43–55. Madrid: UNED, 1990.

Litvak, Lily. *Musa Libertaria*. Barcelona: Antoni Bosh, 1981.

Lomnitz, Claudio. *The Return of Comrade Ricardo Flores Magnón*. Zone Books. Cambridge, MA: MIT Press, 2014.

Lonsdale, Laura. "Don Juan in Exile." In *Stages of Exile: Spanish Republican Exile Theatre and Performance*, edited by Helena Buffery, 95–106. Oxford: Peter Lang, 2011.

López Campillo, Evelyne. "Vanguardia burguesa y cultura anarquista en la *Revista Blanca* (1923–1936)." In *El anarquismo español y sus tradiciones culturales*, edited by Bert Hofmann, Pere Joan i Tous, and Manfred Tietz, 237–242. Madrid: Iberoamericana, 1995.

Lorde, Audre. *A Burst of Light*. Ann Arbor, MI: Firebrand Books, 1988.

Loren, Mar. *Texturas y pliegues de una nación: New York City: Guastavino Co. y la reinvención del espacio público de la metrópolis estadounidense*. Valencia: T. C. Cuadernos, 2009.

Lunar, Felix. *A cielo abierto: De Riotinto a Norteamerica*. Mexico: León Sanchez, 1956.

Macdonald, Nancy. *Homage to the Spanish Exiles: Voices from the Spanish Civil War*. New York: Human Sciences Press, 1987.

Marin, Dolors. *Anarquistas: Un siglo de movimiento libertario en España*. Barcelona: Ariel, 2010.

Martin, Rod A. *The Psychology of Humor: An Integrative Approach*. Burlington, MA: Elsevier Academic Press, 2007.

McClennen, Sophia A. *The Dialectics of Exile: Nation, Time, Language, and Space in Hispanic Literatures*. West Lafayette, IN: Purdue University Press, 2004.

Meléndez Badillo, Jorell A. *Voces libertarias: Los orígenes del anarquismo en Puerto Rico*. [Bloomington, IN]: Secret Sailor Books, 2013.

Mendez Montesinos, Delia Leticia. *The Ingenious Simpleton: Upending Imposed Ideologies through Brief Comic Theater*. Lanham, MD: University Press of America, 2014.

Molina, Juan Manuel. *El movimiento clandestino en España, 1939–1949*. Mexico City: Ediciones Mexicanos Unidos, 1976.

Mormino, Gary R., and George E. Pozzetta. *The Immigrant World of Ybor City: Italians and Their Latin Neighbors in Tampa, 1885–1985*. Urbana: University of Illinois Press, 1987.

Muñoz-Rojas, Ritama. *Poco a poco os hablaré de todo: Historia del exilio en Nueva York de la familia de los Ríos, Giner, Urruti: Cartas, 1936–1953*. Madrid: Publicaciones de la residencia de estudiantes, 2009.

Navarro Navarro, Javier. *A la revolución por la cultura: Prácticas culturales y sociabilidad libertarias en el País Valenciano, 1931–1939*. Valencia: University of Valência, 2004.

———. *Ateneos y grupos ácratas: Vida y actividad cultural de las asociaciones anarquistas valencianas durante la Segunda República y la Guerra Civil.* Valencia: Biblioteca Valenciana, 2002.

Neira Vilas, Xosé, and Xesús Alonso Montero. "A cultura galega en Buenos Aires: 1950–1960." Paper presented at the Salón de Actos da Real Academia Galega, November 17, 2001. Tabernas: Real Academia Gallega, 2001, 9–52.

Orleck, Annelise. *Common Sense and a Little Fire: Women and Working-Class Politics in the United States, 1900–1965.* Chapel Hill: University of North Carolina Press, 1995.

Parcerises, Pilar, ed. *Josep Bartolí: Un creador a l'exili: Dibuixant, pintor, escriptor.* Barcelona: Diputació de Barcelona, 2002.

Pauli, Benjamin J. "The New Anarchism in Britain and the US: Towards a Richer Understanding of Post-War Anarchist Thought." *Journal of Political Ideologies* 20, no. 2 (May 2015): 134–155.

Payne, Stanley G. *Fascism in Spain, 1923–1977.* Madison: University of Wisconsin Press, 1999.

Pereda, Prudencio de. *Windmills in Brooklyn.* New York: Atheneum, 1960.

Pérez, Janet. "Fascist Models and Literary Subversion: Two Fictional Modes in Postwar Spain." *South Central Review* 6, no. 2, *Fascist Aesthetics* (Summer 1989): 73–87.

Piqueras, José A., and Rozalén V. Sanz, eds. *A Social History of Spanish Labour: New Perspectives on Class, Politics, and Gender.* New York: Berghahn Books, 2007.

Preston, Paul. *El gran manipulador: La mentira cotidiana de Franco.* Barcelona: Ediciones B, 2008.

———. *The Politics of Revenge: Fascism and the Military in Twentieth-Century Spain.* New York: Routledge, 1995.

———. *Salvador de Madariaga and the Quest for Liberty in Spain.* Oxford: Clarendon Press, 1987.

———. *The Spanish Holocaust: Inquisition and Extermination in Twentieth-Century Spain.* New York: W. W. Norton, 2012.

Requena, Manuel, and Rosa Maria Sepúlveda Losa. *Las Brigadas Internacionales: El contexto internacional, los medios de propaganda, literatura y memorias.* Cuenca, Spain: Ediciones de la Universidad de Castilla–La Mancha, 2003.

Rey García, Marta. *Stars for Spain: La guerra civil española en los Estados Unidos.* Sada, A Coruña, Spain: Ediciós do Castro, 1997.

Rodrigo, Javier. Cautivos. *Campos de concentración en la España franquista, 1936–1947.* Barcelona: Crítica, 2005.

———. "Fascism and Violence in Spain: A Comparative Update." *International Journal of Iberian Studies* 25, no. 3 (2012): 183–199.

———. *La guerra fascista: Italia en la Guerra Civil Española, 1936–1937* (Madrid: Alianza Editorial, 2016.

———. *Hasta la raíz: violencia durante la Guerra Civil y la dictadura franquista.* Madrid: Alianza, 2008.

Rodríguez Barreira, Óscar. "The Many Heads of the Hydra: Local Parafascism in Spain and Europe, 1936–50." *Journal of Contemporary History* 49, no. 4 (2014): 702–726.

Rodríguez Jiménez, Francisco Javier. "La AFL-CIO y el sindicalismo español, 1953–1971." *Hispania* 75, no. 251 (Sept.–Dec. 2015): 863–892.

———. "Trade Unionism and Spain–US Political Relations, 1945–1953." *Ventunesimo Secolo* 12, no. 37 (2016): 96–124.

Rodríguez Jiménez, Francisco Javier, and Haruko Hosoda. "Convidados de piedra o promotores del cambio? Actividades del sindicalismo Anglo-Estadounidense en España, 1971–1977." *Alcores* 16 (2013): 37–60.

Rueda Hernanz, Germán. "El asociacionismo de los españoles en los EE.UU. en los siglos XIX y XX, 57–93." In *El asociacionismo de la emigración Española en el exterior: Significación y vinculaciones*, edited by Juan Andrés Blanco Rodríguez and Arsenio Dacosta. Madrid: Sílex Ediciones, 2014.

———. *La emigración contemporánea de españoles a Estados Unidos, 1820–1950: De "Dons" a "Místers."* Madrid: Editorial Mapfre, 1993.

Said, Edward W. *Reflections on Exile and Other Essays*. Cambridge, MA: Harvard University Press, 2000.

Sánchez-Albornoz, Nicolás, ed. *Españoles hacia América: La emigración en masa, 1880–1930*. Madrid: Alianza Editorial, 1988.

Santiáñez, Nil. *Topographies of Fascism: Habitus, Space, and Writing in Twentieth-Century Spain*. Toronto: University of Toronto Press, 2013.

Sarría Buil, Aránzazu. "Sátira y caricatura desde el exilio: En torno a la figura del general Franco." In *Humor y política en el mundo hispánico contemporáneo*, Marie-Claude Chaput and Manuelle Peloille, coordinators, 77–97. Nanterre, France: Université Paris X–Nanterre, 2006.

Shaffer, Kirwin. *Black Flag Boricuas: Anarchism, Antiauthoritarianism, and the Left in Puerto Rico, 1897–1921*. Urbana: University of Illinois Press, 2013.

Shatz, Marshall S., ed. *The Essential Works of Anarchism*. New York: Bantam Books, 1971.

Smith, Eric R. *American Relief Aid and the Spanish Civil War*. Columbia: University of Missouri Press, 2013.

Solla Gutiérrez, Miguel Ángel. *Una efímera autonomía: El consejo interprovincial de Santander, Palencia y Burgos*. Santander, Spain: Centro de Estudios Montañeses, 2011.

Soriano, Ignacio C., and Francisco Madrid. *Bibliografía del anarquismo en España, 1868–1939*. http://www.cedall.org/Documentacio/IHL/Antologia%20Documental%20del%20Anarquismo%20espanol_Bibliografia.pdf.

Southard, Donna. "Francisco Rivero Gil: Caricaturist, Soldier, and War Correspondent and the Álbum-Recuerdo del Batallón de Valencia en Marruecos Campaña (1921–1922)." In *Ideology, Politics, and Demands in Spanish Language, Literature, and Film*, edited by Teresa Fernandez Ulloa, 380–405. Newcastle upon Tyne, UK: Cambridge Scholars Publishing, 2012.

———. "Rivero Gil's 'Aleluyas de la defense de Euzkadi': Comic Strip Images of Spain's Civil War and the Education of a New Citizenry." *International Journal of the Image* 2, no. 4 (2012): 1–19.

Streeby, Shelley. *Radical Sensations: World Movements, Violence, and Visual Culture*. Durham, NC: Duke University Press, 2013.

Sturman, Janet L. *Zarzuela: Spanish Operetta, American Stage*. Urbana: University of Illinois Press, 2000.

Sueiro Seoane, Susana. "Inmigrantes y anarquistas españoles en EEUU (1890–1920)." In *Conflictos y cicatrices: Fronteras y migraciones en el mundo hispánico*, Almudena Delgado, coordinator, 273–284. Madrid: Dykinson, 2014.

Sumner, Gregory D. *Dwight Macdonald and the Politics Circle: The Challenge of Cosmopolitan Democracy*. Ithaca, NY: Cornell University Press, 1996.

Tavera, Susanna. *Solidaridad Obrera: El fer-se i desfer-se d'un diari anarco-sindicalista (1915–1939)*. Barcelona: Diputació de Barcelona, 1992.

Tomchuk, Travis. *Transnational Radicals: Italian Anarchists in Canada and the U.S., 1915–1940*. Winnipeg: University of Manitoba Press, 2015.

Turcato, Davide. *Making Sense of Anarchism: Errico Malatesta's Experiments with Revolution, 1889–1900*. Oakland, CA: AK Press, 2015.

Turda, Marius, and Aaron Gillette. *Latin Eugenics in Comparative Perspective*. London: Bloomsbury, 2014.

Tusell Gómez, Javier, Alicia Alted Vigil, and Abdón Mateos López, eds. *La oposición al régimen de Franco*. Madrid: UNED, 1990.

Varela-Lago, Ana Maria. "'No Pasarán': The Spanish Civil War's Impact on Tampa's Latin Community." *Tampa Bay History* 19, no. 2 (1997): 5–35.

———. "'We Had to Help': Remembering Tampa's Response to the Spanish Civil War." *Tampa Bay History* 19, no. 2 (1997): 36–56.

Vega, Bernardo, and César Andreu Iglesias. *Memoirs of Bernardo Vega: A Contribution to the History of the Puerto Rican Community in New York*. Translated by Juan Flores. New York: Monthly Review Press, 1984.

Vials, Christopher. "Fight against War and Fascism and the Origins of Antifascism in US Culture." *Cultural Logic*. Special Issue: *Culture and the Crisis* (2010): 309–321.

———. *Haunted by Hitler: Liberals, the Left, and the Fight against Fascism in the United States*. Amherst: University of Massachusetts Press, 2014.

Viñas, Angel. "Natural Alliances: The Impact of Nazism and Fascism on Franco's Domestic Policies." In *Interrogating Francoism: History and Dictatorship in Twentieth-Century Spain*, edited by Helen Graham, 139–178. London: Bloomsbury, 2016.

Ward, Alan W. *Trinity of Passion*. Chapel Hill: University of North Carolina Press, 2007.

White, Matthew C. "'The Cause of the Workers Who Are Fighting in Spain Is Yours': The Marine Transport Workers and the Spanish Civil War." In *Wobblies of the World: A Global History of the IWW*, edited by Peter Cole, David Struthers, and Kenyon Zimmer, 212–227. London: Pluto Press, 2017.

Yaross Lee, Judith. *Twain's Brand: Humor in Contemporary American Culture*. Jackson: University of Mississippi Press, 2012.

Yusta Rodrigo, Mercedes. "Género y antifascismo en España, de la II República a la Guerra Fría (1931–1950)." *Anuario IEHS* 28 (2013): 227–247.

Zimmer, Kenyon. *Immigrants against the State: Yiddish and Italian Anarchism in America*. Urbana: University of Illinois Press, 2015.

———. "The Other Volunteers." *Journal for the Study of Radicalism* 10, no. 2 (Fall 2016): 19–52.

———. "The Voyage of the *Buford*: Political Deportations and the Making and Unmaking of America's First Red Scare." In *Deportation in the Americas: Histories of Exclusion and Resistance*, edited by Kenyon Zimmer and Cristina Salinas, 132–163. College Station: Texas A&M University Press, 2018.

Unpublished Sources

Caminals, Roser. "Salvador de Madariaga and National Character." PhD diss., University of Barcelona, 1988.

Clavijo Ledesma, Julio. "La política sobre la población refugiada durant la guerra civil 1936–1939." PhD diss., University of Girona, 2004.

Feu, Montse. "*España Libre* (1939–1977) and the Spanish Exile Community in New York." PhD diss., University of Houston, 2011.

Kaiser, Wilson. "Partial Affinities: Fascism and the Politics of Representation in Interwar America." PhD diss., University of North Carolina at Chapel Hill, 2011.

Ordaz Romay, M. Ángeles. "Características del exilio español en Estados Unidos (1936–1975) y Eugenio Fernández Granell como experiencia significativa." PhD diss., University of Alcalá, 1999.

Valera-Lago, Ana Maria. "Conquerors, Immigrants, Exiles: The Spanish Diaspora in the United States (1848–1949)." PhD diss., University of California, San Diego, 2008.

Villamil-Acera, Rakhel. "La construcción del diálogo teatral en el teatro cómico español (1898–1936): El discurso humorístico en el contexto social." PhD diss., University of California–Berkeley, 2008.

Winrow Hart, Marion. "La Nación Flamenca: The Influence of Flamenco on Spanish Nationalism." PhD diss., University of California–Irvine, 2013.

Index

Abad de Santillán, Diego, 63, 71, 84
A cielo abierto (Lunar), 42
Adelante, 74
Adriensens, Juan, 56
Aesthetics of Antifascist Film, The (Barker), 113–114
AFL-CIO Free Trade Union News, 43
AFL Journeymen Cigar Makers International Union, 7
Aguirre, Valentín, 104
Alba, Víctor, 48–49
Albanese, Matteo, 5
Albornoz, Sánchez, 59
Albornoz Limiana, Álvaro de, 46, 48, 50; call for transnational coalitions of antifascist exiles, 57
Aldecoa, María Isabel, 85–86
Aldecoa González, Carmen, 14, 26, 65, 177, 178; as female leader, 118, 132; as managing editor of *España Libre*, 72–75, 78; Nancy Macdonald and, 86; refugees and, 93, 95
Aldecoa González, Francisco, 85–86
Aldouby, Zwy Herbert, 30, 44–45, 75

Alexander, Robert, 107–108
Alfarache, Progreso, 34
Alianza Sindical Obrera (ASO), 45, 107–109
Al Margen, 117
Alonso, Daniel, 3, 30, 63; expulsion from the Spanish Communist Party, 54
Alonso, Manolo, 62, 63
Alonso Falero, Antonio, 93
Álvarez Quintero, Joaquín, 135
Álvarez Quintero, Serafín, 135
Amat, Francisco de, 56
American Civil Liberties Union, 43, 88, 94
American Federation of Labor and Congress of Industrial Organizations (AFL-CIO), 32, 34, 43
American Socialist Party, 94, 97
Amo, Julián, 21
anarchism, 15–16, 177–181; in Cuba, 61; *España Libre* bookstore services on, 41–43; heroes of, 114–116; Modern School Network and, 33–35; press and publishing networks in, 29–31
anarcho-syndicalism, 69–71, 78, 109–110
Anderson, Benedict, 42

anticommunism, 153
antifascism: border crossings and, 124–125; cartoons of (*see* cartoons in *España Libre*); Don Quixote as symbol of, 19, 119–122; of *España Libre*, 13, 36–37, 60, 75, 176; evolving exilic representations and, 122–125; evolving migrant representations and, 125–132; gender and, 116–119, 174–175; Hispanic newspapers in the U.S. and, 28–29; interlocked nature of activism and culture in, 16–17; literary representations of, 113–114; plays about, 137–144; voices of, 17–22
Antifascista, El, 46
Apolo, 119
Appeasement's Child (Hamilton), 57
apropósito, 138
Aragonés, Sergio, 14, 15–16, 29, 160, 166–167, 179
Araquistáin Quevedo, Luis, 48, 49
Arenas Ruiz, Jesús, 3 30, 63; Spanish Communist Party and, 54
Argibay, José, 104
Arniches, Carlos, 135
Artajo, Martín, 151
Ascaso, Francisco, 114
Asensio Torrado, José, 63, 64, 80
Asensi Selles, José, 87, 114
astracán, 135–136
Astray, Millán, 159
Ateneo, El, 104
Ateneo Hispano, 3–5
Aurora, 6
Aventura (Martí Ibáñez), 122
Ayala, Francisco, 28, 48, 50
Ayensa y Sánchez de León, Alonso, 28, 48, 50

Bacofra, Juan, 32
Bakunin, Mikhail, 46, 71
Baldwin, Roger Nash, 15, 33–34, 43, 107–108
Barciela, Manuel, 116
Barker, Jennifer L., 113, 124
Baroja, Pío, 74
Barrios, Alberto Lozano, 75
Bartolí Guiu, Josep, 15, 91, 160, 165–166, 168–169, 176
Bartolomé Álamo, Jesús, 92

Batalla, La, 48–49, 74
Beffel, John Nicholas, 43–44
Behrendt, Fritz, 161
Benaño, Onobre, 83
Bencivenni, Marcella, 13
Benedet, Julian, 62
Betanzos Palacios, Odón, 116
Blasco Ibáñez, Vicente, 74
Bombas de mano (Jiménez Colón), 46
bookstore services, *España Libre*, 41–43
Borines, Aldea, 8

Cabet, Étienne, 73
Calle Mancilla, Francisco, 109
Calvo, Antonio, 44
Calza, F., 7–8
Camín Meana, Alfonso, 14, 30–31, 41–42, 119–121
Canada, labor unions in, 31–33
Capetillo, Luisa, 8, 15
Carcagente, Agustín, 65
Cárdenas, Lázaro, 39
Carnero, John, 62, 94
cartoons in *España Libre*, 20, 29, 176–177; misogynistic, 162–163; in response to Imperial Spain and Catholic Nationalism, 163–164; in response to political persecutions, 165–166; transnational, 161–162; about worker's resistance, 166–169
Casals, Pablo, 59
Castilla Morales, José, 14, 15, 31, 75, 126, 132, 135, 175–176, 180; on Antonio Martínez, 60; artistic works and, 20; Aurelio Pego and, 64; as editor, playwright, and satirical chronicler, 60–63; evolving migrant representations by, 126–128; influence of, 53; IWW and, 31; plays written by, 137–140, 143; on preserving the story of the SHC, 21–22; *zarzuelas* written by, 135
Castro, Américo, 26, 48, 59
Castro, Manuel, 41
Castro Barral, José, 62, 64, 84
Castroviejo, Ramón, 56
Catholic Worker, 106
Cazorla Sánchez, Antonio, 150
Cenit, 74
Cervantes, Miguel de, 75, 145
Cesar (cartoonist), 161

270

Chase, Allan, 56–57
Chúmez, Chumy, 161
Cianfarra, Camille M., 108
Civera, Marin, 71, 74
Clariana, Bernando, 28
Clarín, 74
CNT (Mexico), 72, 74
CNT (Toulouse), 67
Cohn, Jesse, 13
Cold War era, 17, 58
Colina, Jerano, 161
Colón, Joaquín, 8
Comité Antifascista Español (CAE), 3, 30
Comunidad Ibérica, 67
Conchado, Carmen, 65
Concheiro, Yuyita, 100–101
Conde, Arturo, 65
Confederación Nacional del Trabajo (CNT), 2, 58, 66–67, 69, 105–106, 114
Copado, Antonio García, 176
Cordellat, Maria, 83, 91–94, 95, 100, 118, 174
Cordellat, Vicente, 91
Costa, Joaquín, 71
Costa Amic, Bartomeu, 73
Crane, Louise, 43
Cristóbal, Hipólito, 62
crónica, 145–146, 149
Crowded Paradise (film), 141
Cuadernos de Cultura, 74
Cuadernos del Congreso de la Libertad de la Cultura, 32, 49
Cultura Obrera, 6, 31, 138
Cultura Proletaria, 6, 46, 119, 138

Darwin, Charles, 75
de Kooning, Willem, 165
Delaney, George, 34
de la Rosa, Matías, 7
Delegación del Gobierno de Euzkadi, 107
del Hierro, Pablo, 5
del Moral, Armando, 28
de los Ríos, Fernando, 56, 68–69
del Río, Ángel, 4, 26
Del sentir y pensar (Aldecoa), 73–74, 178
del Valle, Adrián, 30
de Pereda, Prudencio, 1, 8
Devesa, Jaime, 39
Diario de la Marina, 119

Diario Montañés, El, 73
Díaz, Manuel, 55–56
Díaz Pestaña, Ramón, 87
Dicenta, Joaquín, 135
Díez, Paulino, 61
Díez, Pedro, 60, 61
Don Quixote, 19, 119–122, 132
Dorado, Manuel, 32, 40, 90–91, 146
drama de Calderón, Un (Muñoz Seca), 135–136, 143
Dubinsky, David, 48
Duffy, Edmond, 161
Dumenio, Baldomero, 61
Durruti, Buenaventura, 114

Echegaray, Miguel, 56
Eco de la Clase Obrera, El, 74
editors of *España Libre*, 53–54; Aurelio Pego as, 63–64; Carmen Aldecoa González as, 72–75, 78; editorial evolution and, 54–60; Jesús González Malo as, 14, 15, 32, 42, 59, 65–72, 77–78; José Asensio Torrado as, 64; José Castilla Morales as, 60–63; during the last years, 75–77
Einstein, Albert, 40, 88
Eisenhower, Dwight, 155, 163, 164
el Arrecio, Francisco, 116
El Cid, 133
el de la Boeguilla, Juan, 116
el Erizo, José Antonio, 116
Encarnación, Virgilio de, 116
España Libre, 2–3, 6; advocacy for refugees by, 82–83; anarchism and, 15–16, 177–181; anarchist heroism depicted in, 114–116; antifascism of, 13, 36–37, 60, 75, 176; articles on Franco in, 41; artistic works reviewed by, 19–20; bookstore service of, 41–43; on Cándido Villa, 6–7; cartoons of (*see* cartoons in *España Libre*); commemoration of important events by, 115; editors and editorial process of (*see* editors of *España Libre*); English pages, 43–45; evolving exilic representations in, 122–125; evolving migrant representations in, 125–132; fiction in, 15, 176–177; fundraising and advertising in, 7–8; gender and racial hierarchies in, 116–119, 174–175; humor in, 20; labor unions and, 31–33;

España Libre (continued): legacy of SHC and, 171–181; main characteristics of, 37–40; makeup of, 40–41; Modern School Network and, 14–15, 33–35; political prisoners and (*see* political prisoners); refugees and (*see* refugees); regular contributors to, 45–52; satire and commentary in (*see* Pego, Aurelio); solidarity and protest against Spanish fascism in, 10–16, 105–110; tools used to challenge fascism by, 175–176; as voice of antifascist workers, 17–22. See also *Frente Popular*; Sociedades Hispanas Confederadas (SHC)
Espí, Salvador, 31
Espoir, 47
Esteve, Pedro, 15, 30, 31
Estudios, 74, 104
Etcheverria, Salvador, 90

Fabas García, Federico, 87
Falange: The Axis Secret Army in the Americas (Chase), 56, 57
Falange Española, 5, 55–57, 148, 152; and JONS, 5
Falange, 56
Faldella, Emilio, 9
Fascist Italy, 5, 10, 46, 58
Fascist Spain. *See* Franco, Francisco; Spanish Civil War
Federación, La, 74
Federal Bureau of Investigations (FBI), 13, 66–67, 146
Feduchy, Martínez, 94
Feinsohn, Jacques Simon, 44
FE-JONS, 5
Fernández, Jiménez, 59
Fernández Escobés, Antonio, 79
Fernsworth, Lawrence, 44
Ferrer i Guàrdia, Francesc, 14–15, 33, 35
Ferrer Sanmartí, Sol, 35
Fleischman, Ernest, 44, 89–90, 95, 174
Fleischman, Josephine Teresa Bridge Cowan, 90
Floreal, 47
Flores Magón brothers, 15
Forges (cartoonist), 161
Fourier, Charles, 73
Franco, Francisco, 1, 2, 9; ascension to power of, 5, 18; cartoons of, 159, 162–163; diplomatic relations with the United States, 57, 58; economy under, 150–151; *España Libre* editorials on, 59; executions of dissidents by, 34, 110, 113, 116; Falange and, 56; fascistization under, 12, 146–148; mocked by Aurelio Pego, 148–150; National Catholicism under, 12, 41, 45, 145, 151–152, 163–164; satirical sketches of, 133; worker union suppression by, 36. See also Spanish Civil War
Fraternidad, La, 74
Freedom, 43
Freedom House, 107
Freedom Ride (Peck), 43
Free Labor World, 43
Frente Popular, 3, 6, 30, 46, 54, 55–56; political prisoners and, 104; public protests and, 97, 99; refugees and, 83, 84. See also *España Libre*
Frontera, La, 43
fundraising and advertising in *España Libre*, 7–8

Gaceta Hispana, 104
Galíndez, Jesús de, 34, 81
Gallego, Ferran, 5, 149
Gallego, Juan, 56
Galván, Tierno, 59
Gandhi, Mahatma, 75
Garagarza, Luis, 140
Garay, Gregorio, 61–62
García Copado, Antonio, 126, 128–129, 132
García Duran, Juan, 59
García Fernández, Adolfo, 40
García Gómez, Julián, 49–50
García Lorca, Federico, 139
García Olay, Pelayo, 107
García Oliver, Juan, 84
García Polanco, Bernabé, 95
García Pradas, José, 71, 74
García Rubiera, Marcelino, 55–56
García Vallín, Antonio, 63
Gaston Leval, A., 71–72
Gavinet, Ángel, 74
gender and the antifascist movement, 116–119, 174–175; misogynistic drawings and, 162–163
George, Henry, 71
George School, 71–72

Gilman, Charlotte Perkins, 33
Giménez Igualada, Miguel, 15, 75, 113, 132, 178–179; on antifascist women, 19, 117–118; on disparagement of anarchism, 119
Giráldez, Manuel, 91
Glondys, Olga, 48
Goldman, Emma, 33
Gómez, Antonio María, 116
Gómez, Josefina, 65
Gómez, Laureano, 133
González, Domingo, 7
Gonzalez, Joaquin, 83
González Cárdenas, Antonio, 90
González Malo, Jesús, 11, 44, 50, 132, 165, 166, 174, 177, 178–179; advocacy for political alliances, 109; AFL-CIO and, 32, 34; anarchist community and, 30; anarcho-syndicalism and, 69–71, 109–110; on anticommunist hysteria, 39; books and pamphlets written by, 67–68; communication mechanisms with sailors and, 13; in Cuba, 27; death of, 60, 65, 70, 110; at demonstrations in front of Spanish Consulate, 43; as editor of *España Libre*, 14, 15, 32, 42, 59, 65–72, 77–78; FBI interviews of, 66–67; influence of, 53; Juan Reyes Ramos and, 87; labor unions and, 32; Maria Cordellat and, 93–94; Miguel R. Ortiz and legacy of, 75; monitored by the FBI, 13; refugees and, 87, 93–95; on solidarity, 107; work with professors, politicians, and professionals in exile, 28
González Moscoso, John, 89, 95
González Prada, M., 71
Gorkin, Julián, 32, 48, 59
Government of the Second Spanish Republic, 25, 26, 30, 36–37, 45, 54; featured in *España Libre*, 40
Granell, Eugenio F., 48, 54, 75–76, 78
gran manipulador, El (Preston), 10
Grant, Francis, 95, 107
Gritos de carne (Prado Rodríguez), 47
Grupo Antifascista del Bronx, 79
Guarner, Vicente, 114
Guerra Cuoto, Rafael, 88
Guyau, Jean-Marie, 75

HaBoker, 44
Haekel, Ernst, 75

Hamilton, Thomas J., 57
Haya, Ignacio, 8–9
Hayworth, Rita, 39
Heraldo, El, 49
Herald Tribune, 43
Hércules, 7
Hispanic press in the United States, 28–29
Hitler, Adolf, 10, 116–117, 122–123; cartoons of, 161–163
Holiday, 165
Homage to the Spanish Exiles (Macdonald), 86
Hoover, J. Edgar, 13
humor in *España Libre*, 20, 176–177

Ibérica, 43
Ibérica Publishing Co., 41
Iglesias, Avelino, 61, 63
Iglesias, Pablo, 74
Immigrant World of Ybor City, The (Mormino and Pozzetta), 14
Imperial Spain, cartoons of, 163–164
incorporación de las masas, La (González Malo), 67–68, 70, 71, 78
Industrial Workers of the World (IWW), 6, 31, 32, 61–62
internacional, El, 7
International Association for Democracy and Freedom, 107
International Ladies' Garment Workers Union (ILGWU), 32
International League for Human Rights, 43, 95
International League for the Rights of Man, 107
International Rescue and Relief Committee (IRC), 87–88

Javits, Jacob K., 106
Jiménez Colón, Adolfo, 14–15, 45–46, 50, 100
Johnson, Lyndon, 95
Juntas de Ofensiva Nacional-Sindicalista, Councils of the National-Syndicalist Offensive (JONS), 5

Kahlo, Frida, 165
Kanellos, Nicolás, 29
Kennedy, John F., 106
Kent, Victoria, 41, 43

Keynes, John Maynard, 71
Kinna, Ruth, 178
Kline, Franz, 165
Krause, Karl, 68
Krishnamurti, Jiddu, 75
Kropotkin, Peter, 71, 75
Kropotkin's Revolutionary Pamphlets, 43
Kuppinger, Eldred D., 83

labor unions, 31–33, 108; cartoons of worker's resistance and, 166–169; in Cuba, 61–62; Santander Dock Workers, 65, 67
Lanza, Peter G., 63
Larcegui, Francisco, 56
Largo Caballero, Francisco, 80–81
Larra, José Mariano de, 145–146
League for Industrial Democracy, 107
League for Mutual Aid, 34, 43
Ledesma Ramos, Ramiro, 133
Leónidas Trujillo, Rafael, 81
Leval, Gaston, 71
Liberación, 28
Libertarian League, 106
Lirón. *See* Jiménez Colón, Adolfo
Llorden, Demetrio, 83
London, Jack, 33
London Times, 44
López, Alfredo, 61
López, Carmen, 143
López Becerra, Anastasio, 91
López Gallarta, Eusebio, 81
López Moyano, Juan, 92
Lorde, Audre, 16
Lorenzo, Anselmo, 69, 71, 74
Lovestone, Jay, 32, 34, 48
Lunar, Félix, 7, 42–43

Macdonald, Dwight, 43, 68–69, 108
Macdonald, Nancy, 15, 44, 85–86, 95, 118
Machado, Gerardo, 61
Machete, El, 6
MacVeagh, Lincoln, 36
Madariaga, Salvador de, 48, 59
Mad magazine, 16, 166, 179
madre española, La (Castilla Morales), 139
Malatesta, Errico, 71
Mari, Marcos C., 53–54, 75, 78, 84
Marshall Plan, 58

Martí Ibáñez, Félix, 15, 65, 71, 113, 134, 172, 177, 179–180; Don Quixote and, 121; exilic representations in writing of, 122–124; on hearing Benito Mussolini speak, 55; pro-Republic tour by, 33
Martín, José, 56
Martínez, Antonio, 60
Martínez, José María, 66, 134
Martínez, Manuel P., 63
Martínez Augusto, Emilio, 87
Martínez Barrio, Diego, 86
Martínez Gil, José, 7
Martínez Novella, José María, 104–105
Martínez Ybor, Vicente, 8–9
Más allá del dolor (Giménez Igualada), 75
Mauldin, Bill, 161
Maurín Julià, Joaquim, 54, 65, 75–76, 78
McCarran, Patrick Anthony, 153
McCarthyism, 17, 178
McClennen, Sophia A., 11–12
McCook, Philip, 99
MD, 15, 180
Mella, Ricardo, 69, 70, 71
Memoirs of Bernardo Vega (Vega), 8
Miaja Menant, José, 114
Midstream, 43
migrants and exiles, Spanish: community networks of, 8, 30–31; companies established by, 8–9; evolving representations of, 125–132; Government of the Second Spanish Republic in exile and, 25, 26, 30, 36–37, 54; Hispanic press in the United States and, 28–29; labor unions and, 31–33; as members of SHC, 5–9, 79; mocked by Aurelio Pego, 154–156; professors as, 27–28, 47–48, 50–51, 56; as refugees of World War II, 57–58; as regular contributors to *España Libre*, 45–52; voices of, 17–22. *See also* Spanish diaspora
military power, cult of, 12
Mill, John Stuart, 71
Mingorance, Juan Eugenio Domingo, 4, 47, 100
Mingot, Miguel, 139
Mingote Barrachina, Ángel Antonio, 161
Miqueli González, Violeta, 98
Modern School Network, 14–15, 33–35, 69
Molina, Miguel de, 163

Index

Molina Mateo, Juan Manuel, 44
Monrós, Alfredo, 161
Montero López, Manuel, 7
Montes, Eugenio, 55
Montés, Luís, 46, 50
Montseny, Federica, 40, 63
Moreno, Consuelo, 142–143
Moreno Barranco, Manuel, 106
Morente, Francisco, 5
Mormino, Gary R., 14
Morning World, 43
Morodo, Raúl, 59
Movimiento Nacional, 147
Múgica Arbelca, Juan, 91
Muñoz Seca, Pedro, 135–136, 143
Mussolini, Benito, 5, 10, 55, 140, 162

Nacional, La (mutual aid society), 39, 44, 62
Nation, The, 43, 44, 106
National Catholicism, 12, 41, 45, 145; cartoons of, 163–164; mocked by Aurelio Pego, 151–152
Nationalism and Culture (Rocker), 78
NATO, 155
Nazi Germany, 10, 33, 46, 56, 57, 58, 147, 148
New Masses, 6
New York Daily Call, 43
New York Post, 34
New York Times, 44, 91, 108
New York World, 43
Nieto Ruiz, José, 29–30, 41, 65, 81; on the execution of Manuel Moreno Barranco, 106; refugees and, 89
Noche, La, 119
Norte, 42
novedades, Las, 49
novela española, La, 119

obra impresa de los intelectuales españoles en América 1936-1945, La (Amo & Shelby), 21
Olay, Maximiliano, 33
Onís, Federico de, 4, 26
Ortega y Gasset, José, 67, 71, 132
Ortiz, Miguel R., 44, 65, 75, 78

Paco, Benito y Adolfo (Sugrañés), 140
Pact of Madrid, 58

Pagès, Pere, 48–49
Palmer Terrassa, Sebastián, 62–63, 82, 104
Palomo, Manolito, 116
paraíso fascista, El (Sugrañés), 140
Páramo, Félix Lorenzo, 58
Parsons, Lucy G., 15
Partisan Review, 48
Partit Obrer d'Unificació Marxista (POUM), 48
Patín, José, 3, 63
Pauli, Benjamin J., 178
Payne, Stanley G., 10
Peck, Jim, 43
Pego, Aurelio, 14, 20, 47, 75, 116, 133, 142, 176; Americans mocked by, 152–154; as correspondent for Spanish and Latin American newspapers, 29; *crónica* and, 145–146, 149; Eugenio Montes and, 55; exiles mocked by, 154–156; Francoist economy mocked by, 150–151; Franco mocked by, 148–150; influence of, 53; as journalist and staunch antifascist with *España Libre*, 63–64, 146; National Catholicism mocked by, 151–152; Pedro Díez and, 60; Roque Barca character created by, 156–158; Vicente Cordellat and, 91
Peirats, Josep, 42
Peiro, Juan, 71
Pemán, José María, 148
Pepoti (cartoonist), 161
Pereda, Prudencio de, 1, 8
Pérez de Ayala, Ramón, 74
Pérez Galdós, Benito, 74
Perich Escala, Jaume, 161
Pesotta, Rose, 44
Pestaña, Ángel, 71
Pi i Margall, Franscesc, 46, 70
Poland, Romain, 75
political prisoners, 96–97; cartoons on, 165–166; fundraisers for, 99–103; mainstream press and, 104–105; protest on the pages of *España Libre* and, 105–110; public protests and, 97–99; radio programming protests and, 103–104
Politics, 69
Pollock, Jackson, 165
Polvo y camino (Prado Rodríguez), 47
Pozzetta, George E., 14

Pradal, Gabriel, 40
Prado Rodríguez, Jesús, 46–47, 48, 51
Prego Vieiro, José, 84
prensa, La, 28, 46, 49, 73, 88–89, 141
press, Hispanic, 28–29
Preston, Paul, 148
Prieto, Indalecio, 59, 93
Primo de Rivera, Miguel, 1
Pritchett, Victor Sawdon, 71
professors, Spanish, 27–28, 47–48, 50–51, 56
progreso, El, 61
Progress and Poverty (George), 71
Prosas de razón y hiel (Rubia Barcia), 47
protests, public, 97–99
Proudhon, Pierre-Joseph, 46, 71, 73
Pueblos hispanos, 28
Puig, Teresa, 61
Puig Antich, Salvador, 96
Pupo, Georgina, 44

Quevedo, Francisco de, 120

radio programming, 103–104
Ramirez, Tina, 141
Ramón (cartoonist), 161
Rappaport, Harry, 34
rebelión de las masas, La (Ortega y Gasset), 67
Reclus, Élisée, 71
refugees, 57–58, 79–81; aid sent for, 83–86; American laws on, 81–82; Ernest Fleischman and, 89–90; exceptional activism of SHC's executive members on behalf of, 90–95; relocations of, 87–89; SHC advocacy for, 82–83
región, La, 65
Rego, Emilio, 63
Reid, Mary, 14, 118, 134, 135, 140–142
Relatos fronterizos (Sender), 179
Renovación, 74
República no ha muerto, La (Castilla Morales), 139–140, 143
Republicanos Exiliados en Estados Unidos, 107
Reuther, Victor, 15, 32, 34, 48
Reuther, Walter, 48
revista blanca, La, 74
Reyes Ramos, Juan, 87
Ridruejo, Dionisio, 59

Rivero Gil, Francisco, 161, 165
Rocker, Fermín, 70
Rocker, Rudolf, 15, 33–34, 69–70, 78
Rodó, José Enrique, 75
Rodrigo, Javier, 159
Rodríguez Barbeito, Andrés, 63, 80, 104
Roig, Esteban, 8, 41, 100, 139
Roosevelt, Franklin, 80
Roque Barca, 156–158
Rosenberg, Jesse, 66, 89–90, 95
Rothko, Mark, 165
Rubia Barcia, José, 26, 28, 47–48, 50–51
Ruiz, Alberto Luis, 75
Russell, Bruce Alexander, 161
Ruta, 74

Said, Edward, 125–126
sainetes, 135
Salazar, Antonio, 161
Salvochea, Fermín, 69
Samblancat Salanova, Ángel, 47, 48, 51
Sánchez, Antonio, 7–8
Santamaria, Antonio, 115
Santamaría Cortiguera, Roque, 86
Santander Dock Workers Union, 65, 67
Santos, Mateo, 58
Saturday Review, 43
Seibel, Fred, 161
Sellarés, Pedro, 61
sembrador, El, 61, 104
Sender, Ramón J., 15, 28, 121, 124–125, 132, 177, 179–180
sentido humanista del socialism, El (de los Ríos), 68
Shelby, Charmion, 21
Shum (Alfons Vila i Franquesa), 90–91
Simó i Badía, Ramón, 74
Sinclair, Upton, 33
sindicalista, El, 121
Socas, Ricardo G., 91
socialista, El, 40, 74
Socialist General Union of Workers (UGT), 33
Social Research (academic journal), 56
Sociedades Hispanas Confederadas (SHC), 2–3; aid sent to Spain, France, and the Dominican Republic by, 83–86; anarchism and, 177–181; collaboration with other groups, 108–109; commemoration

of important events by, 115; Cuban groups and, 61; disagreements within, 173–174; editorials on Franco, 59; foundation of, 3–5; fundraising by, 18, 39–40, 99–103; global reach of, 14–15; Government of the Second Spanish Republic in exile and, 26; interlocked nature of antifascist activism and culture in, 16–17; labor unions and, 31–33; legacy of, 171–181; migrants and exiles in, 5–9, 79; Modern School Network and, 14–15, 33–35; political prisoners and (*see* political prisoners); postmodern approach by, 180; preserving the story of, 21–22; refugees and (*see* refugees); and shared membership with other unions, 6–7, 172–173; struggle to find common ground with other groups, 54–55; theater of (*see* theater, SHC); transnational networks of (*see* transnational networks, SHC); visits to Spain by members of, 6. See also *España Libre*
Sociedad Gallega, 7
Solidaridad, 31, 74
Solidaridad Internacional Antifascista (SIA), 86, 97
Solidaridad obrera, 47, 63, 74
Spanish Civil War, 1, 2, 5; antifascism in response to (*see* antifascism); featured in *España Libre*, 40; powerful factions in, 54–55; refugees of (*see* refugees); resistance groups in Spain and, 65–66; solidarity and protest against Spanish fascism after, 9–16. See also Franco, Francisco
Spanish diaspora, 1–3; importance of *España Libre* in, 173–174. See also migrants and exiles, Spanish
Spanish Popular Front, 36
Spanish Refugee Aid (SRA), 44, 85, 95
Spanish Temper, The (Pritchett), 71
Sturman, Janet L., 141
Sugrañés, Manuel, 140
Sunyé, Joaquin, 56

Taengua, Pascual Tomás, 86
Tarrida del Mármol, Fernando, 69
theater, SHC, 133–135; influenced by popular theater in Spain, 135–137; original antifascist plays in, 137–144

Thomas, Burt, 161
Thomas, Norman, 34, 80, 106–107
Tierra, 61
Tierra y libertad, 47, 74
Tolstoy, Leo, 75
Torrado, Adolfo, 64
Torres Perona, José María, 56
Torriente Brau, Pablo de la, 6
Toryho, Jacinto, 63
transnational networks, SHC, 25
Tresca, Carlo, 33
Truman, Harry S., 58

Unamuno, Miguel de, 71, 159–160
Underground Passages (Cohn), 13
UNESCO, 154
Unión General de Trabajadores (UGT), 2
United Auto Workers (UAW), 32, 109
United States, the: avoiding deportations of refugees from, 87–89; diplomatic relations between Franco and, 57, 58; Hispanic press in, 28–29; labor unions in, 31–33; mocked by Aurelio Pego, 152–154; Spanish migrants and exiles to (*see* migrants and exiles, Spanish)
Uriarte, Alberto, 44, 53–54, 62, 65, 75, 78

Valera Aparicio, Fernando, 26
Vázquez Gayoso, Jesús, 46
Vázquez Montalbán, Manuel, 81
Vega, Bernardo, 6
verdad de los presos, La (Castilla Morales), 138
Viadiu, José, 71
Via libre, 43, 119
Vials, Chris, 15
Vidal, Fabián, 79
Vidal y Planas, Alfonso, 113, 121–122, 126, 129–130, 132, 176
Villa, Cándido, 6–7
Villamil-Acera, Rakhel, 135
Villar Mingo, Manuel, 11, 71
Viñas, Ángel, 147, 148
Vivas, Emilio, 58
Vives, Eduardo, 41
Voice of America (radio service), 62
von Faupel, Wilhelm, 56
voz, La, 61, 119
"voz de Sociedades Hispanas Confederadas, La" (radio program), 103–104

277

War Resisters League, 43
Whitelaw, George, 161
Windmills in Brooklyn (de Pereda), 1, 8
worker resistance, cartoons of, 166–169
Workers Defense League, 88, 106, 107
World War I, 119
World War II, 10, 54, 57, 79–81; cartoonists during, 161; refugees of, 57–58, 79–80

Young People's Socialist League, 106

Zimmer, Kenyon, 177–178
Zionism, 44–45
Zorrilla, José, 140
Zugadi Garmendia, Ignacio, 63, 138
Zugadi Garmendia, Luis, 3, 6, 127

MONTSE FEU is an associate professor of Hispanic studies and co-advisor of graduate studies for the Spanish program at Sam Houston State University. She is the author of *Jesús González Malo: Correspondencia personal y política de un anarcosindicalista exiliado (1943–1965)*.

The University of Illinois Press
is a founding member of the
Association of University Presses.

―――――――――――――――

Composed in 10.75/13 Arno Pro
with Avenit LT Std display
by Lisa Connery
at the University of Illinois Press
Cover designed by Jim Proefrock
Cover illustration: Sociedades Hispanas Confederadas stamp.
Courtesy of José Nieto Ruiz.

University of Illinois Press
1325 South Oak Street
Champaign, IL 61820-6903
www.press.uillinois.edu